Using Assessment Results

Career Development

NINTH EDITION

Debra S. Osborn
Florida State University

Vernon G. Zunker
Southwest Texas State University (retired)

CENGAGE
Learning®

Australia • Brazil • Japan • Korea • Mexico • Singapore • Spain • United Kingdom • United States

For product information and technology assistance, contact us at **Cengage Learning Customer & Sales Support, 1-800-354-9706.**

For permission to use material from this text or product, submit all requests online at **www.cengage.com/permissions** Further permissions questions can be emailed to **permissionrequest@cengage.com**.

ISBN: 978-1-305-39777-4

Cengage Learning
20 Channel Center Street
Boston, MA 02210
USA

Cengage Learning is a leading provider of customized learning solutions with office locations around the globe, including Singapore, the United Kingdom, Australia, Mexico, Brazil, and Japan. Locate your local office at: **www.cengage.com/global**.

Cengage Learning products are represented in Canada by Nelson Education, Ltd.

To learn more about Cengage Learning Solutions, visit **www.cengage.com**.

Purchase any of our products at your local college store or at our preferred online store **www.cengagebrain.com**.

Printed in the United States of America
3 4 5 6 7   23 22 21 20 19

BRIEF TABLE OF CONTENTS

TABLE OF CONTENTS

CHAPTER 10: CARD SORTS AND OTHER NON-STANDARDIZED APPROACHES IN CAREER COUNSELING **163**

Pleasure in the job puts perfection in the work.
—Aristotle

Dream-makers. This is one of the main roles of career practitioners. We create an environment that is safe and accepting, and we provide tools for clients to identify and give voice to their dreams. Finally, we help them identify the steps necessary to turn those dreams into reality.

It is not always the case, though, that the dream is apparent to the client. Sometimes, the starting point is in helping the client identify, understand and appreciate the unique aspects that make them up as an individual. This is the role of career assessment. Too often, clients (and sometimes counselors) want to take a test because it is the fast way to land a list of potential occupations. But career assessment is personal assessment, and involves both a standardized look at the individual along with personal reflection.

We begin this book with the introduction of a model for using career assessments. To use career assessments effectively, a career practitioner should couch them as part of the career advising process. It is not a one-shot deal. Just as career counseling techniques are grounded in career theory, how a practitioner uses a career assessment should be a reflection of his or her theoretical perspective.

We cover several types of career assessments in this book, providing detail on a handful of inventories for each chapter, and then a brief description of other inventories at the end of the chapter. We describe and review individual tests and provide sample protocols that may be used by career practitioners. These reviews cover a description of the instrument, its purpose, some technical information, where to find other extensive reviews, and case studies. Our principal motive in writing this book has been to provide practitioners with a tool for understanding how to use a variety of inventories in counseling. The case studies offer examples of how each instrument can be introduced and how the results can be interpreted. Each chapter also features a list of suggested activities and questions so that readers may apply the information to practical situations.

CHAPTER 1

A CONCEPTUAL MODEL FOR USING ASSESSMENT RESULTS

Career counseling is both an art and a science. Deciding if, when and how to incorporate the use of assessments into the process can be complicated, involving factors such as the client's needs and the reason/desired outcomes for testing. A practitioner might choose to have a client complete an inventory as part of their session, or as an activity for the client to complete outside of the session and to bring for discussion at the next meeting. With many inventories being online, it is plausible that clients might come to their first session with results in hand from a reliable, or in some cases, a questionable virtual inventory.

A recent (2014) online search in the Mental Measurements Yearbook yielded 96 test results for the word "interests" alone. If you did a search on abilities, skills, values, or decision, you'd add substantially to that list. If you expand that to an Internet search on any of those terms, the number of related sites is in the hundreds of thousands. The ever-increasing number of sophisticated assessment instruments requires that career practitioners continually upgrade their skills in using assessment results to meet the demands of a wide range of individuals. Being a regular consumer of test reviews, journals, professional associations and even professional social media groups (e.g., there is a "Career Assessments" as well as a "Career Counselor Technology Forum" group in LinkedIn) will ensure that you are up to date with information relevant to career assessments. With the multitude of available inventories on the market, career practitioners are challenged to understand and apply the statistics associated with test data into meaningful information.

As an integral component of the career counseling process, assessment is also changing and growing in complexity. For instance, computer-assisted career guidance programs and online testing have grown in popularity. Career service providers must be aware of potential errors and misleading results or inappropriate interpretations of computer-generated statements or results from a questionable inventory or career quiz that was taken virtually. In the next section of this chapter, the practitioner's responsibilities associated with using standardized assessment instruments will be emphasized, along with suggestions for improving the general use of assessment instruments.

We recognize from our current perspective that the use of assessment results for career counseling have gone through significant changes that are thoroughly discussed in a number of textbooks, including *Career Counseling: Applied Concepts of Life Planning* (Zunker, 2014). No doubt the use of assessment for career counseling will make further changes in the 21st century, along with advances in technology and refinement of career counseling models.

Advanced Organizer

In this chapter, we will cover the following topics:
- Conceptual Perspective: Career Development Through Assessment
- Rationale for Assessment
- Preparing the Practitioner for Using Assessment Results
- A Model for Using Career Assessments in Career Counseling
- Using the Model for Individual Career Counseling: A Case Example
- Using Career Assessments to Stimulate Career Exploration in Groups
- General Overview of the Book
- Summary
- Questions and Exercises

Conceptual Perspective: Career Development Through Assessment

In early counseling approaches, assessment results were used primarily as analytical and diagnostic instruments (Prediger, 1995). A general transition from trait-and-factor approaches in career counseling practices to an emphasis on life stages and developmental tasks has created a different perspective for practitioners using assessment results. For instance, in career decision-making approaches, assessment results are considered as only one facet of information. A practitioner uses other sources of information such as what the client shares, and observations about how the client is sharing (are they getting excited when talking about making a difference or shifting uncomfortably when talking about getting additional education). Career theories also suggest key information that should be discussed in a career counseling session and for specific career needs (e.g., initial choice, transition, job loss). These may include self-esteem, the impact of negative thinking on career decision-making, values, as well contextual issues such as cultural influences, poverty, and socioeconomic status, and even mental health concerns such as depression or anxiety. With all of these,

1

assessment results are used to stimulate dialogue about important issues involved in finding an occupational fit, and they are used to encourage individuals to evaluate themselves, including their self-concepts and their self-efficacy development. While in mental health settings, assessment results are used to support diagnoses, more often with career counseling, assessment results are used as a tool to promote career exploration, identify barriers to decision making, and enhance discussion, rather than serving as the primary or sole basis for decisions. They can also help counselors determine what type of intervention will be most meaningful to a client. For example, and introverted client would most likely prefer to do online research about a career option while an extraverted client might be more excited and gain more information from a networking event. Most importantly, we believe that the client should be an active participant in the discussion about their career concerns.

The increasing complexity and diversity of assessment results suggest the need for a systematic model that will permit practitioners to make an effective analysis of the assessment procedures and results appropriate for specific counseling needs. This chapter discusses a conceptual model for using assessment results in career counseling, followed by suggestions for how practitioners can improve and sharpen their skills when using standardized assessment measures. In addition, we present a rationale for using assessment results before discussing the use of a model in individual counseling. Finally, we illustrate how the model can be used to stimulate career exploration among groups.

Rationale for Assessment

In this model, the use of assessment results is conceptualized as a learning process emphasizing the development of self-knowledge. Identification and verification of individual characteristics are the main information provided by assessment results. This information is used with other information in career decision-making. Although assessment results are used in a variety of ways, career practitioners are encouraged to look beyond the score report to facilitate meaningful learning experiences that will enhance self-awareness and lead to effective career exploration and ultimately, successful career decision making.

Thus, assessment results should be only one kind of information used in career counseling. Testing and interpreting score reports should not dominate the counseling process. Other factors, such as work experiences, grades, leisure activities, skills, attitudes toward work, as well as contextual issues such as cultural influences and external demands should receive equal attention. A counselor should always be aware of the mental health status of the person with whom they are working. If a client is struggling with depression or highly anxious, this will likely impact how they approach an assessment, and how they receive the interpretation of the results. Assessment results are best used when they can contribute information that is relevant within this overall context.

The process is complex in that individuals must consider their own values, interests, aptitudes, and other unique qualities in making decisions. Although the method of career decision-making is a relatively easily learned skill, one's application of the scheme involves considering one's complex and unique characteristics. The process usually begins when an individual recognizes a need to make a decision and subsequently establishes an objective or purpose. Then the individual collects data and surveys possible courses of action. Next the individual uses the data in determining possible courses of action and the probability of certain outcomes; estimating the desirability of outcomes centers attention on the individual's value system. The final step involves individual decisions that require specific courses of action. Possible outcomes should be specified and evaluated for optimal fit with an individual's personal characteristics. Individuals with the same objectives (e.g., I want to choose a career that fits my interests, or I want to find a job) will undoubtedly reach decisions by different paths based primarily on personal values and self-knowledge.

Case Example: Sari

Brown (2002) reviewed other examples of decision models. Some models specifically use assessment results to identify and clarify individual characteristics in order to enhance the decision process. For example, Sari, a high school senior, is attempting to decide which college to attend. She collects information concerning entry requirements, costs, faculty/student ratios, academic programs, and other data from five colleges. Using assessments of her skills and abilities, she weighs her chances of being accepted by the colleges under consideration and the probability that she will be able to meet academic requirements at those institutions.

In determining a major at the college chosen, Sari considers results of value inventories. These are among the questions she asks herself: "How much do I value a high salary? And if I do value a high salary, which college major would most likely lead to a high-paying job?" Values assessment is essential for making satisfactory decisions here. She also considers where her family has attended college, and how close geographically she wants to be to them. She decides to visit her top choices, and is also paying attention to her "gut feeling" when there. After Sari selects an institution and major, she once again evaluates the possible outcomes of the decision. In sum, decision-making requires the client's self-knowledge of abilities, interests, values, relevant past experiences, cultural and familial influences, emotions, and the application of this knowledge to the consideration of alternatives.

Information is a key variable in making an effective career decision (Peterson, Sampson, Reardon, & Lenz, 2002). For Sari, tests that measure scholastic aptitude and achievement were used with other data such as earned grades, feedback from others, and her internal feelings to make adequate predictions. These assessment results provided support information that is not easily attained by other means, such as through interviews or from biographical data. Assessment data have the distinct advantage of stimulating discussion of specific individual characteristics that can be linked to educational and occupational requirements. However, you can see the benefit of having both assessment results and other information to help Sari as she weighs through her decision.

Preparing the Practitioner for Using Assessment Results

Throughout this book, we urge the practitioner to inform each client about the purpose of testing and how the results match the goals set out by the practitioner and the client. Thus, the practitioner must be well informed about each measurement instrument used in the client's career development counseling.

Ethical guidelines for using tests responsibly are outlined by several professional associations, including the American Counseling Association, the Association for Assessment and Research in Counseling, the National Career Development Association, the Alliance of Career Resource Professionals, National Board of Certified Counselors, and others. These guidelines describe standards for test selection, administration, interpretation and management, and should be carefully reviewed and followed. In addition, the following are some more strategies for learning about measurement instruments:

1. Take the instrument yourself. Have a trained professional review your results.
2. Thoroughly read the professional manual.
3. Administer the instrument to a friend or colleague. Practice explaining the purpose of the instrument.
4. Look for any flaws in how the instrument is administered.
5. Learn to interpret the instrument by going over the results of a friend or colleague with them.
6. Practice going over the interpretive report and seek additional information to make scores more meaningful. Consider whether it would be helpful to create a summary page, or to highlight certain terms.
7. Search educational journals or even the developer's website for empirical research using that inventory.
8. Join relevant social media boards of practitioners using career assessments, or follow the publishers' social media sites to keep abreast of updates.
9. Attend trainings at professional conferences or webinars on the career assessments that you use often.

By following this general approach, the practitioner can build both skills and confidence in identifying appropriate assessments, and then administering and interpreting the test and results.

A Model for Using Career Assessments in Career Counseling

The effective selection and implementation of assessment tools in career counseling can best be attained by using a conceptual model. Such a model provides a systematic method for establishing the purpose of testing and the subsequent use of assessment results. To be operationally effective, a model must be flexible enough to meet the needs of a wide variety of individuals in different stages of their lives. In essence, a model should provide guidelines that are applicable to individuals at all educational levels, in all population groups, of both sexes, and of all ages.

The Importance of Relationship

Repeatedly, research has shown that the key to a client's evaluation of counseling as being effective goes back to the relationship with the practitioner. The client must feel heard by the practitioner, and this sense of being heard comes through the practitioner's use of basic counseling skills, including reflection of feelings, paraphrasing, summarizing, and confrontation. Establishing the relationship also means acknowledging the diversity of both the practitioner and the client. This may include racial, gender, ethnic or cultural differences, but may also include religious viewpoints, geographic differences, sexual orientation, or disability. Practitioners should acknowledge and incorporate the individual attributes of each client throughout all the stages of counseling, including establishing a relationship, understanding core issues and the client's world views, choosing and interpreting inventories and interventions, and in closure. A simple example would be when a person gets her inventory results and a field of study/major is suggested that is not offered at the local university. This student wants to stay close to home because of a strong family value. Instead of encouraging that student to be willing to go anywhere to achieve her goal, and not let her family ties stand in her way, a career counselor should acknowledge the struggle between her career interests and her values. Appropriate self-disclosure can be a way to begin this conversation.

3

Zunker's Model for Using Career Assessments

Drawing from the works of Cronbach (1984), Anastasi (1988), and Super, Osborne, Walsh, Brown, and Niles (1992), Zunker conceptualized a model for using assessment results in developmental career counseling as having four major steps. As shown in Figure 1-1, these steps are Analyzing Needs, Establishing the Purpose of Testing, Determining the Instruments, and Utilizing the Results. The process is cyclical and continuous. One may return to the first step during career exploration, after a period of being employed, or after completing an educational/training program. For example, an individual who is exploring careers has discussed general interests with a practitioner and, after reviewing occupational requirements, has identified a need for an assessment of abilities. It's possible and often occurs that a client may come in with one need (such as choosing a career) and after getting the results of an inventory and through discussions with the counselor,

Figure 1-1: Zunker's Model for Integrating Assessment Results

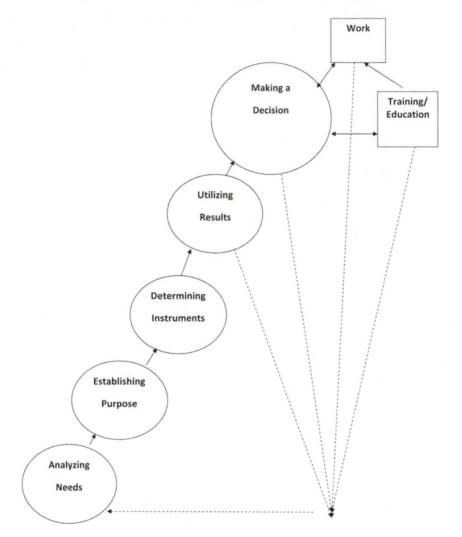

realizes that negative career thinking may be getting in the way of that process, or that in addition to exploring interests, looking at values may be useful, and so, cycle back in at different points.

An individual who is dissatisfied with her current career wishes to begin the process anew and to select a different career based on her increased understanding of needs that are not being met. After completing a training program for licensed vocational nurses, another individual has decided that this occupation is not what he wants; he wishes to meet with a practitioner to analyze why he is dissatisfied and to reassess his career decision. Because career development is a continuous process, assessment may prove to be useful at any point in the life span. See Zunker (2014) for more information on the use of assessment results with career counseling models.

Super and colleagues (1992) consider career maturity to be an important index to an individual's readiness for making career decisions. In an assessment model labeled the Career-Development Assessment and

4

Counseling model (C-DAC), Super and colleagues suggest that measured preferences, such as interest inventory results, should be viewed as basic status data or level of career maturity. Cognitive Information Processing theory (Peterson, Sampson, Reardon, & Lenz, 2002) identify two components of readiness as being the capability of an individual to make a career choice as it interacts with the complexity going on in that individual's life at the time. These are two components that a practitioner should also keep in mind when determining whether an assessment tool is appropriate, and if so, which one and how much support the individual may need in understanding the results and continuing through the career counseling process.

Other measures, such as value inventories and life role importance questionnaires, should be used as moderator variables in the career counseling process. The basic logic underlying this approach is to measure developmental stages according to Super's (1990) scheme and the individual's tasks or concerns to determine the client's needs plus his or her readiness to make career commitments. With this information and additional data gathered through interviews and self-reports, practitioners can determine developmental counseling intervention strategies for each client. Developmental strategies are thus suggested throughout this text.

Step 1: Analyzing Needs

The first step in any counseling encounter is to establish the counseling relationship. As part of the first meeting, the goal is to understand what the client hopes to accomplish as a result of career counseling. To ensure that a practitioner is on an effective course for meeting individual needs, a needs analysis may be accomplished by using interviews, a biographical data form, education and work records, discussions with family or a significant other, or a combination of these methods. The underlying goal is to encourage client participation. Clients who recognize their needs are likely to participate actively and enthusiastically in all phases of preparing for and using assessment results. For example, when Beth recognizes that she needs a structured approach for career exploration, she can be shown how assessment results can assist her.

Likewise, when Raj recognizes the need for help in predicting his chances of success in an educational program, he should be motivated to do his best. Thus, the first key to effective use of assessment results is the practitioner's skill in aiding the client in identifying needs and in relating needs to the purpose of testing.

Four Objectives in Identifying Needs

The following four objectives outlined in Table 1-1 are designed to assist the practitioner in identifying needs: establish the counseling relationship, accept and adopt the client's views, establish lifestyle dimensions, and specify the needs. Accomplishing these objectives may take more time than the initial interview.

KENYA: As you were talking, I saw some things that are similar in our stories. My family is most important to me. I know that I can choose any career that I want, but really, I don't want a career that is going to take me far away from my parents and my sisters and aunts. I would feel lost without them. I see them every day, and we get together on weekends. I really listen to them when they give me advice—especially advice from my grandmother. She's almost always right, and is very wise. Everyone says I should get out on my own, and make my decisions, but that doesn't sound all that exciting to me. I like my life now. I just want to figure out what I can do as a career that will help me provide for my family.

Through this opening discussion and self-disclosure, the practitioner made it safe for Kenya to share some of her values of inter-dependent decision-making. This leads into the second step, accepting and adopting the client's views.

Step 2: Establishing the Purpose of Testing

Following the needs analysis, the practitioner and client decide on the purpose of testing. Both should recognize that testing cannot be expected to meet all identified needs. Testing can be used for diagnosis, prediction, and comparing individuals with criterion groups. The results can be used to stimulate further study of individual characteristics relative to potential career choices. In some instances, the purpose of testing is to answer a specific question, as in predicting chances of success in a training program or an occupation.

In other instances, the purpose of testing may be less specific, as in establishing a direction for career exploration for an individual who is floundering. In cases such as this, where the purpose of testing is less tangible, the practitioner may be tempted to prescribe a battery of tests without obtaining the client's agreement on the purpose of the tests. To avoid this pitfall, the practitioner should establish the policy of explaining the purpose of each measuring instrument selected and making sure that the results of the testing relates to either the overall or specific goal(s).

Table 1-1: Four Objectives in Identifying Needs

Goal	Purpose	Steps to Accomplish	Sample Questions
To establish a counseling relationship	To foster a sense of trust and mutual respect	• Establishing a relationship • Communicate a sincere desire to help the client • Provide hospitality by being friendly • Arrange for personal introductions of staff members • On time for the appointment • Establish a warm, friendly atmosphere • Give undivided attention to the client	• What brings you by today? • What are the client's expectations of career counseling? • Where is the client in the career decision-making process? • Are tests indicated or contraindicated? • Will the client be willing to invest the time necessary for career counseling? • Does the client understand the practitioner versus the client role? • What is the client hoping to achieve by the end of this meeting? • Are these goals realistic, and do they match services available in the setting?
To accept and adopt the client's views	To assist clients in becoming aware of their viewpoints and in recognizing how their viewpoints can affect their career decision making	• Recognize that individuals are unique and have the right to their own commitments, self-awareness, and priorities • Pay attention and explore the role of culture in the client's worldviews	• Does the client have realistic expectations about the world of work? • Has the client experienced discrimination? What impact do those experiences have on his/her current perspective about career choice? • What is the client's level of sophistication in regard to career considerations? • Has the client established short-term and long-term goals? • How committed is the client to his or her viewpoints? • Would value clarification be helpful? • What stereotypes and biases does the practitioner have that may impact his or her counseling approach?
To establish the dimensions of lifestyle	To help clients explore how their career decisions can greatly influence their individual's style of life	• Discuss place of residence, work climate, family responsibilities, use of leisure time, leadership opportunities, financial needs, mobility, and the desire to contribute to society • Encourage clarification of priorities for lifestyle, and through this process realistic alternatives and options can be developed.	• Does the client recognize how career choice will affect lifestyle? • Has the client set lifestyle priorities? • Would an interest, value, or personality inventory help clarify the client's needs? • Would it help to bring in family members or spouses/partners in this discussion? • Are there significant discrepancies between lifestyle dimensions and the needs most likely to be met by the careers under consideration?
To specify needs	To determine if a career assessment will help meet the client's specific need(s).	• As the client states needs, the practitioner summarizes and records the statements for later use in reinforcing the purpose of testing. • Needs analysis	• "Tell me more about your desire to explore interests." • "You mentioned earlier you would like to more about your aptitudes." • "How might this career help you meet your personal goals?" • "What is it about this kind of job that makes it interesting?" • "How would you describe an individual who chooses jobs that help others?" • "Would you like to know more about your interests?" • "How do the needs of your family play a part in this career decision?" • "Would you like to bring in a family member or others as we talk about your needs, your family's needs, and the community's needs?"

6

The purpose of each test, inventory and intervention should be explained in terms that the client can comprehend. For example, the purpose of an interest inventory may be explained to a high school student as follows:

- "This inventory will help us identify your interests. We can then compare your interests to the interests of groups of individuals in certain jobs."

- "These test scores will give us some idea of your chances of making a C or better at the college you are considering."

- "This achievement test will show us how well you can read, spell, and do arithmetic problems. We can use the scores to help us choose a job or a training program for you." (In this example, the practitioner simplifies the language for a student with language difficulties).

In all instances, to make assessment results meaningful, we should attempt to relate the purpose of testing to the needs the client has identified (Cronbach, 1984). The client should also be made aware of how assessment results are used with other data in the career decision-making process. The following dialogue illustrates how a practitioner can accomplish these objectives.

Example of Establishing the Purpose of Testing

PRACTITIONER: As you will recall, we agreed to record your needs for information, materials, programs, and tests. Let's review our comments on testing possibilities. Do you remember any of the testing needs agreed on?

CLIENT: Yes, I want to take an interest inventory.

PRACTITIONER: Do you remember why?

CLIENT: I am not sure about what I want to do. I believe knowing more about my interests would help in choosing a career.

PRACTITIONER: Do you recall specifically how the results of an interest inventory would help the career decision-making process?

CLIENT: Yes, I believe that I will be able to compare the interests of people in different occupations with my own interests.

PRACTITIONER: Go on.

CLIENT: This will give me information about personal traits that I can use with other things I've learned about myself.

Step 3: Determining the Instruments

If a patient tells a doctor her throat is hurting, it is unlikely that the doctor will prescribe a foot ointment, unless she was also complaining of a foot irritation. If the doctor *did* prescribe foot ointment for a sore throat, the patient might question whether the doctor was listening, whether the doctor was qualified, or whether the doctor knew more than she did about her own needs (i.e., maybe there is something in foot ointment that also cures sore throats). This example may sound extreme, but consider the possibility of the following scenarios:

- Jari wants to research careers related to math, and is given an interest inventory

- Reese, who engages in a great deal of negative self-talk and doesn't believe she is capable of much, is asked to rank order her skills

- Hank wants to find out what occupations would best match his skills, and is given a personality inventory

- Jackson has narrowed his options down to two, and is prescribed a vocational identity inventory

In each of these examples, the assessment doesn't match the client needs. What might be the result? Frustration? Anger? Confusion? In our patient example with the sore throat, it might take the patient longer to recover. In the career examples above, more time will pass before the real need is met—and, the client may not return to career counseling, sensing that the practitioner wasn't listening or wasn't qualified, or worse, that they themselves are the cause for the poor results and that they are a lost cause.

Once the needs have been specified, and the practitioner and client have determined that an assessment is appropriate, the next step is to identify which instrument will be best suited. Hopefully, the instruments that a

7

practitioner has available are valid, reliable, current and culturally appropriate. So, the basic considerations for deciding upon an instrument include the construct the instrument purports to measure, reliability, validity, availability, culturally appropriate and fair, practitioner competence in administering and interpreting the assessment, and finally, cost. The types of reliability and validity that should be established for a test are determined by the purpose and use of the test. A review of the procedures for determining and comparing different types of reliability and validity may be found in several texts, including Cronbach (1984), Drummond (2009), Groth-Marnat (2009), Kaplan and Saccuzzo (1993), Zunker (2014), and Whiston (2000). We also cover this information in chapter 3.

What Different Tests Measure

In this book, we concentrate on tests of ability and achievement and on inventories that measure career development, interests, personality, and values. While the classification titles of tests provide a fairly clear indication of what they measure, Table 1-2 more clearly specifies the constructs measured by each type of test.

Results from interest, personality, and value inventories promote discussion of the client's relationship to the working world and the satisfaction the client may derive from a career. In the chapters that follow, each of the test categories mentioned here is discussed in detail. In addition to standardized tests, we will also be exploring non-standardized approaches such as card sorts and genograms.

Table 1-2: Sample Instruments for Specific Constructs

Type of Test	Construct(s) Measured
Ability Tests	Skills, aptitudes
Achievement Tests	Educational strengths and weaknesses; can be used to select appropriate remedial educational programs and other educational intervention strategies such as skills training
Interest Inventories	Interests, preferences
Values Inventories	Motivations, priorities
Personality Tests	Individual differences in social traits, motivational drives and needs, attitudes and adjustment
Career Decision Inventories	Vocational development in self-awareness, planning skills, decision-making skills, decidedness levels and career beliefs

Step 4: Using the Results

Because individual choice patterns are unique and can be influenced by economic conditions and experiences over the life span, assessment use varies greatly. More than likely, individuals will find that assessment results can assist them at various stages of their lives, particularly in clarifying needs and in developing self-awareness. Contemporary thought places considerable importance on the individual's responsibility for finding satisfaction in the ever-changing world of work. This concept was succinctly stated by Shakespeare in *Julius Caesar*: "The fault, dear Brutus, is not in our stars, but in ourselves, that we are underlings."

The use of assessment results in career counseling should be carefully calculated and systematically accomplished through established operational procedures. In general, assessment results identify individual characteristics and traits, which in turn point to possible avenues for career exploration. In the case of making a career choice, the practitioner and the client discuss potential career fields using assessment results to facilitate the dialogue. Interpreting assessment results is the focus of this book, and thus will be addressed in remaining chapters with practical examples and case studies. In addition, general steps for interpreting results will be discussed in Chapter 2.

Step 5: Make a Decision

Ideally, after completing an inventory and discussing the results, the client will be ready to make a commitment to a career decision, which will lead them to finding a job or getting the necessary training. This is not always the case, though. As part of the discussion of the results, the client and practitioner should re-evaluate whether the purpose for testing was achieved and the career need met. How satisfied is the client with the results? Either way, a decision is the next step, and could be:

- To research occupations that were generated
- To identify majors or programs of study related to career fields of interest
- To take a different assessment to further build self-knowledge
- To address negative thinking that might have impacted the test results

The model includes some bi-directional arrows as well, suggesting that the client and practitioner are regularly examining if the needs have changed, and if so, begin the process again. Also, as a client commits to a decision by either trying out the career choice or beginning training, she or he is likely engaging in a re-evaluation of that decision, and also whether the initial need still exists or if a new need has arisen.

Using the Model for Individual Counseling: A Case Example

The following counseling case illustrates the use of a conceptual model using assessment results in a senior high school counseling center. Each step in the model is illustrated by dialogue between practitioner and client and by occasional notations made by the practitioner. Standardized assessment instruments used in this case were not identified. In later chapters, other counseling cases describing the use of models employing assessment results are described, citing specific standardized assessment instruments. In the following illustration of the conceptual model, both major and minor components of the model are identified to demonstrate a sequential order of events. Notations and dialogue between practitioner and client were created for the purpose of illustration.

Amy, a self-referred 17-year-old Hispanic female high school senior, reported to the counseling center that she was undecided about plans after graduation. She filled out a questionnaire and was introduced to Gretchen, her practitioner.

Step 1: Analyze Needs

A. Establish the Counseling Relationship

PRACTITIONER: Amy, I'm Gretchen, welcome to the Counseling Center. I believe you have met Carla, our secretary, who will help us with appointments and records. Please call either one of us if you need any information as we go `along. My office is the first door to the left, here. Please come in and have a seat.

After a brief discussion of current events, the practitioner explained the order of procedures and assured Amy of client confidentiality. The practitioner shared some of her personal background and invited Amy to do the same. Amy shared that she was a first generation American, and that at times, she felt somewhat torn between "the old ways" and the "new way." Her parents had always stressed the importance of a good education, and not taking for granted the opportunities before her. While they were generally supportive of any career path she might choose, there was an unspoken emphasis on being "successful." The conversation shifted easily to Amy's indecision concerning her plans after high school.

AMY: I'm not even sure I'm ready to go to college. I don't know what I want to be and I can't decide about a major. All my friends have this settled, but not me. I don't want to disappoint my family. They have been saving for my college since I was born. I don't want to waste my time or their money by making a bad choice.

The practitioner assured Amy that the counseling center could help her make these decisions. The practitioner continued to build the relationship by not immediately challenging the family values, but by saying, "You're right. This is an important decision, and you want to make the best choice that you can." Gretchen also informed Amy of their career counseling time commitment of five to six counseling sessions with some additional time for testing, if appropriate. The practitioner also established a counseling goal by asking Amy if she could make a table that compared her ideas about possible majors/careers with those of her parents and family.

B. Accept and Adopt the Client's Views

The practitioner encouraged Amy to discuss her academic background, general interests, leisure and work experiences, and values. Amy informed the practitioner of her previous work experience, which consisted of two months as a swimming instructor and four months as an assistant program director in a home for the elderly. Amy indicated that she liked both jobs.

PRACTITIONER: Could you explain how the experiences of these two jobs might influence your future choice of a career?

9

AMY: Well, I never thought about it, but I do enjoy working with people. I like to teach, also, but I don't believe I would like to be a schoolteacher.

PRACTITIONER: I would be interested in knowing how you've come to those conclusions.

AMY: I'm not sure I could handle all the discipline problems that teachers have to deal with. Besides, I want to do other things helping people. I really enjoyed the work I did with the elderly.

Amy continued to express interests and aspirations while the practitioner made the following notations:

- Good rapport has been established
- Amy feels free to express herself
- Amy likes working with people
- Has some limited exposure to careers
- Has developed tentative expectations of the future, but needs help in clarifying interests
- Some pressures to make a "wise" choice, and not disappoint others
- Family influence and input highly valued

C. Establish the Dimensions of Lifestyle

PRACTITIONER: Now, let's take a look at the future. In fact, I would like you to project yourself into the future. For example, think about where you would like to live five or ten years from now and what kind of leisure activities such as travel you would like.

AMY: Okay, let me see (pause)... Hmm, someday I would like to be living in an apartment on my own, of course, with my own car right here in the city, I think. I would like to have a nice place, but I really don't want a fancy car, just a fairly new one. I guess one of the most important things to me is having good clothes and being able to eat out in nice restaurants. I also like to travel. I've been overseas on vacation with my parents, and I would like to go back some day. About money ... I want enough to be able to do these things.

PRACTITIONER: That's a good start, Amy. We will be discussing lifestyle preferences again. I think we can sort out more specific aspects of your lifestyle choices and how they may influence career decisions in one of our future sessions.

During the course of the counseling session, the practitioner thought that the following assessments might be helpful:

1. Measure of college aptitude—Information for predicting success in selected colleges
2. Measure of interests—General interest patterns are needed to stimulate dialogue about future goals. Specific interests will be used to link college majors with potential careers
3. Measure of lifestyle preferences—Lifestyle measures will introduce another dimension for consideration in the decision-making process
4. Invite Amy's parents in for discussion of their vision for their daughter's career path

The practitioner's overall goal was to provide Amy with relevant information that could be used in the decision-making process

Step 2: Establish a Purpose

PRACTITIONER: Our discussion has been very productive and, before you leave today, let's summarize some of the needs you have expressed. One of the first topics we discussed was your indecision about college. Remember you questioned whether you should attend or not.

AMY: Yes, that's right. Maybe I was just blowing off steam; I know I should probably go to college. Really, it's not an option. I will be going—I just want to know why I'm going.

PRACTITIONER: Would you like to take an aptitude test to see how prepared you are for college?

AMY: Yes ... okay... (pause)... I did take one of the required exams for college a few months ago.

PRACTITIONER: Good, we probably have the results in our files and we can use these to help us with our decision. I'll check the files and if we need another test, I'll let you know at our next appointment.

10

(Amy nodded approval.)

PRACTITIONER: Another need you mentioned is choosing a college major.

AMY: Yes, I don't really know what I want to do. I've had subjects I like, but nothing grabs me.

PRACTITIONER: One of the things we discussed was comparing the options you're considering with options your parents see for you. You can extend that to family members as well. After all, they've seen you develop through the years and have a much more thorough view than I do or any inventory. That being said, we do have several interest inventories that might confirm some of your choices and suggest new ones. Would you like to take one?

When Amy agreed to complete the table, and also that an interest inventory would be fine with her, the practitioner turned her attention to the last of the list of indicated needs—lifestyle preferences.

PRACTITIONER: Today I also asked you to project yourself into the future and you were able to express some of your goals. Do you think it would be helpful to further clarify your lifestyle preferences?

AMY: That's something I really haven't thought about very much. I think it might help, but I'm not sure just how.

PRACTITIONER: Okay, that's a good question. Let me briefly explain that career and lifestyle are closely related. For example, your career choice will determine to some extent the kind of lifestyle you will have in the future. One illustration involves the financial returns you get from a job. Remember, you said you wanted a new car, to have the opportunity to travel to Europe, and to have a nice apartment. In order to be able to have and do these things, you will need a job that provides the necessary resources.

AMY: I see. Well, yes, I probably should talk more about my future.

After the practitioner was certain that Amy understood the purpose of each assessment instrument, an appointment for the next counseling session was set.

Step 3: Determine the Instrument

The practitioner discovered that Amy had taken a nationally administered college aptitude test and the results were on file in the counseling center. Composite scores indicated that Amy was well above the national norm for college-bound students. These test scores were current and could be used to predict chances of making a C or better at several colleges, so the practitioner decided that another aptitude test was unnecessary.

The practitioner chose an interest inventory providing measures of general and specific occupational interests. The goal was to stimulate discussion of general interests and to verify preferences Amy had previously expressed. Moreover, the practitioner's primary objective was to stimulate dialogue that could help Amy clarify her interests. Finally, the practitioner chose a lifestyle measure that would assess Amy's preferences for a variety of lifestyle factors. The practitioner was particularly interested in assessing Amy's preferences for work achievement and leadership, work environment, and leisure orientation. As with the interest inventory, the practitioner's objective was to stimulate discussion to help Amy clarify values and lifestyle preferences.

Step 4: Use the Results

During Amy's next appointment, the interest inventory and lifestyle preference surveys were administered. After they were scored, the results of these inventories and aptitude tests were carefully reviewed by the practitioner during pre-interpretation preparation. The practitioner made notes on several items she felt would stimulate discussion. For example, on the interest inventory, she made a notation that Amy had a very high score on the general occupational theme—social—and on such specific occupations as social worker and school counselor.

Highest scores on the lifestyle preference survey were educational achievement, work achievement, and structured work environment. The practitioner was particularly interested in having Amy link lifestyle preferences to high-interest occupations and general occupational themes. Priorities for lifestyle preferences would be used to introduce another dimension of Amy's values in the decision-making process.

Finally, the practitioner obtained studies of students' expectancies of making a C or better at several community colleges and universities. This information would provide an index to predict Amy's chances of matriculating at several two- and four-year institutions of higher learning.

The practitioner began the utilization-of-results session by explaining the purpose of the college aptitude test Amy had taken. The scores were explained as follows.

PRACTITIONER: Since you have said you want to go to college, we will interpret your scores by using National College Bound Norms. These norms are derived for students who have indicated that they intend to enroll in a college or a university. Your total score places you in the 86th percentile among college-bound students. This means that 86 out of 100 college-bound students who took the test scored lower than you did and 14 out of 100 scored higher than you did.

AMY: Wow! That's better than I thought I would do on that test. Does this mean that I could do okay at City College?

The practitioner was able to answer Amy's question by referring to an expectancy table that had been provided by City College. On the basis of Amy's total test score, the practitioner was able to inform Amy that her chances of making an overall C average during her freshman year at City College were very good. The practitioner was also able to point out the chances of making a C or better in specific courses offered to freshmen at City College. These data not only provided an index for predicting Amy's chances of matriculating in City College, but also could be used for suggesting an academic major.

The practitioner's next step in using assessment results was to outline the organization of scores on the interest profile. She explained the various scales on the test, including general occupational interest scores and scores on specific occupations. The scores were interpreted as follows.

PRACTITIONER: Amy, you scored in the high category on the general occupational theme—social. People who score high on this theme like to work with people, share responsibilities, and enjoy working in groups. Do you feel that this is an accurate representation of your interests?

Using this procedure, the practitioner encouraged Amy to discuss other scores on the general occupational theme part of the profile. Likewise, this procedure was used to enhance the discussion of scores measuring specific occupations. Then the practitioner asked Amy to share the table she had completed. Amy shared that there was a lot of agreement with her own ideas as well as that with her family, and even some friends, about what career options might be best for her. Some of the options included teaching, counseling, nursing, human resource development and hospitality. Amy was encouraged to jot down occupations of interest for further exploration in the career library and on the computerized career information system. A discussion of lifestyle orientation related to interests helped Amy crystallize her projections of future needs and desires.

Step 5: Make a Decision

Amy ultimately decided that she should pursue a college education, and that now was a good time to do so. She decided to attend City College and tentatively major in human resource development, an area that met her interests and values, and also was within the prestige and "success" level expected by her family. Zunker's model proved to be a useful framework for guiding her through the process of career counseling, and made the integration of assessment results rather seamless but also helpful in the discussion.

Using Career Assessments to Stimulate Career Exploration in Groups

Group counseling, classroom "guidance" and workshops allow a practitioner to meet the needs of many clients or students than would be possible with one-on-one appointments. Other benefits of group career counseling include: enhancing career counseling outcomes, increased efficiency and cost-effectiveness, enhanced feedback for group members, personalizing information and for the career practitioners, enjoyment and variety (Pyle, 2007). A meta-analytic study of 50 articles has demonstrated that structured career counseling groups and career workshops are effective as interventions (Whiston, Brecheisen, & Stephens, 2003). Some career assessments can also be administered and interpreted successfully in group situations.

Adapting the Assessment Model to Groups

The model for using assessment results proposed in the previous section can easily be adapted to groups. The same steps apply. However, methods used in applying the model may have to be altered. For example, a needs analysis can be accomplished through group discussion or as part of a screening inventory, with each individual noting his or her own needs. Some will find that testing is not necessary at this point in their career

12

development. Those who decide that testing is appropriate will move to the next step of establishing the purposes of testing. After testing purposes are identified, different types of tests and inventories can be selected. Small groups may be formed for administering the tests and sharing results. Individuals or entire groups may then go back to the first step, to reestablish needs, at any time in career exploration.

A modification of the model for groups could include the following procedures:

1. Introduce the concepts of career development
2. Explain the use of assessment
3. Introduce the types of measuring instruments
4. Interpret the results
5. Introduce support material

Interest inventories are especially effective in promoting group discussions and are usually less threatening than aptitude or achievement tests. Who wants to broadcast to a group that they are two standard deviations below the mean on their technical skills? However, other types of measuring instruments can also be used effectively to generate activities for groups. The following example illustrates the use of an interest inventory in a classroom setting.

Example of Group Career Exploration

Ms. Alvarez, a high school practitioner, was invited to a high school class that was working through a career education program. She was asked to present the types of measuring instruments available and to explain how the students could use the career resource center. Before the presentation, Ms. Alvarez asked the teacher's permission to introduce the steps in career decision-making and to make some comments on the basic elements of career development. As she presented this material, she emphasized the purpose and use of assessment results.

The students requested that an interest inventory be administered. Afterward, the practitioner explained how to interpret the score profiles. Ms. Alvarez spent considerable time answering individual questions concerning the results. The practitioner emphasized that interests are one of the important considerations in career decision-making.

Following the interpretation of results, the practitioner introduced the next step in the career decision-making process. Some of the students decided to take additional tests and inventories. Others took different courses of action. Several decided to collect information about selected careers in the career resource center, and some members of the group chose to visit work sites.

In this case, interest inventory results stimulated students to generate further activities within the framework of a decision-making model. This example illustrates the importance of clarifying the role of assessment within a career decision-making model. The practitioner emphasized that career decision-making involves a sequence of steps and support materials. By placing assessment in proper perspective, the practitioner was able to enhance the group's usage of assessment results.

General Overview of This Book

Regardless of the theoretical approach of the practitioner, a common activity in which those providing career counseling often engage is that of administering and interpreting the results of an assessment to a client or a student. The purpose of this book is to review a variety of such inventories, provide basic information about the psychometric properties of these tools, and demonstrate how the results of such inventories might be used in practice. This book begins where courses in assessment and appraisal methods usually end. Instead of emphasizing the procedures used for standardizing tests and inventories and the methods used to develop them, this book illustrates the use of assessment results in the career counseling process. The material is presented with the assumption that the reader has a basic foundation in tests and measurements. In each chapter, we review representative examples of tests, inventories, and self-assessment measures and explain how results are used.

Fictitious cases further illustrate the use of many of these instruments. These cases resemble actual counseling encounters that we have had or that practitioners we have supervised have had. The cases do not include descriptions of the entire information-gathering process and all counseling encounters. In each case, we have included only the material relevant for illustrating the use of assessment results. All standardized assessment instruments mentioned in this book are listed in the "List of Publishers' Names and Websites."

The introduction of new measuring instruments and the refinement and revitalization of established tests and inventories provide further information to the career practitioner. In addition, technology and a global economy has created a variety of new occupations, while national and international economic struggles resulting in layoffs and closings require many to re-evaluate and re-package their skills in order to find work, sometimes in a job or occupational field very different from the one they previously had. We will also explore the use of social media tools in relationship to career testing.

The stereotypes of the breadwinner father and the homemaker mother have undergone significant modification. Women will continue to enter the labor force at a rate faster than men, and will comprise 47.5% of the entire workforce in 2016, based on the Bureau of Labor Statistics (http://www.dol.gov/wb/stats/main.htm). The look of the labor force will be older, with workers ages 55 and older projecting to make up ¼ of the labor market (BLS: http://www.bls.gov/news.release/ecopro.nr0.htm) in 2018. While Whites will continue to make up the majority of the labor force in 2018 (79%, BLS), Asians will increase by almost 30% to comprise 5.6% of the labor force, Blacks will increase by 14.1% to comprise 12.1%, and Hispanics (any race) will grow by 33.1% to comprise 17.6% in 2018.

The variety of clients a counselor sees may include a former executive who is a victim of downsizing in an organization, a homemaker and divorcee who is entering the work force for the first time, a high school dropout, an undecided college student, and a graduate who is unable to find an appropriate career path. In addition, with technological advances, a counselor may not "see" a client at all in the traditional sense, but may conduct career counseling over the Internet. Special instruments have also been developed for individuals who are disadvantaged or who have disabling conditions. All these factors have made it necessary for practitioners to reevaluate if, when, and how they can most effectively use assessments within the context of career counseling. We believe that the model described in this chapter provides a useful backdrop for that evaluation.

Chapter 2 will provide a context for interpreting assessment results in general. In Chapter 3, we will review some basic measurement concepts that will aid in the interpretation of the specific inventories and case presentations. Chapter 4 will explore ethical considerations with respect to career assessment. With these foundational chapters as our backdrop, the remaining chapters will review a variety of tests and inventories selected because they are widely used or provide innovative methods of presenting score results or both. They are representative of the tests and inventories available. For a general evaluation of tests, consult the following references: A Counselor's Guide to Career Assessment Instruments, 6th ed. (Wood & Hays, 2013) and The Mental Measurements Yearbook.

Each review in this book follows approximately the same format and provides the following information: purpose of the instrument, description of subtests, description of reliability and validity studies when appropriate, description of profile and score results, and method for interpreting the results. Case studies illustrate how the instruments may be used for career development. The cases demonstrate the use of assessment in career counseling with clients ranging in age from high school youths to middle-aged adults. At the conclusion of each chapter are discussion questions, some of which have assessment result profiles for the reader to explore. Through this, we hope that the reader will gain a stronger understanding and a deeper appreciation for how different assessment results can enhance the career counseling process.

Summary

Assessment results can be effectively used to enhance the development of self-knowledge and occupational knowledge, identify barriers and to enhance career decision-making. Within a career decision-making model, assessment results are used to clarify individual characteristics and to generate further activities. The decision to include an assessment should be a mutually agreed-upon choice that ties into the client's goal(s) for career counseling. A model for using assessment results has the following steps: analyzing needs, establishing the purpose of testing, determining the instruments, and utilizing the results. Clients should be actively involved in all steps of the model, which may be used for individual or group counseling.

Questions and Exercises

1. What evidence can you give for the rationale that assessment results are used to enhance self-awareness? Using an example, illustrate how the model for using assessment results described in this chapter is cyclical.
2. Why is the model of using assessment results only one part of the career decision-making process?
3. Why might it be necessary to retest an individual after two or three years?
4. How are assessment results used in the total-person approach to career decision-making?
5. Describe how and when you would incorporate the assessment model into the career counseling theory you follow and your career counseling approach.
6. How would you address issues of diversity into a model of career assessment and career testing?
7. How do you believe traditional test results might complement information gained from open-ended questioning and active listening (or vice versa)?
8. What might be some reasons for deciding that an assessment is not appropriate for a client?
9. What assessments have you taken? How useful were they? What information did you learn about yourself? How were the results presented to you? Putting yourself in the counselor's role, what might you have done differently?

CHAPTER 2

INTERPRETING ASSESSMENT RESULTS

How many times have you made or heard statements like these?

These statements are representative of what many career practitioners hear from students and clients who need or want some clarity on their career goals, and see taking a career assessment as a means of achieving that clarity. Often, these statements are among the first that clients say when asked about their reasons for seeking career counseling. Career testing is often an integral part of career counseling, whether the purpose is to identify interests and prioritize careers, discover negative thinking that might be hindering the career decision-making process, or to help clients brainstorm other career options. In order to help individuals evaluate and make decisions about their careers, some type of assessment, whether formal or informal, standardized or non-standardized, may be merited. The goal of this chapter is to better understand the use of assessments within the career counseling process.

Individuals evaluate their choices internally by considering values, interests, achievements, and experiences and externally by seeking acceptance and approval within the work environment. Individuals must deal with self-doubts concerning the appropriateness of their choices in the process, making a careful examination of cognitive and affective domains. The significance of choosing a career parallels other major choices in an individual's life; assessment results can provide useful information in the career decision-making process.

Advanced Organizer

In this chapter, we will cover:

- A Trait-Factor Approach to Assessment Interpretation
- Connecting Career Assessments and Career Development Theories
- Four Uses of Assessment
- How, When and Whether to Use Career Assessment Results
- Culturally Appropriate Career Assessment
- General Steps to Interpreting Results
- Using Holland Codes for Interpretation
- International Career Testing
- One-Shot Career Counseling
- Career Counseling and Testing: Science, Education or Art?
- Summary
- Questions and Exercises

15

A Trait-Factor Approach to Assessment Interpretation

Various approaches to assessment interpretation have been reported in the literature since Parsons' (1909) seminal work. The trait-and-factor approach advocated by Parsons and later by Williamson (1939, 1949), and reviewed by Prediger (1995) was straightforward—it matched individual abilities and aptitudes with the requirements of a job. Parsons originally defined these requirements as "conditions of success." Do the person's abilities and aptitudes line up with what it takes to be successful in this particular job? This approach has been drastically modified over the years toward considering, for example, many different individual characteristics and traits. In other words, individuals are being encouraged to consider many aspects of themselves in the career decision-making process, including their abilities, interests, personalities, values, needs, hobbies, past work and leisure experiences, and total lifestyles. In fact, more emphasis is being placed on integrating all life roles in the career counseling process. Specifically, individuals are encouraged to evaluate the effect work roles will have on other roles such as family, civic, and leisure roles. In addition, while individuals often come to career counseling to make a specific choice at a given point in time, it is advisable to encourage clients to think of their skills as vibrant, changing over time, even after the immediate decision has been made.

This broad approach that originated with Frank Parsons and others has today been accompanied by computer scoring, online administration of valid (and not-so-valid nor reliable) tests, new assessment instruments, and economic/societal changes, all of which have complicated the issues of measurement and certainly the interpretation and use of assessment results. Computerized reports provide an almost unlimited amount of assessment information, and mirror the matching that Parsons attempted on a much larger scale, made possible through large occupational databases such as O*NET (http://www.onetonline.org). Counselors should be aware that interpretive statements in many computerized reports have likely not gone through the validation process that inventory itself has.

Connecting Career Assessments and Career Development Theories

Assessment results are counseling tools for fostering career exploration and serving as a springboard for deeper discussion. All career theories, systems, and strategies underscore the inclusive and complex nature of the career choice process. The use of assessments should fit within the practitioner's career theory. For example, see Table 2-1 for a sample of how assessments might fit in with different career theories.

Table 2-1 Testing Related to Career Theories

Theory	Theoretical Aspects/Types of Testing
Brown's Values-Based, Holistic Model of Career and Life-Role Choices and Satisfaction	Values
Career Constructivism	Values, beliefs, lifeline, autobiography, card sorts
Chaos Theory	Career thinking
Circumscription and Compromise	Occupational aspirations, self-concept, intelligence, barriers (perceived and real), values
Cognitive Information Processing	Knowledge Domain: Interest, values, skills Decision Making Domain: Decision making abilities Executive Domain: Negative career thoughts, vocational identity, career beliefs, self-esteem, readiness
Holland RIASEC	Interests, abilities, vocational identity
Learning Theory of Career Counselling (Krumboltz)	Beliefs
Parsons' Trait/Factor	Aptitude
Person-Environment Correspondence	Skills, needs/values
Super's Life-Span, Life-Space Approach to Careers	Career maturity, self-concept, abilities/traits, readiness, needs, values, intelligence

Other examples might include aptitude testing for Parsons' approach, values/needs and work environment testing for Person-Environment Correspondence theory, values inventories and card sorts for Brown's Value-Based Holistic model, and interest inventories for Holland's RIASEC theory. Even the more person-centered, narrative or developmental approaches include an opportunity for assessment—whether using standardized tests or directive questioning. For example, Super's concept of career maturity might be tested with the Career

16

Maturity Inventory, and other portions of his archway model might be tested with various values, interests, and skills inventories. Or, a practitioner might simply show the archway model and ask about each of the constructs such as needs, economic factors or personality.

As a practitioner, the decision to use an inventory shouldn't be random, or because you're not sure what else to do. There should be a reason for testing, and that reason should stem from the career theory of the practitioner and the client needs. For example, if a person wants to know about the likelihood of being successful in engineering, an interest inventory is not the appropriate choice, while an aptitude test would be. Or, if a client is wanting to narrow down between two options, it may be possible that a values prioritization inventory or card sort is appropriate, or it may be that no inventory is necessary, and the counselor can help the client generate a pro/con list for the two options.

Four Uses of Assessment

Two of Williamson's steps in the career counseling process included diagnoses and prognosis. Similarly, assessments can be classified as either a diagnostic or a predictive tool, and can also provide a means of comparing an individual to criterion groups, and, most important, as relevant information for fostering career development over the life span.

Diagnostic Uses of Assessment

A diagnostic test is one that defines or labels a construct. While labeling may have a bad reputation in some circles, it does serve a helpful purpose, in that it helps the practitioner know more about what the client is experiencing. For example, knowing whether a client is undecided-developmental, undecided-multi-potential, or undecided-deferred, versus indecisive-acute or indecisive-chronic, or even decided-confirmation, decided-implementation, or decided-conflict avoidance (Peterson, Sampson, Reardon, & Lenz, 2002) should have an impact on the interventions that are chosen. A similar example would be a person's Holland Code. If you know a person is Artistic, you might choose more creative interventions versus having them complete an occupational comparison table. While achievement and aptitude tests are most often seen as diagnostic tools, interest, value, personality, and career inventories can also be used diagnostically. Typically, these measures are used to raise an individual's level of self-awareness and to indicate to practitioners when clients are lacking in self-awareness or have personal views that are inconsistent with assessment results.

Achievement and aptitude assessment results, in particular, are often used to evaluate individual strengths and weaknesses in order to determine preparedness and potential for training and for beginning work. The identification of skills and aptitudes may broaden the client's options for careers and education. In the same sense, the assessment of academic and skill deficiencies may help identify the need for treatment, remedial training, or skill development.

Example

Jake, a high school senior, was among a group of students participating in career exploration with his high school counselor. During the initial interview, Jake told the counselor that he wanted to go to college but that he had many interests and was not sure which one to pursue. Also, he expressed concern about his ability to succeed academically in college. After further discussion, they agreed that he would complete an aptitude battery. The assessment results identified several academic strengths and a few specific deficiencies. Next, they spent several sessions relating Jake's strengths to career fields and college majors that might be explored. Finally, they reviewed the curricula of nearby colleges and decided, in light of Jake's academic deficiencies, which remedial courses he might take during his freshman year. By the end of counseling, Jake, though still undecided, had narrowed his ideas about a career choice. Moreover, he indicated that he felt positive about his initial academic plan. In this case, having a clear picture of both Jake's abilities and weaknesses allowed the counselor and Jake to create a plan that would help him increase the likelihood of achieving his goals.

Predictive Uses of Assessment

Assessment results may also be used to predict future academic and job performance. The probability of performing well on a job, in a training program, or in an educational program is relevant information on which to base further exploration. However, currently available ability measures primarily provide broad measures of an individual's experience and ability at the time of testing (aptitude tests), whereas achievement tests assess present levels of developed abilities. What is vitally needed is a measure of the occupational significance of abilities—that is, how important it is to have certain abilities to perform successfully in specific occupations. Until we have more data about prediction of occupational success and prediction of training and occupational performance, we should limit these references to more general terms in the counseling dialogue. Given that there is always some amount of error in any test, we will want a client to consider many forms of data when making a career decision, instead of relying solely on any test result.

Case 1. Herb wanted to know whether he could qualify for a machine operator's job in a local industrial plant. Fortunately, Herb's career practitioner had worked closely with the personnel division at the plant and had assisted in gathering data for selection and placement. Based on this information, the career practitioner administered the test that had been used to develop cutoff scores for a variety of jobs in the plant. Herb's score was sufficiently high for him to qualify for a machine operator's job. In this case, Herb was provided with information that helped him evaluate his chances of meeting the requirements of a specific job.

Case 2. Noelle decided that she would like to attend the local community college. However, she was concerned about her chances of being a successful student in that college. Her practitioner had developed an expectancy table (see Chapter 3) based on test scores and grades earned at the college by students who had attended the high school from which Noelle was graduating. Noelle agreed to take the test used in the study, and the practitioner was able to assess her chances of getting a C or better at the college. The prediction of success based on local data was vitally important in Noelle's career exploration.

When assessment results are used to predict subsequent performance, the practitioner should ensure that relevant predictive validity has been established for the tests that are used. For example, a test used to predict job performance should have a previously established high correlation with performance criteria for that job. Likewise, tests for predicting academic performance should be used only when relevant expectancy tables have already been established.

Comparative Uses of Assessment

Comparing one's personal characteristics (abilities, interests, values) with those of a criterion group is a stimulating part of career exploration. For example, it can be enlightening for individuals to compare their interests with the interests of individuals in certain occupational groups. The similarities and differences found can encourage discussion of the relevance of interests in career exploration.

The Strong Interest Inventory provides an example of an interpretive report that compares an individual's interests with those of people in a wide range of occupations. Although an individual may be pleased to find that her interests are similar to those of social science teachers, she should also be encouraged to pay attention to interests that are similar to those of other occupational groups. In addition, knowing that people with her interest code tend to experience satisfaction in certain types of jobs as opposed to others will be very helpful to her in the career exploration process.

Some inventories also show a client's scores as compared to gender-specific scores. This information can also be very helpful. If a client is considering going into a non-traditional career (i.e., when the majority of workers in that field are different gender from the client), exploring strategies on how to break into and be successful in that field will be a helpful discussion to have.

Another comparison that might be made could be intra-personal. That is, a client may take the same inventory more than once to evaluate changes. This is especially relevant for constructs such as dysfunctional career thinking, career decidedness, career maturity, or career satisfaction. A client might want to compare how s/he has progressed over several sessions, and thus a re-take would be warranted.

Developmental Uses of Assessment

Career development as a continuous process is enhanced by relevant assessment results used to increase awareness of career exploration opportunities over the life span. Learning to link measured aptitudes, interests, and values to work requirements and lifestyle preferences are good examples of using assessment results to foster career development. Meaningful assessment during all phases of career development involves the diagnostic, predictive, and comparative use of assessment results.

The American School Counselor Association has outlined three main career goals for students. Table 2-2 shows possible career development activities at elementary, middle and high school levels for each of the goals.

Table 2-2 ASCA Career Goals for Students

	Career Goal A	Career Goal B	Career Goal C
	Students will acquire the skills to investigate the world of work in relation to knowledge of self and to make informed career decisions.	Students will employ strategies to achieve future career goals with success and satisfaction.	Students will understand the relationship between personal qualities, education, training and the world of work.
Elementary	Encouraged to develop hobbies.	Work on teams to accomplish a task.	Create a collage of hobbies or have them construct career ladders related to O*NET career groups.
Middle	Create a concept wheel with self at the center, and interests, skills and hobbies generating outward, followed by possible career paths.	Have students create an informational interview form and use with five working adults. Compare the information collected in class.	Research occupations related to courses at websites such as Career Information for Kids, available at bls.gov/k12/index.htm.
High School	Take interest inventories, identify career options.	Assign student pairs three different occupations and require them to create a specific career plan for each. In the large group, write out the strategies and compare for similarities. Finally, have them create their own career plan.	Create a diagram that links personal attributes with career fields and possible training paths.

The college student is challenged with assessing personal aptitudes and preferences when determining a major or a career. The career development objective for an adult in career transition requires an evaluation of learned skills from previous work and leisure experiences in determining new career directions. For the older adult, measured interests and leisure activities, skills needed in part-time or volunteer work, and assessment of established values are relevant developmental uses of assessment results. In all the examples of career development objectives, assessment results provide vital information for enhancing individual growth. The career practitioner needs to be aware of a wide range of assessment instruments to meet individual needs at various stages of career development.

In addition to these guidelines are the National Career Development Guidelines, which are suggested for student and adult career development competencies, currently maintained by the National Career Development Association. Three main areas of emphasis and related goals are outlined in Table 2-3.

Table 2-3 Career Goals Associated with the National Career Development Guidelines

National Career Development Guidelines	Goals
Personal Social Development	• Develop understanding of yourself to build and maintain a positive self-concept • Develop positive interpersonal skills including respect for diversity • Integrate personal growth and change into your career development • Balance personal, leisure, community, learner, family and work roles
Educational Achievement and Lifelong Learning	• Attain educational and achievement and performance levels needed to reach your personal and career goals • Participate in ongoing, lifelong learning experiences to enhance your ability to function effectively in a diverse and changing economy
Career Management	• Create and manage a career plan that meets your goals • Use a process of decision-making as one component of career development • Use accurate, current, and unbiased career information during career planning and management • Master academic, occupational, and general employability skills in order to obtain, create, maintain, and/or advance your employment • Integrate changing employment trends, societal needs, and economic conditions into your career plans

Knowledge of these developmental guidelines will give a practitioner confidence in administering and interpreting career assessments. Knowledge about what individuals should know and be able to do with respect to their career choices informs the career practitioner about appropriate interventions, including career assessments.

How, When and Whether to Use Assessment Results

How, when, and whether to use assessment results are decisions made preferably in collaboration between the practitioner and the client. The decision should be based on the purpose or desired outcome for using instruments. Prior to selecting a specific assessment, the counselor should ask, "Can the results from this assessment provide the information sought, and is that information relevant for the decisions that the client needs to make?" This principle is followed when using assessment results for individuals as well as for groups. Tests are not to be given indiscriminately, and the same tests are not to be given routinely to everyone. Individuals in different phases of career development have different needs, which must be considered when determining whether to use an assessment. One individual may need assistance in developing an awareness of her interests; another may need to clarify his values so s/he can establish priorities. Personality conflicts may be a deterrent for another individual who is considering a job change. Yet another may need assistance in clarifying expectations about work in general.

A careful analysis of the purpose for using measurement devices would answer these questions:
- Is now the best time to introduce a career assessment?
- What information would be useful in helping the client move forward in her/his choice?
- What are testing options are available, and which is most likely to provide the needed information?
- What are the psychometric properties (e.g., reliability, validity, normative sample) for the tests I am considering?
- Are there any mental health concerns or cognitive issues that might impact the client's ability to make the best use of a given inventory? (For example, someone who is depressed may indicate that they have no interest in any activity, and someone who has severe dyslexia might find a longer career inventory frustrating or need an accommodation).
- If a group is being counseled, will the results from the inventory introduce pertinent information for group discussion?

Because career exploration follows paths determined by individual needs, the use of assessment results in career counseling will vary and should be geared toward meeting specific objectives. Later chapters show how the use of assessment results in counseling can be designed to meet individual objectives.

Culturally Appropriate Career Assessment

Career practitioners should always consider the cultural background of a client when engaging in career counseling and career testing. Flores, Spanierman and Obasi (2003) identified a four stage linear model for culturally appropriate career assessment (see Figure 2-1). They also encouraged a multilevel and multi-method approach to career assessments with diverse clients.

Figure 2-1 A Model for Culturally Appropriate Career Assessment

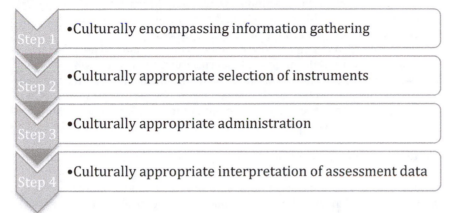

Step 1 •Culturally encompassing information gathering

Step 2 •Culturally appropriate selection of instruments

Step 3 •Culturally appropriate administration

Step 4 •Culturally appropriate interpretation of assessment data

Multilevel includes not only information at the individual level, but also at the cultural and societal levels. Multi-method suggests using various approaches to assessment. In addition, Leong and Hartung (2000) encouraged practitioners to consider cultural validity (how valid an instrument is for specific cultures) and cultural specificity (how cultural variables such as language and world view impact the assessment process) when selecting a career assessment.

As with culturally appropriate career counseling, *culturally appropriate* career assessment should be synonymous with career assessment. That is, career assessment (and career counseling, for that matter) that is culturally enriched is beneficial for all clients. To self-assess cultural competency, a practitioner might complete Ward and Bingham's (1993) Multicultural Career Counseling Checklist, which includes a section on exploration and assessment. Some examples include understanding the client's view of the ethno-cultural identification of her/his family, as well as any limitations that the client may be associating with her/his race or culture.

Culturally competent practitioners strategically consider whether an inventory is appropriate for diverse clients. Some questions to consider include:

- Does the technical manual provide normative information on diverse groups?
- Does the assessment under consideration match the client's concern?
- Does the inventory show cross-cultural reliability? For which groups?
- Have there been articles published on the use of the inventory with diverse groups and what do those results suggest?
- Do any of the items seem to elicit a repeated response among diverse clients? (Best assessed by using local normative data)

The process of deciding is indeed complex and unique for each individual, dependent on cognitive factors and the social structure of the individual's milieu. Understanding a client's racial and cultural experiences, as well as expectations from significant others and family, will help the career practitioner better understand the contextual issues impacting a career decision, as well as draw upon strengths within that client's environment to help the client achieve their goals.

General Steps To Interpreting Results

Most inventories will provide suggestions on how to interpret the test results to a client. Many manuals will also include case studies that a counselor can review to see how to interpret common as well as unusual test results. The steps below are general steps that can be applied to interpreting any test results. There is an assumption that the counselor is following ethical guidelines, such as taking the test in question, having the results interpreted, and observing an interpretation prior to administering and interpreting the test to a client. In addition, the counselor should consider the developmental level of the client (Whiston & Rose, 2013), to make sure that terminology is appropriate. Interpreting results to a middle school student may differ drastically from interpreting results to an adult. Once these have occurred, the following steps are recommended:

21

a. **Review results privately.** If at all possible, the practitioner should review the results prior to interpreting them to the client. This way, the practitioner can determine if the scores are valid, if there are any unusual or difficult results (such as no differentiation among scores, or very few career options listed), and decide how to best approach this with the client. It is not always possible for the practitioner to have preview time. For example, a client might come to a session with test results in hand, or the client might complete a brief inventory during a session. The practitioner should not feel "put on the spot" to interpret the results immediately, and can ask for a few minutes to look over the results, or recommend discussing the results the following week after the practitioner has had adequate time to review the results. This allows time for the practitioner to research the psychometric properties of the inventory, research studies conducted with the inventory, determine potential follow up questions, and to receive feedback from a supervisor on the results, if necessary.

b. **Review the purpose of the inventory.** Even if you followed Zunker's model, selected an inventory that matched the client's needs, and discussed the purpose of that specific inventory and what it would and would not provide, you will find that once the results are in hand, the client will say, "the test told me I should…". Begin the interpretation with restating the client's needs, the reason this inventory was select, and the type of results expected (e.g., generating a list of options to consider versus identifying the one best career choice for you, or identifying potential barriers that are getting in the way of a career decision).

c. **Ask for general reactions to the inventory.** Before diving into the results, gain an understanding of the client's perception of the inventory, and listen for any statements that might give clues as to how they approached the test. For example, "I'm not a negative person, so I said that I basically liked everything." Likely outcome: high undifferentiated profile and not very useful results. Or, "That test was really long. In the end I just wanted to get through it." Interpretation: fatigue and irritation might have impacted level of seriousness in responding to items, especially at the end.

d. **Provide a quick view of the report.** Show how the report is organized. In most cases, reports will provide an overview of the constructs being measured, indicators of how a person scored on specific scales, a list of corresponding occupations, and information on additional resources. Think of this step as being similar to picking up a map at a theme park before beginning down any specific route. This allows the client to have an overall sense of the "lay of the land."

e. **Review main constructs.** While many clients may want to jump to the end of the report to see a list of occupations, providing a quick overview is a good idea. For example, the 16PF measures 16 factors of personality, and also five global factors. If a report has a description of the different constructs, and the client has peaks and valleys (clear indicators of preferences and dislikes), the career practitioner might have the client read through the descriptions of the clear constructs and highlight or star the attributes with which the client most identifies. This step can be useful in later discussions, as the practitioner can pull in those specific attributes, such as "Now that we're talking about job searching, remember how you highlighted 'shy and quiet' in that report? How do you think those characteristics might play out at the upcoming career fair?" In addition, by having clients identify which descriptors do and do not fit their personality, it creates a more individualized report.

   If a client has an undifferentiated pattern, the career practitioner may try to gain an understanding of where the client's true scores lie by having the client read through all the main constructs and rank order them, as well as highlight and cross out descriptors that match/don't match his or her perception of self. After ranking, the practitioner should ask if there is a clear break between any of the ranked order. For example, is #1 "light years" away from #2, or are they interchangeable? Are the first five in the same realm of "fit," and then #6 through #8 in the second tier? By adding this step, the practitioner can get a better sense of where the differentiation might occur.

f. **Review scores.** Begin by comparing scores with those reported for the norm group, and if major differences occur, discuss why this might have happened. A score of 52 on the Investigative general occupational theme of the Strong Interest Inventory isn't helpful unless the client knows how to interpret that score. On the Strong Interest Inventory, that score would be considered average, but on the Self-Directed Search that score would be considered very high. The practitioner should review the score ranges, and what high, average and low scores are and mean. The meaning may differ for each inventory. For example, a score of 70 on the Career Thoughts Inventory suggests a high level of dysfunctional career thinking, but a score of 10 does not indicate that the client has a high level of positive career thinking—only the absence of negative career thinking. In that case, there is one construct being measured. Personality inventory results usually reflect scores on a continuum between two different constructs, such as Extroversion and Introversion. High scores on one indicate lower scores on the other.

g. **Ask client to summarize results and scores.** Before moving into the list of occupations (if there is

22

one), ask the client to summarize what has been reviewed, and their thoughts about how accurate the results are to this point. If they completely disagree with the results presented, the practitioner should not immediately question the validity and reliability of the inventory. Remember, you chose an inventory that was valid and reliable. If the results don't match the client's perceptions of her or his interests, values, personalities, and so forth, the practitioner should reflect on how the client said they approached taking the inventory, and if that had any impact on the results. The client endorsed items on the inventory that yielded the results. If the client was honest in his or her endorsements (rather than trying to make the results come out a certain way), then even though the client may be unhappy with what the results suggest, it does not invalidate the results. The practitioner should use discretion when discussing this with a client. A gentle confrontation or a "let's withhold judgment at this point" statement might be the best approach.

At this point, a practitioner may decide to go back and review individual items with the client. This is especially true for career development, career decision, and career beliefs inventories, or if significant time has passed since the client took the inventory. Look at items endorsed as "strongly agree" or those rated the highest and ask the client to talk about each of those items. Or, similarly to having them review themes, have the client rank order the strongly endorsed items so that a clearer picture of concerns can begin to emerge.

h. **Review the list of occupations.** For those inventories that provide a list of matched occupations or fields of study, it's best to have a highlighter and pen in hand for this next step. Give the report to the client and ask them to look over the list, highlighting options that are potential choices, crossing through options that are not, and placing a question mark by options that the client may need more information on before placing it on the would/would not choose list. This step can be done outside or during the session. If during the session, the practitioner might ask the client to talk aloud during the process to gain a sense of how the client is making decisions about each of the options. Some questions to consider include:

- Is there a theme emerging (even beyond what the report descriptions suggest) for occupations placed in either category?
- Is negative self-talk beginning to emerge?
- How is the client approaching the task?
- Is the client disappointed that a particular option did not appear on his or her list? (If so, the practitioner can research what the code is for that option and discuss why it might not have appeared.)

i. **Determine next steps.** What happens next is covered extensively in step five of Zunker's model. The practitioner should review the purpose that was determined earlier for taking the inventory, and then determine with the client whether that purpose was achieved. If it was, then what is the next logical step? It might be an assessment that focuses on a different area (e.g., if the first inventory assessed interests and the client also wanted to explore values), or might proceed with gaining information about options of interest. If the goal for testing was not accomplished, the practitioner and client should discuss the possible reasons for this. Possible problems might be inventory selection, a misunderstanding of what the assessment was supposed to do, that the client's stated goals for assessment changed, or that perhaps the client was not ready to take the inventory. Either way, the client and practitioner should re-group to determine what the next step might be, which could be to re-take the inventory, use a different career assessment tool, or focus on a different aspect of career counseling such as exploring career information or a narrative approach.

Emphasis on Dialogue

When interpreting results, the practitioner should aim for balance in the discussion with respect to how much time each person (practitioner and client) talks. If a 20 page report is generated, the temptation is to move into "expert" mode and explain the results for 10, 15, 30 minutes or more. The opposite of this is to be very passive, handing the client the results and letting them read through it, and then to ask "What do you think?" or some other general question. Either direction is less than desirable.

As much as possible, involve the client in discovering and discussing the results. For example, most personality and interests test results have at least one paragraph describing the personality or interest types measured by the inventory. Instead of reading this section of the results or describing the types, a practitioner could say, "Here we have a description of the different types. Why don't you read through them and talk about which one(s) you think is/are most like you?"

At this stage in the interpretation is where career counseling gets the reputation as a "test and tell" activity. As career practitioners, we love problem-solving, and can be easily tempted into giving advice—whether it's about finding career information, job search strategies, or how to interpret a career inventory. Instead, the practitioner should be deliberate about breaking the report into sections, and making sure the client has time to

23

reflect and respond. It will make the interpretation slower, but it will also be much more meaningful if the client is given the space to consider what the results mean personally.

Using Holland Codes for Interpretation

The Holland codes are a common way for presenting information about an individual's interests and personalities. Several inventories, including the Strong Interest Inventory, the Self-Directed Search, the ASVAB, Career Key, the RIASEC Inventory, the Picture Interest Career Survey, and others utilize the Holland types. Having a basic understanding of the six types and the undergirding theory will help the practitioner understand the meanings of the types and implications for clients.

According to John Holland (1997), individuals are attracted to a given career by their particular personalities and numerous variables that constitute their backgrounds. Although Holland's work centered on the development of interest inventories and their interpretation, his concepts are also related to skills, abilities, attitudes, and values that will be discussed in many of the following chapters. It is therefore important to introduce the basic assumptions of his theory (Holland, Powell & Fritzsche, 1994, pp. 5–6):

1. In our culture, most persons can be categorized as one of six types: Realistic, Investigative, Artistic, Social, Enterprising, or Conventional.
2. There are six kinds of environments: Realistic, Investigative, Artistic, Social, Enterprising, and Conventional.
3. People search for environments that will let them exercise their skills and abilities, express their attitudes and values, and take on agreeable problems and roles.
4. A person's behavior is determined by an interaction between his or her personality and the characteristics of the environment.

Central to Holland's theory is the concept that one chooses a career to satisfy one's preferred personal modal orientation. For example, a socially oriented individual prefers to work in an environment that provides interaction with others, such as a teaching position. A mechanically inclined individual, however, might seek out an environment where the trade could be quietly practiced and one could avoid socializing to a great extent. Occupational homogeneity—that is, congruence between one's work and interests—provides the best route to self-fulfillment and a consistent career pattern. Individuals out of their element who have conflicting occupational environmental roles and goals will have inconsistent and divergent career patterns. A brief explanation of Holland's personal styles and occupational environments is seen in Table 2-4. For a more complete explanation, see Zunker (2014).

Many of the chapters in this book refer to Holland's types and codes, and, at times, some of this information will be repeated for a better understanding of his typology. For in-depth coverage of RIASEC theory, read Holland's book about his theory (1997) and the many research articles that support his occupational types.

Table 2-4 Holland Personal Styles

Type	Personal Style	Occupational Environments
Realistic (R)	R types prefer concrete versus abstract work tasks, work outdoors in manual activities, likes to work alone or with other realistic people	Most occupations are blue-collar ones, such as plumber, electrician, and service occupations
Investigative (I)	I types prefer to work in an environment where one is required to use abstract and analytical skills, are somewhat independent, and are strongly oriented to accomplishing tasks	Many scientific professions require high levels of education and are intellectually oriented, such as chemist, biologist, and researcher; examples of other investigative occupations are laboratory technician, computer programmer, and electronics worker
Artistic (A)	A types include imaginative and creative individuals who value aesthetics, prefer self-expression through the arts, and are rather independent and extroverted	Some occupations included in this category are sculptor, artist, designer, music teacher, orchestra leader, editor, writer, and critic
Social (S)	S types are very concerned with social problems, prefer social interaction, are religious, participate in community service, are interested in educational activities, and prefer working with people. There is a strong orientation toward working with others and using interpersonal skills	Occupational categories in this group include those in education, such as teacher, school administrator, and college professor; others are social worker, rehabilitation practitioner, and professional nurse
Enterprising (E)	E types are extroverted, aggressive, adventurous, dominant, and persuasive and prefer leadership roles. Their behaviour is also characterized as goal-directed, and they like to coordinate others' work	Occupational categories are managerial including workers in charge of production and in various sales positions
Conventional (C)	C types are practical, well controlled, sociable, and rather conservative. They prefer structured tasks and are comfortable when working with details	Occupations include office and clerical workers, accountant, bookkeeper, receptionist, teller, and key-punch operator

International Career Testing

While many of the popular career inventories in the United States have been translated into languages other than English, there is a dearth of research reporting the reliability, validity, and normative findings for use of these instruments in other countries. Volume 50 of the Career Development Quarterly is a special issue about career counseling in Asia. Some of the articles addressed the issue of career testing. For example, Leung (2002) identified four factors impacting career testing in Hong Kong:

1. The lack of an official Chinese translation of popular U.S. inventories;
2. The inventories are too expensive;
3. Lack of research proving the reliability and validity of the inventories for the different communities within Hong Kong; and
4. The occupations and structure of occupations that are presented either as part of the inventories or as a result of taking such inventories doesn't match the occupations and occupational structure of Hong Kong.

These issues have an obvious impact on career service providers in Hong Kong. There is a need for career instruments that are relevant in terms of specific inventory items as well as a list of occupations that are available and likely possibilities for people in China.

In Taiwan, Chang (2002) described that for centuries, test results were used to classify people into occupations, and people would follow the career path that was suggested by these results. This highlights a difference in philosophy between Taiwan and most American counselors. A key assumption about career testing in general is that the purpose is to expand, not narrow, a person's career options. Practitioners may find it difficult to change a mindset that has been the reality for decades. This relates back to validity and reliability information. Knowing that a Taiwanese client probably puts a great deal of faith into test results, a counselor must ensure that the test being used meets the highest psychometric standards, and that the client understands the purpose of the test. Chang also described that the government controls testing, funding and staff. Without governmental assistance, developing test norms is difficult to accomplish. Other issues included test security, test over-exposure and conditions of testing as factors that are slowing the development of computer-assisted career guidance in Taiwan.

The issue of international career testing is one that is just beginning to gain some attention. At this point in time, we can identify the following concerns, based on the articles above:

- Translation does not equate with cultural applicability
- Occupations, work tasks and occupational structures of the U.S. are not generalizable to those of other countries
- Culture-specific validity and reliability must be established for each inventory; it is incorrect to assume that because a test has high validity and reliability in the U.S., that it will demonstrate the same in other countries
- The costs associated with test training, purchasing tests, software or licenses can be prohibitive
- The philosophy of how a career choice is made, the power of career tests, and who is in control of making career decisions for individuals need to be addressed before an inventory is selected

While many practitioners may not see themselves as counseling in another country, in today's global workplace, it is easy to see how a practitioner who engages in online career counseling might very well have a career counseling client who is from another country. Another common situation is with providing career counseling to international students who hope to return to work in their home country. It is then that these issues and others (i.e., ethical issues regarding online career counseling and using career assessments online) become more pertinent. Practitioners interested in learning more about international issues with respect to testing should refer to the *International Journal for Vocational and Educational Guidance*.

One-Shot Career Counseling

People have different expectations for career counseling. Some take a realistic approach and expect to spend considerable time in individual study and in counseling encounters. Others expect practitioners to analyze their assessment results and prescribe a career in one counseling session (Cronbach, 1984; Prediger, 1980). At the most, clients seem to expect career counseling to only require a maximum of three sessions (Galassi, Crace, Martin, James, & Wallace, 1992). To illustrate this second kind of expectation, imagine yourself as a practitioner in the following two cases.

Two Examples

Ying, a high school senior, drops by the counseling office one week before graduation and tells the practitioner that he would like to know what major he should select for his first summer session in college: "I would like to take the test that will tell me what to major in." As Ying sees it, the test holds the key to his future.

Ann, a second-semester college sophomore, makes an appointment in the college counseling center during mid-semester break. She explains, "I would like to take those tests that will tell me what career I should choose so I can register for the courses next semester." She has an entire half-day to make this decision!

Often, in more subtle ways than these, parents and students expect one-shot assessment interpretations to resolve the issue of career choice, as if believing that tests have a mystical power to foretell the future. The pressure to declare a major or a career immediately is demonstrated best by college students right before a holiday - when they are headed home and will be expected to have an answer for the question, "So, what are you majoring in?" Some clients may very well have high expectations of what psychological tests can do—that is, solve their problems. From that frame of reference, a practitioner's major responsibility is to test clients and place them in the right job, major or career path.

The limitations of one-shot counseling are apparent. First, in career exploration, many decisions are tentative; one-shot counseling approaches give just the opposite impression. Second, there is little opportunity to confirm the decisions based on assessment results. One-shot counseling does not provide for follow-up through observation, continuous discussion of assessment results, or retesting. Third, a one-shot counseling approach affirms the individual's desire to make decisions without devoting time to gathering information and considering alternatives. There is little opportunity to develop a systematic method of decision-making. In effect, the client is seeking the practitioner's approval to approach career decision making from a single throw of the dice without considering alternative information. When faced with a client who insists on making the career decision within one session, the counselor's best option may be to create an itemized plan with recommended steps for making a career decision – but not try to accomplish it all in one session! To point out the folly of making such an important decision with such little thought, the counselor could have the client pull an occupational title out of a bag, or open the *Occupations Finder*, close her/his eyes and point to one, and ask the client to react to that choice. In most cases, this extreme response isn't necessary. By engaging the client in the process, they will see that it is going to take more than 15 minutes to make an informed career choice.

Ideally, the use of assessment results should be only one phase of career exploration. Individual characteristics measured by tests and inventories should be only one facet considered in the career decision-making process. Assessment results should be combined with background information for making career decisions over the life span. Practitioners and clients can then periodically verify or reevaluate assessment results along with other material and experiences in the continuous process of career development. In the next chapter, we'll explore models other than one-shot counseling for using assessment results in career counseling.

Career Counseling: Science, Education or Art?

Career development professionals are scientists as well as educators and artists.

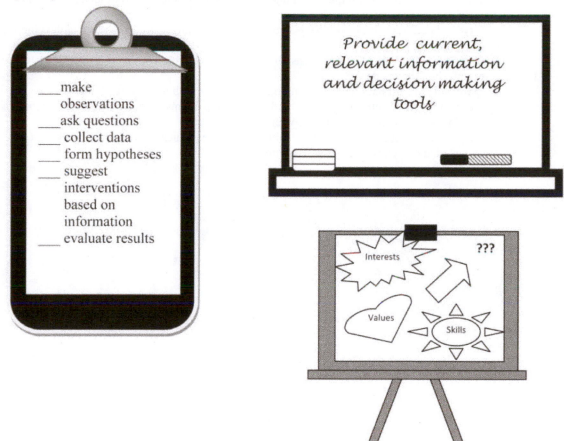

As a scientist, the career practitioner relies on well-researched theories and methods to help a client in their situation. The career practitioner should regularly check the professional literature and other review sources of career assessments. Some of these include professional journals such as *Measurement and Evaluation in Counseling and Development,* the *Career Development Quarterly, Buros' Mental Measurement Yearbooks,* and *A Counselor's Guide to Career Assessment Instruments.* As an educator, the practitioner hopefully employs a learner-centered approach of providing accurate information that is useful to the client. The career practitioner is able to translate research findings into understandable terms, as well as explain the nuances of specific test results to the client. As an artist, the practitioner joins with the client in considering all the unique elements the client and his or her environment (culture, family, and so forth) bring that may be brought out through discussion with the client or through assessment results, and to design the client's current situation and to create a promising career path.

Summary

Many factors should be considered when interpreting assessment results, including the original intention for testing, the theoretical framework for interpreting, the cultural appropriateness and relevancy of career assessments, and how career assessment fits into the overall process of career counseling. General guidelines for interpreting test results, as well as international career testing, and the limitations of one-shot counseling, were discussed. In our next chapter, we look more closely at general measurement issues that should be considered when using career assessments in counseling.

Questions and Exercises
1. How does your preferred career theory impact the way you choose and use career assessments?
2. What kinds of tests are most often used for diagnostic purposes? For predictive purposes? Explain.
3. Describe how you will evaluate your multicultural competencies with respect to using career assessments.
4. What role might culture play with respect to career assessment? What issues should a culturally competent career practitioner be aware of?
5. Describe one circumstance where assessment may be used as (a) a diagnostic tool, (b) a predictive tool, (c) a means of comparing an individual with a criterion group, and (d) for developmental purposes.
6. How would you answer the request of Ying, the high school senior used as an example of one-shot career counseling?
7. What type of activities might you have students and adults engage in to assess and develop their level of career competency?
8. If you are providing online career counseling with a person from another country, what are some of the issues you should consider?
9. Compare and contrast national versus international issues with respect to testing.
10. What type of creative activities might you design to help clients or students accomplish one of the goals outlined in the National Career Development Guidelines?
11. Roleplay interpreting a career inventory with a colleague. Which of those steps was most useful? How would you change your approach with future clients?

CHAPTER 3

SOME MEASUREMENT CONCEPTS

In this chapter, we discuss several basic measurement concepts and methods of interpreting assessment results to help improve the career practitioner's skill in selecting and using standardized instruments. Later chapters will make numerous references to the material in this chapter in describing specific tests and inventories. The information found in this chapter is contained in separate chapters in most assessment textbooks. We have combined this information here to provide, first, an overview of the common elements used in assessment interpretation; second, the information necessary for comparing the strengths and weaknesses of currently used methods of score reporting; and third, definitions of measurement concepts for easy referral.

Advanced Organizer
In this chapter, we will cover the following topics:

- Norms
- Score Profiles
- Transformation of Scores
- Criterion-Referenced Measures
- Accuracy of Measurement
- Correlations
- Summary
- Questions and Exercises

Norms
One of the most important questions a career practitioner must consider when selecting an inventory is whether or not the tool is appropriate for the client. Of course, the first consideration is the client's needs and the instruments available, but the second question must be how appropriate the tests under consideration are for the specific client and their career needs. The determination of test appropriateness should be partially based on whom the test was piloted, or for what groups the test has been shown to have value (through additional research). If the test was normed on college students, using that inventory on elementary or middle school students would be unethical.

The usefulness of assessment results in career counseling is determined by norms. In using norms, the practitioner should consider:

- When norms should be used;
- What kind of norms should be used; and
- How much weight should be given to norms.

Norms represent the level of performance obtained by the individuals (normative sample) used in developing score standards. Norms can thus be thought of as typical or normal scores. Norms for some tests and inventories are based on the general population. Other norms are based on specific groups such as all 12th-grade students, 12th-grade students who plan to attend college, left-handed individuals, former drug abusers, former alcoholics, or individuals with physical disabilities.

Norm Tables
The organization of norm tables varies somewhat from test to test. For example, the manual for the Self-Directed Search lists separate norms for males and females by middle school, high school, college and adult levels for two letter and three letter Holland types (Holland & Messer, 2013). The ASVAB provides norms in terms of gender (male, female, combined gender) and other demographic characteristics.

The normative sample description is critical for understanding if a test should be used. In some manuals, only a brief description is given, leaving practitioners to assume that their clients resemble the normative population. Others, such as the Kuder Career Search, provide specific definitions of normative groups. Such detailed descriptions of persons sampled in standardizing an inventory provide good data for comparing the norm samples with client groups. In many instances, more information would be useful, such as score differences between age and ethnic groups and between individuals in different geographical locations. The more descriptive the norms are, the greater their utility and flexibility.

When using norms, practitioners must carefully evaluate the population from which the norms have been derived to determine whether that population resembles their clients in background and individual characteristics. We would not want to use norms derived from a sample of Puerto Ricans in the Northeast to

29

advise a group of Chinese students on the West Coast. However, norms derived from Puerto Ricans in the Northeast are more appropriate for use with Puerto Ricans living elsewhere in the country than are general-population norms.

National Norms

National norms, sometimes referred to as general-population norms or people-in-general norms, are usually controlled in the sampling process to be balanced in geographical area, ethnicity, educational level, sex, age, and other factors. National norms may be helpful in determining underlying individual characteristics and patterns. For example, an individual whose measured values suggest only an average need for achievement compared with that of business executives and entrepreneurs may exhibit a moderately high need for achievement when compared with people in general. This information suggests an underlying or secondary need for achievement that might not otherwise have been clarified. The identification of lower-order yet important personal traits affords greater depth for career exploration.

In many instances, national norms should not be used. National norms based on a sample of 12th graders are of little value in predicting success in a particular university; appropriate norms would be those derived from students who have attended the that specific university. Likewise, norms based on a general population are not useful in predicting success in a certain job at a local factory. Selection and placement in an industry are usually based on norms derived from workers in a specific occupation or work setting.

Local Norms

Because operational and educational requirements vary from one location to another, using local norms is recommended. For example, you will recall that in Chapter 2, Noelle wanted to know her chances of success at the local community college. In this case, the practitioner had collected data from former students of Noelle's high school to develop an expectancy table based on test scores and grades earned at the college by students who had attended the high school from which Noelle was graduating. This information was very helpful and more personal than national norms.

Although more weight can be given to local norms than to general norms and local norms should be developed whenever possible, practitioners usually do not have the time and resources required to devote to such projects. Most practitioners must rely on the published norms furnished in test and inventory manuals. Most of the counseling cases discussed in later chapters illustrate the use of assessment results with published norms.

Score Profiles

In early counseling approaches, the profile served as the primary tool for making one-shot predictions of vocational choice (Goldman, 1972; Prediger, 1980). Choices were considered definite and irreversible (Cronbach, 1984). Currently, the score profile is considered as only one source of information on individual characteristics. As can be seen in Figure 3-1, score profiles provide a visual representation of the peaks and valleys in a person's test results.

Figure 3-1: Example of Score Profile

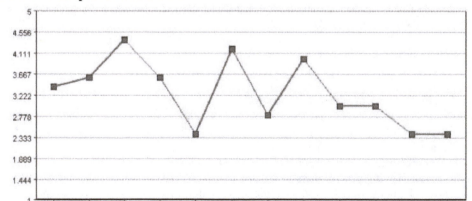

They help to identify what falls within the "normal" range, as well as indicators of where the individual scored higher or lower. Regardless of the instrument, these results should stimulate questions for the counselor, such as:

- Do the results confirm the hypotheses I had about this client?
- Do they provide us with new information or confirm pre-existing information?

- Are there any interesting combination of peaks and valleys? For example, does the combination of high scores on External Conflict and Decision Making Confusion on the Career Thoughts Inventory suggest that significant others might be adding to the confusion an individual is experiencing?
- Do the results provide me, as the counselor, with any ideas of interventions that might better suit my client? For example, I might have originally thought that my client would find researching occupations online useful, but after seeing that the client has a very high *Social* score, I might suggest informational interviewing instead.

To make assessment results as meaningful as possible, computer-generated narrative reports or computer-based interpretations are increasingly being used as supplements to the profile. The computer uses logarithms to interpret the score results in narrative form according to a planned program, and these narrative reports are often sent directly to students and parents, or can be printed out for the clients. Score profiles alone do not always stimulate individuals to explore careers. Exercises such as workbooks or written exercises significantly increase the effectiveness of career interventions such as career assessments (Brown & Ryan Krane, 2000). Although supplements to profiles may prove helpful in stimulating career exploration, the career practitioner should not completely abandon the role of interpreting the profile. In fact, the potential for increasing the number and variety of computer-generated score interpretations in the future is almost a mandate for practitioners to sharpen their skills in this respect. Receiving a generic report can be useful because the client can assume there is no bias evident. The computer is not taking into consideration the unique nuances of the client's background, cultural values, and biases. The report is a strict output of the data that was inputted. However, this is also a weakness of the report. For example, what happens if a client's scores generate a list of 3-5 career options? The counselor may be able to help the client expand her or his list based on their knowledge of the client's preferences or unique background.

Score profiles can be represented in many different ways. Often times, scores will be plotted in a fashion similar to Figure 3-1. At other times, t-scores or percentiles may be reported and presented in a graph. Or, in some cases, just the scores are reported.

Regardless of the format of the score profile, three important principles of interpretation must be followed:

- differences between scores should be interpreted with caution,
- profiles should be interpreted with concern for the influence of norms, and
- scores should be expressed in ranges rather than in points.

Differences Between Scores

Caution must always be used when interpreting differences between scores on a profile. Small score differences are meaningless and should be attributed to chance effects. Clients may be tempted to make much more of small score differences between subtests than is plausible. Still, one should not eliminate second-, third-, or fourth-order measured interests and consider only highest measured interests in career exploration. Although, if one scale is highly elevated above other scales, more weight should be given to that highest scale.

Example

Matteo's scores on the Self-Directed Search were as follows: R=52, I = 30; A=28; S=12; E=14; C=27. Taking the highest scores, his code would be calculated as "RIA". After looking at an initial list of occupations related to that code, the practitioner (or computer) will mix up the codes to be RAI, IAR, IRA, AIR, and ARI. This will likely yield very few additional options that he will like, as Matteo clearly has a preference for "R" type careers. In this case, a better strategy would be to keep the "R" in position one, and look at occupations matching the following: RIA, RAI, RIC, and RCI. "C" was included because it was a close score to "A."

Likewise, when the scores are relatively flat (e.g., R=32, I = 30; A=28; S=21; E=22; C=27), the practitioner should not focus solely on the high score, in this case, "R," but should look at various permutations. At the same time, you might say that the best intervention is to just give the client the *Dictionary of Holland Occupational Codes*. Obviously, that would be overwhelming. A better option would be to ask the client to prioritize the types based on the descriptions of each type provided in the computerized report, and then look at the options represented in the top three types chosen. To point a person narrowly to a slightly higher measured characteristic is counterproductive in developmental counseling.

Relation of Norms to the Shape of a Profile

An individual's profile must be carefully interpreted in light of the norm reference group. The position of scores is determined by the norms used. For example, Miguel, who is interested in architecture, has taken the Differential Aptitude Test. His score profile compared with that of men in general suggests that his general abilities are high enough for him to consider college. To obtain a reliable estimate of his chances of success in a school of architecture, his scores were compared with norms derived from architecture students. The shapes of

31

the profiles were quite different. When Miguel's scores were plotted against those for men in general, all were considerably above average. When compared with scores of architecture students, most of his scores were in the average range (See Figure 3-2).

Figure 3-2: Comparison of Individual Scores with National and Local Norms

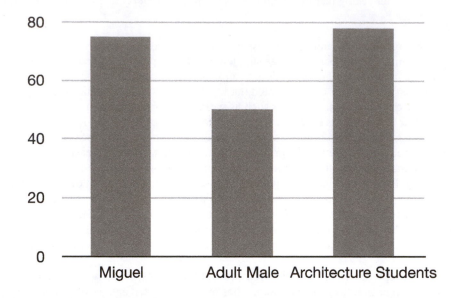

This profile gives a much more valid estimate of Miguel's chances for success in a school of architecture than does the general profile. Whenever possible, score profiles used for predicting performance should be compared with those of competitors (Cronbach, 1984).

Scores as a Range

On some score profiles, results are reported as points on a scale; on others, scores are reported as a range that includes the error of measurement of each test. The range may be represented on a percentile graph by a bar, line, or row of x's, with the obtained percentile at the center. The purpose for this is to show where a person's true score might actually be. We know that the obtained score on a test on any given day likely differs from the person's true score. For example, if a person was praised or criticized, or was feeling unusually good or bad just prior to completing an inventory, the inventory might not reflect the person's real or true score. Showing a range (also known as confidence bands) reflects where the individual's true score more accurately than does the single-point method.

Because career development is a continuous process, the score profile provides information from which only tentative decisions need be made. These decisions, not being binding or irreversible, provide information on which to base a further study of individual characteristics. Therefore, the range is more appropriate as a reference for individual decisions than is a single point. Because we are usually not able to obtain precise measures in career exploration, the standard error of measurement should be considered for all scores recorded as a single point on a scale. An easy way to do this is to transform the scores using the standard deviation of the test or sub-scale

Transformation of Scores

Client raw scores on a test are rarely useful to a career practitioner. Raw scores on their own can be difficult to interpret. What does a 52 mean? Is that good? bad? average? Trying to keep track of what raw scores actually mean, especially when talking about more than one inventory, is near to impossible. That's where transformation of scores comes in handy – and, most computer-generated profiles do this us! Even on the ones that don't, it doesn't take much effort to transform them manually. In this section, we'll review the normal bell curve, as well as how to interpret transformed scores, which may be reported in the form of percentile equivalents, standard T scores, stanines, or grade equivalents.

Bell-Shaped Curve

Two of the most prominently used methods of interpreting assessment results are percentile equivalents and standard scores. To obtain an understanding of the relationship between these two reporting procedures, refer to the well-known normal, or bell-shaped, curve in Figure 3–3. M represents the mean, or midpoint (50th percentile), with 4 standard deviations on each side of the mean.

Figure 3-3: Scores Plotted on a Normal Bell Curve

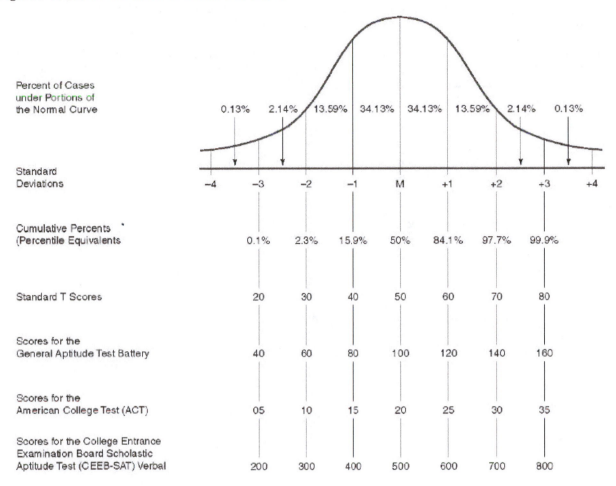

Starting at M, go to the right to +1 standard deviation and note the percentile equivalent of 84 (in rounded numbers). Likewise, go to the left of M to -1 standard deviation and find the percentile equivalent of 16. You will notice that other percentile points can be obtained for each standard deviation. Understanding the relationship of percentile equivalents to standard deviations and their relative positions on the bell-shaped curve helps interpret test scores. For example, a percentile score of 98 is 2 standard deviations from the mean. A score equal to 2 standard deviations below the mean is approximately at the 2nd percentile.

Referring to Figure 3-3 you can see also that a General Aptitude Test Battery (GATB) score of 120 is 1 standard deviation above the mean, or at the 84th percentile. An ACT score of 25 is at the same relative position. These two scores are not to be regarded as equal. The standard scores for each test were developed using samples from different populations, and each test is quite different in content. However, two standard scores can be compared by their relative position under the normal bell-shaped curve. For example, an ACT score of 25 is at the same relative position within its reference group as a GATB of 120.

It is useful at times to compare an individual's score to where the majority of the scores lie. For example, +1 or -1 standard deviation from the mean will capture approximately 68% of the variance. (To obtain the 68%, you add the 34.13% that is contained within-1 standard deviation and the 34.13% that is contained within +1 standard deviation). People whose scores are closest to those of the norm group will score within + or - 1 standard deviation from the mean. As you move out further from the mean, the frequency of people scoring in that range becomes fewer. For example, one of the qualifications of being labeled as gifted is an intelligence quotient of 130 or higher. The mean for most intelligence tests is 100, and the standard deviation is 15. So, to meet that specific criterion for giftedness, a person would need to score 2 standard deviations above the mean. If you learn that a person's score is 2 or 3 standard deviations above or below the mean, you conceptually know that their score is outside of what the normal scores typically are.

This isn't necessarily bad. For example, a person scoring three standard deviations above the mean on career decidedness is someone who has a very clear sense of what they want to do. However, someone who is three standard deviations above the mean on dysfunctional thinking has some major internal barriers to making decisions.

33

Percentile Equivalents

Percentile equivalents are sometimes easier to interpret than standard scores. Using Figure 3-3 and a GATB score of 63, you can determine the exact percentile equivalent. Here's the process:

First, you need to find the 1% increase between 60 and 80. These numbers aren't chosen arbitrarily. 60 lies at -2 standard deviations, and the next GATB number reported is 80, which lies at -1 standard deviation. 63 lies in between those numbers. Steps are required to find the 1% increase, including:

    a. Find how many numbers lie between the range for the observed score.
- 80–60 = 20

    b. Calculate the difference between the standard deviations around the observed score.
- 15.9–2.3 = 13.6

    c. Divide the SD difference by the number of integers between the range surrounding the observed score to determine the 1% increase.
- 13.6/20 = .68

    d. Multiply the 1% increase to the number that you want to increase the score by. This will give you the percentage increase to add to the lower percentage (in this case, 60).
- We want to get to 63, and we already know the percentile for 60. We need to move up from 60 to 63, or by 3. So, we multiply .68 by 3.
- .68 * 3 = 2.04

    e. Determine the percentile equivalent.
- The percentile equivalent for 60 is 2.3.
- To gain the percentile equivalent for 63, you'd add 2.04 to 2.3.
- 2.3+2.04 = 4.34

    f. Double-check your answer. We know that a GATB of 65 = 5.7 percentile. If our calculations are correct, when we multiply .68 times five and add that to 2.3 we should get 5.7 (.68*5 = 3.4 + 2.3 = 5.7).

In Figure 3-4, a typical test profile is constructed to depict percentile equivalents.

Figure 3-4: Percentile Equivalents

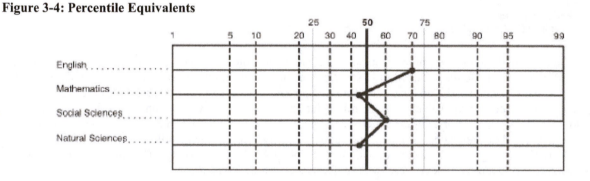

Note the heavy line representing the midpoint and the thinner lines representing the 25th and 75th percentiles, the average range for this particular achievement test. The difference in scores between the 25th and 75th percentiles is not as great as may appear. Refer to the bell-shaped curve in Figure 3-3 and notice that to move several percentile points within the average band does not take as great a performance as it does to move the same number of percentile points beyond the 75th percentile. Thus, the practitioner needs to be cautious when interpreting differences in scores within the average range; the difference in performance within this range may not be as significant as it appears.

      Percentile equivalents are direct and relatively easy to understand, which is a primary reason for their popularity. However, it is important to identify the norm reference group from which the percentile equivalents have been derived. Norm-referenced tests can be based on local, state, regional, or national data or on data for selected groups such as all high school seniors (nationally) who are attending college or all college seniors in the western region of the United States. One of the problems is with the interpretation of percentile equivalents. People tend to interpret a 45% as failing, or a 95% as an "A." We attach labels to these percentile equivalents that aren't always appropriate. Thus, to effectively communicate test results, the norm frame of reference should be established. For example: "From a national sample, 60 out of 100 high school seniors who attended college scored lower than you did, while 40 out of 100 scored higher."

Standard Scores

Normalized standard scores used in tests and inventories are based on standard deviation units in a normal distribution. Test developers determine what the average score is for the norming group and assign a value to it. They then determine where the major differences occur within the norming group by seeing how far off the next group of test-takers are from the mean (i.e., determine the standard deviation from the mean). Figure 3-4 shows the percentage of scores within each standard deviation unit and standard scores used by selected standardized tests. The first, the standard T score, have an average of 50 and a standard deviation of 10. The T score has a range of 20 to 80, extending 3 standard deviations above the mean and 3 standard deviations below the mean. For all practical purposes, the entire range of scores of 99.72% of the cases will fall within +3 and -3 standard deviations. The middle 68% of the scores are within +1 and -1 standard deviations.

Approximately 95% of scores will fall between ±1.96 standard deviation units. A T score of slightly less than 60 is in the top 20% for a given test. Such points of reference make the standard score a valuable tool for interpreting assessment results. For example, a meaningful interpretation can be made of a score that is 1.5 standard deviations from the mean when normalized standard scores and their relationship to standard deviations are understood. Thus, the relative position of the standard score under the normal distribution provides a discernible point of reference for that score's variation from the average.

Sometimes, you may see scores reported as z-scores. Z scores have a mean of zero and range from -4 to +4, with each number landing on the standard deviation. For example, someone who is 2 standard deviations above the mean will have a z score of 2, or if they are 3 standard deviations below the mean, they will have a z score of -3. A frame of reference can easily be established for standardized tests by thinking about their scores in the same way. For example, a GATB score of 120 is 1 standard deviation from the mean, or at the 84th percentile. Likewise, 1 standard deviation below the mean (16th percentile) is equal to a GATB score of 80. The middle 68% of the scores are between the standard scores 80 and 120. A meaningful interpretation can thus be given to any standard score when the mean and standard deviation are known.

Stanines

A stanine (short for "standard nine") is a standard score on a scale with nine approximately equal units, and an average of about 4.5 with a standard deviation of 2. The advantage of the stanine is that scores are presented as a range rather than as points on a scale, as shown in Figure 3-5. In a normal distribution, the lower level (1) represents the bottom 4% of the cases; stanine 5 represents the middle 20%; and stanine 9, the highest level, represents the top 4%. Thinking of a range rather than a point for score interpretation is more descriptive and deters emphasizing small differences. To be of practical significance (a distinction worth talking about with the client or altering interventions), the difference between stanine scores must be 2 or more.

Figure 3-5: Stanines and the Normal Bell Curve

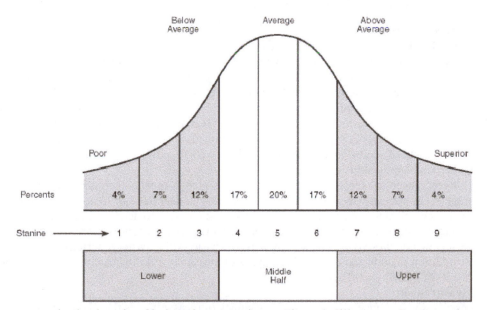

Stanine scores may also be thought of in broader categories, as Figure 3-5 illustrates. For example, stanine scores 1, 2, and 3 are considered below average; stanine scores 4, 5, and 6 are considered average; and stanines 7, 8,

35

and 9 are above average. Cumulative percentile points (Figure 3-5) provide further possibilities for interpreting stanines as lower quarter, middle half, and upper quarter.

Grade Equivalents

Because of the familiarity of grade placement and its frame of reference, grade equivalents are often used to interpret achievement test scores. Norms for grade equivalents are derived from average raw scores of students in each grade level. These equivalents are expressed by a number representing grade level in combination with the ten months of the school year, September through June. For example, 10.0 represents the beginning of the tenth grade in September; 10.5 represents average performance in February of that academic year.

Because of the idea of placement within a grade, misinterpretation of grade equivalents can occur. For example, in Figure 3-6, this 4th grade student received a score of 6.3 on the science portion of the Stanford Achievement Test. This result **should not** be interpreted to mean the student has mastered the science courses taught in the 4th grade and the first half of the 6th grade and can now be placed in the second half of the 6th-

Figure 3-6: Sample Stanford Achievement Test Result

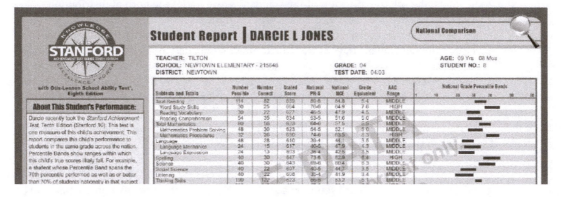

grade science class. No doubt, the student has performed admirably on the science test, but grade equivalent scores are not to be regarded as performance standards. In this example, the student's raw score is close to the median or mean raw score made by students in the middle of the 8th grade. Although the student might have performed very well on the lower primary form of this achievement test, there were no 6th grade level items on the test given to 4th graders (Drummond and Jones, 2009). Also, grade equivalents are not to be considered comparable for all scales. For example, in the fifth grade, growth in learning a particular subject such as mathematics will be much greater than it will be in the ninth grade. Additionally, counselors should remember that a single grade equivalent score, as is true with all instruments, provide a snapshot, not a video of a person's abilities, interests and so forth. For many achievement tests that provide grade equivalent scores, counselors are recommended to use the National Percentile score instead.

Criterion-Referenced Tests

Criterion-referenced tests evaluate a person's knowledge or skill as it relates to an established knowledge base. In these types of tests, there are right and wrong answers (or better answers). In criterion-referenced measures, an individual's score is interpreted by its relative position within the distribution of scores obtained by the standardization sample or other groups of special interest. In other words, the interpretation of criterion-referenced test scores is based on how well the individual's performance matches a set of standards or external criteria judged by the test user to be suitable for the individual's grade level. The focus is on levels of performance within a limited range of specific skills or content. For example, criterion-referenced scores provide an index of how well an individual has mastered arithmetic computations or certain reading skills.

In criterion-referenced tests, specific information is provided as to what the individual is capable of doing: for example, "The subject was able to subtract numbers with decimals" or "The subject used the correct verb form in a sentence." Scales from a criterion-referenced test are used to determine an individual level of performance with reference to a specified content criterion. Examples of criterion-referenced tests that a career counselor might see include those that focus on competency, basic skills, mastery, performance, and credentialing. In addition to understanding different types of measures, a skilled career practitioner must also understand concepts of measurement accuracy.

Accuracy of Measurement

This section presents several concepts regarding the accuracy of measurements that should also aid the practitioner in transforming assessment results into meaningful interpretations. Most importantly, you must consider the reliability and validity of the instrument under consideration. Second, to understand the relative position of a score, the practitioner must be aware of inherent error, which is specific for particular tests. Third, significant differences that may exist among subtests on any one test greatly affect the interpretation that may be given to the test results as a whole. Finally, inaccuracy in interpreting assessment can be reduced by constructing locally based expectancy tables. These concepts and their application to test interpretation are discussed and illustrated in the paragraphs that follow.

Reliability and Validity

Reliability. Reliability is one of the first requirements for good measurement. Reliability looks at how consistently a test measures the construct under consistently, and the degree to which tests scores are free from error. Since no test is completely free from error, the counselor should consider that a client's observed score on a test is actually their true score with some error added in. Reliability coefficients provide an estimate on how stable, reliable or consistent a given test is. Reliability coefficients are correlations of a given instrument with itself, parts of the inventory, or among alternate forms of the same test, and range from .00 to 1.00. Strong reliability usually ranges between .85 and .95. Test-retest reliability occurs when the same test is given more than once over a period of time to see how stable the results are. Of course, the time between the two testing periods can impact the reliability coefficient. If the two testing times are too close together, the reliability is likely to be very high, and if there's too great a distance, the reliability is likely to be lower, because of other events or variables that could influence the score.

Not all tests should have strong test-retest reliability. For example, while you would hope that a person's interest types would remain stable over time, you would hope to actually see changes in a person's career decidedness or career beliefs over time. Cronbach's alpha is a common statistic that is reported for tests that use Likert-scale items (i.e., items that have more than 2 potential responses, such as "always, often, sometimes, occasionally, never"). KR-20 is used for items that have only two response such as true/false or yes/no responses. Factors that influence reliability include the length of the test (longer tests have higher reliability), type of scoring (objective scoring has higher reliability than subjective scores), variability of the group on which the test was given (heterogeneity has higher reliability), and the difficulty of items on the test (questions that are too easy or too hard decreases reliability).

Validity. Validity answers the question, "Does the test measure what it purports to answer?" An inventory that claims to measure interests shouldn't actually be measuring skills, unless it is also claiming to measure skills. The range of validity coefficients often run much lower than that of reliability coefficients, because the test is being compared to other tests (and not itself). Validity coefficients rarely go above .60 and are more typically in the range of .30 to .50. Three types of validity include content, criterion-related and construct. *Content validity* considers the actual items on a test, and is often determined by an expert panel. For example, the statement, "I am good at problem-solving" would be a valid test item for a skills test, but questionable for an interest inventory. Sometimes tests can be misleading in their validity claims. For example, does a test that is supposed to measure math skills REALLY measure math skills, or is it composed of word problems of such reading difficulty that it is actually testing reading ability instead?

Criterion-related validity shows the degree to which the test is related to an outcome. For example, achievement test scores are often used to predict whether a student will be successful in college. To determine the criterion-related validity in this case, a researcher would collect the achievement test scores as well as an indicator of success in college, such as grade point average at the end of the first year in college. Criterion validity can be use either predictive or concurrent in nature. *Predictive validity* is used for situations like the one described earlier, i.e., when we want to use the test scores to predict or estimate future criterion scores, in this case, first year college GPA. *Concurrent validity* is looking at whether one test can be substituted for another test. Basically, a test-taker completes a test and another measurement of the criterion at the same time, and comparisons are made. If there is a strong relationship between the two, the researcher can have confidence that the test is valid to measure the desired criterion.

Construct validity answers the question, "Do the test results make psychological sense?" Another way to put it is, "Does the test actually measure the construct it is intended to measure?" For example, the test says it is measuring career satisfaction. We would expect that test to be strongly correlated with tests or other constructs that are related to career satisfaction (convergent validity) and negatively correlated with tests that are not related to satisfaction (*discriminant validity*). Often times, factor analysis is used to determine these relationships.

Standard Error of Measurement (SEM)

A score on a test should not be considered an exact point without any error. It is important to always keep in mind that the score a person obtains on a given inventory on a given day is not likely to be their true score, but that some "inherent error" exists. It is much more accurate to think of test scores as estimates of true scores. Thus, an individual's performance on a test can best be thought of as falling within a range or a band rather than as a point on a scale. The SEM is an estimate of the amount of error in a particular test score; it is often provided in the test manual. (If it is not in the manual, you can calculate the SEM by multiplying the standard deviation times the square root of 1 minus the reliability coefficient). By using SEMs, we are able to increase our confidence in interpreting scores as we use the SEM to construct "confidence bands" around a person's observed score. This enables us to say, "While your score was 85 today, we are 95% confident that your true score lies between 75 and 90."

Consider the table of fictitious achievement scores on a reading scale below (Figure 3-7). The circles indicate the student's observed score (with the actual number listed in the "Student" column), and the lines going through the middle of the circle show the confidence bands, or where the student's true score is likely to be. The outlined boxes show the average mastery range, and the shading within

Figure 3-5: Demonstration of Standard Error of Measurement

	Student	Average Mastery Range	50	75	100
General Understanding	91	48-70			
Test Analysis	92	52-75			
Comprehension	65	50-70			
Applying meaning	70	45-73			

the circles indicate the student's level of mastery (high is completely darkened, moderate is half darkened). With this understanding, the practitioner can interpret that the student is far above average on General Understanding and Test Analysis areas, and within average on Comprehension and Applying Meaning subscales.

You can calculate for any percent of confidence; however, it is easier to use the percentages represented on the normal curve at +/-1, +/-2 or +/- 3 standard deviations. To determine where someone's true score lies 68% of the time, you would calculate the SEM for +/- 1 standard deviation. To do this, you would multiply the standard deviation by 1 (because you want to know where the true score lies 68%, or +/- 1 SD of the time) and then add and subtract that number to the observed score to get a range. However, being able to predict 68% of the time isn't that impressive. So, you decide that you want to be able to predict 95% of the time (which is +/- 2 standard deviations), you would take that standard deviation and multiply it by 2 (for 2 standard deviations) and then add/subtract that number to the mean to obtain your range. You would follow the same procedures to obtain the confidence bands for 99%.

The traditional approach to using the SEM is illustrated by the following example. An individual, Patricia, receives a score of 105 (observed score) on a test that has a reported SEM of 5. We now want to obtain an estimate of the person's true score. Because of errors of measurement, observed scores are assumed to be normally distributed around the true score. Hence we can refer to standard deviation units to give us the limits of observed scores. In this example, the SEM is used as a standard deviation (SD). Therefore, Patricia's true score can be calculated.

- To determine where her true score lies 68% of the time:
  - Start with her score of 105
  - Add and subtract 1 SD (5) to her observed score.
  - 105 - 5 = 100.
  - 105 + 5 = 105.
This gives us confidence that Patricia's true score lies between 100 and 105 (68% of the time).

- To determine where her true scores lies 95% of the time:
  - Start with her score of 105
  - Add and subtract 2 SD (2 *5 = 10) to her observed score.
  - 105 - 10 = 95.
  - 105 + 10 = 115.
This gives us confidence that Patricia's true score lies between 95 and 115 (95% of the time).

Over all individuals, true scores lie within this band 95% of the time. Therefore, the probability is high that the true score for the student in the example is between 95 and 115, and the probability is somewhat lower that the true score is between 100 and 110. What you can observe from this, is that as our confidence increases (we can say we are 95% certain where her true score lies), the range becomes larger, and thus our statement may lose some of its power. How powerful is it to say that you are 99% confident that a person's age lies between 0 and 100? Obviously, the standard deviation has a large impact on how wide the confidence bands will be. So, you need to determine the best balance between the observed score, standard deviation and confidence bands for each client and test.

38

Standard Error of Differences (SED) Between Two Subsets

In career counseling, it is often necessary to be certain when differences in subtest scores are significant. The differences between scores can be ascertained by computing the SED. The following example illustrates this method.

A multi-aptitude test battery reports T scores (mean = 50 and standard deviation =10) for interpretation of subtest scores. On the abstract reasoning subtest scale, a reliability coefficient of .89 is reported. Another scale has a reported reliability coefficient of .95. To find the SED between the two tests, use the following formula:

$$SED = SD\sqrt{(2 - r1 - r2)}$$

$$SED = 10\sqrt{(2 - .89 - .95)}$$

$$SED = 4$$

Where r1= reliability of subtest 1; r2 = reliability of subtest 2

To determine whether the difference between the individual's scores on the test is a real difference rather than simply chance, the SED is multiplied by 1.96. Because ±1.96 standard deviation units on the normal distribution will include 95% of the cases, scores within that range will occur by chance only 5% of the time. In this case, the result is obtained by multiplying 4 by 1.96, which is 7.84, or approximately 8 points. Thus, we can interpret a difference of 8 points or more between the two subtests in our example as being meaningful.

Consider the Self-Directed Search (SDS) that has a SED of 8. The SED is important, because it helps you interpret the scores. If a person's Realistic score is 40 and their Social score is 35, you know that there isn't any significant difference between those two scores. So, in interpreting the results, you'd know that the two scores are interchangeable, and when looking up occupations by codes, the person should look up RS jobs as well as SR jobs. If, on the other hand, the R score was 40 and the next highest code was S, with a score of 20, that's over 3 SEDs away. Then you know that the person will likely be most interested in "R" jobs, not SR jobs (though the person should consider all combinations, as long as the R is first, so RSE, RIC, RAE, RCI, RES, etc.).

Expectancy Tables

In educational planning, a practitioner often has to advise a student of chances of success in a particular college or university. An expectancy table constructed from the records of previous graduates and their performance at the university being considered provides relevant information. In Table 3–1, a sample expectancy table has been constructed from the first-semester grade point averages and ACT composite scores.

The numbers that are not in parentheses are the numbers of students whose grade point averages are in the designated range. For example, two students whose ACT composite scores were in the range 26–28 earned grade point averages between 1.50 and 1.99. Seven students in this same ACT score range earned grade point averages between 2.00 and 2.49. The numbers in the parentheses are the cumulative percents of individuals within a particular ACT score range whose earned grades are in the corresponding grade point average cell or higher. For example, 88% of the individuals whose ACT composite scores were in the 20-22 range earned grade point averages between 1.50 and 1.99 or higher. Likewise, 92% of the individuals whose ACT composite scores were in the 11–13 range earned first-semester grade point averages of .50–99 or higher.

To demonstrate the chances of success at the university being considered, the ACT composite score provides an index of academic success. For example, 81 out of 100 individuals whose ACT composite scores were 23–25 made a 2.00 grade point average or higher. The chances that individuals with the same ACT scores would make a 2.50 or higher grade point average are 48 out of 100.

Table 3-1 Sample Expectancy Table

American College Test (ACT) Composite Scores	First Semester Grade Point Averages							
	0.00-0.49	0.50-0.99	1.00-1.49	1.50-1.99	2.00-2.49	2.50-2.99	3.00-3.49	3.50-3.99
32-35						(100) 1	(67) 1	(33) 1
29-31					(100) 1	(91) 2	(73) 4	(36) 4
26-28				(100) 2	(89) 7	(50) 4	(28) 3	(11) 2
23-25				(100) 5	(81) 9	(48) 6	(26) 6	(4) 1
20-22			(100) 6	(88) 15	(61) 15	(31) 12	(6) 3	
17-19		(100) 5	(92) 6	(83) 24	(46) 22	(12) 5	(5) 3	
14-16		(100) 5	(86) 9	(62) 13	(27) 8	(5) 2		
11-13	(100) 2	(92) 5	(72) 8	(40) 62	(16) 3	(4) 1		
8-10	(100) 2	(85) 4	(54) 5	(15) 2				
5-7	(100) 1							

Correlations

Understanding how factors are related help a practitioner make appropriate interpretations and interventions. In measurement, we use the term "correlation" to describe relationships among constructs and scales. Correlations can be positive (when one factor is present, it's likely that another is present), negative (when one factor is present it's likely that the other factor is not), strong or weak, significant or insignificant. Correlations range from -1 to +1. A zero correlation would mean that there is no relationship between the two variables. A score of 1 (either positive or negative) means that there is a perfect relationship. If the score is +1, the two variables are always present together, and if the score is -1, they are never present together. Obviously, most correlations fall somewhere between +/- 1. The actual number is also important. A .23 correlation is much weaker than a .94 correlation. Correlations are generally reported with the symbol r.

Figure 3-8 shows visual representations of positive, negative and no correlations between individuals' scores (indicated as dots) on two career inventories. Imagine that the line is not there, and all you can see are the individual dots (scores). You see that in both the positive and negative correlations, the scores tend to fall in a way that would form a line. In the positive correlation example, scores on Career Inventory I mirror those on Career Inventory II. If one increases, the other increases. If one decreases, the other decreases. In the negative correlation example, scores on Career Inventory I are opposite to those on Career Inventory II. If one increases, the other decreases. If one decreases, the other increases. In both of these examples, this is not always the case.

You can see that there are a handful of scores that don't fall into the line. These are called outlier scores. If you were a researcher, you would look more closely at these outliers to see if there is anything consistent about them (such as, these scores were collected in a certain geographic region, or were for a certain age group, and so forth). There may be nothing consistent about the outlier scores, and they are just "not within normal limits." If there is no correlation between individuals' scores on Career Inventory I and II, you would visually see the third graph. You cannot draw any conclusions about how a person will score on one inventory based on the results of how they scored on the other.

Figure 3-8: Examining Sample Correlations

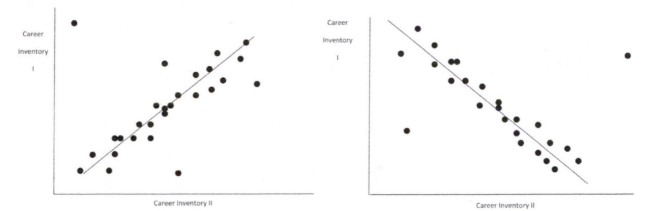

Example of a positive correlation   Example of a negative correlation

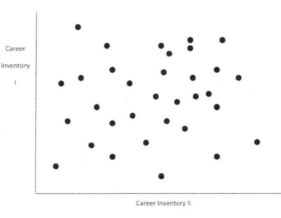

Example of no correlation

Why is this useful? If a practitioner administers a decision-making inventory, and the client's scores indicate a high level of indecision, the practitioner might want to know what other issues might be affecting the career indecision. Through research, the practitioner might discover that anxiety is the number one correlate of career indecision, but depression is a low correlate. So, instead of asking the client questions about depression, the practitioner might ask about stress/anxiety instead and might incorporate stress management techniques, or introduce cognitive reframing exercises. It is important to know that correlations describe a relationship, but do not identify which variable is causing the other.

A final consideration when looking at correlations: you will often see a "p-value" behind the correlation. For example, r = .43, p < .05. The p-value is the amount of likely error in the correlation. Anything below .05 is usually considered statistically significant, meaning the relationship is interpretable and the error is low. If p = .05 or is higher, then the relationship does not mean much, statistically speaking. However, it is important data, because it is just as important to know what is related to a variable as it is to know what is not related to it. For example, let's say a study shows there was no relationship between Holland code and intervention preference (e.g., shadowing, card sort, online research, etc.). That would be helpful to know, in that a career practitioner could then feel free to choose any of those interventions regardless of the client's Holland type and not try to match intervention with the person's primary type (e.g., have an artistic client create a collage or draw a picture of their confusion).

Consider the correlation table (Table 3-2) below of partial findings of a study comparing dysfunctional career thoughts and communication apprehension (Meyer-Griffith, Reardon, & Hartley, 2009). The 1's, perfect correlations, occur because the construct is being compared with itself. In reviewing the table, you can see that total CTI (Career Thoughts Inventory) scores (measuring overall dysfunctional career thinking) were positively and significantly correlated to three aspects of communication apprehension, but in different levels. The double asterisks indicate a p value of < .01, which means a 99% chance that this relationship was not due to chance. The one asterisk indicates a p value of < .05, which means a 95% chance that this relationship was not due to chance. If there is no asterisk, such as in the relationship between communication apprehension and group discussions, it means there is no significant relationship there. You can tell this from the low number, that even though the .18 correlation is significant, the relationship is not very strong.

41

Table 3-2: Sample Correlation Table

	Total CTI	Communication Apprehension	Group Discussions	Public Speaking
Total CTI	1			
Communication Apprehension	.81**	1		
Group Discussions	.18*	.06	1	
Public Speaking	.37**	.26**	.42**	1

So what can the practitioner take from these results practically? If a client scores very high on the Career Thoughts Inventory, the practitioner now has an additional area to discuss with the client, based on the results of this study. The practitioner can hypothesize that the client may also have some communication fears. This correlation may be of more importance when the client begins the job interview process. Try to see the whole picture. An individual goes to an interview and has a high level of negative thoughts about themselves and has a fear of how they communicate (more negative thinking). How well is this client likely to perform in the job interview? But, if the practitioner teaches some cognitive restructuring techniques on how to manage and reframe negative self-talk, and the person's CTI scores (and dysfunctional thinking) decrease, it is very likely that the person's communication fears will also decrease because of the high correlation between CTI scores and Communication Apprehension.

Summary
In this chapter, we have discussed several methods used to interpret assessment results. These methods illustrate how assessment results can be transformed into meaningful information on characteristics and traits—information that can be used in career counseling. The concepts of measurement accuracy further illustrate how tests must be interpreted to enhance the usefulness of information provided in career counseling. Finally, we presented information about understanding basic correlations. Career practitioners should stay abreast of empirical studies that examine relationships among constructs and tests, so as to have a better understanding of test correlates outside of those reported in the manual.

Questions and Exercises
1. From Figure 3-3, what are the approximate percentile equivalents for the following standard scores? GATB: 140, 61, 85; ACT: 15, 23, 36.
2. From Figure 3-3, what is the closest standard deviation to a standard score of 108 for a test that has a mean of 100 and a standard deviation of 10?
3. Why is it important to identify the norm reference group when using percentile equivalents to interpret assessment results? Illustrate your answer with an example.
4. What are the advantages of stanine scores over percentiles and grade equivalents?
5. Use the sample expectancy table (Table 3–1) to answer the following questions.
a. What would be the chances of Bob's making a 2.00 grade point average or better with an ACT score of 30?
b. What would be Joan's chances for a 2.00 grade point average or higher with an ACT score of 16?
c. What advice would you offer to Bob and Joan?
6. If a person receives a 63 on the GATB, what would their score be in terms of percentiles? (Don't estimate, calculate)
7. If a person receives a 90 on the GATB, what would their score be in terms of percentiles? (Don't estimate, calculate)
8. If a person received a 12 on the ACT, what would their score be in terms of percentiles? (Don't estimate, calculate)
9. If a person received a 428 on the College Entrance Exam, what would their score be in terms of percentiles? (Don't estimate, calculate - in this case, you might not want to start by figuring out the 1% increase, but start at the midpoint or a higher percentage).
10. If a person's raw score was 7 on the Decisiveness scale of the Career Decision Profile (that measures how clearly a client views his or her career plan), and the mean is 12 and the S.D. is 3, where does this person's true score lie 68%, 95% and 99% of the time? How decisive is this person likely to be?
11. Consider a person's sten score on the 16PF for Factors A (Reserved versus Warm), C (Reactive versus Emotionally Stable) and I (Utilitarian versus Sensitive) are 2, 3 and 4 (with a mean of 5.5 and S.D. of 2). The factors represent polar opposites, with 5.5 meaning the median, and scores from 1-5 leans toward the first factor listed in the pair, and 6-10 towards the second pair. Where does his/her true score lie 68%, 95% and 99% of the time, and which of the following occupations would you most highly recommend investigating, practitioner, engineer or firefighter?

42

12. Do a literature search on a topic related to career testing or career counseling. For example, a search might include any combination of the following:
    - Anxiety, depression, perfectionism
    - Career choice, career satisfaction, undecided

    Using the article, look for a report of the correlations. Describe your findings to the class. An alternative activity might be to break into small groups and decide on a key construct for each group (career choice, career satisfaction, career decidedness, career change, career major, etc.) and have each member of the group research a correlate. Each group could then present their findings to the class.

13. Which is more desirable, to have 95% accuracy and a larger range in which a true score may lie, or a 68% accuracy and a smaller range in which the true score lies?

14. If a person obtains a 75 on a career indecision inventory (scores range from zero to 100, with high scores indicating higher indecision), and the SEM is reported to be 4.1, where does this person's true score lie 68%, 95% and 99% of the time?

15. What kind of norms should be used to predict an individual's chances of getting a C grade or better at a certain community college? Explain your answer.

16. How can national norms be most effectively used in career counseling? What are their limitations?

17. What is the difference between reliability and validity?

18. Given the profile below from the Gordon Personal Profile, how would you interpret this student's scores?

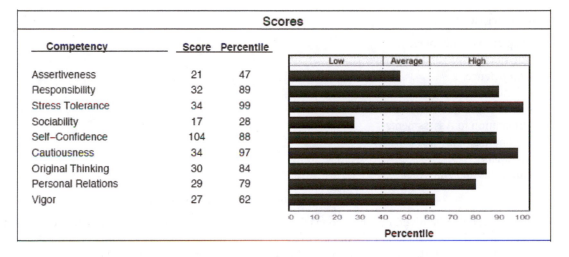

43

CHAPTER 4

ETHICS AND ASSESSMENT

What do the following have in common?

- An employer asks you to share the results of an employee's personality inventory to help in a promotional decision.
- A client brings in assessment results from an inventory that you've not seen and asks you to help interpret, but you notice that the information is presented in Holland codes.
- You determine that a client could benefit from a career maturity inventory, but the only one your center has was not normed on a sample similar to your client.
- You offer online career services, and you want to provide an online intake form as a preliminary assessment that e-mails the completed form to your e-mail account.

In each of these examples, an ethical dilemma is being presented. Issues of competence, confidentiality, and appropriateness are presented above. Many other ethical issues are associated with testing. In this chapter, we will address the major issues.

Advanced Organizer

In this chapter, we will cover:
- The Purpose of Ethical Standards
- Competence
- Client Needs
- Confidentiality
- Orientation to Assessments
- Technology and Assessments
- Summary
- Questions and Activities

The Purpose of Ethical Standards

As a profession, those involved in career counseling and career counseling activities are bound by a set of ethical standards. These standards help define what we should and should not be doing. They serve as reminders, but also as guidelines for appropriate behavior with respect to the many aspects of career counseling practice, such as individual and group counseling, confidentiality, diversity, testing, and advertising. As career counselors and practitioners, our professional boards include the American Counseling Association and the National Career Development Association. If you are a nationally certified counselor, then you must adhere to the NBCC code of ethics as well. In addition, the Association for Assessment and Research in Counseling has published the *Multicultural Assessment Standards* (2012). Even if a career counselor or practitioner is not a member of a professional association, they are still responsible to act within the boundaries of those standards, and their actions held up against the standards of these professional associations. Website addresses (which house ethical standards) for the American Counseling Association (ACA), National Center Development Association (NCDA), National Board for Certified Counselors (NBCC), and Association for Assessment and Research in Counseling (AARC) standards are listed below:

- American Counseling Association: counseling.org
- National Career Development Association: ncda.org
- National Board for Certified Counselors: nbcc.org
- Association for Assessment in Counseling: http://aarc-counseling.org

The most common guidelines include the following recommendations for ethical use of assessments:
- reviewing the validity and reliability of the instrument,
- being aware of your boundaries of competence (only give and interpret tests that you are qualified for and have had experience giving and interpreting),
- providing an orientation in which you describe how the test results will be used and stored (including confidentiality and test security),
- considering whether the test is appropriate for your client (based on client needs and the norm

group for the test),
- explaining all test limitations,
- obtaining informed consent,
- ensuring that any advertising that your school or agency distributes about the test is accurate and not misleading,
- following standardized instructions, and
- providing correct and easy-to-understand interpretations.

The professional associations identified in this chapter can provide additional information on these specific guidelines. In addition, having a basic knowledge of testing is required. For example, when you see a bar with a dot somewhere in that bar, knowing that the dot is the person's individual score on the construct and that the bar represents a certain amount of variance (error) around the score indicating where the person's "true score" might exist will be very helpful when interpreting results. Finally, practitioners should remember that career assessment results, whether standardized or non-standardized, only provide one piece of the puzzle and should be interpreted in the larger context of what the individual is presenting.

Competence

As a counselor or practitioner, you agree that you will act within your own "boundaries of competence" (BOC). Every practitioner has areas of expertise, and other areas in which they do not have the skills or necessary training to provide adequate service. Multiple areas of counseling foci exist, including family counseling, marital counseling, career counseling, eating disorders, depression, anxiety, sexual abuse, and g/l/b/t issues, to name a few. With hundreds of assessments in existence, it is probable that a practitioner will not be aware of or skilled in using every one. In order to become competent in an area or with an assessment, a practitioner must have training and supervised experience. The ethical standards state that a practitioner should not provide services or assessments that exceed the practitioner's existing training and skills. At a minimum, providing assessments ethically includes practitioners:

- Taking the assessment themselves and receiving an interpretation of their inventory results prior to administering it to a client;
- Reading the manual; and
- Practicing administering/interpreting the results on a peer or another practitioner to build competence and confidence.

In addition to these, knowing the validity, reliability and normative information about the assessment will help the practitioner determine if the inventory is appropriate for a given client.

Client Needs

Any intervention that a practitioner selects should be based on the client's characteristics, needs and the stated goals for counseling. A common expectation of clients regarding career counseling is that they will take a test (Galassi et al., 1992), while many prefer reading about careers or other activities over testing. In some cases, administering an inventory might not be appropriate. The practitioner should take into consideration a client's comfort/desire to engage in any intervention before recommending it. Some clients, being more "Social" in nature, will prefer to rely more on conversation with a counselor or an expert in a given field of interest. A practitioner who is aware of Holland types might ask directed questions and then suggest looking at a list of "S" occupations. Or, if a client is deciding between two occupations, giving an interest inventory would not be the logical next step, but helping the client to evaluate the options, either through providing more information, or a pro/con analysis, would be a better intervention. In other words, assessments should not be the immediate answer for any need that the client presents, but should be recommended when the client's career needs suggest that it would be helpful. In addition to career needs, practitioners should also consider client characteristics such as cultural differences, gender, and sexual orientation.

Cultural Differences

Career practitioners should strive to be culturally competent, and this competence should be demonstrated through sensitivity when recommending, administering and interpreting tests. They should "recognize the importance of social justice advocacy" and "integrate understanding of age, gender, ability, race, ethnic group, national origin, religion, sexual orientation, linguistic background and other personal characteristics in order to provide appropriate assessment and diagnostic techniques" (AACE Standard for Multicultural Assessment, 2012, p. 2).

According to Flores, Spanierman and Obasi (2003), a culturally competent career assessment "integrates culturally relevant information about the client; attempts to understand the client in his or her cultural, personal and career contextual realities; and takes into account the limitations of traditional assessment and assessment tools" (p. 80). In addition, they suggested that the practitioner should deliberately evaluate each step of the career assessment process to ensure they are acting in culturally appropriate ways. Leong and Hartung (2000) encouraged practitioners to consider cultural validity (how valid an instrument is for specific cultures) and cultural specificity (how cultural variables such as language and worldview impact the assessment process) when selecting an assessment.

Other considerations should include:
- *Norm groups for a test.* If the client's norm group was not included, the results should be interpreted with caution. If there is a certain population that has a higher percentage of representation at a practitioner's site, the practitioner should consider developing local normative data on the test results for comparison. This would require masking identifiable information about the client. In addition, practitioners should not just assume that because a particular ethnic group is mentioned in the normative data, e.g., Asian females, that the results of the norm group are comparable to all Asian females. For example, many times test developers will use college students as a large base for their norming sample. It would be wrong to assume that the results of a college-educated sample are generalizable to those even in the same ethnic group who are not college-educated (Flores et al., 2003).
- *Incorporating standardized and non-standardized, formal and informal assessment approaches.* Using multiple approaches to assessment attends to different learning styles and can yield different types of useful information.
- *Equivalence.* This includes linguistic, conceptual, scale and normative *equivalency* associated with an inventory (Fouad, 1993; Marsella & Leong, 1995). It is important that score differences among culturally different groups are not interpreted as deficits (Flores et al., 2003).
- *Test security* (Flores et al., 2003). This involves being clear about with whom test results will be shared.
- *Above all else, focus on the therapeutic relationship.* If the client senses there is a strong working alliance, the client would have been involved in the decision to incorporate the assessment into the counseling session, and might be more willing to state concerns or disagreement with the results if the results did not seem to correspond with what the client expected. In some cultures, disagreement is seen as a sign of disrespect, and the practitioner should be alert to this possibility, and even model some healthy questioning of the results.

Client's culture should also play a part during the interpretation phase of career assessments. Culturally competent counselors should explore the potential impact of individual differences (e.g., culture, background, experience, familial expectations) and external events such as oppression and discrimination on how the client may see the assessment results.

PRACTITIONER:	So, what did you think about the inventory you completed?
LI:	It was good. It showed me things I should do and things I shouldn't do.
PRACTITIONER:	Do you think that a test like this one should be the ultimate authority on whether or not you choose one career or another?
LI:	I don't know – you talked about how this was a valid test – so the answers must be right. Maybe the test picked up on something I didn't know myself.
PRACTITIONER:	You make a good point there – maybe the results grouped your interests together in a way you hadn't seen them grouped before. So were there any surprises?
LI:	Well, I would have never considered myself to be a politician, and it's listed in there. So is salesperson and fundraiser. I would have never thought of any of these. Maybe I should learn a little more about these jobs and consider changing my major?
PRACTITIONER:	I think you're wise to consider each of the options carefully before discarding them. However, remember, this inventory was a measure of your interests. There's a lot more to you than what was on that inventory – your personality, your values, your skills, and goals – all of these also play a part. You know, one of the inventories I took had physician listed as an option. It was picking up on the fact that I like to problem-solve and help people. What the inventory didn't pick up on was that I didn't want to spend that much time in college, I didn't really like the sight of blood, and I didn't want to work on-call. What do you think the inventory might have been tapping into, in terms of your interests, when listing politician and those other occupations?

LI:	Maybe that I'm a good leader? I guess I also can be persuasive if there's something I really believe in. But, I don't like to be pushy, and I think some of that has to come out if you're in those occupations.
PRACTITIONER:	OK. So you can see how those might fit some of your interests and skills, but is not such a good match in other areas. What were some of the occupations that were on your list that you felt good about?
LI:	There was a project manager listed, and a small business owner. I liked those.
PRACTITIONER:	I can see you highlighted some others as well. Instead of focusing on the ones that you already feel are not a good fit for you, why don't we spend some time on the ones that seem to be better fits?

In this conversation, the practitioner modeled the appropriateness of questioning the results of the inventory, without negating the results altogether. In addition, the practitioner used self-disclosure as a way to demonstrate how the inventory might not pick up on all aspects of a person. By asking what interests the inventory might have found that resulted in some "surprising" occupations being listed, the practitioner gave Li the opportunity to strengthen his self-knowledge, by causing Li to re-state his interests and clarify some of his work values.

Gender Issues

The questions of sex bias within an instrument and in the results of an inventory, as well as the way in which the data is reported by norm group appear to be the primary issues of concern with respect to gender issues and assessment. A practitioner should read the manual of any assessment prior to administering it, to gain a better understanding of the assumptions made by the test developer and to determine if it is an appropriate inventory to administer to a particular client (considering client needs and psychometric properties, including norm group data).

While using same-sexed norms is often recommended (Whiston & Bouwkamp, 2003) especially with interest inventories, not all assessments report different results for women and men. Betz (1992; 2000a) suggested that the practitioner help the client evaluate suggested options with respect to opportunity and socialization. For example, did a client score lower in mechanical interests or skills because she actually has no interests or skills in that area, or could it be because she was never given the opportunity to develop those interests/skills, and was even socialized against those interests/skills, because those activities were seen as being more "boyish"?

Consider including non-standardized approaches, such as a values clarification exercise (Hackett & Lonborg, 1994), an ideal day exercise, and card sorts (see chapter 10). With respect to card sorts, make sure that gender and ethnic bias are not evident in the cards (especially if pictures are used). In addition, given the research that shows that women tend to have lower self-efficacy, especially with respect to math skills (Betz & Hackett, 1997), practitioners should not just accept it when a female client says, "I'm not good at math," but should be prepared to gently challenge that statement. For example, "What makes you think that you aren't good at math?" or "Are there certain areas of math that you are better in?" or "Do you think that it's a matter of skill or that you aren't as interested in math?"

Sexual Orientation Issues

Normative data on assessments do not generally include information on the sexual orientation of the norm group. This may stem from an assumption that career interests and skills do not differentiate according to a person's sexual orientation. While limited research has been conducted on this topic, Chung (2003) has outlined some ethical considerations associated with testing and lesbian, gay and bisexual (LGB) clients. For example, testing that includes information about barriers may bring up concerns of discrimination, victimization, and harassment. LGBT clients may lean toward stereotypically appropriate LGBT careers, or may lean for stereotypically heterosexual careers. While a practitioner should not discourage a client from pursuing a career that is a real interest, the practitioner might want to help the client evaluate how their perception of their career options are "related to social pressure, internalized stereotypes, or perceptions of limited occupational opportunities" (p. 100).

A practitioner might also want to include the LGBT client's significant other, parents, families and friends in the assessment/career counseling process as the client desires. Before choosing an inventory to use with a LGBT client, the practitioner should review the inventory to make sure that there is no evidence of heterosexist bias. For example, if a practitioner wants to help the client identify potential barriers to making a career choice, does the inventory include an item such as "My spouse disapproves of my current choice" versus the more inclusive term of "partner"? Another consideration is that given the lack of standardized inventories for LGBT individuals, a practitioner might use non-traditional assessment methods (Chung, 2003), such as card sorts or an ideal day, as described in other chapters of this book.

Confidentiality

Part of the power of counseling comes from the trust that develops between a client and the practitioner. The client is free to share hopes and dreams, fears and doubts, with the confidence that the information shared is confidential, with a few caveats. Confidentiality also extends to test results. For example, test results can only be released with the client's consent (or client's legal representative), and then can only be shared with other professionals that are able to interpret the results. In addition, if a client uses a computer-assisted career guidance program or a computer inventory, the practitioner is required to make sure that the data stored on the computer is confidential and that the records are periodically destroyed.

While this seems straightforward, the issue can become convoluted when someone else is paying for the assessment or the career counseling. For example, if a client is technically still a minor, FERPA rules allow disclosure to parents if a child is under 21 (or over 21 if the child is still dependent on the parents). Another example would be if an employer wants to have employees complete a personality measure so as to determine group strengths and weaknesses, or if an employer requires an intelligence or aptitude test as part of the selection process? While assessment results should be confidential, in these cases, the practitioner should make sure that the test-takers are informed about what and with whom the results will be shared.

Orientation

If you follow the model described in Chapter 2, the client and the practitioner should both know why a certain assessment is being suggested. You have discussed the client's needs and, working collaboratively, have decided that a certain inventory would best help achieve the next step towards meeting a goal. Even so, prior to administering an assessment, you should review why the assessment is occurring, and how the results will be used.

PRACTITIONER: Sandy, do you remember the reason that you are taking this interest inventory today?
SANDY: Yes, it's going to show me what career I should follow.
PRACTITIONER: Well, not quite. The results are going to help give us an idea of where your main interests lie. You'll also receive a list of occupations, but it won't do the work of narrowing down for you. That will be our next step, taking the suggested occupations, brainstorming from it, and getting some information to narrow those down so you can make a good choice about a career path. How does that sound to you?

One of the common misperceptions by clients is that they can take one test that will tell them what they should be. In the example above, Sandy and the practitioner had already discussed why an inventory would be useful, but as is often the case, Sandy had kept the misperception that the result would be an almost magical appearance of *the* occupation that will satisfy her forever. Instead of beginning the assessment by simply reviewing the purpose, the practitioner chose to let Sandy describe the purpose to gauge how accurate her perceptions were, and then reinforced the purpose and made a link between what she was about to do (take an assessment), the next step, and how that would help accomplish the overall goal. In addition to correcting a faulty perception, the practitioner also demonstrated ethical behavior by accurately describing the purpose for and expected results of the assessment.

Along with confirming that the client and the practitioner are on the same page about how the assessment will fit into the overall career counseling goals, the practitioner needs to determine that the client is emotionally and mentally able to complete the administration. Someone who is feeling down, or having a great deal of negative thoughts, might approach an interest inventory with all negative responses, and thus skew the results. A vicious cycle can begin, starting with negative thoughts, that lead to negative responses on the inventory, which leads to poor options being suggested, which then leads back into negative thoughts again ("I knew there wouldn't be any good options for me"). Obviously, the validity of responses from a client who is under the influence of alcohol or drugs, or someone who is experiencing mania, paranoia, depression, anxiety, etc., will be questionable.

Technology and Assessments

Technology has had a major impact on career assessments. Computerized tests and online assessments are now not only possible, but are also the norm. When a client completes an inventory, a common expectation is to see, as a result, some type of written interpretation of the results, along with a list of suggested occupations. Computerized assessments are subject to the same reliability and validity requirements as traditional paper and pencil assessments. However, many computer-assisted career guidance programs incorporate and combine various assessments (e.g., values, interests and skills) that make it difficult to calculate reliability and validity coefficients.

In addition to computerized assessments, a computer-based test interpretation report is an efficient and many times effective way to deliver a general interpretation and to pull a list of occupations from a database that match specific items endorsed by the client on the test. However, very rarely do you see validity information in an inventory manual about the interpretive report. Sampson, Purgar and Shy (2003) summarized the opinions of several authors about the role of CBTI. In a nutshell, they stated that CBTI should never be used as a replacement for a practitioner, or as a "data dump" from a stand-alone computer or an online inventory, but should be used in a consultative manner between practitioner and client. Sampson et al. (2003) outlined an 8-step sequence for integrating CBTI into career counseling in an ethical manner, and several strategies for establishing and evaluating the validity of CBTI.

The 8-step sequence is similar to the model described in Chapter 2, in that they recognize that test results should be part of the overall counseling process, related to career theory, appropriate to the client' needs and contributing to the overall plan of action. To use CBTI ethically, a practitioner should thoroughly understand the construct being tested (such as career indecision, interests, etc.); psychometric properties of the inventory; how to interpret the results and make appropriate interventions; and supervised experience with the CBTI. For more specifics on these steps and strategies, the reader is referred to Sampson et al. (2003).

Another expansion in the area of technology and assessment is with online career assessments. A keyword search on the phrase "career test" on a popular search engine yielded 500,000,000 hits/results. In the 2011 edition of this text, that same search yielded 23,000 hits/results, which shows how quickly the information has expanded. Alongside the many high-quality online assessments are thousands with questionable psychometric properties. Test results from an inventory with questionable or non-existent psychometric properties can lead to individuals making career and educational choices on faulty information.

Even those online inventories that are valid and reliable have to face certain ethical concerns. For example, if a person takes the online Self-Directed Search and ends up with a list of suggested occupations that don't seem like a good fit, who is there to offer possible explanations or inquiries to determine if a high skill set (such as conventional skills) might have inflated the total score on one typology? Similarly, a person with limited reading skills might begin to complete a computer-assisted career guidance program online, only to find that they don't understand the directions. Some may not read the instructions or descriptions of the test purposes or norm group information at all, and then misapply or misinterpret the results.

Barak (2003) outlined several ethical concerns associated with online assessment, including:

- the effects of a person's computer and Internet skills (or lack thereof);
- lack of preliminary screening—does this person need to take an inventory, and is this particular inventory the one they need to take;
- uncontrolled intervening personal psychological factors (technophobia, reading level, etc.);
- risk of cultural bias;
- secrecy of personal information and assessment results;
- unprotected, unregulated use of assessment results;
- lack of monitoring;
- technical failures;
- lack of contracted relationship between test-taker and test owner;
- lack of relevant information on a test;
- improper use of an online assessment by professional unaware of limitations;
- lack of assessment standardization;
- questionable construct validity;
- effects of digital divide (those who have regular access to a computer and the Internet versus those who do not);
- lack of information on test-taking behavior;
- common use of a single assessment method;
- problems relating to test interpretation;
- the use of non-professional tests on the Internet;
- outdated tests;
- easy violation of test copyrights (a criminal act);
- lack of qualifications of test administrators;
- lack of personal assistance and support relating to assessment results; and
- implementation and use of assessment results; and existence of hidden commercial agenda (gaining personal information to add to mailing or spam lists).

Some clients will come to career counseling with results from an online inventory in hand, or memories of having taken an online inventory. The career practitioner should be cautious about giving too much credibility to questionable sources, but also should avoid dismissing them completely, as this might communicate to the client that s/he made a "stupid" decision to take an online inventory. Instead, the career practitioner could use the results as a starting point for discussion. The career practitioner should also model "Internet savvy" by sharing with the client a checklist and/or resources such as the Mental Measurements Yearbook that the career practitioner uses to evaluate such inventories.

49

A sample checklist, created with the NCDA/ACSCI standards, as well as the criteria used in a recent special issue of the Journal of Career Development for online assessments is shown in Table 4-1.

Name of Career Website:		
Standard/Guideline	Yes	No
Does the site follow NCDA's "Guidelines for the Use of Internet for Provision of Career Information and Planning Services, as well as the ethical guidelines for Internet-based counseling services endorsed by ACA& NBCC: • www.ncda.org/about/polnet.html#guidelines (NCDA Guidelines) • www.counseling.org/gc/cybertx.htm (ACAs Ethical Guidelines for Online Counseling)		
Does the site contain a clear identification of the name and address of the organization for which the website was developed?		
Does the site have the title of the website prominently displayed near the top of the page?		
Does the site include a short statement about the purpose of the site?		
Does the site contain an index near the beginning of the site which can be internally linked back (e.g., return to index, return to top) to various locations on the page?		
Does the site have correct grammar, punctuation, and spelling throughout?		
Does the site contain a link to the home page (if any) of the organization for which the web site was developed?		
Does the site include enough images to be attractive but not so many that the page takes excessive time to load when using modems?		
Are the graphics used appropriate?		
Is an email address listed for further questions or comments and/or a link to Frequently Asked Questions (FAQ)?		
Is the target audience clearly identified (e.g., adults, children, international, school, businesses)?		
Is the career development content up-to-date and accurate?		
Would the content hold the attention of the target audience?		
Does it appear to be free from bias or stereotyping (e.g., gender, ethnic, age)?		
Does it appear to be user-friendly (i.e., easy to use and navigate by target audience)		
Does it include a date when the site was last updated?		
Does the site provide information about the qualifications of the developer of the content for the web site and/or persons who provide services?		
Is the content concise and use a clear vocabulary?		
Is information provided for user support and/or technical assistance?		
Does the site provide access to persons with disabilities?		
Is an evaluation plan of the site included?		
Is information provided on how user feedback is incorporated?		
Is data security and confidentiality addressed?		

Summary

As ethical, culturally competent practitioners, we must be aware of and adhere to the ethical codes of our profession. This extends to career counseling as well as career testing. Gender and racial bias, the use of the Internet, and other ethical concerns affect not only counseling, but testing as well. We must know and educate other practitioners as to the ethics associated with career testing.

Questions and Activities

1. A student comes into session with the results of an online inventory summarizing interests and a list of possible careers to consider. You have not seen this inventory before. How do you proceed?
2. A client who is an ethnic minority and has been seeing you to help her make a career choice is interested in taking an interest inventory. However, the interest inventory that is available at your site (school, agency, center) does not include the normative information by racial distribution. What should you do?
3. Choose 2 websites that provide online testing. One test should be a well-known inventory, such as the Self-Directed Search, Strong Interest Inventory, Myers-Briggs Type Indicator, etc. and the other test should be one that you identify via an online search. First, evaluate the two websites on two general factors: what you liked and what you disliked. Then, complete an in-depth analysis of the two websites on some of the ethical criteria identified in this chapter.
4. Create a table comparing and contrasting the ethical standards for testing as set forth by ACA, NCDA AACR, and NBCC. For example, see below:

Standard	ACA	NCDA	NBCC	AARC
Orientation to testing	Prior to testing, practitioner gives an explanation as to the purpose, in language the client can understand – unless an explicit exemption has been agreed upon in advance.	Practitioner must provide orientation to the client prior to and following test administration, describing the purpose of the test and how the results will be used.	Must provide instrument specific orientation prior to and following testing, so the results can be placed in context. Clients must know before they take the assessment the purpose for testing and how the results will be used.	Prior to assessment, practitioners explain the nature and purposes of assessment and the specific use of results in language the client (or other legally authorized person on behalf of the client) can understand, unless an explicit exception to this right has been agreed upon in advance.

5. How do the ethical standards relating to gender, diversity and sexual orientation compare and contrast?
6. A client wants to take a well-known inventory with which you have not had experience administering and interpreting. What should you do?
7. Many times, computer-based programs allow students to save their data. What steps can you take to ensure confidentiality for students who choose this option at a computer terminal in your setting?
8. What ethical standards would apply specifically to non-standardized career assessments?

CHAPTER 5

APTITUDE AND ACHIEVEMENT TESTS

One of the most enjoyable aspects of career counseling is helping clients and students explore their interests and goals, and to give voice to their dreams. However, if the exploration of interests was the only area of personal exploration, we would have a lopsided view of the person. We need the reality of a person's skills, aptitudes, and knowledge to increase the likelihood of their making an occupational selection in which they are most likely to be successful.

Every year, thousands of students enter pre-med schools with the dream of becoming doctors - and then reality hits as they take their first chemistry course. This course is often seen as the thinning-out course. If a student cannot pass this course, they will not be admitted to the pre-med program, and they will not become a doctor. Some students faced with this problem will seek tutoring or re-take the course in hopes to then be successful. Some are, but many are not successful in passing the course and are forced to consider options that better fit their knowledge, aptitudes and skills. While this may seem cruel, consider your own physician. Would you rather have a surgeon who was passionate about his or her work, and yet did not have the knowledge or skills to perform the work well, or a less passionate doctor who did have the skills? Ideally, your physician would have both, but certainly in this case, skills are favored over interests.

Advanced Organizer

In this chapter, we will cover:
- Aptitudes
- Aptitudes & Skills Through the Lens of Theory
- Aptitude Tests
- Multi-Aptitude Tests: Limitations and Suggestions for Use
- Other Aptitude Tests
- Aptitude Tests Summary
- Achievement
- Using Achievement Test Results for Self-Concept and Self-Efficacy Development
- Suggestions for Career Development
- Other Achievement Tests
- Summary
- Questions and Exercises

But first, let's hear from a sergeant who regularly uses an aptitude test to help adolescents identify career and educational opportunities linked to their aptitudes and interests.

We mainly use the ASVAB for entry into Armed Forces. We are invited into the local high schools by the school counselors and then proctor a large group administration of the ASVAB. Once we have the results, we offer a basic 5-10 minute interpretation of the overall results with students in a large group format. We show them their percentile scores and how to see where they stand among their peers. There's a booklet that comes with the ASVAB that guides the students through selecting their likes and dislikes, and as they progress through the booklet, a table develops to show what skills of employment would be best suited for them. Usually, this process takes about an hour. Following this, we offer individual follow-ups to those students who are interested.

The ASVAB is more than just a recruitment tool for the Armed Services. The career assessment program has 72 questions that doesn't involve the armed services - about everyday things in which they might be involved and enjoy. It's incredibly beneficial to juniors, in that if they can identify their career goals based on their interests and aptitudes, they can be deliberate in their academic planning and what they need to emphasize in their studies for their senior year in order to pursue that career.

I remember one student I worked with who scored very well on the ASVAB. As we were going through interpretation, it came to light that he liked the idea of working in medicine and that he had a strong aptitude for it. However, according to his mother, he had never shown an interest in the medical field. The last I heard, he had obtained a medical position within the army and was doing well. The ASVAB Career Exploration Program helped him discover his aptitude and interest in medicine, and the military provided him with the opportunity to pursue that dream.

Sergeant Charles E Kitchens

Aptitudes

An aptitude is thought to be specified proficiency or the ability to acquire a certain proficiency. Aptitudes differ slightly from abilities, in that abilities represent existing skills while aptitudes include potential skills (Drummond and Jones, 2009). Aptitude may also be defined as a tendency, capacity, or inclination to do a certain task. A common misconception is that aptitudes are inherited, unchangeable characteristics that need to be discovered and subsequently matched with certain job requirements. Such an assumption is misleading for the interpretation of aptitude test results (Drummond and Jones, 2009). Rather, aptitude should be viewed as the result of both heredity and environment; an individual is born with certain capacities that might or might not be nurtured by the environment.

Aptitudes & Skills Through the Lens of Theory

Most career theories acknowledge the role of aptitudes and skills as critical factors to consider when helping someone make a career decision. The trait-and-factor approach matched the individual's traits with the requirements of a specific occupation (see Figure 5-1). Parsons' (1909) theory relied upon true reasoning between an understanding of an individual's abilities and specific job requirements, what he called, "conditions of success." The more agreement between the two, the greater likelihood a person would be successful in that occupation. Note that in Figure 5-1, the occupation listed, i.e., Chemistry, with the corresponding conditions of success, is an example of an occupation most likely to use the person's skills. Other possible occupations might include mechanic, doctor, electrician, and so forth. Less likely are social worker, professional dancer, or politician. It's not to say that these occupations are completely off the list, but the knowledge of a person's aptitudes and knowledge base help to narrow what can be an exhausting list of occupational possibilities.

Figure 5-1: Demonstration of Parsons' Theory

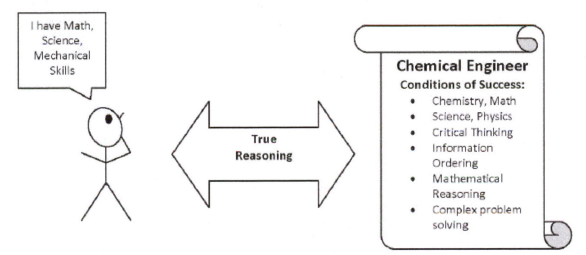

Person-Environment Correspondence theory (Dawis, 2002) describes the two possible outcomes of the interaction between skills and work expectations (See Figure 5-2). From this perspective, a job has certain demands or requirements, and a person has specific skills and knowledge. If the person's skills/knowledge match the demands of the job, the person will perform satisfactorily, and will continue on the job. If the person's skills don't match the job requirements, the person will perform unsatisfactorily and likely be fired. This is not the only option, especially if the employee is well-liked. One alternative to being fired would be for the employee to address the skills and/or knowledge gaps with specified training.

Job performance depends greatly on one's understanding the demands as well as one's ability to perform those demands. In addition, most employers want their employees to continue to progress in knowledge and skills specific to their jobs. It's in the best interest for employers to invest in their employees, as this will likely positively impact performance. Consider a pre-med student who could not pass Chemistry after repeated attempts. An aptitude or achievement test would provide the practitioner with critical information on the knowledge and skills the client brings to the table. If the client's expressed interests are very different from his or her measured abilities or knowledge, this discrepancy should be discussed.

53

Figure 5-2: Job Demand/Skill Interaction via Persona-Environment-Correspondence Theory

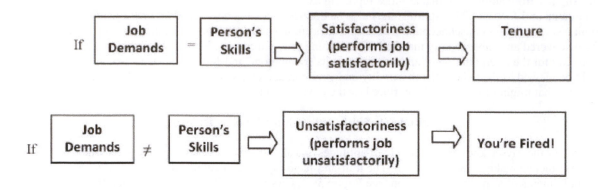

Depending on the test results, tutoring might be a viable option. If the person's scores are significantly lower than average, e.g., in stanines 1-3 (10-30% percentiles), or more than one standard deviation below the mean, it is very probable that even with tutoring, the client will not be successful in that specific area. In this example, the practitioner might proceed in the following ways:

1. Ask what attracted the student to medicine in the first place (interests and values), and if the client is interested in identifying and exploring other medical careers.
2. Explore related occupations. Many computer-assisted career guidance programs and information sources, such as the Occupational Outlook Handbook (bls.gov/OCO/) and O*NET (onetcenter.org) allow users to search for related occupations by inputting an occupation of interest.
3. Administer a general aptitude or achievement inventory and explore occupations that are generated.
4. Discuss potential external forces such as family, teachers or others that might be placing pressure on the client to choose this career path.
5. Explore and address any negative career beliefs or dysfunctional career thinking that the client might be engaging in, such as "I will only be successful if I am a doctor," or "There is only one career for me."
6. Consider using the narrative approach to identify life themes that might provide a more holistic view of the individual.

Other theories also emphasize the exploration of aptitudes and skills. Cognitive Information Processing theory (Peterson, Sampson, Reardon, & Lenz, 2002) identifies skills as one element that should be explored within the realm of the self-knowledge domain. Similarly, Social Cognitive Career theory (Lent & Brown, 2008) suggests the inter-correlation of values, interests and skills. RIASEC theory (Holland, 1997) and specifically, the *Self-Directed Search*, includes self-estimates of skills. Finally, the Career Construction approach (Savickas, 2012), and specifically the *Career Story Interview* (http://www.vocopher.com/CSI/CCI.pdf), address perceptions of skills (and other elements of self) through the question about role models. Having an understanding of how aptitudes and skills fit into the theoretical model you are using provides a roadmap for what happens next. For example, with CIP theory, the next step after analyzing skills would be Synthesis Elaboration, or expanding career options. With these theoretical frameworks in mind, let us now turn our attention to aptitude tests.

Aptitude Tests

Aptitude tests have been associated with career counseling since the time of the early trait-and-factor approach to career guidance (Zunker, 2011). Aptitude and achievement tests identify existing knowledge and skills, and are also used to predict the ability to be successful in future training or education and to learn new skills within a certain aptitude (such as verbal reasoning). As mentioned earlier, a career practitioner should be cautious about using aptitude or achievement test results as being written in stone. Rather, aptitude tests reflect the interaction of heredity and environment and predict the capacity to learn. In this discussion of aptitude tests, it is important to understand the difference between measured and expressed skills.

Measured Versus Expressed Skills

Measured aptitudes and skills differ from expressed statements of one's aptitudes and skills. "Measured" means that a test required the individual to demonstrate a skill. "Expressed" means an individual stated their skills, likely in response to a request, such as, "What are you good at?" Many inventories ask a person to self-rank their abilities. Is this always an honest estimate? Is it possible that a person would over- or under-estimate his or her own capabilities? Is it possible that a person's current mental health might impact these ratings? How would depressed individuals respond to questions about their abilities? Prediger (1995) cautioned practitioners to be careful of assuming that ability scores are indicators of true ability. Self-efficacy has been defined as "an individual's estimate of his or her ability to successfully perform a particular behavior" (Darcy & Tracey, 2003, p. 221). The question of what is actually being measured speaks to the issue of inventory validity. Ability inventories that require an individual to perform a task (such as geometry, typing, etc.) are likely to have greater validity, as compared with those that require a person to rate his or her proficiency at the task. With inventories that utilize self-estimates of skills, a career practitioner should look for other evidence of both high and low scores. IS a person TRULY poor in math or are they closing that option off because of a perception that "math isn't cool" or "girls aren't good at math?"

History Impacts on Aptitude Testing

World Wars I and II provided additional pressure on filling positions based on a person's true abilities and aptitudes. After World War II, the use of aptitude test results to select applicants for colleges and professional schools increased significantly as college applicants increased. The armed forces have sponsored ongoing research programs to develop aptitude test batteries for their use. Given the time, expense and critical nature of many of the positions in the armed forces, being able to accurately predict who will be successful in those positions becomes not only an economic matter but also one of national security.

Early vocational counseling programs advocated psychological testing in vocational counseling specifically to analyze an individual's potential in relation to requirements of training programs and occupations. These early approaches to career counseling inspired the study of job descriptions and job requirements in an attempt to predict success on the job from the measurement of job-related traits.

Multi-trait Measures

The attention to specific job requirements revealed the need for multi-trait measures. In particular, there was a need for a differential assessment of an individual's abilities. Multi-aptitude test batteries evolved to fill this need. Table 5-1 provides a comparison of aptitude scales covered by the most widely used multi-aptitude tests.

The statistical technique of factor analysis provided the tools for measuring individual abilities and thus provided the foundation for multi-aptitude test batteries. The growth of career counseling and the need for selecting and classifying industrial and military personnel increased the demand for differential measures. A number of multi-aptitude tests have also been developed for career counseling (Drummond and Jones, 2009; Whiston, 2000). The use of aptitude test results remains a prominent part of career counseling.

Table 5-1 Comparison of Multi-Aptitude Subscales

ASVAB	DAT	OASIS-III: AS	MAB-II
General Science	Abstract Reasoning	General Ability	Information
Arithmetic Reasoning	Language Usage	Numerical Aptitude	Comprehension
Word Knowledge	Mechanical Reasoning	Verbal Aptitude	Arithmetic
Paragraph Comprehension	Numerical Ability	Perceptual Attitude	Similarities
Mathematics Knowledge	Space Relations	Spatial Aptitude	Vocabulary
Electronics Information	Verbal Reasoning	Manual Dexterity	Digit Symbol
Auto and Shop Information	Spelling		Picture Completion
Mechanical Comprehension	Clerical Speed		Spatial Picture Arrangement
			Object Assembly

Types of Aptitude Tests

There are two types of aptitude tests: multi-aptitude test batteries and single tests measuring specific aptitudes. Multi-aptitude test batteries contain measures of a wide range of aptitudes and combinations of aptitudes, while single aptitude tests are used when a specific aptitude needs to be measured, such as

55

manual dexterity, clerical ability, artistic ability, or musical aptitude. More simply stated, multi-aptitude tests provide information on a breadth of aptitudes, while single aptitude tests provide depth on a specific aptitude.

Review of Specific Aptitude Tests
In this section, we provide a snapshot view of the Differential Aptitude Test (DAT), the DAT paired with the Career Interest Inventory, Armed Services Vocational Aptitude Battery (ASVAB), and the Multidimensional Aptitude Battery–II. We'll begin with the DAT. The DAT has the option of being paired with the Career Interest Inventory. Information on this combined assessment is provided in Tables 5-2 and 5-3. Kelley (2013) has provided a recent detailed review of the DAT and CII.

Table 5-2 Differential Aptitude Test – Fifth Edition

Author/Publisher	Pearson Assessments
Copyright date	1990
Test Purpose	To identify candidates for hiring, training and career development in any organizational setting.
Versions	English and Spanish
Administrator Requirements	B level
Appropriate Age Range	Form C consists of two levels: Level 1: Grades 7 – 9 Level 2: Grades 10 – 12 and adults
Norms	Separate sex norms were derived from a stratified random sample of more than 60,000 students. Percentile Ranks, Stanines, and Scaled Scores presented separately for males and females, as well as combined. The major purpose for separate sex norms was to allow comparisons between the sexes when significant differences occurred.
Administration	Group
Completion Time	About three hours
Test Scales & Subscales	General Cognitive Abilities: Verbal Reasoning + Numerical Ability Perceptual Abilities: Abstract Reasoning, Mechanical Reasoning & Space Relations Clerical & Language Skills: Spelling, Language Usage, Clerical Speed & Accuracy
Reliability	Consistently high reliability coefficients (.82 to .95) are reported by sex and grade level, with SEM ranges from 26 to 55 for each scale.
Validity	An impressive amount of validity data correlates test scores with various course grades and achievement test scores. Although sufficient evidence indicates the DAT (specifically the VR + GR) is a good predictor of high school and college grades, there are limited data concerning the ability of the test to predict vocational success.
Interpretation	The DAT provides 2 types of individual reports for interpretation. One type is a computer-produced profile and the other is hand-plotted. Raw scores, percentiles, stanines and national percentile bands are included. The bars indicate high, average, and low ranges of percentiles, and give an overall sense of the individual's strengths and weaknesses. Observe whether the ends of any bars overlap. There is a significant difference between any two that do not overlap. Two bars having an overlap of more than one-half their length are not significantly different. If the overlap is less than half their length, a difference should be considered as probable and should be specifically determined by retesting. Identify the individual's scholastic aptitude by exploring the verbal reasoning and numerical ability scores.
Supporting Materials: Research/Reviews	The verbal reasoning score is highly correlated with grades in a number of academic courses, especially English courses. The numerical ability score is highly correlated with grades in mathematics courses. Extensive research has been done with other combinations of DAT scores for predicting success in academic subjects and vocational courses (Linn, 1982; Pennock-Roman, 1988). Kelley (2009) cites a lack of recent research on the DAT, particularly in the area of predicting beyond GPA and a need to further establish construct validity and retest reliability. A number of reviews of the DAT have been published, including Anastasi (1988), Hattrup (1995), Kelley (2009), Linn (1982), Pennock-Roman (1988), Schmitt (1995), Wang (1993), and Willson and Stone (1994).

Table 5-3 Differential Aptitude Test and Career Interest Inventory

Author/ Publisher	Pearson Assessments
Copyright date	1990
Test Purpose	To stimulate career exploration for students, including those who are interested in attending college, non-college-bound students, at-risk students, and adults. When the DAT and CII are given together, interest and aptitude comparisons can be made.
Versions	English and Spanish
Administrator Requirements	B-level
Appropriate Age Range	Grades 7-12 and adults
Norms	The norm group for the CII was based on 100,000 students from 520 school districts in grades 7 through 12. The norm group for the DAT with the CII was based on 2000 adults from 43 programs (vocational technical, prison, community college, and adult basic educational programs) in 17 states.
Administration	CII results are reported by occupational-group consistency index and raw scores. Scoring is available via machine or by hand scoring.
Completion Time	Although the CII is not timed, on average it takes about 30 minutes to complete.
Test Scales & Subscales	The CII provides measures of the following occupational groups (linked to the Dictionary of Occupational Titles): <table><tr><td>Social Service</td><td>Educational Services</td></tr><tr><td>Clerical Services</td><td>Legal Services</td></tr><tr><td>Health Services</td><td>Transportation</td></tr><tr><td>Agriculture</td><td>Sales</td></tr><tr><td>Customer Services</td><td>Management</td></tr><tr><td>Fine Arts</td><td>Benchwork</td></tr><tr><td>Mathematics and Science</td><td>Machine Operation</td></tr><tr><td>Building Trades</td><td></td></tr></table>
Reliability	Internal consistency scores for the occupational groups ranged from .82 to .94 for Level 1, and .87-.94 for Level 2. KR-20's, which provide conservative estimates of reliability or consistency, were used to determine test-retest reliabilities, which ranged from .80 to .90.
Validity	The manual presents several examples of concurrent validity, with the DAT being compared with various achievement tests, although Willson and Stone (1994) state that reliability and validity information was inadequately provided. More recently, Kelley (2009) noted that construct validity was provided by matching CII items with the Dictionary of Occupational Titles career fields and comparing CII scales with OVIS II scales, yielding "generally strong" correlations (p. 135).
Interpretation	The report shows an individual's profile for occupational groups, in order from highest to lowest. Also reported are subject areas and school activities, with the report linking these three (occupational groups, subject areas and school activities) together. In addition to using the CII, the developers suggest using the Guide to Careers Portfolios: Student Workbook (Willson & Stone, 1994) as a tool to help students with the career planning process. Willson and Stone (1994) suggest that practitioners should be familiar with a client's needs and purposes for taking the DAT/CII before interpreting the results, and practitioners must be sensitive to how a client might interpret and integrate "low" scores.
Reviews/ Research	Kelley (2009) suggests that while the CII is easy to interpret, it needs to be updated to link items and scales with the O*NET Standard Occupational Classification taxonomy that is currently being used. For further reviews of the DAT and CII, refer to Bennet, Seashore and Wesman (2002), Wang (1993), Stone (1993), Hambleton (1985), Pennock-Roman (1988), and Sander (1985). An international comparison between high school American and Netherlands students demonstrated that the subtests of the DAT equally measured their cognitive abilities with the exception of mechanical knowledge (Te Nijenhuis, Evers & Mur, 2000).

DAT Case Study: Case of a Male High School Student Interested in Legal Services

Adam, a high school freshman, came to the counseling center to see if a career in the field of law matched his skills. Although he was not an honors student, he excelled in courses such as creative writing and speech. The practitioner and Adam decided that it would be worthwhile for Adam to take tests that would provide specific information about his skills and interests. They selected the DAT/CII primarily because the DAT provides an index of scholastic aptitude and measures of specific skills, and the CII would provide preferences for occupational groups, subject areas, and school activities. Following the descriptions of the DAT and DAT/CII below, Adam's results are presented in Table 5-4.

Table 5-4 Adam's DAT Scores

Scale	Percentile	Stanine
Verbal Reasoning	65	6
Numerical Reasoning	69	6
Abstract Reasoning	97	9
Perceptual Speed & Accuracy	77	7
Mechanical Reasoning	47	5
Space Relations	50	5
Spelling	91	8
Language Usage	73	6

Adam's Scholastic Aptitude score (VR + NR) was the 68th percentile (6th stanine), and his Career Interest Inventory scores are shown in Table 5-5. In discussing the results with the practitioner,

Table 5-5 Sample CII Results

Occupational Groups	Subject Areas	School Activities
Moderately high interests in Legal Services, Social Services and Fine Arts. Medium interests in Math and Science, Health Services, Management, Clerical Services and Agriculture. Low interests in Building Trades, Sales, Educational Services, Benchwork, Customer Services, Transportation and Machine Operation.	He indicated liking Speech or Drama, Creative Writing, and Metal Shop or Woodworking. He was neutral towards Bookkeeping/Office Practices, English or Literature, Health Career, Newspaper Writing, Science, Social Studies, Typing or Office Machines. He disliked Computers, Mathematics, Art or Music, Auto Repair, Cooking or Sewing, and Farming or Livestock Care.	He liked Photography Club, School Play and Speech or Debate Team. He was neutral towards Automobile Club, Business Club, Farming Club, School Officer, Science Fair, and Student Government. He disliked Computer Club, Literary Magazine, Mathematics Club, School Newspaper, Office Helper or Assistant, School Library Aide and Teacher's Aide.

Adam expressed pleasure with his scores on abstract reasoning and spelling but concern about his average scores on verbal reasoning, numerical reasoning, and language usage range.

ADAM: How am I ever going to get into college with average scores in English and math? And if I'm only average in the way I use language, does that mean that I won't make a good lawyer?

PRACTITIONER: The skills that you mentioned are important in applying to college and in many professions such as law. Although they are important, they present only one part of the puzzle. Colleges and employers look for many things when considering applicants, such as GPA, work and volunteer experience, and letters of recommendation. With regards to your performance in these areas, you still have three more years to strengthen your skills. Can you think of some ways to do that?

ADAM: Well, I guess I could get a tutor, or study harder.

PRACTITIONER: True. What else could you do?

ADAM: I could take some extra classes, or harder ones, to make myself stronger.

PRACTITIONER: Now you've got the idea. Let's take a look at your CII report. What do you think that's telling us?

ADAM: Well, legal services is definitely my top interest, and it says here that some of these

58

courses I'm good at, as well as some of my activities, are related to that field. It also says that I need a college degree to get a job. How hard will it be for me to get into college?

PRACTITIONER: You have a lot of time between now and graduation to create and implement a strategy that will make going to college a more probable occurrence for you. It is very possible that you could go to several colleges with your current scores. However, if you know that college is a long-term goal for you or that law is the field in which you want to work, it is in your best interest to start working toward reaching your goals now.

ADAM: Yeah, that makes a lot of sense.

The practitioner and Adam then worked together to create a general four-year plan. The plan listed educational goals as well as career goals, steps, and an estimated timeline for completion. In this case, the DAT/CII helped confirm Adam's areas of strength, as well as highlight areas in which he had room to improve. Because he took the DAT/CII in his freshman year, he had plenty of time to take steps toward strengthening himself academically and vocationally.

Armed Services Vocational Aptitude Battery (ASVAB)

The ASVAB was originally developed to replace the separate Army, Navy, and Air Force classification batteries for selecting and classifying personnel and was first available to schools through the U.S. Department of Defense in 1968. This battery is designed primarily for high school seniors. The armed services have developed cooperative programs with school systems for administering this battery and furnish test results at no cost. Table 5-6 presents detailed information on the ASVAB.

Table 5.6 Armed Services Vocational Aptitude Battery (ASVAB)

Author/Publisher	Department of Defense
Test Purpose	"The goal of the ASVAB Career Exploration Program is to give students the opportunity to explore a variety of careers using knowledge they have gained about their interests and skills through assessment components and structured activities. Career development during adolescence and early adulthood is an ongoing process." (ASVAB Counselor Manual, 2012, p. 1)
	The ASVAB test and composite content was selected to facilitate prediction of success in training and entry-level performance across a wide array of military occupations.
Administrator Requirements	US Department of Defense or US Office of Personnel Management Employee
Appropriate Age Range	10th-12th grades, and those in post-secondary schools
Norms	The norming samples were obtained from aptitude test data collected as part of the Profile of American Youth (PAY97) project. The Enlistment Testing Program (ETP) included an assessment of about 6,000 American youth, aged 18-23 as of June 1, 1997, with oversampling for Hispanic and Non-Hispanic Black youth. The Career Exploration Program (CEP), which included an assessment of approximately 4,700 youth who expected to be enrolled in grades 10, 11, and 12 as of fall 1997. The ASVAB norms for grades 10, 11, and 12 were derived from CEP data. Norms for students in postsecondary schools (2-year colleges) were derived from the ETP data.
Administration Time to Complete	FYI – self-scorable paper version and online. ASVAB paper-based administration. Multi-Aptitude Test: 170 minutes Find Your Interests Inventory: 90 minutes
Test Scales & Subscales	Multi-Aptitude Test: General Science Mathematics Knowledge Arithmetic Reasoning Electronics Information Word Knowledge Auto and Shop Information Paragraph Comprehension Mechanical Comprehension Three composite scores: Verbal, Math, and Science & Technical Skills Military Entrance Scores (AFQT) Find Your Interest Inventory

Reliability	Item Response Theory was used to calculate reliability estimates. The reliability estimates for the ASVAB composites range from .88 to .91 across gender and grade level, while the estimates for the individual tests range from .69 to .88. The Counselor Manual (2005) reports internal consistency of the FYI 6 Holland scales as ranging from .92 - .94.
Validity	Extensive research demonstrates that the ASVAB is a valid predictor of success in military training and entry-level military job performance. However, Patrick, Blosel and Gross (2009) state that additional research needs to be done to establish the validity of the ASVAB in predicting civilian jobs. Holmgren and Dalldorf (1993) examined the criterion-related validity of the ASVAB for eleven popular civilian occupations (e.g., firefighter, cosmetologist, electronics technician, operating engineer). For eight of these occupations, there were statistically significant correlations between the measures of occupational success and appropriate ASVAB scales and composites. The Counselor Manual also reports numerous validity studies that support the construct validity of the ASVAB. The Counselor Manual reports validity for the FYI using 2 different analyses: FYI item and scale internal relationships, and relationships between FYI item/scales and the various scales in the 1994 version of the Strong Interest Inventory. Correlations at the scale level ranged from .68 to .85. Patrick, Samide, Muth, Comito and Gross (2013) state that substantial evidence for the construct validity of the FYI exists.
Interpretation	Practitioners are provided a summary score report that describes standard and percentile scores on individual ASVAB tests, Career Exploration Score composites (Verbal, Math and Science & Technological Skills), and Military Entrance score (composite of Arithmetic Reasoning, Mathematics Knowledge, Paragraph Comprehension, and Word Knowledge). Explanations for each of the scores are in the report. Standard scores have a mean of 50 and standard deviation of 10. The actual standard score is given, and the error range is also provided visually on the graph. Percentile scores are provided for the FYI by gender.
Supporting Materials	The website, asvabprogram.com contains the online FYI and the OCCU-Find as well as other links to descriptions of civilian and military occupations. Skills Importance Ratings (in OCCU-Find) allow comparison of personal skills with the skills required for certain occupations as outlined by O*NET.
Research/Reviews	Issues have been raised about major differences between the scores of Black students and those of Caucasian students. In the 2005 manual, however, details have been provided on how these concerns were addressed, and that in a comprehensive study (Wise, Welsh, Grafton, Foley, Earles, Sawin, & Divgi, 1992), that the ASVAB scales and composite scores are 'highly sensitive and predictors of training and job performance for all applicant groups' (p. 58). For a detailed description of validity studies, see Armed Services Vocational Battery (ASVAB): Integrative Review of Validity Studies (Welsh, Kucinkas, & Curran, 1990). Rogers (2002); Patrick, Blosel and Gross (2009); and more recently, Patrick et al. (2013).

Case of a High School Student Interested in the Armed Services

Corrina resided in a small rural community; the nearest city was 50 miles away. She had considered a career in the army and took the ASVAB during her senior year in high school. Her results from the 12th grade administration are shown in Figure 5-3.

Corrina reported to the practitioner that she was considering the armed services because her family's military history as well as a lack of jobs in her community and the nearby city. Because an army recruiter was not available in the community, the practitioner had been provided with ASVAB materials for counseling purposes. The practitioner explained each of the scores in the following manner: "Your score on verbal skills is at the 65th percentile. This means that 65 students out of 100 in the eleventh grade scored lower than you did, while 35 out of 100 scored higher than you did. The band on the profile indicates the range of your score. In other words, your true composite score for verbal is somewhere within this range. The verbal composite is a measure of word knowledge and paragraph comprehension." The practitioner reviewed the rest of the higher scores to identify strong aptitudes, and then moved on to her Find Your Interests (FYI) results.

Figure 5.3 - Corrina's ASVAB Results

Print No.:XXXXX

ASVAB Results	Percentile Scores 12th Grade Females	Percentile Scores 12th Grade Males	Percentile Scores 12th Grade Students	12th Grade Standard Score Bands	12th Grade Standard Score
Career Exploration Scores					
Verbal Skills	97	95	96		65
Math Skills	22	17	19		42
Science and Technical Skills	81	48	64		53
ASVAB Tests					
General Science	91	81	86		61
Arithmetic Reasoning	43	30	37		47
Word Knowledge	98	95	96		66
Paragraph Comprehension	92	91	91		62
Mathematics Knowledge	14	12	13		37
Electronics Information	13	10	11		38
Auto and Shop Information	53	21	37		45
Mechanical Comprehension	95	76	85		59

Military Entrance Score (AFQT) 57

Corrina's FYI results included R (88%), I (65%), A (13%), S (58%), E (0%), and C (62%). The practitioner stated, "Based on your FYI scores, your main area of interest is Realistic, following by Investigative and Conventional." After describing the different Holland types, the counselor confirmed with Corrina that her primary fits seemed to fit her well. The practitioner then provided Corrina with a copy of the OCCU-FIND.

The OCCU-FIND allowed Corrina to identify those occupations that best matched her primary interests, and Verbal, Math and Science/Technical Skills. As she looked through OCCU-FIND, Corrina checked off several occupations that she would like to explore further. She read through various descriptions of occupations found in the online OCCU-FIND, and made plans to visit an army recruiter for more information about her career plans. In Corrina's case, the ASVAB results were used to stimulate career exploration. This information encouraged Corrina to relate her skills and interests to job opportunities in the armed services.

Aptitude Testing and People with Disabilities

Practitioners should be aware of issues with aptitude testing for people with disabilities, and should remember to focus on a person's strengths, rather than areas of deficit, in that people get hired because of their strengths, not their weaknesses. Many people with disabilities are already aware of how their disability impacts their ability to perform tasks. Therefore, when interpreting a client's profile to the client, a practitioner should help the client focus on his or her strengths and how to enhance other skills.

During the past ten years, two main public laws, the Carl D. Perkins Vocational Education Act (P.L. 98-524) and the Individuals with Disabilities Education Act (IDEA) (PL. 94–142), were passed, requiring equal access to training and employment for people with disabilities and people who are disadvantaged. These and other legislation, including the American with Disabilities Act of 1990 (PL. 101–336), have led to intense scrutiny of assessment methods and procedures. Thus, a practitioner should be aware of personal biases about the client's abilities and disabilities and, in addition, focus on exploring occupations of interest and any necessary accommodations the client might need to successfully complete the job tasks.

Practitioners can use several different ways to help a person with a disability explore career options and make career decisions. These interventions include interviews, observations, written tests, performance tests, work samples, and situational assessments (Levinson, 1994). Performance tests are "manipulative tests that minimize the use of language . . . usually designed to assess specific abilities related to the performance of a job" (Levinson, 1994, p. 95).

Work samples involve having an individual complete selected tasks that are required by a particular occupation, such as typing a letter or answering a phone (secretarial work sample) or changing a tire (automotive work sample). Work samples usually include three phases:

1. Demonstration of the work
2. Training
3. Performance of the tasks

Situational assessment techniques involve placing clients in either a real or a simulated work setting and then having them be evaluated by peers or supervisors via observation, interviews, and rating scales.

61

The purpose of situational assessment techniques is to identify a person's interests and aptitudes and demonstrated work habits. They are best used in conjunction with formal assessments. In this section of the chapter, we will review three aptitude/skill inventories designed for people with disabilities, including the AVIATOR 3, SkillTRAN, and the Talent Assessment Program, starting first with a presentation of AVIATOR 3 in Table 5-7.

Table 5-7 AVIATOR 3

Author/Publisher	VALPAR; http://www.valparint.com
Test Purpose	AVIATOR 3's multifunctional approach encompasses aptitude assessment, two pictorial/audio interest surveys, and two databases - the standard and O*Net databases each with approximately 1000 jobs.
Appropriate Age Range	Adolescent through adult
Components	Academic and aptitude assessment, two pictorial/audio interest surveys
Administration	Self or individually administered
Time to Complete	About 60 minutes
Psychometric Properties	Aviator 3 is a criterion-referenced test. Test items are tied to an external set of standards. In this case, the Department of Labor's job standards contained in the Revised Handbook for Analyzing Jobs were used, meaning test results aren't compared to any specific norm group. Rather, Aviator reports the skills that an individual has demonstrated during the testing. Because it is a criterion-referenced instrument, Aviator can be used by most populations.
Interpretation	The reports provide tables and bar graphs. The graphs reference the individual's 3 main interest levels, highlight academic grade level scores and skills assessment results. The report also shows the person's general educational development (GED) levels, compares to 12 GOE interest areas and presents occupations based on an O*NET search. The compares individual skills to the skills required by the occupations on this list.

Case of a Client with a Visual Impairment

Nadeen, a first year college student who has a visual impairment, has taken the AVIATOR 3 Interest Survey and Skills Assessment as a way to explore possible career paths. Her career advisor is meeting with her to talk about her results.

ADVISOR: Hi, Nadeen. I have the results from your assessment here. But first, what did you think about the assessment process?

NADEEN: I was really excited about the audio, and that I could listen to it in Spanish. You know I have trouble with reading because of my impairment. So, being able to hear the items while I was looking at the screen was really nice.

ADVISOR: That's great, Nadeen. I'm glad that was a useful feature for you. Now let's talk about your results. What are you expecting the results to show?

NADEEN: I'm not really sure. I guess I hope there isn't anything business-related. I hated working in sales over the summer.

ADVISOR: The results did show that you weren't interested in sales or business. It did show your strongest areas of interest were in Scientific, Accommodating, and Leading/Influencing. What do you think about that?

NADEEN: I always liked science, so that's not surprising, and I guess I like helping people, too. I never really considered myself a leader, though. That's surprising to me.

ADVISOR: Really? From what you've told me, you're already involved in student government, are active in a student ministry group, and volunteered to be a mentor for incoming students with disabilities. That sounds like leadership to me.

NADEEN: Well, I guess you're right. I just never thought of it that way.

ADVISOR: So, we'll keep those interest areas in mind as we look at your skills assessment results. It looks like your lowest skills are in reading, which we anticipated. You scored very high on the other tests, with the exception of discriminating shapes and sizes. Your highest score was in problem-solving. So, keeping in mind your interests that we just talked about, what career options come to mind?

NADEEN: Something that involves science, helping others and problem solving.

ADVISOR: What careers come to mind that incorporate those three?

NADEEN: Medicine? Research?

ADVISOR: Sure, and engineering as well. Let's take a look at the options that were listed on your printout, and then we'll start researching the ones that interest you most.

In this case, AVIATOR 3 was useful to Nadeen, especially with the auditory assessments. She had confidence in working through the printout with the advisor. The advisor balanced the conversation between Nadeen's understanding of herself as well as the results of the assessments. Next, we will explore SkillTRAN. Table 5-8 provides a brief glance at this tool.

Table 5-8 SkillTRAN

Author/Publisher	www.skilltran.com
Test Purpose Versions	To provide software and online services for Rehab, Forensic and Career Services Placement Planning Service (PPS): identifies feasible occupations for an individual using residual post-injury capacities, transferable skills from past work history, preferences, and/or interests. PREPOST-Pre-Injury/Post-Injury Analysis: used by vocational experts and attorneys in litigated cases including: worker compensation, personal injury, medical malpractice, and product liability.
Appropriate Age Range	These instruments analyze past work experience to identify transferable skills and similar occupations. While an age range is not specified, SkillTRAN is designed for those who have worked.
Interpretation	PREPOST provides an analysis of transferable skills based on previous work history. Past job titles are inputted into the system, which are analyzed for skills, after which possible alternatives are generated. PREPOST provides a comparison of abilities pre and post injury, and shows the number of occupations available to the individual pre and post injury that are directly, generally and indirectly similar to the previous occupations held. Neither takes into account possible accommodations, so this should be discussed during counseling.

Forensic Case in which a CRC Has Been Asked to Be an Expert Witness

Dan is a 29-year-old male who was involved in a severe car crash that rendered him paralyzed from the waist down. Prior to his injury, he was a construction worker. His certified rehabilitation counselor (CRC) has been asked to make a presentation in court about the impact of the injury on Dan's future employability. The CRC uses the PREPOST software from SkillTRAN to determine the impact and to provide an estimate of loss of wages. A portion of the report is shown in Figure 5-4. The CRC was able to demonstrate the tremendous decrease in possible job options post-injury.

Figure 5-4: PREPOST Sample Report

```
==========================================================================================
PRE-INJURY / POST-INJURY                 PRE-INJURY     POST-INJURY
   OCCUPATIONAL SERVICE                  OCCUPATIONAL   OCCUPATIONAL
                                         ACCESS (PRE)   ACCESS (POST)   LOSS *
------------------------------------------------------------------------------------------
   DIRECTLY TRANSFERABLE OCCUPATIONS          65             10         84.7%

   CLOSELY TRANSFERABLE OCCUPATIONS          116             18         84.5%

   GENERALLY TRANSFERABLE OCCUPATIONS        437            106         75.8%
------------------------------------------------------------------------------------------
                            TOTAL            618            134         78.4%
------------------------------------------------------------------------------------------
              UNSKILLED OCCUPATIONS         2675           1591         40.6%
```

* OCCUPATIONAL LOSS is the percentage of occupations which the worker is no longer able to perform due to injury. CAUTION should be exercised in generalizing from this figure, since this calculation assumes that occupational titles occur with equal frequency.

63

The CRC also used local employment information to show that the availability of directly and closely transferable jobs was even more limited. Based on the client's interests and abilities, the counselor recommended training in a new occupational field that would generate additional career options.

The Talent Assessment Program will be reviewed next, with a brief snapshot in Table 5-9.

Table 5-9 Talent Assessment Program

Author/Publisher	Talent Assessment, Inc.
Copyright date	1988
Test Purpose	System for assessing career aptitudes quickly and fairly.
Versions	The Talent Assessment Program does not require any reading ability. Instructions may be given in any format. Oral, written, signed, or simply demonstrated.
Administrator Requirements	On-site training
Appropriate Age Range	Middle school to adult
Norms	Normed with Adult, Middle School/Junior High and Mentally Challenged.
Administration	Individually-administered or to groups of 8
Time to Complete	2 - 2 1/2 hours
Test Scales & Subscales	Consists of a battery of 10 hands-on tests, focusing on three areas: ***Visualization & Retention*** Form and spatial perception is an essential aptitude to have in the mechanical, industrial and building trades. (TEST 1) The ability to follow flow patterns is needed in many areas, especially electronics and computer programming. (TEST 9) The retention of form and special details indicates potential for reconstruction devices and repeating tasks without supervision. (TEST 10) ***Discrimination*** The fine discrimination of similar objects is needed in such jobs as electronics and small parts assembly. (TEST 2) Strong color discrimination is an attribute important to many occupations including artists, paper hangers, cosmetologists, auto body workers and laboratory technicians. (TEST 3) Tactile discrimination is vitally important to such occupations as upholstering, auto body work, woodworking, physical therapy and dental modeling. (TEST 4) ***Dexterity*** Fine motor control is needed in many fields that work with small materials including assembly line operations, as well as, dental technicians, counter parts men and surgical and jeweler display arrangers. (TEST 5) Manual dexterity plays a large part in the building trades and material handling. (TEST 6) Quality performance with small tools is required in mechanics, electronics and medical profession. (TEST 7) The ability to use large tools is an advantage in industrial and mechanical work. (TEST 8)
Reliability	The manual reports a .86 test-retest reliability with a 6 month interval between tests for 8th grade students.
Validity	The manual reports content validity as the tests are comprised of tools and materials used in the fields being tested. The test developers provide several strong reasons as to why the series have not undergone intense validity checks, and point to the longevity of the test as being indicative of its predictive validity.
Interpretation	The results are correlated both to the D.O.T., the Worker Groups of the Guide to Occupational Exploration (G.O.E.) and the occupational data of the D.O.L.

Case of an At-Risk Student Considering College
Catalina, a junior in high school, is interested in going to work right after graduation, but is not sure which occupational field would best match her skills. She is considered "at-risk" academically, and works very

hard to maintain her average grades. She meets with her practitioner to review her Talent Assessment Program (TAP) results in Table 5-10 and discuss her plans.

Table 5-10 Sample TAP Test Results

	TAP Test	Time (Minutes)	Percentile
1.	Structural and Mechanical Visualization	8.7	92
2.	Discrimination by Size and Shape	5.4	86
3.	Discrimination by Color	1.9	99
4.	Discrimination by Touch	3.2	77
5.	Fine Finger Dexterity	7.8	94
6.	Gross Manual Dexterity	6.5	20
7.	Fine Finger Dexterity with Tools	9.3	22
8.	Gross Manual Dexterity with Tools	7	85
9.	Visualization of Flow Patterns	5.9	18
10.	Retention of Mechanical and Structural Detail	8.2	86

After completing the TAP, Catalina and the career practitioner discuss the results.

CATALINA: So what did my results show?
PRACTITIONER: You seem really excited. What did you expect them to show?
CATALINA: I'm not sure – probably that I'm good with my hands?
PRACTITIONER: Actually, you're right. The results do show that you are good at details and working with your hands. Let's read through your highest scores, and you tell me what you think about each.

The practitioner and Catalina took turns reading the descriptions, and Catalina would comment on the descriptions, agreeing with some, and disagreeing with others. They went through the occupations corresponding to her TAP and Catalina was excited to see some jobs listed that were closely related to her hobbies. During a previous session, Catalina had shared that at home, she enjoyed putting together models that had very tiny pieces, and playing with electrical circuits, and she spoke enthusiastically about a science fair project she was working on that involved manipulating circuit boards.

In this case, the TAP results helped Catalina identify key strengths that she already possessed, and then linked them to occupations. She was surprised to find that the hobbies she was currently involved with might lead to similar occupations. Following the discussion of the results, she was able to engage in some career planning, and decided upon a work study arrangement where she could attend school part time and work in a circuit board factory to gain experience.

Multi-aptitude Tests: Limitations and Suggestions for Use
Although multi-aptitude tests provide differential measures of ability, expectations for the predictive value of the results may be too high. The scores from multi-aptitude test batteries should not be expected to pinpoint careers. The tests cannot answer specific questions such as "Will I be a good architect?" or "Will I be a good mechanical engineer?" or "Will I be a good surgical nurse?" Only partial answers to these questions can be expected. For example, a space-relation score on an aptitude battery should provide an index of the individual's ability to visualize the effect of three-dimensional movement, which is one of the aptitudes required of architects. However, many other factors, not all of which can be measured by a multi-aptitude battery, need to be considered by the prospective architect. It is therefore important to determine the individual's objectives before testing is accomplished.

"Should I consider being a mechanic?" "Do I have the aptitude to do clerical work?" "Is my finger dexterity good enough to consider assembly work?" Reasonable answers to these questions can be obtained from the results of aptitude tests. More important, however, a meaningful career search may begin once test results are evaluated. The results of multi-aptitude test batteries provide valuable suggestions and clues to be considered along with other information in career decision-making.

Many of the following suggestions for fostering the career development of students and adults can be modified and used interchangeably to meet the needs of both groups. These suggestions should not be considered exhaustive of all possibilities of using assessment results to enhance career development; rather, they should be viewed as examples from which exercises can be developed to meet local needs and needs of other groups.

For Schools:

- Provide a list of reading-level appropriate words that represent various abilities and aptitudes for elementary students. Provide written directions that tie into the teacher's curriculum and goals. For example, following 3 step directions might be a goal for a kindergarten or first-grade class. Consider how the following directions meets that goal: "Put your name on the paper, circle all the words that best describe you and put an x on the words that do not describe you at all."
- Create a crossword puzzle using a puzzle maker at a site such as discoveryschool.com, using definitions of traits as the descriptors.
- Use appropriate magazines to allow students to create a collage of what they are good at doing.
- Ask students to write a short paragraph on the subject of their personal strengths and weaknesses. Ask students to explain how they can improve their weaknesses.
- Increase awareness of occupations that are related to specific skills by dividing students into teams and giving each team the task of filling in a concept wheel specific to one trait. For example, a team might have "organization" written in a circle in the middle of their worksheet, and their task would be to draw lines coming out of that circle and adding a related occupation at the end of each of the lines.
- Divide students into groups according to abilities and ask them to identify and then brainstorm other occupations that match their measured ability scores. Share their findings.
- Conduct a contest to determine who can find the most occupations that match ability subtest scores.
- Play "My Strengths" by having students make a list of the courses and hobbies in which they do best.
- After reviewing ability test results, have them determine what potential matches there are between the results and course electives, clubs, and volunteer opportunities.
- Ask students to share "These Are My Skills," in which selected ability scores are used as a basis for describing their skills. Using O*NET, have them match the skills with occupations.
- Construct a job box or a service file that has pictures of various occupations. Ask students to match and identify job skills with their ability test results.
- Construct various displays that contain listings of occupations under categories such as verbal aptitude, numerical aptitude, spelling, and mechanical reasoning. Ask students to go to the display that contains occupations that match their test results. Find one or more and discuss.
- For elementary grades, have them create (or instructor or counselor can create) a concentration game matching the picture of the occupation with job description and abilities required.
- Ask students to read a vocational biography of someone in an occupation selected on the basis of ability test results.
- Using an ability test profile, ask students to make a list of several occupations to be considered for further evaluation.
- Ask students to construct resumes that outline their measured abilities.
- Distribute job notices from local newspapers. Have students choose three occupations and then classify each of the jobs into a primary Holland type. If there aren't enough options from the local newspaper to represent each Holland type, search online job notices. Then, have students identify the abilities that the employers are looking for. Create a table (on the board) that has each Holland type as a header. As the practitioner calls out each Holland type, have students who had an occupation classified as that type report the job skills required. After all the types have been addressed, have the class note themes, such as which type had the most skills, was there overlap of skills within each type (do they see "S" type skills in an occupation that is mostly "R"), was there overlap across types (did "C" type work show up across all the RIASEC categories) and what do these themes suggest about the world of work and how they should prepare?

For Adults:

- Ask adults to compare requirements of occupations with their ability test score results. Consider informational interviewing with employers to learn more about the actual job.
- In groups, discuss skills needed for certain occupations. Use test results as examples.
- Ask adults to discuss individual strengths and weaknesses. Use test results as examples.
- Ask adults to develop personal profiles of developed abilities.
- Ask adults to discuss the relevance of identified abilities in the career decision-making process.
- Ask adults to share how abilities were developed from previous work and leisure experiences.
- Use current resume to identify skills.
- Ask adults to share identified abilities that can be linked to emerging and changing occupational requirements.
- Have adults compare their aptitude test scores with those of other results, such as an interest

inventory or values card sort.
- Ask adults to discuss the relevance of developing abilities in learning over the life span. Use current test results as examples.

Other Aptitude Tests

In addition to the multi-aptitude batteries discussed in this chapter, a number of other batteries are on the market. Here are some examples:

- **Ability Explorer-3rd Edition**. Taking about 15 minutes to complete, the Ability Explorer measures 14 abilities (Artistic, Clerical, Interpersonal, Language, Leadership, Manual, Musical/Drama, Numerical/Mathematical, Organizational, Scientific, Persuasive, Spatial, Social, Technical/Mechanical) with 140 questions. An individual's strengths are linked to courses, activities and careers.
- **Career Ability Placement Survey**. This test is used to measure abilities of entry requirements for jobs compiled by the authors in 14 occupational clusters of the COPSystem. It can be self-scored or machine-scored for junior high school, senior high school, college, and adult populations. The eight 1-page tests are timed for five minutes each, and scores are reported in percentiles, stanines and stanine ranges. National normative data provide comparisons of scores for mechanical reasoning, spatial relations, verbal reasoning, numerical ability, language usage, word knowledge, perceptual speed and accuracy, and manual speed and dexterity.
- **Flanagan Aptitude Classification Test**. This test consists of 16 separate tests: inspection, coding, memory, precision, assembly, scales, coordination, judgment/comprehension, arithmetic, patterns, components, tables, mechanics, expression, reasoning, and ingenuity. Each test measures behaviors considered critical to job performance. Selected groups of tests may be administered. The entire battery takes several hours. This test is designed primarily for use with high school students and adults.
- **Highlands Ability Battery**. Consisting of 19 different work samples which are designed to measure how quickly an individual can complete a series of tasks, the tests shows the level of difficulty for each task. The report contains information on how a person's skills relates to four personal dimensions including work environment, personal style, learning and problem-solving, and decision making and communication.
- **Kuder Skills Confidence Assessment**. The Kuder Skills Confidence Assessment (KSCA) provides a self-efficacy estimate (e.g., I can do this well, it would be hard for me to do this well) of about 50 abilities (depending on version) related to six Holland types, that can then be linked to occupations in O*NET. Results are shown with bar graphs ranging from low to medium to high scales. Results can also be linked to the Person Match sketches, which are interviews in a question and answer format with people who have similar interests as the client's results. Gibbons (2013) provides a recent review of the KSCA.
- **Modern Occupational Skills Test-2nd Edition**. The MOST is an aptitude test from London designed to assess applicant's skills for office, sales and managerial work. The MOST includes nine areas of assessment with three increasingly difficult levels. Level 1 includes Verbal Checking, Numerical Checking and Filing; Level 2 includes Numerical Awareness, Spelling & Grammar and Word Meanings; and Level 3 includes Numerical Estimation, Technical Checking and Decision Making.
- **OASIS-III Aptitude Survey**. The OASIS-III Aptitude Survey is a self or group administered inventory that was developed to assist students in grades 8 through 12 and adults in making career decisions. Specifically, the results provide information about relative strengths through two subtests, an aptitude survey and an interest survey. The OASIS-3 Aptitude Survey consists of the following subtests: General Ability, Verbal Aptitude, Numerical Aptitude, Spatial Aptitude, Perceptual Aptitude and Manual Dexterity. The inventory takes about 30-45 minutes to complete and may be hand or machine scored. Validity coefficients ranged from .6 to .8 when compared to General Aptitude Battery subtests of similar nature. Median alpha reliabilities were reported as ranging from .70 to .91. Blackwell and Lutyhe (2003) reviewed the OASIS 3 and stated that the instrument was both time and cost effective in helping career-undecided students in assessing their aptitudes and interests.
- **O*NET Ability Profiler**. A paper and pencil inventory for individuals age 16 and older that measures the following abilities: verbal ability, arithmetic reasoning, computation, spatial ability, form perception, clerical perception, motor coordination, finger dexterity and manual dexterity. The O*NET Ability Profiler results can be scanned or inputted into software available on the O*NET website, resulting in a computerized report and linked to over 800 occupations in O*NET.
- **PRO3000**. This is a modular assessment software for aptitude and interest testing. It is useful for work skill profiling, employment screening, and transferable skill analysis. It can import many paper/pencil results such as VTES, TABE, ABLE, and DAT, and assesses all Department of Labor aptitudes, 11 temperaments, 20 physical demands, 14 environmental conditions, and 12 interest categories, as well as math, reasoning and language. There are multiple components available, such as COMPASS, which uses adaptive testing techniques for on-computer subtests, as well as several specialized Work Samples, to measure a person's

67

knowledge and skills. COMPASS measures the three GED factors and all eleven aptitude factors of the DOT.

- **Wiesen Test of Mechanical Aptitude**. This test is an example of a single aptitude test, focusing on mechanical aptitude of individuals 18 years and older. Its format is paper and pencil, and it takes about 30 minutes to complete. The developers state that the design of the WTMA has resulted in minimal gender and ethnic bias on the measure, and that individuals do not need to have previous experience in a shop class to understand the test. The multiple-choice questions include drawings of basic mechanical concepts.
- **Wonderlic Personnel Test**. According to the website, this test measures a job candidate's ability to "understand instructions, learn, adapt, solve problems and handle the mental demands of the position" (wonderlic.com). The online administration takes eight minutes to complete, and can link to 700 job profiles or to a job profile designed by the employer.
- **Workkeys**. WorkKeys (ACT Inc., 2012) is a job skills assessment system intended to compare an individual's current skill set with the skills required for specific positions within a company. There are eight "foundational skills assessments" (Applied Mathematics, Applied Technology, Business Writing, Listening for Understanding, Locating Information, Workplace Observation, Reading for Information, and Teamwork), and three "soft skills" assessments (Talent, Performance, and Fit).

Aptitude Tests Summary

Early trait-and-factor approaches to career counseling used ability measures. Multi-aptitude batteries evolved from a growing interest in intra-individual measurement. Ability measures can be used to stimulate discussion of personal characteristics and traits relevant for career decision-making. An aptitude is a specific proficiency or an ability to acquire a certain proficiency. The aptitude tests discussed in this chapter measure a variety of skills and abilities.

Achievement Tests

Consider the following:

- Jorge wants to become a teacher, but consistently earns poor scores on verbal portions of achievement tests.
- Terry wants to determine which program of study is likely to best fit her.

In both of these cases, the main concern is academic achievement. Levels of competence in reading, language usage, and mathematics may be the key to rejection or consideration of certain educational and vocational plans. Career planning is often related to academic proficiency. Educational doors open and close based on grade point averages, course grades, and standardized achievement test scores.

Many jobs that do not require college training do require that the individual be able to read, do arithmetic, and write coherently. Training and additional education are key ways for individuals to keep their skills and knowledge sharp, and to make them marketable. One's level of basic skills often determines future training and career-planning opportunities.

Outcomes of achievement tests have been related to students' academic grades (Cooper, Lindsay, Nye, & Greathouse, 1998). Achievement tests provide results that can be linked to most occupational requirements, not to mention that achievement tests can identify potential areas needing remediation (such as vocabulary), which might impact a person's job search (resume, cover letter and interviewing capabilities). As always, practitioners should review normative data and research on specific achievement tests when using or interpreting for diverse clients.

Difference Between Aptitude and Achievement Tests

Career practitioners should understand the difference between achievement tests and aptitude tests. Both measure learning experience. However, achievement tests measure learning of relatively restricted items and in limited content areas—that is, learning related to an academic setting. Achievement tests measure knowledge that a person has, and the results are compared to others' scores who are at the same grade level to identify whether that person's scores are below, equal to, or above grade level. Many times, achievement tests results are also used in a way similar to aptitude tests, to predict who will be successful in college or graduate school.

In a review of the literature, Petrill and Wilkerson (2000) reported that achievement test results are affected by genetics and environmental influences. Two key environmental influences that show gains in academic achievement have been smaller classrooms and spending more time in those smaller classrooms (Konstantopoulos & Chung, 2009). While we have little control over genetics, we can encourage students with lower achievement scores to seek out environments that will be smaller in terms of class size.

Do Beliefs Impact Achievement Scores?

Earlier in this chapter, we raised the question of how one's measured aptitudes can differ from their perception of his or her abilities, and we suggested that one's beliefs might affect a person's self-estimates

68

of abilities. This has also been a concern of researchers interested in the use of achievement tests (See Table 5-11).

Table 5-11 Research on Achievement Test Scores

Study	Topic	Findings
Abu-Hilal, 2000	Attitudes toward testing and academic aspirations	Attitudes significantly and directly influenced the standardized achievement scores of high school seniors.
Brown & Josephs, 1999	Beliefs about the test purpose	If they believed the test's purpose was to show weakness in math, women scored worse. If they believed the test's purpose was to show strength in math, women scored better while men scored worse.
Cole, Bergin & Whittaker, 2008	Beliefs about usefulness and importance of the test	The less students (N=1000) believed the test to be useful or important, the poorer their effort and test scores.
Hay, Ashman, & Van Kraayenoord, 1998 Other researchers have reported similar findings (Bouffard, Markovitz, Vezeau, Boisvert, & Dumas, 1998; Marsh & Yeung, 1998; Rangappa, 1994)	Self-concept	Low self-concept has also been found to correlate with lower scores on 9 to 11 year olds' standardized achievement scores on math, reading, and spelling.
Moller, Pohlmann, Koller, & Marsh (2009)	Internal/External frame of reference	Meta-analytic study showed positive paths from achievement to academic self-concept, but not when self-esteem was used instead of self-concept
Raju & Asfaw, 2009	Academic self-concept	A significant positive correlation between perceived general academic self-concept and achievement test scores.

Do Achievement Tests Predict Success?

Yes and no. ACT and SAT test results have been found to correctly predict college grades 25% of the time (Popham, 2006). Two studies focused on the success of students in MBA (Master's of Business Administration) programs, and have found that scores on the GMAT do predict academic success of students (Fish & Wilson, 2009; Ragothaman, Carpenter, & Davies, 2009). Park, Khan and Petrina (2009) found that Korean middle school students' aspirations for science careers increased following an intervention of computer-assisted instruction, with increased science achievement test scores. However, most studies show that achievement test scores combined with other factors (such as high school or undergraduate GPA, motivation, age, study habits and so forth) offer the best predictors. Despite mixed findings, Zwick (2007) stated that almost 90% of colleges and universities require SAT or ACT results for admission. They continue to be an important consideration for admission for colleges (high school grades and academic rigor of courses were more important; Clinedinst & Hawkins, 2013).

Achievement Tests and Women

Practitioners need to evaluate the degree to which negative beliefs about self may impact the student's achievement scores. Betz (1994; 1997) identified this as a crucial issue for women's career development. If girls embrace the idea that they are inferior in math and science, they will opt out of those classes— classes that would eventually lead to jobs in traditionally higher-paying fields such as medicine and engineering. Betz pointed out that currently women make up 45% of the work force, yet only 16% of scientists and engineers. Another study confirmed that women in high-level college math courses who endorse stereotypical thinking had lower math test performance scores, even though they were performing well in the classes (Good, Aronson, & Harder, 2008). As discussed earlier, relying on the results of any one test as the sole basis for career decision-making would be unwise. Instead, the practitioner should employ various tools in assisting with a person's career decision and always be listening for and challenging negative self-talk that might be hindering the client's performance and subsequent options.

Achievement Tests and Cultural Concerns

There has been ample concern about the "achievement gap" between minority and majority cultural groups, with Whites typically outperforming Blacks and Hispanics on achievement tests. Haile and Nguyen (2008) used national data to analyze test scores among ethnic groups and found that Blacks and Hispanics did not

69

achieve the same results in the highest quartile of scores, especially science, as compared to Whites. They also found that family factors such as parental level of education or parent's profession did not provide an adequate explanation for the gap. The Journal of Blacks in Higher Education (2003) noted that Whites are five, seven and twelve times more likely to outperform Blacks on the MCAT, the GMAT and the LSAT (respectively).

Standardized achievement test scores are often seen as a gatekeeper for certain educational programs. There are cutoffs and considerations of combinations of subscales and GPA that help academic programs narrow their pool of applicants quickly. Most programs will consider multiple factors, including standardized scores, GPA, leadership, letters of recommendation, experience, fit with the program, and so forth. Many programs actively seek to diversify their student body, so some of the effects of lower test scores may be offset for a person of color if they are high in other areas. Researchers have found that achievement test results alone do not predict the success of at-risk students, and that other factors such as gender, high school GPA, and leadership experience were better predictors (Mattson, 2007). Thus a practitioner working with a student of color whose standardized scores are lower should encourage enhancing his or her application through gaining experience (work or volunteer), taking leadership roles, focusing on GPA and so forth.

Interpreting Scaled Scores for Achievement Tests

Table 5-12 contains fictitious scores for illustrating how raw scores are converted to scaled scores on a math computation test. By using such a table, you can compare performance in grade 9, for example, with the score in math computation in grade 12. However, the table should not be used to compare performance in one subject with performance in another. The advantage of scaled scores is that they provide equal units on a continuous scale for making comparisons.

Table 5-12 Interpreting Scaled Scores for Any Achievement Test

Number Right (Raw Score)	Reading Comprehension Scaled Score	Reading Number Right (Raw Score)	Reading Comprehension Scaled Score	Number Right (Raw Score)	Comprehension Scaled Score
40	284	26	258	13	226
39	284	25	257	12	221
38	283	24	255	11	216
37	282	23	254	10	214
36	280	22	251	9	210
35	279	21	249	8	205
34	276	20	248	7	201
33	275	19	245	6	195
32	274	18	242	5	193
31	273	17	238	4	188
30	269	16	237	3	184
29	268	15	231	2	181
28	262	14	228	1	178
27	261				

Types of Achievement Tests

Numerous achievement tests are on the market today. They are usually either general survey batteries covering several subject areas or single-subject tests. They can be criterion-referenced or norm-referenced or both. Achievement tests are usually identified by grade level. When deciding which type of achievement test to use, it is useful to establish the specific purpose for giving an achievement test. The general survey battery should be chosen when comparisons of achievement in different content areas are needed. The survey battery provides a relatively limited sampling of each content area but, as the name implies, covers a broad spectrum of content areas. More items and more aspects of the subject are usually covered in a single-subject test than in a survey battery. The single-subject test should be chosen when a precise and thorough evaluation of achievement in one subject is needed.

In educational planning, it is often desirable to choose a single-subject test when detailed information about a person's capabilities in that particular subject is necessary. The saving in testing time is also a major consideration in the decision to use a single-subject test. Both types of tests can be used as diagnostic instruments when measurement of specific skills or abilities and proficiencies can be related to occupational requirements. Detection of a specific deficiency is also valuable for referral to remedial programs.

Review of Specific Achievement Tests

The 10th edition of the Stanford Achievement Test (STAT) is a good example of a survey battery. This test was first published more than 50 years ago and has undergone numerous revisions. The test may be hand-scored or computer-scored. The publisher provides a comprehensive, computerized reporting service to assist local administrators with instructional planning and reporting to the public. The purpose is to inform about what students know and are able to do.

Table 5-13 Stanford Achievement Test (Tenth Edition)

Author/Publisher	Pearson Assessments
Copyright date	2008
Test Purpose	To help educators find out what students know and are able to do
Versions	Complete and abbreviated M-C battery by grade and subject
Administrator Requirements	Teachers
Appropriate Age Range	Kindergarten-12th Grade
Norms	Scaled scores, national and local percentile ranks and stanines, grade equivalents and normal curve equivalents
Administration	Group administered
Time to Complete	Untimed, although timing guidelines are included
Test Scales & Subscales	Complete Battery Spelling Total Reading Science Total Math Social Science Language Listening Plus 67 clusters
Reliability	Reliability established by split-half estimates for each subtest range from .87 to .95. Reliability estimates based on KR-20 range from .86 to .94.
Validity	Content validity is well documented by a thorough explanation of the evaluation and editing process for test items. Construct validity is based on correlations with prior editions of the test, internal consistency of items, and evidence of the decreasing difficulty of items with progress in school.
Interpretation	Stanine and percentile equivalents are used for reporting scores. A practitioner can refer to how stanines and percentile equivalents are positioned under the normal distribution s a good frame of reference. A multiple-score report such as this one lends itself to meaningful interpretations for career counseling because the combination of scores displayed provides the practitioner and the client with an overview of achievement by subject. Particular attention should be given to the scaled scores, which provide an index for comparing growth from one grade level to another.
Supporting Materials	Preview for Parents – a guide to help parents prepare their children for the STAT Understanding Test Results – includes sample score reports, and how the results can be used Practice Tests Guide for Classroom Planning Compendium of Instructional Standards Strategies for Instruction: A Handbook of Performance Activities, Second Edition
Research/Reviews	A study of the eighth version of the STAT and gender differences (among 7th to 12th graders) in scores revealed only minimal differences (Slate, Jones, Sloas, & Blake, 1998). Other reviews include Drummond and Jones (2010), Brown (1993), and Stoker (1993).

The first high school battery of the STAT was published in 1965. Developers of this test thoroughly reviewed textbooks and many different curriculum patterns. Items were edited by individuals from various minority groups and were evaluated in trial programs involving 61,000 students in 1445 classrooms in 47 different school systems. Frequent revisions of the test have been made to stay abreast of changing curriculum patterns. Several guides designed to aid in the interpretation of results enhance the general use of the test. Because of the high level of the skills assessed, this test is particularly useful for helping individuals make plans for college.

Case of a High School Student Referred to a Practitioner Because of Poor Grades

Li, a junior in high school, was referred to the career practitioner by his English teacher, who reported that Li was a poor student in English and, even with tutoring, had difficulty maintaining the level of performance necessary to pass the course. Earned course grades and comments from previous teachers reflected the same concerns. The teacher reported that Li's parents were insisting that he attend college, and Li was trying to meet their expectations of him. According to the teacher, Li was making a maximum effort but was having little success.

The practitioner reviewed the results of an achievement test survey battery that had been administered during the current semester. A summary of Li's scores is shown in Table 5-14.

Table 5-14 Achievement Test Survey Battery Results for Li

Test	National Percentile Equivalent	National Stanine
Reading comprehension	17	3
Vocabulary	20	3
Math reasoning	38	4
Math computation	57	5
Language usage	24	3
Spelling	09	2
Grammar	11	3
Social science	19	3
Science	32	4

The practitioner concluded that the reported weaknesses in language usage were certainly verified by Li's recent achievement test results. The practitioner found that previous test data for Li followed the same pattern —a weakness in language skills and average or better performance in mathematical computation.

Li spoke softly and volunteered little information. He seemed proud of, but also somewhat threatened by, the fact that his two older brothers were attending college. He reported that his father owned and operated a manufacturing firm. Both his parents were college graduates.

When the practitioner asked Li about his plans for the future, he answered with a well-rehearsed, "I want to be an accountant." The practitioner acknowledged Li's response positively and explored in more detail Li's interest in the field of business. During the course of the conversation, it became apparent that Li possessed little knowledge about the work activities of an accountant. To Li, the job was the same as bookkeeping. However, the practitioner had established rapport with Li and had been able to get him to project into the future and to talk about what he perceived as a good job.

Before the next counseling session, the practitioner consulted with Li's math teacher: "Li has good computational skills and really tries hard; he certainly is not my top student in mathematics, but he does well in applications." This information confirmed the results of the previous test data and of the recently administered achievement test. The practitioner was encouraged, for now he could include some positive facts when giving Li the test results.

At the next session, after a brief period of small talk designed to reinforce the rapport already established, the practitioner suggested that they discuss the achievement test results. "Your score is at the 17th percentile on reading comprehension. This means that in a national study, 17 out of 100 11th graders scored lower than you, while 83 out of 100 11th graders scored higher." The practitioner explained the other scores in the same manner and then discussed groups of scores.

Li was particularly sensitive to his low scores in language usage. He commented that he had always had problems with English courses. The practitioner asked that he explain how this problem could affect his plans for educational training and a career. Li acknowledged that he would have problems in college; his brothers had told him the English courses were difficult.

The practitioner sensed that it was the right time to introduce encouraging information and an alternative potential career goal: "The field of business is broad and has many opportunities for you, particularly with your good math skills. We can explore some careers that require math skills, but that do not necessarily require a college degree. A couple of occupations that I can think of offhand are bookkeeping and bank teller." Li appeared hopeful with this new information, and in subsequent counseling sessions made reports on several careers he had researched in the career resource center. He seemed most interested in bookkeeping.

In a meeting with the practitioner, Li's parents expressed their appreciation for Li's enthusiasm and interest in career exploration. Li had shared some of the occupational information he had found on bookkeeping with them. They said they had hoped that Li could attend college as his brothers had, but they recently came to the realization that Li was not as academically inclined. They now planned to encourage and support Li's interest in alternative careers.

In this case, the achievement test results were linked easily to educational planning and occupational information. Li and his parents recognized that his weak English skills would make it difficult for him to be a successful college student, but that his relatively higher skills in mathematics opened other occupational opportunities as shown in Table 5-15.

Table 5-15: Achievement Test Survey Battery Results for Li

Test	National Percentile Equivalent	National Stanine
Reading comprehension	17	3
Vocabulary	20	3
Math reasoning	38	4
Math computation	57	5
Language usage	24	3

Case of a School Dropout Interested in Changing Jobs: Using the WRAT4

Diana, 24 years old, dropped out of school when she was in the seventh grade. She had worked at a number of odd jobs but mainly as a nurse's aide and came to the career-counseling center to find out what the requirements were for becoming a licensed vocational nurse (LVN). After reviewing the requirements, she asked the practitioner whether there was some way of determining how she would "do" in LVN training and in classes that prepare individuals to obtain a high school equivalency diploma.

The practitioner suggested that she take an achievement test to get a rough estimate of her educational level in arithmetic, reading, and spelling. The WRAT4 was selected because it specifically measures basic achievement in those areas and can be quickly administered and scored. Table 5-16 provides a brief snapshot of the WRAT4.

Table 5-16 Wide Range Achievement Test-Revision 4 (WRAT4)

Author/Publisher	Psychological Assessment Resources, Inc.
Copyright date	2006
Test Purpose	Allows educators to examine students' development of reading, spelling, and arithmetic, and to diagnose learning disabilities in reading, spelling, and arithmetic when given with a comprehensive test of ability
Versions	Green and Blue Forms (alternative forms)
Administrator Requirements	B
Appropriate Age Range	5-94
Norms	It was standardized on a stratified, representative national sample of over 3,000 individuals ranging in age from 5-94 years. They stratified the sample with respect to age, gender, ethnicity, geographic region, and socioeconomic status (as measured by obtained education by parent). Norm-referenced: standard scores, percentiles, age equivalents, and grade equivalents
Administration	Group and individual (differs for subtests)
Time to Complete	Approximately 15-25 minutes for individuals ages 5-7 years. Approximately 35-45 minutes for individuals ages 8 years and older.

Test Scales & Subscales	Four subtests: Word Reading Sentence Comprehension Spelling Math Computation Reading comprehension score (Word Reading + Sentence Comprehension)
Reliability	By age, the median coefficient alpha subtest reliability coefficients range from .87 to .93 for the subtests for an age-based sample, and from .83 to .98 for a grade-based sample.
Validity	The publisher reports content and construct validation studies supporting the WRAT4 with a variety of inventories, such as Woodcock Johnson III, KTEA-III Brief, WAIS-III and the WISC-IV.
Interpretation	Standard scores are based on a mean of 100 and SD of 15.
Research/Reviews	Dell, Harrold & Dell (2008)

The results of the WRAT4 for Diana are listed in Table 5-17. The practitioner recognized Diana's disappointment with her performance. However, the practitioner pointed out that a high school diploma was not a prerequisite for entering the local LVN training program. In discussing why she wanted to be a LVN, Diana expressed a sincere desire to help people and to be in a career that made a difference.

Table 5-17 WRAT4 Results for Diana

Test	Stanine	Percentile	Standard Score
Math Computation	3	12	82
Reading Composition	2	09	80
Word Reading	2	05	75
Sentence Comprehension	2	05	67
Spelling	2	08	79

Before Diana returned for her next appointment, the practitioner reviewed the items Diana had missed on the test. It was obvious that Diana's spelling skills were poor, but an item analysis of the arithmetic test revealed that she made a number of careless mistakes. A review of the reading test revealed that Diana's word attack skills were poor, probably because she had not been exposed to many of the words she missed.

At the next counseling session, the practitioner reviewed her item analysis of Diana's test results by pointing out careless mistakes and a lack of self-confidence in attempting words on the oral reading test. Diana appreciated being given concrete examples of her mistakes; she realized that she might do better with greater exposure to academic materials. In subsequent meetings, Diana agreed to enter a remedial program sponsored by the high school learning assistance center. When Diana was asked about the decision, she stated, "I've always been afraid of tests. Now—could you believe it?—the test scores helped me see the light!" Diana's career exploration was enhanced in a number of ways by the test. First, she was encouraged to upgrade her vocational skills by further academic training. Second, she gained self-confidence by diagnosing the mistakes on her test. By encouraging her to upgrade her skills through educational programs, the practitioner helped make other work opportunities available to Diana.

The Test for Adult Basic Education (TABE) is a type of achievement tests that examines basic levels of knowledge in adults. Table 5-18 provides a brief snapshot of the TABE.

Table 5-18 Test for Adult Basic Education (TABE)

Author/Publisher	CTB-McGraw Hill
Copyright date	2007
Test Purpose	Assess adult basic skills in vocabulary, reading, language, language mechanics, mathematics, and spelling.
Versions	9/10
Administrator Requirements	Adult educators who have a general knowledge of measurement principles and who are willing to abide by the assessment standards of the American Psychological Association
Appropriate Age Range	High school and above

Norms	Normed on 14 year olds and above.
Administration	Group, individual, computer
Time to Complete	The complete battery takes 3.5 hours. Other times vary depending on test being administered.
Test Scales & Subscales	The complete battery consists of five levels (L, E, M, D, and A), two forms (9 and 10), and a Locator Test. Subtests cover reading, math computation, applied mathematics, and language. Vocabulary, Language Mechanics, and Spelling are optional tests. Also available in Braille and Spanish.
Reliability	Reliability coefficients for subtests range from .73-.95 (Prins, 2009).
Interpretation	Uses percentile, scale scores, and grade equivalent scores.
Supporting Materials	Student instructional workbooks, individualized lesson plans, staff development products, links and correlations to other studies.
Research/Reviews	Burck (2013); Prins (2009)

Consider Ric, a ninth grade student whose goal is to receive a GED. He completes the TABE, and the grade equivalent scores are presented in Table 5-19.

Table 5-19 Sample TABE Results

	Grade Equivalent Scores	National Percentile
Reading Comprehension	9.9	99
Math Comprehension	9.9	95
Math Application	9.9	99
Language	2.2	12
Vocabulary	12.9	99
Language Mechanics	2.3	18
Spelling	2.3	7

PRACTITIONER: Your TABE results are in, and I think they'll provide us with a good picture as to where your strengths are in preparing to take the GED, and what areas you need to focus on in the coming weeks.

RIC: So what do the results show?

PRACTITIONER: Well, you are right on target in four areas: reading and math comprehension, math application, and you are particularly strong in vocabulary. There are three areas that seem to be providing you with a great deal of challenge: language, language mechanics and spelling.

RIC: Those scores look really low – do you think there's any way that I can get the scores up?

PRACTITIONER: Yes, I do. You need to focus your energy on these three areas, and not expect for it to come overnight. If you take your time, but stay on task in studying these specific areas, I think you are sure to see progress.

In this case, the TABE helped RIC to narrow down his studying focus specifically to the lower scores, and also provided encouragement as to what he already knows. The practitioner was able to help Ric save time by addressing the subjects in which he scored poorest.

Using Achievement Test Results for Self-Concept and Self-Efficacy Development
The last two case studies in this chapter do not have specifically named achievement tests. The focus in these two cases is on how the results of achievement test scores are used for career development. Career practitioners will find that numerous achievement tests on the market will meet individual and group needs.

Case of the Client with Limited Educational and Vocational Experience
Rita was referred to the career practitioner by a local social service agency. She had been deserted by her husband after ten years of marriage and left with three children. She had little work experience. Her school grades were poor, and she had dropped out of school while in the seventh grade to get married.

The practitioner was not surprised to find that Rita was depressed. It became quite clear during the intake interview that Rita had developed a very poor self-concept; she was especially critical of her academic basic skills. She simply felt that she had little or nothing to offer an employer.

Although the practitioner recognized that there might be many reasons for Rita's poor self-concept, an

75

outstanding problem was her inability to identify functional skills and abilities that could be used to establish career goals. The practitioner noticed that Rita was able to express herself fairly well and used proper grammar. Perhaps, he thought, Rita may have more ability than she realized. Her alertness gave at least some positive clues that she could, under the right circumstances, improve her basic skills.

As the interview continued, the practitioner realized that he must build counseling strategies that focus on building a more positive self-concept. He reasoned that Rita's poor self-concept might make it very difficult for her to build enough self-confidence to aggressively pursue a training program or seek employment. It became clear that many hard recent personal experiences would make it difficult for Rita to project into the work world in a positive manner. Furthermore, she had experienced social forces that were major determinants of poor self-concept formation. As Rita saw it, an active life role in society was at this point an unattainable goal.

Counseling Plan for Rita
The major focus of the counseling plan was the development of skills that could be used for employment to help meet the needs of her family. The first step would include developing a more positive self-concept through skill assessment and development. The practitioner would emphasize positive aspects of measured skills and establish goals to improve them. Rita's strengths and weaknesses both would be approached in a positive manner; that is, strengths would be identified with required skills in occupations and weaknesses would be used as starting points for improving skills. Following is a summary of the counseling plan:

1. Suggest an assessment instrument designed for adults that evaluates basic skills in language usage, mathematics, reading, and writing.
2. Criterion-referenced scores would be used. Link the needs for basic skills to employment.
3. Use the results of assessment to determine an appropriate training program.
4. Ask Rita to describe a plan of action for improving basic educational skills.
5. Direct Rita to identify and appreciate personal interests and skills.
6. Assist Rita to clarify career and life goals based on an understanding of self.
7. Ask Rita to describe the relationships between personal behavior and self-concept.
8. Offer other counseling services as needed.

In this case, the importance of self-concept formation was stressed, and the practitioner decided that a direct link to employment was the best approach to use. Adults often react favorably to counseling programs that are clearly delineated and demonstrate how counseling goals are related to future employment. For Rita, it seemed particularly important to design a counseling program that provided a means of personal improvement to restore the self-confidence she was lacking. Like all clients, Rita must be able to project her self-concept into a work role.

Case of the Girl Who Had Difficulty with Math
When Evita reported to the counseling center, she was confused about why she had been referred by her teacher. "So I have trouble with math like all other girls; so what?" she thought. "It doesn't make sense that because I can't get the problems in class, I'm sent to a counselor," she confided to a friend.

Although Evita's teacher had carefully explained that she believed Evita's poor performance in math was symptomatic of an underlying problem, Evita refused to accept that explanation. Realizing Evita's reluctance to visit the counseling center, Evita's teacher had a conference with a counselor.

Evita's teacher explained the problem as she saw it: "I have been trying to figure out why Evita's grades have been significantly dropping this year. She seemed to be an outstanding student, but when she started this last math course it seems that all of her grades dropped. I am not aware of personal or family problems, but this girl needs your help!" Evita had never been a problem student, and, as instructed, she reported to the practitioner's office. The counselor immediately tried to comfort Evita by telling her that teachers often sent students to see her. After a briefing of the services offered at the counseling center and small talk design to establish rapport, Evita became more comfortable and begin to express herself.

During the course of several counseling sessions, the counselor made note of the number of times that Evita mentioned "girls are just not good in math." However, this feeling of lack of confidence in math seemed more pervasive. Evita begin to express doubts about her ability in other subjects and skills as well. The counselor remembered the teacher's remark that Evita's grades had been dropping in all subjects. The practitioner scanned the results of several achievement tests over the past three years. A clear pattern of low achievement in all subjects was obvious from Evita's recent records. Yet, in further probes of Evita's activities during this time period, there was no evidence of any significant event that could be responsible for home or personal problems. There was also no evidence of substance abuse or poor health.

The counselor had established an excellent counseling relationship with Evita but had difficulty in

76

finding underlying problems that could be contributing factors to a significant change in academic achievement. The practitioner began to research specific problems in women's career development and found that self-efficacy was a significant problem for many women. For instance, Betz (1992b) defined career self-efficacy as "the possibility that low expectations of efficacy with respect to some aspect of career behavior may serve as a detriment to optimal career choice and the development of the individual" (p. 24). Furthermore, self-efficacy deficits may lead to procrastination in or avoidance of making a career decision.

The practitioner believed that she had found Evita's underlying problem, but she was cautious. In counseling sessions, she carefully led to the subject of career choice and found that Evita was quite undecided about the future, which she expressed with overtones of lack of confidence and confusion about what the future might hold in store for her. It seemed clear that Evita had poor planning skills and had given little thought to career decision-making. In fact, she seemed to want to avoid these subjects as though she was not ready to tackle them.

Before talking to Evita's teacher and developing any counseling strategies, the practitioner decided to wait for the next administration of achievement tests, which were to begin in a few days. When the results came in indicating another significant drop in achievement for Evita, the practitioner developed a counseling plan.

Counseling Plan for Evita
The major thrust of this plan would be to increase Evita's expectations of efficacy by the following methods:
1. Provide opportunities for performing successfully, especially in math.
2. Select positive role models for visits and discussions.
3. Provide ways to deal with stress and anxiety.
4. Provide support and encouragement from significant others.
5. Discuss the problems of self-efficacy, especially as they affect women and their career development.
6. Discuss the impact of negative thinking on feelings and behavior, and introduce cognitive reframing exercises.
7. Develop a personal agency perspective that suggests that all individuals be responsible for their career development (Zunker, 2014).

In this case, achievement test results played an important role in providing objective data that ultimately led to the development of a counseling plan. The practitioner and the teacher collaborated to help a very confused student regain momentum for completing course work in a timely manner. Evita discovered that what she told herself about herself greatly affected her behavior. She learned that when you expect positive results through self-evaluation, your performance usually improves.

Suggestions for Career Development
Many of the following suggestions for fostering the career development of students and adults can be modified and used interchangeably to meet the needs of both groups. These suggestions should not be considered an exhaustive means of using assessment results to enhance career development; rather, they are examples from which exercises can be developed to meet local needs and needs of other groups.

For Schools:
Ask students to identify personal strengths and weaknesses as measured by achievement test results. Using this information, identify related work tasks for selected occupations or career clusters. Ask students to identify relationships between ability and achievement.
- Ask students to develop a plan for improving their academic skills.
- Form discussion groups for the purpose of linking basic skills to occupations.
- Ask students to identify and compare levels of achievement to selected occupations. Ask students to discuss the relationships between student roles and work roles.
- Ask students to relate academic skills to interests and values.
- Ask students to identify basic skills used in selected occupations in the community and compare them with their own.
- Ask students to discuss the relationship of academic achievement and self-concept development.
- Ask students to discuss how one's self-talk impacts how he or she would describe his or her abilities and academic skills.

For Adults:
- Form groups and ask adults to discuss and identify the relationship of obsolescence to achievement

results.

- Ask adults to identify the changes in training requirements for selected occupations. Match their achievement results with some new or different occupations.
- Ask adults to identify the necessity of acquiring basic skills for many occupations. Have them make a list of occupations with matching basic skills. Then compare achievement test results with requirements of selected occupations.
- Ask adults to identify and discuss the limitations of advancement in many occupations because of poor basic skill achievement. Using assessment results, have them develop plans for improving basic skills.
- Ask adults to discuss the necessity of training for making career transitions. Relate achievement to training requirements.
- Using achievement test results, have them develop educational plans to meet requirements of selected jobs.
- Have adults develop a positive view of self by assessing strengths, and potentials, from achievement test results.
- Ask students to compare self-rated achievement results with the results of a standardized test and share their conclusions.

Other Achievement Tests

Because many published achievement tests are currently available, the following list is far from complete. The following seven examples of various achievement tests include four survey batteries and three diagnostic tests.

- **Basic Achievement Skills Inventory (BASI).** A comprehensive achievement test for ages 8 to 80 that consists of 6 timed subtests, including Vocabulary, Spelling, Language Mechanics, Reading Comprehension, Math Computation and Math Application. The BASI was normed on a sample matching 2000 U.S. Census data and can be group or self-administered.
- **Kaufman Test of Educational Achievement, Third Edition (KTEA-III).** The KTEA-II is an individually administered battery that includes 5 composites (Reading, Math, Written Language, Oral Language and Comprehensive Achievement) and one Reading-related subtest that consists of six areas. The Comprehensive Form can be used on ages 4.6 through 25, and the Brief Form can be used on ages 4.6 through 90+. Scores are presented via standard scores, with a mean of 100 and a standard deviation of 15, age and grade equivalents, percentile ranks, stanines and normal curve equivalents.
- **Peabody Individual Achievement Test—Revised-Normative Update (PIAT-R/NU).** This test provides grade equivalents, age percentile ranks, and standard scores by age or grade for reading comprehension, reading recognition, written expression, mathematics, spelling, and general knowledge (science, social studies, fine arts, and sports). The Reading Recognition subtest measures the ability to recognize that sounds that go with printed letters and to read words out loud. The Reading Comprehension subtest measures the ability to understand a reading passage. The Written Expression subtest measures ability to understand mathematical concepts and procedures, to perform calculations and to solve problems. The Spelling subtest measures the ability to recognize letters from their names or sounds and to recognize the standard spelling of words. The PIAT is designed to be used with individuals from age 5 to adulthood. It takes 30 to 50 minutes to administer.
- **Stanford Diagnostic Mathematics Test—4th Edition.** A group-administered test, this test measures knowledge in basic concepts of math that are critical to future success in math, and also problem-solving strategies. The test has six levels, ranging from grades 1.5 to 13.0 and ranging in total time from 145 to 155 minutes.
- **TerraNova-Second Edition (TerraNova CAT6).** An achievement test series used in public and private schools that provides results on Reading, Language, Mathematics, Science and Social Studies. Five performance levels are identified - Advanced, Proficient, Nearing Proficiency, Progressing and Step 1/Starting Out. Item content was developed after consultation with national, state and local standards.
- **Woodcock Johnson IV.** The complete battery consists of achievement tests, tests of cognitive abilities and oral language tests. There are multiple sub-tests for each of these, such as phonological processing, pattern matching, verbal attention, oral reading, reading comprehension, picture vocabulary and rapid picture naming.

Summary

Academic achievement is a primary consideration in educational and vocational planning. For educational planning, there is a direct relationship, and almost all jobs are linked to achievement of basic skills. Compared with aptitude tests, achievement tests measure much narrower content areas and more limited learning experiences. Aptitude tests measure broader areas of abilities and experiences. There are two types of achievement tests: general survey batteries and single-subject tests. Achievement test results are reported as norm-referenced scores, criterion-referenced scores, or both. Practitioners should be aware of the potential of self-concept to affect an individual's performance on an achievement test.

Questions and Exercises

1. Define aptitude and achievement, describe the difference, and illustrate how aptitude and achievement scores are used in career counseling.
2. Review the profile of the CAPS in Figure 5-5. The abbreviations can be interpreted as MR = Mechanical Reasoning; SR = Spatial Relations; VR = Verbal Reasoning; NA = Numerical Ability; LU = Language Usage; WK = Word Knowledge; PSA = Perceptual Speed and Accuracy; and MSD = Manual Speed and Dexterity. How would you characterize this student's strengths and weaknesses? What recommendations might you make to this student? In what kind of career activities might this person excel? How might this person present in counseling? What changes might you make in your counseling approach with this individual?

Figure 5-5: Sample CAPS Results

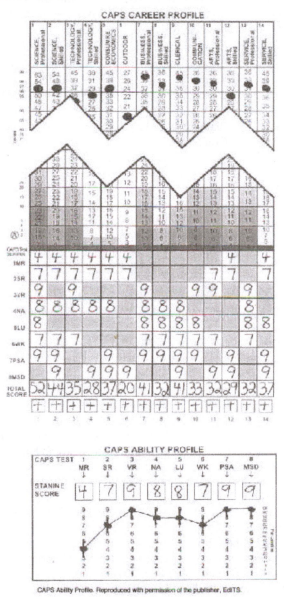

CAPS Ability Profile. Reproduced with permission of the publisher, EdITS.

79

3. What are the major differences between the DAT and the ASVAB? Give an example of a case and specify why you would choose one of these tests over the other to assess an individual's abilities.
4. How would you counsel an individual who claimed that she was not interested in the occupations suggested as a result of her aptitude test, or the areas of study suggested by her achievement test scores?
5. Is it important for aptitude and achievement tests to provide separate sex norms? Why or why not?
6. How would you prepare high school students to interpret the results of the ASVAB? Develop a list of major points you would cover for a presentation to a group or to an individual, parents, teachers and students. (The website for ASVAB has fact sheets for parents and students that might provide a great springboard for discussion).
7. Corrina is struggling with post-graduation plans. She is currently in ROTC, and although she enjoys the discipline and the group's activities, she is not certain that she wants to pursue a military career. She has taken the ASVAB, and her results are presented in Figure 5-3. How would you summarize her results, and how would you proceed?
8. An adult client has completed the Highlands Aptitude Battery. Her Work Type results are shown in Table 5-19. What would you guess her Holland code to be, based on these results? How would you summarize her strengths and weaknesses? What types of occupations might fit her skills best?

Table 5-19 Highland Aptitude Battery Results

Strong Match With Your Abilities	Good Match With Your Abilities	Moderate Match With Your Abilities	Weak Match With Your Abilities
Problem-Solving, Diagnostic Research	Problem-Solving, Consultative Creative Structural/ engineering Technical/ abstract Planning, Strategic Communicating, Speaking/Listening Paying Attention to Details Creating, Artistic Managing People Managing Processes Decision-Making, Directional/Strategic	Managing, Structural/Engineering Facilitating Interactions Connecting at Feeling Level	Making Contact With Others Teaching Coaching Performing Motivating Selling

9. A teacher has referred a tenth grade student, Ken Jones, to you for help with career decision making. The Individual Profile Report of the Terra Nova (a standardized achievement test) indicate the following percentiles:
   a. Reading subtest scores range from 70 to 91
   b. Language subtest scores range from 50 to 78
   c. Mathematics subtest scores range from 61 to 83
   d. Science subtest scores range from 47 to 52
   e. Social Studies subtest scores range from 74 to 84
   How might his scores be related to his career interests and abilities? What are his apparent strengths and weaknesses? What type of interventions (career and other) might you make with this student? How might a parent feel in receiving this information? Knowing that this information will be sent home, design an introductory sheet to aid parents in the interpretation. What other interventions might you do, pre- and post-testing, to prepare student and parents for the results?
10. Kieta, a 2nd grade (8 year, 7 month) student, has completed the PIAT. Her mother wants to talk with you about her adjustment to the second grade. In her previous school, her grades were on a "C" or average level. Her results are presented in Figure 5-6a and Figure 5-6b on the next page. Summarize her strengths and areas for improvement. Speak to the grade equivalent scores, age equivalent scores, standard scores and percentile ranks. If she was seeing you in a career-counseling group, how might you vary your interventions, activities or information, based on these results? What type of interpretations and suggestions can you make, based on her results?

Figure 5-6a

04/05/2001 Peabody Individual Achievement Test - Revised/NU

Examinee: Obatu, Kieta
School/Agency: North Community School
Teacher/Counselor: Karla Liebowitz

Sex: Female
Grade: 2
Examiner: Emilio Juarez

Test Date: 01/04/2001
Birth Date: 05/19/1992
Age: 8-7

Reasons for testing
Experiencing difficulties in reading

SCORE SUMMARY

Standard scores were derived from Age norm tables.

Subtest or Composite	68% Conf. Level	Raw Score	Grade Equiv.	Age Equiv.	Standard Score	%ile Rank	NCE
General	+1.00 SEM	33		7-9	90	25	36
Information	Obtained Score	30	2.0	7-5	86	18	30
Subtest	-1.00 SEM	27		7-1	82	12	25
Reading	+1.00 SEM	25		7-2	82	12	25
Recognition	Obtained Score	23	1.5	6-11	80	9	22
Subtest	-1.00 SEM	21		6-8	78	7	19
Reading	+1.00 SEM	23		6-10	81	10	23
Comprehension	Obtained Score	20	1.2	6-7	77	6	18
Subtest	-1.00 SEM	17		6-4	73	4	12
	+1.00 SEM	47		6-11	79	8	21
TOTAL	Obtained Score	43	1.3	6-9	77	6	18
READING	-1.00 SEM	39		6-6	75	5	15
	+1.00 SEM	31		8-5	99	47	49
Mathematics	Obtained Score	29	2.6	8-1	95	37	43
Subtest	-1.00 SEM	27		7-10	91	27	37
	+1.00 SEM	24		6-7	80	9	22
Spelling	Obtained Score	22	1.0	6-5	77	6	18
Subtest	-1.00 SEM	20		6-2	74	4	13
	+1.00 SEM	130		7-1	79	8	21
TOTAL	Obtained Score	124	1.5	7-0	77	6	18
TEST	-1.00 SEM	118		6-11	75	5	15

Written Expression II (Prompt A)
Raw Score = 17 Developmental Scaled Score = 2 Grade-based Stanine = 2

WRITTEN LANGUAGE Scaled Score Sum = 2 + 2 = 4
Age Standard Score = 74 +/- 4 %ile Rank = 4 %ile Range = 2 - 7

APTITUDE ACHIEVEMENT

Aptitude Test: K-ABC MPC
Aptitude Standard Score: 94 Aptitude Ach. Correlation: .65

Expected TOTAL READING Standard Score: 96
Standard Score Discrepancy: 19 Frequency of Occurrence: 5%

COPYRIGHT 1998, AMERICAN GUIDANCE SERVICE, INC., CIRCLE PINES, MN 55014-1796

Figure 5-6b

EXAMINEE:Obatu, Kieta

```
                        DEVELOPMENTAL SCORE PROFILES
                             68% Confidence Level

                          Age Equivalent Profile
            Age       !
Equivalent Range!  4    5    6    7    8    9   10   11   12   13   14   15   16   17   18   19
----------------!--+----+----+----+----+----+----+----+----+----+----+----+----+----+----+----+
General Info.   !                 ****
     7-1 to 7-9 !                      A
----------------!--+----+----+----+----+----+----+----+----+----+----+----+----+----+----+----+
Reading Recog.  !                ***
     6-8 to 7-2 !                      A
----------------!--+----+----+----+----+----+----+----+----+----+----+----+----+----+----+----+
Reading Comp.   !               ***
     6-4 to 6-10!                      A
----------------!--+----+----+----+----+----+----+----+----+----+----+----+----+----+----+----+
TOTAL READING   !              **
     6-6 to 6-11!                      A
================!--+----+----+----+----+----+----+----+----+----+----+----+----+----+----+----+
Mathematics     !                 ***
     7-10 to 8-5!                      A
----------------!--+----+----+----+----+----+----+----+----+----+----+----+----+----+----+----+
Spelling        !               ***
     6-2 to 6-7 !                      A
----------------!--+----+----+----+----+----+----+----+----+----+----+----+----+----+----+----+
TOTAL TEST      !              **
     6-11 to 7-1!                      A
================!--+----+----+----+----+----+----+----+----+----+----+----+----+----+----+----+
```

11. Nick is a seventh grade student who recently completed the BASI. His results are included in Table 5-20. How would you interpret his results to him, and to his parents? How would you interpret each of the following: confidence interval, percentile rank, performance, grade and age equivalents? Write up a brief summary of his results addressing these key factors.

Table 5-20 BASI Results

	Standard Score (mean=100; SD = 15)	Confidence Interval	Percentile Rank
Reading Total	116	108-122	86
Vocabulary	112	102-120	79
Reading Comprehension	121	109-128	92
Written Language Total	114	106-120	82
Spelling	123	110-130	93
Language Mechanics	108	100-115	70
Math Total	109	99-117	73
Math Computation	109	98-118	73
Math Application	109	96-120	73

12. Eleanor worked with her hands all of her life, until she had a stroke which severely impacted her fine motor skills. She has asked for an evaluation to see what other jobs she could perform that would be hands-on but not require intricate finger work. In the past, she worked as a carpenter, a tool maker and a drill press operator. You enter the occupational history into the Job Browser Pro from SkillTRAN. The preliminary list of options is presented in Figure 5-7. How will you help Eleanor narrow down the list from 674 to a manageable number? What would your next steps be?

82

Figure 5-7: Job Browser Pro Results

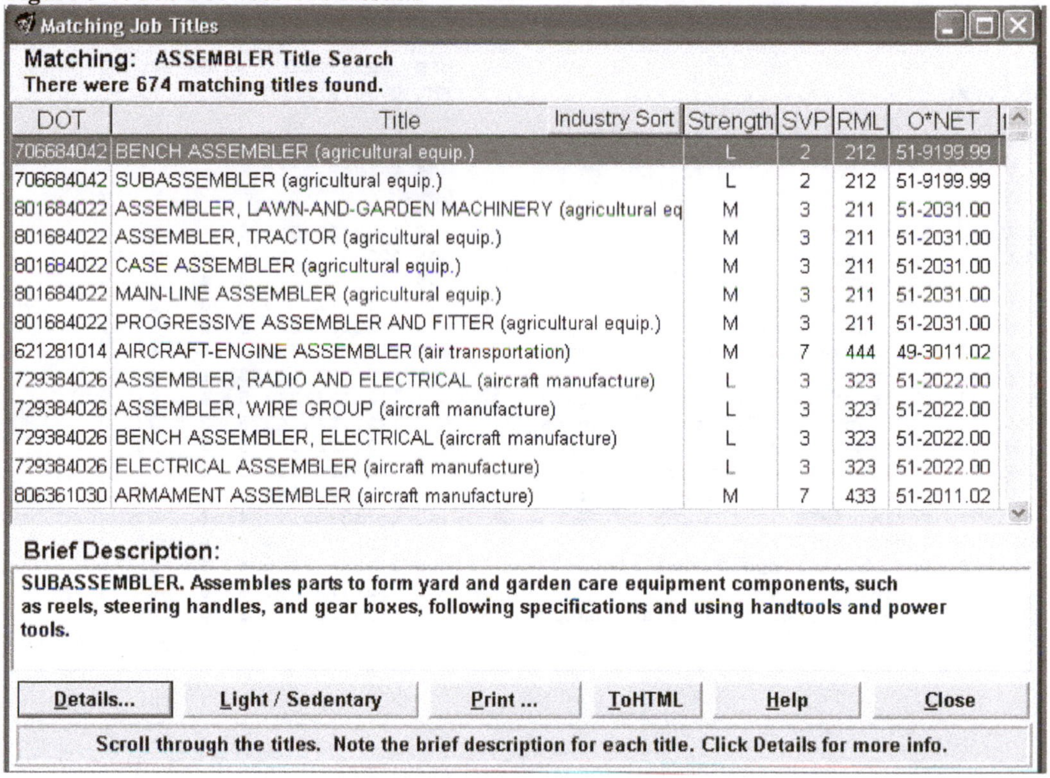

Matching Job Titles

Matching: ASSEMBLER Title Search
There were 674 matching titles found.

DOT	Title	Industry Sort	Strength	SVP	RML	O*NET
706684042	BENCH ASSEMBLER (agricultural equip.)		L	2	212	51-9199.99
706684042	SUBASSEMBLER (agricultural equip.)		L	2	212	51-9199.99
801684022	ASSEMBLER, LAWN-AND-GARDEN MACHINERY (agricultural eq		M	3	211	51-2031.00
801684022	ASSEMBLER, TRACTOR (agricultural equip.)		M	3	211	51-2031.00
801684022	CASE ASSEMBLER (agricultural equip.)		M	3	211	51-2031.00
801684022	MAIN-LINE ASSEMBLER (agricultural equip.)		M	3	211	51-2031.00
801684022	PROGRESSIVE ASSEMBLER AND FITTER (agricultural equip.)		M	3	211	51-2031.00
621281014	AIRCRAFT-ENGINE ASSEMBLER (air transportation)		M	7	444	49-3011.02
729384026	ASSEMBLER, RADIO AND ELECTRICAL (aircraft manufacture)		L	3	323	51-2022.00
729384026	ASSEMBLER, WIRE GROUP (aircraft manufacture)		L	3	323	51-2022.00
729384026	BENCH ASSEMBLER, ELECTRICAL (aircraft manufacture)		L	3	323	51-2022.00
729384026	ELECTRICAL ASSEMBLER (aircraft manufacture)		L	3	323	51-2022.00
806361030	ARMAMENT ASSEMBLER (aircraft manufacture)		M	7	433	51-2011.02

Brief Description:

SUBASSEMBLER. Assembles parts to form yard and garden care equipment components, such as reels, steering handles, and gear boxes, following specifications and using handtools and power tools.

Details...	Light / Sedentary	Print ...	ToHTML	Help	Close

Scroll through the titles. Note the brief description for each title. Click Details for more info.

13. Neal, a client with a physical impairment in his right hand, used the AVIATOR 3 to learn about his interests and skills. He was able to use an adaptive device provided by VALPAR instead of the mouse. Figure 5-8 shows a summary of his assessment as compared to an occupation of interest chosen by Neal. How would you describe Neal's GED scores, with 6 representing the highest level of ability? How does this compare to the GED level required for the position Neal chose (hint: the top line is the client's assessed level, and the bottom bar is the minimum level required for the job)? How would you describe his aptitudes (with 1 representing the highest level of aptitude)? How do his aptitudes compare with the job he has chosen to research? How would you address the issue of Neal's disability in the discussion? Points on the Growth scale range from zero to 7, with 0=not rated; 1=decline rapidly; 2=decline slowly or moderately; 3=little or no change; 4=slower than average growth; 5=average growth; 6=faster than average growth; 7=much faster than average growth. What implications does the growth indicator suggest for this career? How would you proceed with Neal?

Figure 5-8: Sample AVIATOR 3 Occupational List

```
                                          GED .APTITUDES. ZO GR SCO
O*NET.Code.   Job.Title.......................  RML GVNSPQKFMEC NE OW  RE

Interest Areas Searched - 02, 09, 11
Your Levels. Search items underlined           445 22233233222


29-1061.00   Anesthesiologists                 656 12221222253 5  4   4
29-1121.00   Audiologists                       545 22222333354 4  0   0
29-1011.00   Chiropractors                      545 22322422244 5  4   0
29-1029.99   Dentists, All Other Specialists    655 12111321143 0  0   2
29-1021.00   Dentists, General                  655 11212221243 5  2   2
29-1062.00   Family and General Practitioners   656 11212221253 5  4   4
29-1063.00   Internists, General                656 11211221143 5  4   4
29-1064.00   Obstetricians and Gynecologists    656 11211231243 5  4   4
29-1022.00   Oral and Maxillofacial Surgeons    655 12211221143 5  2   2
29-1023.00   Orthodontists                      655 11211321244 5  2   2
29-1065.00   Pediatricians, General             656 11211221153 5  4   4
29-1069.99   Physicians and Surgeons, All Other 656 11211221243 0  4   4
29-1081.00   Podiatrists                        545 23333443355 4  3   0
29-1066.00   Psychiatrists                      656 11212344454 5  4   4
29-1127.00   Speech-Language Pathologists       555 22332333355 4  5   2
29-1067.00   Surgeons                           656 11211221143 5  4   4
31-9096.00   Veterinary Assistants and Laboratory 434 33333233343 3  4   0
```

CHAPTER 6

INTEREST INVENTORIES

"What do you like to do? What do you hate doing? What do you do for fun? How do you spend your free time? If you could be doing anything, what would it be?" In one way or another, almost everyone has been involved in the exploration of interests to decide which activities to pursue in leisure, in a career, or in both. In fact, interests have been found to be better predictors than personality variables for matching with specific job characteristics as well as matching with occupations (Ehrhart & Makransky, 2007).

Strong (1943) pioneered the development of interest inventories by introducing innovative principles for measuring interests. He gathered data concerning individuals' likes and dislikes for a variety of activities, objects, and types of persons commonly encountered. He found that individuals in different occupations have common patterns of interests that differentiate them from individuals in other occupations. In this way, the results of interest inventories provide the opportunity for individuals to compare their interests with those of individuals in specific occupational groups. A review of the history of interest inventories in career counseling is provided by Harrington and Long (2012). Before diving into this chapter, let's first start with the reflections of two practitioners on their use of a well-known interest inventory, the Strong Interest Inventory, with a male college student.

Fred is a 19-year-old African American male in his sophomore year. He is currently majoring in business, but is unsure if business is the best option for him. Fred suffers from a low GPA (lower than 2.5) and doesn't enjoy most of his classes in business. According to Fred, the only reason he entered business in the first place is that the career opportunities in business "sounded more promising than other majors." Fred describes himself as a very organized person who attends to details. He enjoys leading and helping people, but does not know much about what majors fit with his interests.

Based on the conversations we had in our sessions, I used the Strong Interest Inventory (SII) as a supplementary tool to help Fred with his major decision. I briefly talked with him about Holland's personal-environmental fit theory and how SII assesses one's interests, not abilities. Additionally, I asked Fred to self-rate on the Holland types and he ranked his top three as Social, Conventional and Enterprising. I also shared that information obtained from SII can be helpful to assist his career and education exploration, work environment preference, and reassurance of interests if applicable. Fred took the online SII and reported that he had no difficulty understanding the questions, and it took him about 20-minutes to complete it. He also said that simply by doing the inventory he found a potential interest in training others.

Results of Fred's *General Occupational Themes* showed that he scored high on Social, Enterprising, and Conventional, medium in Investigative, and very low in Artistic and Realistic. As a result, Fred's measured Occupational Themes were rather consistent with his earlier self ratings. I shared with him that these interest levels are relative levels compared to working adult men. When asked how well the results reflect his ideas, he said that the values and skills described in Social, Enterprising, and Artistic are quite consistent with what he likes and values. One of the top areas of his *Basic Interest Scales* - Human Resources and Training - is something that he had not considered in the past but finds it to be interesting. Also, Fred scored similar to several Occupational Scales including: Human Resource Manger, Training and Development Specialist, Career Counselor, Instructional Coordinator, Administrative Assistant as well as Paralegal. I used O*NET to help Fred better understands the relevant occupations, work activities, skills, education, as well as employment trend in the Human Resources field. Regarding Fred's work environment preference, the *Personal Style Scales* showed that Fred enjoys working with others, prefers practical learning environments and taking on leadership roles, but does not like risk-taking. We discussed how his personal style preferences may manifest itself in his fields of interest. Finally, we used the *College Profile* to look for majors and courses that relate to his interests. We discussed the courses, activities, and internship recommended by SII. We also identified that the requirement for a human resource specialist is a bachelor's degree combined with work experience in the field. After several sessions, Fred decided to register for courses in Human Resources, Organizational Psychology and Labor-Industrial Relations to get a better sense of the field. He also joined a programming committee in a student group to gain more experience working with others.

Ivy Li and Jeff Garis
Doctoral Student and Senior Director, Career Services & Affiliate Professor, Counselor Education
Pennsylvania State Career Services

Advanced Organizer

In this chapter, we will cover:

- RIASEC Theory
- Other Career Theories and Interests
- Stability of Interests
- Racial and Cultural Bias of Interest Inventories
- Interpreting Interest Inventories
- Interpreting Flat and Elevated Profiles
- Profile Elevation
- When RIASEC Codes Differ Across Inventories
- Review of Specific Inventories
- Suggestions for Career Development
- Other Interest Inventories
- Summary
- Questions and Exercises

RIASEC Theory

The most well known theory for examining interests is John Holland's RIASEC theory, and is based on four assumptions, including:

Assumption 1:	Personality can be classified into six distinct "types": Realistic, Investigative, Artistic, Social, Enterprising, and Conventional. Each personality is a combination, to some degree, of the six types.
Assumption 2:	There are six types of environments that share the same characteristics as the six personality types.
Assumption 3:	People are most satisfied in their environment when their three-letter personality code, derived from their interests and skills, matches that of the environment in which they are engaging.
Assumption 4:	Certain predictions can be made about the outcome of a certain personality combining with a certain environment.

The main goal of RIASEC theory is the achievement of a "fit" between a person and his or her environment. An environment can be any arena in which a person finds himself or herself. Job titles, work place, majors or fields of study, and leisure activities are all examples of environments. RIASEC is the acronym for six interest types. These types are utilized in many other inventories, and so a description of the six types is provided in Table 6-1.

Every career counselor should know the basic descriptions of the RIASEC types, and the types of occupations that accompany those types. In addition to seeing the RIASEC types used in many inventories, career information systems such as the Online O*NET (http://online.onetcenter.org/) also include Holland types for each occupational description.

Other Career Theories and Interests

Most career theories emphasize the importance of examining interests when making a career decision. For example:

- Super emphasizes exploration and understanding of self-concept as a main goal of career counseling, and part of this self-concept includes interests explored within the context of the person's environmental influences.
- Constructivist theory focuses on how a person implements self-concept in the occupation chosen. Questions such as "What is your favorite movie or book?" or "What are your hobbies" suggested by the Career Style Interview (1989) help to identify vocational "personality" and life themes.
- Cognitive Information Processing Theory suggests examining interests as part of the self-knowledge domain. During the decision making process, CASVE cycle, individuals analyze themselves (including their interests) in the "A" stage, and then generate related options in "S" (Synthesis) stage.
- Social Cognitive Theory suggests that a person develops interests when they are involved in activities in which they are competent, and when they believe those activities will yield an outcome they value or find positive. It creates a cycle in which interests can become strengthened and stabilized, or, if the outcome is not seen as positive, will prompt the individual to re-evaluate the activity and possibly the interest.
- In Gottfredson's theory, Circumscription and Compromise, she identifies interests as one of three items under consideration when a person is faced with making a choice. The other two are sex-type and prestige. She states

that when there are small discrepancies between two options, a person will not sacrifice their interests, but will sacrifice interests first when the stakes are raised and there are major trade-offs between two options.

Table 6-1: Descriptors of Holland Types and Interests

Type	Sample Occupations	Interests	Typical Activities/ Hobbies	Preferred Work Environments
Realistic	Carpenter, rancher, engineer, forester, veterinarian, and welder.	Hands-on activities, outdoors, mechanical, athletic, working with things.	Fishing, camping, sports, and mechanics.	Outdoors and work in rural areas.
Investigative	Biologist, mathematician, psychologist, pharmacist, and dental hygienist.	Science, math, abstract tasks, problem solving, working independently.	Collecting data, conducting research, analyzing data.	Office settings such as laboratories.
Artistic	Artist, music teacher, photographer, and interior designer.	Aesthetics, self-expression, creating original works, using imagination.	Creating, Composing, and designing while working independently.	Museums, theaters, galleries, and concert halls.
Social	Teacher, guidance counselor, playground director, social worker, and juvenile probation officer.	Helping people with their problems, teaching, working with people.	Informing, teaching, coaching, and leading discussions.	Social service agencies, schools, religious establishments, and personnel offices.
Enterprising	Corporate executive, sales manager, elected public official, computer salesperson, and stockbroker.	Leading, persuading, politics, influencing others, making money.	Selling, managing, giving speeches, and leading groups of people.	Marketing agencies, investment banking firms, retail & wholesale firms, and small businesses.
Conventional	Bookkeeper, accountant, secretary keypunch operator, cashier, and banker.	Organizing, routines, meet clear standards.	Keeping records, scheduling, and maintaining adopted procedures of an organization.	Large corporations, business offices, and accounting firms.

In addition to identifying interests as a vital piece of information for individuals making career decisions, most theorists would also assert that if a person is in an environment (or job) that is very different from her or his interests, they are going to be unhappy. Research does support this. Logue, Lounsbury, Gupta and Leong (2007) found that business students whose primary codes were Investigative, Artistic or Realistic were less likely to be satisfied with their major. However, the converse was not true – having a primary code of Enterprising did not relate to being satisfied with their business major.

Stability of Interests

In her chapter entitled "Stability and Change in Vocational Interests," Jane Swanson (1999) summarizes 5 themes that can be drawn from the review of 30 studies focusing on the stability of vocational interests. The five themes include:

1. Studies consistently show that interests are incredibly stable over long periods of time, regardless of the types of measures used to identify interests, statistical measures given, or types of people tested.
2. For some people, interests do change dramatically over time and that this observation merits additional investigation to determine the causes for this.

87

3. Interest stability appears to increase with age and higher differentiation and consistency as defined by John Holland's theory, while instability seems to be related to career decision making difficulty.
4. Attempts to predict who will have stable interest scores have not yielded consistent information.
5. It appears that after a certain age, interests tend to stay the same, although they may become further clarified.

In a 30 year follow up study on the predictive validity of the Kuder Occupational Interest Survey (now known as the Kuder Career Planning System), researchers (Rottinghaus, Coon, Gaffey, & Zytowski, 2007) found very little change in interests over time for the 107 participants. Fouad (1999) extended this finding, stating that regardless of which specific measure is used, interest inventories appear to be generalizable across time. Tracey and Sodano (2008) reviewed several studies and found that research seems to support that the "relative stability of interests exists not only for ages 12 to 16 years old, but also for ages as young as 8 years old" (p. 53).

Finally, Swanson raised some interesting questions to ponder with respect to interest stability. She first asks, "How much stability is desirable?" This question requires some thoughtful reflection. Should a first grader have stabilized interests? What about a sophomore in college who has not engaged in many activities? Is it possible that someone who presents very stable interests is stating that because she or he wants to avoid the unpleasant feeling of being undecided or admitting that she or he might not know her or himself completely? Certainly, as a person begins to commit to a career, whether through a career path or training, some stability of interests is required. How unnerving it would be to commit oneself to a career of medicine, only to decide, one year later, that anthropology is the field that holds her interest. But what about later years in life? Gottfredson's theory posits that we make compromises along our career path. Could it be that at some point, individuals may want to revisit those compromises and explore their interests anew?

Racial and Cultural Bias of Interest Inventories

Counselors should be concerned with racial and cultural bias, not only with interest inventories, but with all inventories. Most professional manuals will include information on how the inventory was tested for gender, ethnic and racial bias. In addition, researchers extend this understanding by using various inventories with specific racial, cultural, gender and other groups. Some examples are included in Table 6-2.

Table 6-2: Gender, Racial, and Other Findings for Interest Inventories

Instrument/ Construct	Findings	Researcher
Harrington-O'Shea Career Decision Making System	In a 20-year follow up study, the researcher found no significant gender differences.	Harrington, 2006
RIASEC Model	Proven to be valid for several American ethnic groups;	Tak, 2004
	A circular RIASEC model fit for Asian Americans, Middle-Eastern Americans and Native Americans	Kantamneni, 2014
RIASEC themes	They compared self-efficacy to the RIASEC themes between European American and African American college students, and found very few racial differences.	Betz and Gwilliam, 2002
RIASEC/ Strong Interest Inventory	RIASEC order and general occupational themes (GOT) were supported for females but not for male Mexican American high school students.	Flores, Spanierman, Armstrong and Velez, 2006
	Minimal differences for congruence and differentiation among 5 racially diverse groups on Holland themes and specifically the SII were found.	Fouad and Mohler, 2004
Strong Interest Inventory	Results support using this instrument with Asian American college students.	Hansen and Lee, 2007

As mentioned in chapter 1, a counselor should consider the culture from which a client comes and compare that to the normative data before administering any inventory. Considerations should include the amount of likely exposure by the client to the activities/interests being presented, and whether the occupational database of the inventory is similar to the occupational realities within the client's world.

88

Interpreting Interest Inventories

"Interpretation of interest inventories deepens self-knowledge, promotes career exploration, and assists counselors in understanding a client" (Healy & Chope, 2006, p. 247). Most interest inventories come with a manual that has suggested steps for successful interpretation. Hundreds of interest inventories exist, however, and countless more are emerging as the Internet provides new avenues for aspiring test writers. Wouldn't it be helpful if there were some standard approach to interpreting interest inventories?

Imagine sitting with a counselor who provides you with an excellent lecture of the background of the interest inventory you just took, how to go about interpreting each of the scales, the theory behind each scale, what each scale is related to, and so on. Although the information might be helpful, the likelihood is that you'd be bored to death after the first couple of minutes. There has to be a better way.

Zytowski (1999) identified five general principles that a counselor should follow when providing an interpretation of interest inventories, that will decrease the likelihood of you losing a client in mid-interpretation. They include:

1. Prepare for the session.
   a. Know what the test results are, terms associated with the theory and report, and how that person's scores relate back to the normative group.
   b. Have an understanding of all special scales, and be able to explain the test results in understandable terms.
   c. Review current research on correlations made about scales. For example, if a client has a very low flat profile, the counselor should be aware that one of the possible reasons for this is depression and should ask questions during the session to ascertain if depression is occurring. In addition, in this case, before the interpretive session, the counselor should know related symptoms of depression and recommended treatments.
2. Actively involving the clients in the results.
   a. Help clients view the occupations as tentative hypotheses that should be examined alongside of previous experience.
   b. Two questions Zytowski suggested include: "What kinds of things like this have you done in the past?" or "How does this fit with what your friends say about you?" (p. 282).
3. Use "simple, empathetic communication" (p. 282), whether verbally or through the use of graphs, checkmarks, other graphics or body language.
4. Ask the client to restate their results using their own words. Why?
   a. One reason is to make sure that the client is not holding onto myths, such as "The test says I should be …" or "It says I'm not good at…".
   b. Zytowski suggests that this step helps the individual translate the information received from the inventory into the person's developing self-concept. A role-play in which the client is asked to call a parent or friend and share his or her interest results is another recommended approach.
5. Use the inventory as a springboard to continuing career development. Some strategies might include:
   a. Narrowing the occupational list, action planning, examining the positives and negatives, shadowing, or reading career information.
   b. An additional strategy that we've found helpful is to have the client go back through his or her list of occupational alternatives and give reasons for crossing off items from the list. The counselor should keep a running list of the reasons, and then looking for "avoidance themes." A second list can be created of the reasons a client gives for finding other occupations appealing. A third list can be made as the client discusses occupations that she or he is somewhat conflicted about considering.
   c. In discussing occupations, what are the positives and the drawbacks of each one? If the client had to make a choice today to keep that occupation on the list or to drop it, which would be the choice and why? This activity can help confirm and expand the client's understanding of his or her knowledge about self, identify where potential conflicts of interests and values might lie, and unearth misperceptions, such as, "There are no real jobs in art."

When providing an interpretation of results, the counselor should aim for a balance in the quantity of talking from both the counselor and client. It's very easy to slip into "expert mode" when providing an interpretation. Most reports have natural breaks in the information, such as a brief introduction about what the instrument measured, followed by a summary of the person's scores and a description of the scores. Alternately, the counselor could pause at the end of each page to ask the client's thoughts so far. The counselor has several options on how to begin the interpretation:

1. *Client-led interpretation.* The counselor gives the client a copy of the report prior to the session with limited instructions. "Here is the report generated by the inventory you completed. Why don't you take a few minutes and look it over before we begin?" This would be followed with "What did you learn from the report?" or a similar question. The client may start with the list of occupations, or at other places in the report, and the counselor would follow the client's lead on what was important to the client to discuss.

2. *Counselor-led interpretation.* The counselor starts the session with the statement, "Here is the report generated by the inventory you completed. The first section of the report states the purpose of the inventory, which was to identify occupations that relate back to your interests." The counselor would go through describing each section in a linear fashion, stopping if the client had questions or comments with each section.

3. *Collaborative interpretation.* This approach may be a combination of the first two approaches, but the key difference is that the counselor purposely seeks to actively involve the client in each step of the interpretation. For example:

COUNSELOR:	We have the results of your inventory back. How are you feeling about that?
CLIENT:	Curious, a little nervous, I guess.
COUNSELOR:	Curious and a bit nervous?
CLIENT:	Yeah. I'm curious as to what's going to come up on the list. I guess I'm nervous that there won't be anything on it that I like.
COUNSELOR:	I'm thinking that there will probably be at least some occupations on the list that you'll like, since it's based on what you said you liked and didn't like doing. Well, let's see what came up! So, this first section describes the purpose of the inventory. Do you remember why we decided on this one?
CLIENT:	Yeah, because I wanted to see what jobs might be out there that match my interests, while the computer one looked at a lot of different things all at once. I wanted to start with just what I like to do.
COUNSELOR:	That's right. So, we'll expect to see a list of options, not "the perfect option for you." In this next section, they go over how you scored on the different scales. You can see that this is your highest, and your second highest and so forth. Then here, they describe what each of the scales mean. Why don't you take a minute and read through the scales and see how similar each of those are to you?

This example shows how a counselor might be deliberate in balancing the discussion between counselor's interpretation, client reactions, and the use of silence/reflection in the interpretation. On a related note, many inventories have subscales, and unique nuances that may be of great interest to a counselor, but less so to a client. Some clients will be very interested in knowing every detail, large and minute, about their inventory results. The counselor shouldn't assume this to be so of the majority of clients. Anseel and Lievens (2007) found that students preferred only learning about the most important and most stable dimensions of the results, rather than the less important dimensions. Best rule of thumb – ask your client!

Interpreting Flat, Depressed, and Elevated Profiles

One problem that causes confusion for clients and counselors are flat or elevated profiles. Flat, or depressed, profiles consist of scores around the average range with little differences among scores. In contrast, elevated profiles have a large number of scores that are considered to be high in interest levels. These types of profiles can be used productively, as discussed by Hansen (1985).

Flat, depressed profiles may indicate one of the following:
1. *A narrow interest range and an individual with highly defined interests. A* profile with a narrow interest range will more than likely show high scores in one or two interest areas. Such an individual may be completely satisfied with an occupation and may have achieved significant positive feedback.
2. *A client with very little knowledge about the world of work and the workplace.* Such an individual may be reluctant to respond aggressively to questions about the work world.
3. *Mood swings.* An individual may be unwilling to differentiate among offered choices just because he or she is having a "bad" day.
4. *Indecisiveness.* An individual who is unwilling to make a commitment or a change could indicate a lack of readiness to respond to an interest inventory.
5. *An unwillingness to work.* Persistent negativity can create a flat depressed profile.

Flat, elevated profiles may indicate the following:

1. *Individuals who are reluctant to say "dislike" or "indifferent" to items.* Some may feel such responses would type them as negative individuals, and so their results show a high percentage of "like" items.
2. *A wide diversity of interests.* Focusing on only a few interests may be difficult for these individuals.
3. *Clients who are multi-potential or gifted in many areas.* Most people enjoy doing things they are good at. For clients who are good at many things, they may honestly endorse the majority of inventory items, resulting in an elevated, but flat profile. Negative thinking might need to be addressed, especially if the person is feeling pressured by others to choose. For example, a gifted client may receive much positive feedback from teachers in different fields (science, math, English, history) and parents, and may fear disappointing any of them.
4. *Clients with a great deal of experience.* Sometimes experience can help strengthen a person's view of what they truly like and truly dislike. At the same time, it can add complexity to the overall picture. If a client has worked in a variety of areas and developed skills in those areas, their inventory results may resemble those of the multi-potential or gifted client. We have found that in addition to examining current interests, including an exploration of work and life values with this type of client to provide useful information and direction.
5. *Client who have an inflated view of self.* Occasionally, a client may have some narcissistic tendencies, and test results, such as an elevated flat profile may be evidence of this. (This can be confirmed if the client asks for more and more tests, with a "tell me more about me" attitude). A counselor may decide to investigate whether a personality disorder is present, or may decide to point out during the interpretation that no one is equally good at every option or equally interested in all options, and that the task is to figure out which are the main interests and skills that the person would like to use on the job.

Knowledge of some of the reasons and causes for flat or elevated interest profiles prepares the counselor for suggesting intervention strategies. Although profiles of this type may seem to provide little in the way of counseling opportunities, this information can be of significant assistance in career planning. Some general questions to consider asking to someone with a flat profile include:

- Do you remember how you were feeling when you took the inventory?
- What kind of strategy (if any) did you use when completing the inventory?
- When deciding whether you liked or disliked something, or made a rating, what criteria did you use in making the decision?
- How do you think your work experience (having a lot or very little) impacted the way you answered the questions?
- If you were to rank order these categories to create the truest picture of your interests, what order would you choose?

Profile Elevation

Profile elevation has provided a new way to look at interest inventory results. Profile elevation is different from the flat depressed or flat high scores, in that with profile elevation, we are looking at how high the total profile score is across all subscales. So, with the Self-Directed Search, a counselor would add up the six summary scores for the RIASEC types and end up with one total score. In the most recent SDS Technical Manual (Holland & Messer, 2013), low scores are defined as less than 54, average scores are from 99 -205, and high scores are greater than 205 (See Table 6-3).

Table 6-3: Profile Elevation for Interest Inventories

	Low Evaluation	Average Evaluation	High Evaluation
Men	<128	129-149	> 150
Women	<127	128-146	> 147

So what may you expect to see with elevated profiles? Table 6-4 answers this question. While the research on profile evaluation is just starting to emerge, the consistency among many of the findings provide the counselor with some additional areas to consider when reviewing a client's profile. Those with high elevation are described as having a positive response set (basically, liking and endorsing most items in a positive way), and "are more likely to value new experiences and react to the results in an open, accepting way" (Reardon & Lenz, 2013, p. 23). Because the information presented in Table 6-4 are correlations, as profile elevation decreases, a counselor would expect to see the factors presented in the first column to decrease as well. So, if a client has a lower profile elevation, the counselor might expect more depressive tendencies, less openness to options and more introversion. Clients with a low profile on the SDS might have been more negative when responding to items and to the results, and may be less open to considering options suggested by the results (Reardon & Lenz, 2013). Bullock and Reardon (2008) suggest that this type of client might require a more "intense collaboration" with the counselor.

Table 6-4: Correlates of Elevated Profiles

Correlates	Instrument	Citation
Openness to experience, extraversion, and lower depressive personality	Self-Directed Search	Fuller, Holland, & Johnston, 1999
Openness, Conscientiousness, Extraversion, Consistency. Correlation with differentiation not conclusive	Self-Directed Search	Bullock & Reardon, 2008
Extraversion and openness; decreased neuroticism in men	Self-Directed Search	Holland, Johnston, & Asama, 1994
Consistent profiles	Strong-Campbell Interest Inventory	Swanson & Hansen, 1986
Higher grades, likelihood to persist in college, and better prediction of college majors by the instrument	Strong-Campbell Interest Inventory	Swanson & Hansen, 1986
Higher scores on expressiveness, enthusiasm or impulsive general style	Vocational Preference Inventory	Gottfredson & Jones, 1993

When RIASEC Codes Differ Across Inventories

Given the popularity of RIASEC codes, it is likely that clients or students taking more than one interest inventory will have more than one report that provides a RIASEC summary code. In fact, Savickas and Taber (2006) compared RIASEC summary codes across five different inventories and found that almost half of the 99 participants had RIASEC profiles in the less similar to most dissimilar range, and only 19 had profiles in the quite similar to very similar range. These researchers concluded that the inventories measure different aspects of personality, and that those with more stable interests (or traitedness) were more likely to have higher consistency across the inventories.

It would seem likely that if a person has an extremely high code on one type on one inventory, that the same type would end up being listed as first on the other inventory. When there is less differentiation among the highest three codes on an inventory, a counselor might not be surprised to see a different ordering of the three types on another inventory. But what if the highest code on two inventories ends up being the exact opposite?

Healy and Chope (2006) suggested using the inconsistencies as a springboard for discussion. Some questions might include:

- What does the client say about the discrepancy in scores?
- What is their attitude about the discrepancy? Are they amused by it, able to explain it, open and flexible about it, or dissatisfied and frustrated with the inventories overall?
- Does the client have experience in each of the types (interests and skills) or is there a large gap evident anywhere?
- Is it possible that the client is feeling pulled or pressured to go into different directions?

In addition to these questions, and exploring the occupations generated by each inventory, the counselor should remember that ultimately, inventory results are only one way to assess interests.

Review of Specific Inventories

Hundreds of interest inventories exist, and there is not enough space in this book to provide an adequate review of each of them. The following popular career inventories will be reviewed: Campbell Interest and Skill Survey (Campbell, 1992), Career Decision Making-Revised (Harrington & O'Shea, 2000), the Kuder Career Interest System, the Self-Directed Search, and the Strong Interest Inventory. We will also review the PIC and the Reading-Free Vocational Interest Inventory, interest inventories designed for people with disabilities. The reader is referred to *A Counselor's Guide to Career Assessment Instruments, 6th Edition* (Wood & Hays, 2013) for additional reviews of interest inventories.

We will first turn our attention to the Campbell Interest and Skill Survey (CISS). A brief snapshot of the inventory is provided in Table 6-5.

Table 6-5: Campbell Interest and Skill Survey

Author/Publisher	Pearson Assessments
Copyright date	1992
Test Purpose	Measures self-reported vocational interests and skills, that provide estimates of an individual's confidence in his or her ability to perform various occupational activities.
Versions	One form, available in English and in Spanish
Administrator Requirements	B or Q2 Level (Formal supervised mental health, speech/language, and/or educational training specific to working with parents and assessing children, or formal supervised training in infant and child development).
Appropriate Age Range	Adolescents (age 15) and older
	Norms for the Orientation and Basic Scales consisted of 1790 women and 3435 men representing 65 different occupations and various ethnic backgrounds. Given that item responses were found to differ for women and men (e.g., women choosing more artistic activities as opposed to mechanical), unisex norms were developed by separating separate raw score means by gender and then giving each gender equal weighting.
Administration	Self-administered
Time to Complete	30 minutes
Test Scales & Subscales	7 Orientation Scales, which have a similarity to RIASEC: Influencing, Organizing, Helping, Creating, Analyzing, Producing and Adventuring **Basic Interest and Skills Scales:** Breaks the Orientation Scales into 25 categories, split into interests and skills **Occupational Scales:** Compare client's scores to those of workers in several occupations **Academic Focus Scale:** Estimates how comfortable and successful the client will be in a formal educational setting **Extraversion Scale:** Shows the amount and intensity of interpersonal interactions the individual is likely to seek out daily.
Reliability	For the interest and skill scales of the Orientation Scales, the median alpha coefficient was .87, and the median alpha for the 29 Basic Scales was .86. Median test-retest coefficients at a three-month interval included interest and skill scales of the Orientation Scales, .87 and .81; Basic Scales, .83; and Occupational Scales, .87 (interests) and .79 (skills).
Validity	Sullivan and Hansen (2004) found the constructive validity of the interest scales of the CISS to be strong when compared with the Strong Interest Inventory. With respect to predictive validity, Hansen and Neuman (1999) found that the CISS interest component had good to excellent predictive validity for student choice of college major. When comparing the CISS and the Strong Interest Inventory, these researchers found a similar concurrent validity for the interest component and a lower validity for the skills component of the CISS.
Interpretation	Scores used in the reports are standardized, reported as T-scores with a mean of 50 and a standard deviation of 10. Reports are generated either by computer software, online or via a mail-in service. Because the CISS emphasizes the relationship between interests and skills, scores compare interests and skills on each scale. Interests are represented by a black diamond, and skills are represented by a clear diamond.
Supporting Materials	CISS pattern worksheets CISS Career Planner

Research/Reviews   Campbell (2002) describes the development of the CISS. For a thorough review of the CISS, see Boggs (2002), Fuqua and Newman (1994b), and Severy (2009; 2011; 2013).

Using the CISS in Counseling

A career counselor may find it useful to use the following four-cell table (Table 6-6) with a client when discussing the results of the CISS. Using this module, there are four possible outcomes.

Table 6-6: Implications Suggested by the Interaction of Interests and Skills

		Interests	
		High	*Low*
Skills	*High*	Pursue	Explore
	Low	Develop	Avoid

- *Pursue*: if a person has high interests and high skills in a certain area, the client would be encouraged to *pursue* those options, in that these are most likely to be satisfying options for the person.
- *Develop:* Someone with high interests and low skills would be encouraged to *develop* their skills or get training in the area(s) in which they are interested. For example, a person may think that they are interested in a certain area, but they can't know for sure until they get some experience in that area.
- *Explore:* If a person has low interests but high skills, as often happens when a person has had extensive experience in an area but have grown tired of using those skills and are ready to try something new, based on this model, the person would be encouraged to *explore* other career options that use those skills that might also interest the person.
- *Avoid:* Finally, if a client has low interests and low skills in an area, they would be encouraged to avoid careers in those areas.

The information in Table 6-5 provides a game plan for what is to occur next in counseling, with possible strategies outlined in the section below.

Developing a Game Plan

Pursuing Strategies: The client might choose to pursue occupations by gaining more information about them, doing informational interviews, researching on the Internet or shadowing.

Developing Strategies: A client who is really "set" on one career but doesn't have the required skills may be encouraged to identify training opportunities, volunteering or finding part-time employment to gain the desirable skills.

Exploring Strategies: A client who is trying to escape his or her current employment and try something totally new should use inventories such as the CISS or some of the inventories described in chapter 5 that help clients identify how their current skills might be transferable into other occupations and industries. After all, why completely ignore a set of well-developed skills when, with exploring how those skills might transfer to other occupations and industries might yield a new acceptable and exciting career possibility?

Avoiding Strategies: Strategies for avoiding certain occupations? It doesn't seem that much planning is needed to accomplish this. A counselor could say, "Oh, these are the occupations that won't likely interest you. Let's move on." In doing so, however, the counselor might be missing out on an opportunity to help the client enhance her or his self-knowledge, by asking the client to reflect on the occupations listed in that category for common themes and to see if values or avoidance themes emerge.

The next inventory we will examine is the Harrington-O'Shea Career Decision Making System-Revised. A brief snapshot is provided in Table 6-7.

Table 6-7: Career Decision Making Revised (CDM-R)

Author/Publisher	Arthur J. O'Shea and Rich Feller/Pearson Assessments
Copyright date	2010
Test Purpose	The CDM, in its self-scored and Internet editions, is a comprehensive and multidimensional systems approach to career decision making that uses an individual's self knowledge of interests, stated career choices, work values, and future training plans to suggest career options for further exploration. This contemporary tool yields results that can be linked directly to career clusters. The theoretical basis for this linkage is the Holland theory of career development. The CDM, which in 2002 received the Exemplary Practices Award from the American Counseling Association's Association for Assessment in Counseling, has been successfully used by millions of users, including secondary and college students, those returning to the workplace, and workers considering changing career directions.
Versions	*CDM Level 1:* self-scored; designed for middle school students through grade 10, and those with limited reading ability; a single booklet combines the interest inventory and interpretation; English and Spanish. *CDM Level 2:* self-scored booklet and separate interpretive folder for those in senior high school through adult; English, Spanish, Canadian English, and French editions *CDMInternet:* www.cdminternet.com; English. A full assessment that provides a printable summary of survey results and a comprehensive interpretive report, as well as briefs for all 800+ O*NET occupations, many with videos and photos, based on U.S. Department of Labor data.
Administrator Requirements	Qualification Level: A Can be self-administered and self-interpreted
Appropriate Age Range	CDM Level 1: Middle school range CDM Level 2: High school and adult CDMInternet: all ages
Norms	The sample used in the 1991 CDM normative studies was controlled for age, gender, race/ethnicity, and geographic region, based on the 1990 U.S. Census.
Administration	All of the CDM materials can be self-administered. Those in charge of the administration should determine the need for supervision.
Time to Complete	*CDM Levels 1 and 2*: 20-40 minutes *CDMInternet*: 20-30 minutes
Test Scales & Subscales	The CDM reports on the six RIASEC interest scales, some re-named for vocational understandability: Crafts (similar to R) Scientific (similar to I) The Arts (similar to A) Social (similar to S) Business (similar to E) Office Operations (similar to C)
Reliability	Alpha reliability coefficients for ages 11 through 20 revealed a median of .90 for 965 who completed Level 1 and .93 for 996 who completed Level 2. The Spanish edition also shows strong internal consistency ($\alpha = .85$).
Validity	The authors base the validity of the CDM interest scales on the correspondence of scale correlations to the pattern hypothesized in Holland's (1997) theory regarding the hexagonal ordering of interests. The authors compared the inter-correlations for four separate samples. Campbell and Perry (2013) report several studies supporting the validity (construct, and predictive) of the CDM-R.
Interpretation	CDM uses raw scores. Results are reported independently of sex. For Level 2: Results can either be hand scored by the client or counselor. The results (raw scores) are then transferred to the interpretive folder, which includes a summary profile, a career clusters chart, a guide to majors and training programs based on major interests, and tips for continuing career exploration. The **CDMInternet** provides the following links: Find a College, Job Search Skills, STEM, The Occupational Outlook Handbook, and Job Openings.

Supporting Materials	The CDM Manual
	Tour of Your Tomorrow DVD
	CDMInternet (www.CDMInternet.com):
Research/ Reviews	Campbell and Perry (2013); Campbell and Raiff (2009); Harrington, and O'Shea (2000); Kelly (2005); Rounds and Tracey (1996); Shaffer (1995); Vansickle (1994).

Using the CDM-R in Counseling

Leesa, a ninth-grade student was very impressed by a recent career speaker that the counseling center brought to school. What really appealed to her was not the field that the speaker came from, but the advice she gave on identifying, preparing for and following one's own dream. Leesa said that she wanted to start now, to figure out a general career direction, so that she could plan her summers and even the clubs she would join to help her develop in that area. Her CDM-R profile revealed the following total scores:

Test Scales	Score
Crafts	18
Scientific	22
The Arts	15
Social	10
Business	25
Office Operations	17

Based on the CDM-R profile, her Career Code was determined as Business-Scientific. She completed the rest of the profile as follows:

1. Career choices: Math-Science, Technical
2. School subjects: Math, Science, Management, English
3. Work Values: Creativity, Good Salary, High Achievement, Work with Your Mind
4. Abilities: Computational, Scientific, Mathematical, Language
5. Future Plans: 4 year college or university
6. Career Clusters: Management, Sales, Math-Science, Technical

After reviewing the summary profile with Leesa, the counselor asked Leesa to work on the Career Clusters Chart for homework. When Leesa returned for her follow-up session, she described the activity to the counselor.

LEESA:	Well, here's what I've narrowed it down to: math-science and maybe the technical clusters.
COUNSELOR:	That's interesting—it kind of goes along with what you've been considering all along. But even though you've narrowed it down in terms of general fields, there are quite a lot of possibilities within each of those areas.
LEESA:	Don't I know it? I was hoping that this was going to get easier, and that I'd figure out the right career for me.
COUNSELOR:	So you are seeing a variety of career options related to your interests. What do you think that means?
LEESA:	That there's more than one choice for me?
COUNSELOR:	Sure! Remember, the purpose of taking the CDM wasn't to help you choose one career, but to see different options related to your interests. So let's talk about the jobs that jumped out at you in these areas. Were there any surprises?
LEESA:	Engineering! That seemed to come up a lot. I really never considered that before. Metallurgic Engineer? That just doesn't seem like me.
COUNSELOR:	Now, hold on … remember our deal? We're not going to cross off any alternatives until you know enough about them. Do you know what a metallurgic engineer does?
LEESA:	Well, no…OK, you're right. I don't want to close off any options just yet. OK, so I did like some of the engineering jobs. I also think I might like some of the jobs in the life sciences group.
COUNSELOR:	So what common themes do you think these groups share?
LEESA:	Besides science, they both involve math, agriculture, art and technology, and I'm pretty good at those classes. They share similar values, such as Good Salary, Job Security, Work With Hands and Work with Mind. Outdoor work is also pretty common, but I don't know if I'd want to be outdoors a lot, especially if the weather was bad.
COUNSELOR:	Which group is more like you?

LEESA:	Well, the Math-Science group has all the values I listed, and all of my abilities.
COUNSELOR:	So, what do you think the next steps are for you?
LEESA:	I think I want to give myself a goal of reading about each of these fields. Then I can start identifying occupations that seem to match me on interests, values and skills, and narrow the list as I find those that don't.
COUNSELOR:	I think that's a great idea. Let me highlight a website that goes along with the CDM where you can research these occupations. In fact, let's go there right now and do a search on a job, so you can see how it works. Which occupation would you like to look at?
LEESA:	How about that metallurgic engineer?
COUNSELOR:	Sounds good!
LEESA:	This is great! It even has a video on it! Oh, good. I can even just look at those in my career zone, instead of typing each one of them in. Cool!
COUNSELOR:	All right! Why don't we spend the last few minutes here creating an empty table for you to complete, and then you get back to me, say, in a month, and tell me what you're leaning towards?
LEESA:	Sounds great to me!

The counselor and Leesa proceeded to make a table (Figure 6-1) for her to complete as she reviewed the different occupations. She decided the information she wanted to keep track of, and they inputted that into the table. "If I read the job description and don't like it, I just won't put it in the table." The counselor saved the document and put it into a shared folder (such as Dropbox) so that Leesa could continue to work on it in between sessions and it was easy to access when in session as well.

Figure 6-1: Example of Organizational Table

Occupation	Education	Money	Job Outlook	What I liked best about it
1.				
2.				

During the weeks that followed, Leesa was able to narrow her list from her research. In this example, Leesa was able to work closely with the counselor and use the CDM website to identify and explore options that matched her interests, values and skills. The CDM served as a stepping stone from which Leesa was able to create her own organizational table for career development.

We will now turn our attention to the Kuder Career Interests Assessment. A brief snapshot is provided in Table 6-8.

Table 6-8: Kuder Career Interests Assessment (KCIA-32)

Author/ Publisher	JoAnn Harris-Bowlsbey, Spencer Niles, Donald Zytowski, Jack Rayman, & Jerry Trusty/Kuder, Inc.
Test Purpose	To match an individual's interests in the RIASEC areas to O*NET occupations, 16 national career clusters and pathways.
Versions	English, Spanish, Arabic, Korean and Chinese. Note that it is one of three assessments included in the Kuder Career Planning System.
Appropriate Age Range	Grade 7 through adult
Norms	About 2000 employed adults were used to develop cluster raw scores, and 8,785 males and females (age 14-adult) in 30 states were used to determine percentile scores.
Administration	Self-administered.
Time to Complete	About 9 minutes.

Test Scales & Subscales	Holland RIASEC Categories
Reliability	According to Suen (2012), reliability coefficients ranged from .73 to .86 for the RIASEC categories of working adult sample ($N = 958$), and from .74 to .87 for the high school sample ($N = 142$).
Validity	Suen (2012) reported that "formal iterative content validation exercises" were used, retaining only items with 81% or higher consensus. Suen also described how formal sensitivity reviews were conducted that resulted in the removal or modification of 20% of the items.
Interpretation	The KCIA-32 was designed as one leg of a 3-part assessment tool that then feeds into the overall Career Planning System. Clients can either take an assessment online or enter their assessment scores. The next step would likely be to review the assessment results, which are presented within the context of the six Holland RIASEC themes. Counselors can use a similar approach as described earlier to help clients understand the meaning of the themes. Next, a client could either view occupations that are suggested by the assessments, explore related occupations, view sample plans of study, or see "person matches" (i.e., learn about individuals who have similar interest patterns as the client does). Other options within the system allow for an individual to make educational plans, create a portfolio, plan for work and job search.
Supporting Materials	www.kuder.com
Research/ Reviews	Gibbons, 2013; Ihle-Helledy, Zytowski, & Fouad, 2004; Shenck (2009); Zytowski (2001).

Case of a High School Senior Rebelling Against Parental Expectations

Ann, a high school senior, had been the topic of conversation during many coffee breaks in the teachers' lounge at City High School. The teachers' major concern was her complete lack of interest in academic courses, although Ann's parents were well educated and were prominent members of the art and music groups in the city. Ann's grades reflected her lack of interest, and she had successfully resisted receiving any counseling assistance. Her parents finally convinced her to see the school counselor.

As expected, Ann approached the counselor in a casual manner and quickly admitted that the visit was her parents' idea. The counselor spent several sessions with Ann attempting to build trust and to get her to respond positively. Ann showed enthusiasm only when the counselor brought up the subject of future plans. The counselor decided that she might be able to win Ann's confidence through career exploration.

Ann had taken the Kuder Career Interests Assessment (KCIA) during her junior year, and a review of the results revealed a low, flat profile. The counselor showed the results to Ann, and asked her what she thought was going on at the time she was taking the KCIA. Ann said, "I didn't care about that test. What's the use of taking an interest inventory when you don't have many choices in the first place?"

When asked to explain her remarks, Ann indicated that she had completed the inventory haphazardly without even reading some of the options. When the counselor asked her to explain her statements about not having many choices, Ann was rather hesitant. After a brief pause, she responded, "Nobody cares or understands, so why bother?" Ann eventually revealed that she felt hemmed in and unable to identify with her parents' expectations. She expressed a negative view of their lifestyle and emphasized that she wanted something different. She felt her parents were unaccepting of her needs and interests. Ann summed up her feelings: "So what's the use of saying what I want?" In the sessions that followed, the counselor encouraged Ann to express her interests and individuality.

Nevertheless, Ann remained confused about a career. The counselor asked, "Do you think it would be helpful to see the types of career paths that people who have similar interests to you choose?" Ann agreed to retake the KCIA but with a changed attitude and a different approach to responding to the choices.

Ann completed the KCIA and had her printed results with her at the next session. Ann seemed eager to discuss the results. The counselor cautioned Ann that these scores would not solve all her problems but would provide vital information that could be used for career exploration. They looked at her top career pathways, shown in Figure 6-2.

Figure 6.2: Top Career Pathways

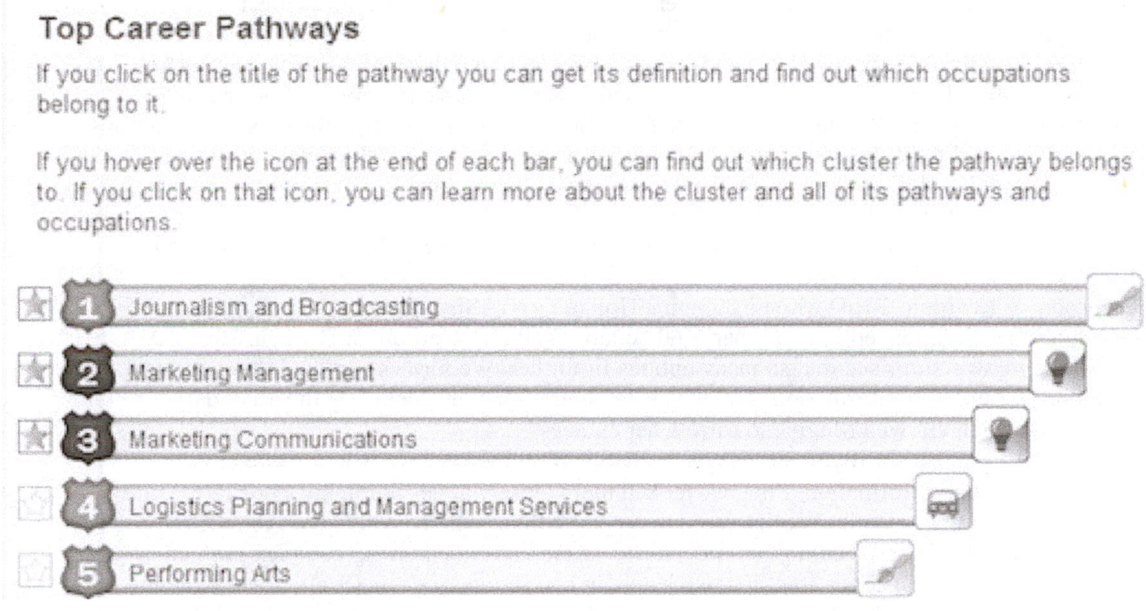

Top Career Pathways

If you click on the title of the pathway you can get its definition and find out which occupations belong to it.

If you hover over the icon at the end of each bar, you can find out which cluster the pathway belongs to. If you click on that icon, you can learn more about the cluster and all of its pathways and occupations.

⭐ 1	Journalism and Broadcasting	
⭐ 2	Marketing Management	💡
⭐ 3	Marketing Communications	💡
4	Logistics Planning and Management Services	🚗
5	Performing Arts	

The counselor asked Ann to reflect on what she thought the graph showed.

ANN:	Well, it shows what I've been feeling all along. I really am different from my parents. I guess I'm more like people who are into management and marketing.
COUNSELOR:	You seem relieved.
ANN:	I guess. But they're not going to be happy that I'm soooo different from them.
COUNSELOR:	What about the top match?
ANN:	You saw that I skipped that one (smirking). Those seem somewhat like them, in that they are kind of creative careers, but they are also sort of sales-like, aren't they?
COUNSELOR:	So, there's some overlap between your interests and those of your parents, but there's also some interests that are unlike them. I know you're concerned about how they will feel, but we don't really know how they're going to react. Plus, you may not be as different as you think. Let's not jump to conclusions. Why don't we take a look at some of the Person Matches you printed out, to see how similar they sound to you? Here's a highlighter – I'd like you mark the activities, skills, rewards and other things that jump off the page at you, that you think are very similar to you.

Although Ann seemed interested in the results of the KCIA, this was the first time she had given serious thought to exploring a career on her own, and she was going to need a great deal of reinforcement and guidance from the counselor. She expressed an interest in working with people in some capacity but also recognized that her knowledge of careers and working environments was extremely limited. She agreed to become a part of a career decision-making group that was made up of students who were also trying to figure out career possibilities. The counselor created a structured group that met weekly and used the KCIA as a foundation for discussion and activities.

The Self-Directed Search (SDS) is the inventory designed by John Holland that corresponds with RIASEC theory. Before we look more closely at the SDS, let's hear from a practitioner about how she uses the SDS in her practice.

Several years ago, I taught an undergraduate student, "Maggie," in a career development course. Maggie stands out because she was an enthusiastic freshman who wanted to choose a major that she loved as opposed to making an immediate decision due to academic pressures. After discussing an approach to making career decisions (Cognitive Information Processing; Sampson, Reardon, Peterson, & Lenz, 2004), she reported that the most important thing she learned from the course was to integrate her self-knowledge when making career, academic, and life decisions. Maggie knew that she wanted to travel and help people, but she felt overwhelmed about how to begin exploring options.

We chose to identify options with the Self-Directed Search (SDS; Holland, 1994b) because research indicates that the SDS helps individuals to expand their options (Dozier, Sampson, & Reardon, 2013) while integrating Holland's RIASEC theory (Holland, 1997) which has been referenced in more than 1,600 citations (Ruff, Reardon, & Bertoch, 2008). At first, Maggie was surprised that so many options fit for her. We further explored these options by closely examining information from the professional summary including the secondary constructs which allowed Maggie to narrow her choices.

The process for reviewing Maggie's SDS is discussed generally to remove any unique identifying information. First, we looked more closely at her Summary Code (SAI) and Aspirations Summary Code. We discussed the specific things she enjoyed about each letter in these codes (helping and meeting new people, being creative, and solving complex problems). Upon reviewing Consistency (the first two letters in her Summary Code [SA]), it was evident that her interests were closely related according to Holland's hexagon (Holland, 1997). Her closely aligned interests helped to normalize that it was difficult to make a decision and narrow her options because her interests were so closely related to one another. Furthermore, Differentiation was low which indicated that she was nearly equally interested in areas that were already closely related. Next, Congruence (Average) indicated that her aspirations code was consistent with her Summary Code from the SDS which helped solidify that her interests were all closely related. We reviewed her occupational dreams which were all similar as evidenced by the average score for Coherence of Aspirations. After reviewing the information from Maggie's SDS results, she not only chose a major in International Affairs, but she also set additional goals. She hoped to become fluent in Spanish because she wanted to work for the United Nations. She also planned to obtain a Global Pathways certificate which would enhance her ability to collaborate with others globally. Maggie reported that the combination of an approach to making decisions (CIP; Sampson et al., 2004) and the SDS helped her expand and then narrow her options.

Emily Kennelly, Ed.S., NCC
Senior Assistant Director, Career Advising & Counseling
Florida State University Career Center

snapshot of the SDS is provided in Table 6-9.

Table 6-9: Self-Directed Search

Author/Publisher	Holland/Psychological Assessment Resources, Inc.
Test Purpose	Taking the Self-Directed Search will determine a person's 3-letter Holland code to help them find the occupations and fields of study that match well with their interests and personality.
Versions	5th Edition (high school, college, adult), CE (Career Explorer, Middle School), E (for those with limited education or poor reading skills; audiotape available), Available in paper/pencil, Internet, PARiConnect. Available in English, English-Canadian, French-Canadian, and Spanish
Administrator Requirements	Level A
Appropriate Age Range	High school and above (CE is for middle school)
Norms	The 2013 version of the SDS norm sample was composed of 1,739 students and working adults, equally divided among females and males, and ranging in age from 11 to 70. The sample included 61% Caucasian, 13% African American, 17% Hispanic, 7% and from other ethnic backgrounds.

Administration	SDS can be self-administered, self-scored, and self-interpreted.
Time to Complete	15-20 minutes
Test Scales & Subscales	Aspirations Occupations Interests Competencies Self-Ratings of Skills
Reliability	Internal consistencies for the Activities, Competencies, and Occupations Scales ranged from .71 to .93, and the summary scales ranged from .88 to .94 (Holland & Messer, 2013). Test-retest reliability also appears to be strong, ranging from .78 to .98 over different periods of time.
Validity	The manual (Holland & Messer, 2013) provides information that demonstrates the validity of the SDS with respect to face validity, inter-correlations among the scales, equivalence of prior editions, between print and online versions, and convergent validity.
Interpretation	The interpretive report (either generated from the computer program once scores are inputted or delivered when the individual completes the SDS online) provides a brief description of Holland's RIASEC theory, including a hexagon for visual interpretation, and a description of the six types. A person's summary code scores are presented on the first page, and on the following pages, occupations that match the first three codes are presented, first in order of score (three highest scores), and then by mixing up the scores. For example, a person's highest three codes might be SIA (in order). A list of occupations matching that code would be provided first, followed by a list of occupations that match the code SAI, ISA, IAS, ASI and AIS. In addition, fields of study and leisure activities are also included. The Occupations Finder accompanies the paper/pencil version and has a list of occupations associated with the SDS code combinations.

When interpreting the SDS, the counselor should look for secondary constructs of Congruence, Consistency, Differentiation and Profile Elevation. *Congruence* has to do with how well a person's summary code matches his or her environment. In other words, how do a person's current interests compare with the occupations being considered? Another assumption of Holland's theory is that the agreement between person and an environment can be estimated through a hexagonal model. A distinct difference between these two codes might indicate a need for further information about the occupational aspirations, a need for more experience within related fields (a counselor should examine the three skill sections and look for lower scores), or further exploration regarding the attractiveness of those occupations. A counselor could also examine the degree of congruence between a person's summary code and current occupation. A large difference might help explain lack of satisfaction in the current situation.

By examining the *aspirations* listed and seeing the amount of *Coherence* among those aspirations, a counselor can gain a picture of how stable a person's ideas are relative to occupational options. A person who has listed occupational aspirations that don't have a lot in common with each other might need special assistance, including information about these specific occupations, a schema for organizing the world of work, or more information about self, self-concept, and self-efficacy.

Another assumption is that the degree of *Consistency* between views of self and work environments can be determined through the hexagonal model. Consistency has to do with how close the letters of the summary code are to each other. Codes that are closer together have more in common, whereas codes that lie opposite on the hexagon have much less in common. Therefore, a person whose code comprises opposite types (such as Social-Realistic) is expressing very distinct descriptions of self. By exploring the professional summary, a counselor can identify whether this report is the result of a difference in background, such as the previous example of a person with a large amount of clerical experience versus actual interests, or if the summary code is a true reflection of the person's interests. Someone whose first two codes are opposites could explore how they might satisfy one of their primary types through leisure or volunteer activities.

The amount of ***Differentiation*** between codes provides a counselor with a clearer picture of a person's code. This assumption suggests that the amount of differentiation in a person's code affects any prediction a counselor might make from a person's code. A "true" code would be one where the first letter is separated by 8 points from the next letter. Glavin and Savickas (2011) found that in a sample of 2397 students, the rule of 8 was strongly supported. A person whose scores are well differentiated has identifiable interests that are unlikely to shift drastically, whereas a person whose letters are less differentiated might be less clear as to what area truly interests him or her. If the top three codes are close together, then the person is more likely to find satisfying occupations when looking under various combinations of his or her initial code. On the other hand, a person who is highly differentiated will be more likely to be interested in those occupations that have the same primary code (first letter). See earlier discussion on how to interpret high and low flat profiles.

Supporting Materials	Dictionary of Holland Occupational Codes Educational Opportunities Finder Leisure Activities Finder Making Vocational Choices, 3rd Edition Occupations Finder Veterans and Military Occupation Finder
Research/ Reviews	The SDS is one of the most researched instruments. Lindley and Borgen (2002) found generalized self-efficacy related to the RIASEC types. A search on Self-Directed Search will yield hundreds of articles. Extensive reviews of the SDS include those by Anastasi (1988), Baker (2013), Ciechalski (2002), Dumenci (1995), Manuelle-Adkins (1989), and McKee and Levinson (1990). Other helpful references are Brew (1987), Ciechalski (2009), Hansen (1985), Levin (1991) and Reardon and Lenz (1998).

Case of a Group Program in a Community College

A community college counseling center regularly offered seminars in career exploration, and a major component of the program involved interest identification. In one all-female group, the paper/pencil version of the SDS was administered with the counselor monitoring the scoring.

After each student had recorded her own SDS code, the counselor explained Holland's six modal personal styles and their corresponding codes. The counselor referred the students to the summary profile of the SDS assessment booklet, and used the sample table in Table 6-10 to demonstrate the interpretation.

Table 6-10: Sample Summary Table Created by Counselor

	R	I	A	S	E	C
Activities	4	8	9	8	6	1
Competencies	9	2	2	3	4	12
Occupations	3	7	0	9	5	1
Self-Estimates	6	1	9	2	3	7
	6	2	2	1	3	7
Summary Scores	27	20	23	23	21	28

COUNSELOR: Compare your scores on the Activities and Occupations rows. These represent your interests. You would expect to see low scores in the columns for types you are least interested in, and higher scores in the columns for types you are more interested in. Did anyone find that to be true?

MARY: Yes, I have high scores in both those rows for S and E, but low scores for R and C.

COUNSELOR: Good example. Now, look at the Competencies and Self-Estimate rows. Those should be similar as well.

ANGELA: I have high scores on all four rows for E and A.

COUNSELOR: Let's go there next. The first and third rows are getting at interests, the 2nd and 4th are getting at skills. If you have all high scores or all low scores down a column, then you either really like and are good at that type, or you really dislike and aren't so skilled at that type.

ELSIE: But what if the scores down a column are different?

COUNSELOR: Great point. Look at our example, in the R and C columns. This person has low interests in R and C types, but high skills. What do you think that means?

REESE: That maybe they are skilled in those areas but they don't like those areas? Like being good at typing but not wanting that as a job?

COUNSELOR: Exactly. It's possible that you have had jobs or experiences where you built up a certain skill set, but you're not really interested in using those skills in your next career. And look what happened on the sample profile – her first RIASEC type, "C," has been skewed because of the high level of skills. Do you think she will be satisfied with the list of jobs that are matched with her interest types? Probably not. One option would be to ignore the high "C" code and go with the three types she has more of a blended score of interests and skills on, such as S and E. On the other hand, look at her I scores – her interests are high in that area, but her skills are low. Maybe that's an opportunity for her to get some training or experience to figure out if that's an area worth pursuing.

Calculating the Aspirations Summary Code

At that point, the counselor asked the students to review their summary profiles to see if they noted any discrepancies between interests and self-estimates, and to give an opportunity for them to ask questions. The counselor explained the concepts of consistency and differentiation, and then asked them to determine how consistent their codes were and the level of differentiation. She also had them calculate their aspirations summary code by assigning points in the following way:

COUNSELOR: What you want to do is to look at the list of your aspirations and the RIASEC code that goes with each. (As she demonstrated on a whiteboard (Table 6-11), she said): So let's say you had five aspirations, and their codes were SAI, SAE, ASE, IRA, and IAS. You will give every first letter a 3, every second letter a 2, and every third letter a 1, and then add up the scores for each type. In this example, R=2 (because there is 1 R and it is in the second position), I = 7, A=10, S=8, E=2, C = 1, so the Aspiration Summary code is ASI. Now we can compare that code to your summary code on the inventory. Hopefully, there is a good degree of overlap, because you're comparing the jobs you said you'd like to do with the activities and skills you like to be involved with and use.

Table 6-11: Counselor-created coding of aspirations

	R	I	A	S	E	C
Speech pathologist (SAI)		1	2	3		
Career Counselor (SAE)			2	3	1	
Drama Teacher (ASE)			3	2	1	
Surgeon (IRA)	2	3	1			
Art Appraiser (IAS)		3	2	1		
Summary	2	7	10	9	2	0
Aspiration Summary Code:	ASI					

After this activity, the counselor explained how to use The *Occupations Finder* for locating specific occupations by summary codes. For an outside activity, the counselor asked the students to look through the *Occupations Finder* and highlight occupations of interest. When the students returned the next week, their session was held in a computer lab. Before getting online, the counselor asked them to share what they thought of their lists, whether there were any surprises or disappointments.

Following that discussion, the counselor showed students how to research occupations of interest online and gave them sample questions to consider as they read about occupations. She encouraged the students to work quickly to narrow the list down to 3-5 occupations. The following session involved the members sharing the results of their research and talking about next steps to further clarify their career options. The counselor had taken note of the students' RIASEC types, and made sure to include potential strategies similar to each person's type. For example, some suggestions included having the students shadowing/interning (R), doing more in-depth research (I), creating a collage or creative expression on Pinterest to show the person's SDS results and occupational options (A), talking with those already in the field (S), creating a career management plan (E) or organizing the information in a meaningful way (C).

Another well-known career interest inventory is the Strong Interest Inventory (SII). A table presenting pertinent information on the SII is presented in Table 6-12.

Table 6-12: Strong Interest Inventory

Author/Publisher	Consulting Psychologist Press
Test Purpose	To help clients identify, understand and expand career options based on their interests in occupations, work activities, leisure activities, and school subjects.
Versions	Examples of different report options include: iStartStrong (interactive report for those without a counselor) Strong Profile Strong Profile, College Edition Strong Interpretive Report Strong Profile and Skills Confidence Inventory Strong and MBTI® Career Report Translated into Korean, Portuguese, Argentinian Spanish
Administrator Requirements	Master's degree in counseling or related field; SII credentialing offered by publisher
Appropriate Age Range	14 and older
Norms	2,250 employed adults; 30% non-white
Administration	Self-administered. Paper/pencil, computer, online
Time to Complete	About 45 minutes
Test Scales & Subscales	6 General Occupational Themes (RIASEC) 30 Basic Interest Scales 244 Occupational Scales 5 Personal Style Scales 3 Administrative Scales
Reliability	GOTs .90 or greater (Chronbach's alpha); retest reliabilities average .85 OS scales .71-.93 (retest reliability, 2-23 months) PS subscales range from .82-.87 (Chronbach's alpha) Reliabilities also provided by gender
Validity	Construct and concurrent validity of subscales with previous SII version ranging from .80 to .98. Also used correlations among the scales, such as GOT scales and specific Occupational Scales to determine validity. Jenkins (2008) reported in detail how the validity of the specific subscales was measured, and it is evident that the SII continues to be a valid instrument for its purposes.
Interpretation	*GOTS* When interpreting the GOTs, the counselor should focus on the client's general interests and use that information as a bridge to the world of work. Because the GOTs are reported in terms of Holland codes, they should be interpreted in the context of that theory. Hansen (2000) suggested once the client understands the difference in the six Holland types, the counselor should ask where and how the client expresses those interests in life, including work, leisure, relationships, and so on. In addition, Hansen recommended an integration process by which clients compare what they already knew about their interests (from past experiences, how they spend their time, etc.) and the inventory results. *BIS* Generally, a client's highest BISs will fall within one or two of the RIASEC areas. The purpose of the BISs is to further clarify a person's interest within the GOTs. For example, a person may have a main GOT theme of Social and have a high interest in teaching but a low interest in medical services. The BISs serve another purpose as well: They help expand the client's understanding of the world of work via this "branching effect." A study on the ability of the BISs to predict major choice demonstrated that the BISs have impressive power when added to the six GOTs in predicting 22 of 24 majors of the 17,074 in the norm group (Ralston, Borgen, Rottinghaus, & Donnay, 2004). The information provided by the GOTs and BISs is useful in exploring a person's general interests, but also serve as an easy springboard into discussion of non-vocational interests, such as leisure activities and living environments (Hansen, 2000).

OS

The next step is to examine the client's occupational scales in search of interest patterns or scores that show a degree of likeness between the client and individuals who are in particular occupations. According to Hansen (2000), these scales are the most useful in predicting future occupational choices. The rationale behind the OSs is the comparison of how similar an individual's interests are to the interests of others in specific occupations. The mean standard score of each occupation is 50. The interpretive comments range from similar to mid-range to dissimilar interests (with a negative score indicating strong dissimilarity). Hansen (2000) recommends that the counselor and client collaborate to identify common interests among the similar occupations.

PS

Also a part of the Strong instrument, is the Personal Style Scales, which consist of the Work Style Scale, the Learning Environment Scale, the Leadership Style Scale, Risk Taking Scale, and Team Orientation Scale. Some ways to use this information in counseling include helping a client understand how their style affects his or her career decision-making process, identifying training alternatives that are appropriate to the client's learning style, and exploring the degree to which the client is willing to take risks in choosing or changing careers. Clear scores, where a strong preference is indicated are classified as below 46 or above 54. Mid-range scores, between 46 and 54, suggest that there is not a strong preference, and that the person endorsed descriptors on both sides.

A person who gains a high score on the *Work Style* scale prefers working with people to working with data, ideas, or things. The *Learning Environment* scale identifies the setting in which a person prefers to learn. Some clients may jump to the conclusion that a low score on this scale means that they are poor learners, when what it does suggest is that they are likely to be more interested in hands-on, practical, and applied knowledge as opposed to learning from lectures and books. The counselor should make sure to fully describe what this and every scale is measuring. The *Leadership* Scale measures the preference of individuals to either work by themselves (lower scores) or managing the work of others (higher scores). This preference has also been related to Introversion and Extraversion preferences (Harmon et al., 1994). The *Risk Taking* separates those who prefer to have a high degree of adventure in their lives (high scores) from those who prefer consistency and lower degrees of risk (low scores). The newer scale, *Team Orientation*, measures the degree to which an individual prefers to work, make decisions and share responsibility and accomplishments individually or on a team. According to Hansen (2000), men and younger people (Hansen, 1990) tend to score higher on this scale than women and adults.

AS

Other information provided on the report includes the Total Responses (how many items the person responded to), Items Omitted and Typicality Index. If the client indicates that he or she understood the directions, responded honestly, and had a positive attitude toward taking the Strong instrument (the client was not taking it to please someone else, for example), then the counselor should proceed with the interpretation. By adding the percentages of the Strongly Like and Like columns, the Like Percentage (LP) is calculated. The IP stands for Indifferent Percentage, and the DP is calculated by adding the Dislike and Strongly Dislike percentages. According to Hansen (2000), most people average 32% (with a standard deviation of 12%) across all indexes. She also states that elevated and depressed profiles can be identified by either a 65% or higher response rate (for elevated) or 10% or lower response rate (for depressed). In addition, very high scores on the IP Index suggest indecisiveness. For flat profiles, Hansen recommends looking at the profile as a whole; if a consistent pattern of interests exist, the counselor should continue the interpretation. However, if the results appear random, then the counselor should use caution in interpreting or discontinue the interpretation.

Research/Reviews   Betz, Schifano, & Kaplan, 1999; Jenkins, 2008, 2013; Tuel & Betz, 1998; Vacc & Newsome, 2002. Donnay (1997) provides a review of the history of the development of the Strong instrument.

Case of a College Freshman Undecided About a Career

Robyn, a second-semester freshman in college, told the career counselor that she needed help in determining her interests. She added that none of the college courses she had taken so far had grabbed her interests, or prompted her to consider a specific career. As a result, she felt as though she were drifting. Her father, successful in business, was putting pressure on Robyn to make up her mind. Robyn appeared to be serious about wanting to determine her interests for career considerations.

COUNSELOR: We will gladly administer and interpret an interest inventory for you. However, I want you to understand that the results of the inventory may not pinpoint a career for you to consider.

ROBYN: Oh! I thought it would tell me what I should do for the rest of my life.

COUNSELOR: Many students share your belief. They have high expectations of interest inventories and are disappointed when they get their results. Realistically, we can expect to find some occupations for you to explore further or an occupational group you may wish to investigate. I should add that we also often find that a student will simply have his or her interests confirmed by a test.

ROBYN: Okay, that's fair enough. I need some information to help me get started toward making a career decision.

The counselor continued with an explanation of the career decision-making process. After she was satisfied that Robyn understood that interest inventory results are to be used with other factors in career exploration, the counselor discussed the selection of an interest inventory: "The Strong Interest Inventory provides a comparison of your responses to responses of individuals in a number of career fields. With these results you can determine how similar your interests are to those of individuals who have made a commitment to a specific career. You will also be able to identify some of your general occupational interests and some of your basic interests." The counselor and Robyn selected the SII because it includes many careers that require a college degree and suggests many occupational groups for further exploration.

The counselor began the interpretation session with a review of the career decision process. She then presented Robyn with the profile of the results. Her standard scores on the GOTs were as follows: R=37, I = 56, A = 71, S = 51, E = 48, C = 43. The counselor briefly reviewed the snapshot summary and then asked Robyn to read over the descriptors of the six types, including interests, work activities, potential skills and values, and had Robyn highlight the words she felt best described her.

The counselor directed Robyn's attention to the summary code of her three highest general occupational themes. The counselor emphasized the importance of considering combinations of interests rather than considering just one high-interest area. In Robyn's case, the AIS summary code suggested an interest in occupations that involve art, writing, solving abstract problems, conducting research, teaching, and caring for people. The counselor suggested that consideration be given to different combinations of the summary code: ASI, SIA, SAI, IAS and ISA.

The counselor then went to the next part of the report and explained that the basic interest scales are also grouped according to one of the six themes. Robyn's top five interest areas were mostly in the artistic area, and identified as Writing and Mass Communication, Performing Arts, Visual Arts and Design, Culinary Arts and Law. The counselor asked Robyn to mark the basic interest areas she was most interested in exploring further.

Next, the counselor discussed the occupational scales and her top ten strong occupations, which included:

Librarian (A)	Reporter (A)
Technical Writer (AIR)	Chef (ERA)
Broadcast Journalist (AE)	Attorney (A)
Graphic Designer (ARI)	Editor (AI)
Photographer (ARE)	Translator (A)

Finally, the counselor pointed out occupational scales with scores of 40 and higher as being similar to Robyn's interests. Several of the occupations seemed to interest Robyn and she highlighted those. They also talked about occupations listed that were dissimilar to her interests, to gain additional knowledge about what might be unattractive about those occupations.

Finally, they reviewed the Personal Style Scales and Robyn's scores, which were:

- Work Style: 47
- Learning Environment: 65
- Leadership Style: 54
- Risk Taking: 44

The counselor and Robyn discussed the implications of her preferences in making decisions in general as well as career decisions. The counselor suggested that they conclude the interpretation of the results of the Strong

106

instrument by having Robyn summarize what she learned about herself: "I seem to be interested in artistic kinds of work. At least this was my highest general occupational theme. I also have an interest in investigative activities and socially related activities. I like working with people but also working alone at times. Specific occupations that interest me are librarian and legal work. I would like to explore those occupations in more depth." The counselor was satisfied with this summary, as Robyn was able to link the inventory results with potential career fields. The counselor encouraged Robyn to refer to the interest inventory results for other options if she was not satisfied with her career search.

The next set of inventories we will review are those that are designed for individuals with disabilities.

Case of a Relocated High School Graduate

Adriana, having just graduated from high school, wanted to learn more about career opportunities. She was originally from Miami, but her parents had recently moved to a small city for a job change. Fluent in Spanish, but limited in English, Adriana wanted to start working to save money for college. During an interview with a high school counselor, Adriana discovered that the available career tests were in English. Although she could have had a friend translate the statements and the results, Adriana asked if there was another way.

The counselor described the PIC inventory, which requires no reading. Adriana was curious about this and decided to try it. The counselor, who was bilingual, interpreted the results in Spanish since this was Adriana's preference. He began by reviewing her preferences in the 17 occupational areas, shown below in Figure 6-3.

PIC DV2000 CAREER PREFERENCE PROFILE

This is a list in descending order of your preferences to the 17 career clusters in the PIC DV2000 program. The top three (five in the expanded report) are highlighted and indicate your strongest choices.

The (+) indicates career areas that you felt positive about. The (-) indicates career areas that you felt negative about, and the (0) indicates career areas that you felt neither positive or negative about.

PREF	CAREER AREA	SCORE	PCTILE
(+)	Service-Fire Science	35	98
(+)	Service-Barbering/Cosmetology	32	98
(+)	Food Services	29	95
(+)	Business-Data Processing	28	95
(+)	Electrical/Electronics	28	95
(+)	Health Services	28	85
(+)	Science and Laboratory	26	80
0	Communications/Art Graphics	25	80
0	Engineering Technology	24	75
0	Business-Secretarial	19	65
(-)	Criminal Justice	16	55
(-)	Agriculture/Environmental	15	30
(-)	Business-Retailing/Sales	10	5
(-)	Service - Personal	10	10
(-)	Trade & Industry - Construction	10	20
(-)	Trade & Industry - Mechanical	10	30
(-)	Trade & Industry - Metal Trades	10	35

Adriana was excited as she saw her highest preference. "My father and brother are both fire fighters! I guess I always had that in the back of my mind as something I might want to do. Wow, they're going to be surprised!"

COUNSELOR: How do you think they will respond?
ADRIANA: I'm not sure. They're pretty protective of me – but they also know how headstrong I am. If this is what I decide I want to do, they'll have to go along with it.

The counselor, sensing that Adriana understood the complexities and potential family reactions to this choice, decided to move to the next step of having Adriana read the next section of the report, shown below in Figure 6-4. The counselor had her highlight words or phrases that were exciting to her.

You show interest in......

B) Business - working in a public or private store, business or industry; keeping books, managing people and merchandise.

D) Mechanical - working with tools and instruments fixing engines, motors, machines.

F) Office/Clerical - working in an office, at a desk, typing, filing, using the telephone.

I) Physical/Manual - doing work which requires considerable physical effort much of the time.

K) Technical - doing work which requires a lot of special training and frequently involves using complicated tools, instruments and procedures.

YOUR TOP INTEREST CLUSTERS

Service - Fire Science

Workers in this group control and extinguish fires, protect life and property, and maintain equipment as a volunteer or employee of a city, township, or industrial plant. Workers could travel to other areas and fight forest or very large fires. They respond to fire alarms and other emergency calls. Select hose nozzle, depending on the type of fire, and direct streams of water or chemicals onto fire. Position and climb ladders to gain access to upper levels of buildings or to assist individuals from burning structures. Create openings in buildings for ventilation or entrance, using ax, chisel, crowbar, electric saw, core cutter, and other power equipment. Other workers in this group inspect fire damage, investigate fires for arson or other causes. Still others provide service to prevent fires and accidents by informing businesses, schools and individuals on safety. Other workers in this group are involved in hazard waste, chemical waste, and environmental protection caused by some emergency.

She disagreed with the business and office/clerical interests, but agreed with the others, and she highlighted several words and phrases in the description of Service-Fire Science. Next, the counselor showed her the list of suggestions for career exploration. Adriana indicated that she wanted to explore all of the options in the Service-Fire Science list, so they decided to start there, using the O*NET (onetcenter.org) to research the occupations. Adriana added to her list as she read about occupations that were related to her top choices in O*NET, and was also able to delete several. Once she had it narrowed down to fire fighter, fire inspector and paramedic, she decided her next step would be to shadow her father and brothers on the job, and talk with a friend that was a paramedic. In addition, the counselor gave her a list of colleges and training programs that offered scholarships for students with diverse backgrounds, including one for women entering nontraditional career fields. In this case, Adriana was able to use the PIC to help identify her interests and careers that fit her current needs.

The next inventory is the Reading-Free Vocational Interest Inventory. Before proceeding to the example of its use in a classroom with students diagnosed with mild mental retardation, a review of the inventory is presented in Table 6-13.

Table 6-13: The Reading-Free Vocational Interest Inventory—2

Author/Publisher	Elbern Publications
Copyright date	2000
Test Purpose	The R-FVII:2 is a non-reading vocational preference inventory for use with individuals with mental retardation, learning disabilities, the disadvantaged and regular classroom students.
Versions	Paper/pencil
Administrator Requirements	A
Appropriate Age Range	13-adult
Norms	The developers followed a norming procedure similar to Kuder's by dividing the United States into regions and testing samples of educable individuals with mental retardation (MR) and learning disabilities (LD) in grades 7 through 12. The public school norms included 2132 males with MR, 2054 males with LD, 2163 females with MR, and 1967 females with LD from public schools in 30 states. The sample of adults with MR consisted of 1121 males and 1106 females from 36 community-sheltered workshops and vocational training centers in 17 states. Although the manual does not define *disadvantaged,* the norm group for disadvantaged men consisted of 897, with 781 for the female norm group, taken from 24 various centers in 15 states. The R-FVII:2 has separate norms for people who are mentally retarded, learning disabled, and adult disadvantaged/work sheltered.
Administration	Groups or individuals. Instead of verbal symbols or written statements, clients are presented with pictures of three different work activities at a time, from which they circle the one they prefer. The forced choice method results in a ranking within each of the triads.
Time to Complete	administered in about 20 minutes
Test Scales & Subscales	The R-FVII: 2 clusters include mechanical, outdoor, mechanical/outdoor, clerical/personal care, and food service/handling operations for 11 areas of interest, including: automotive building trades clerical animal care food service patient care horticulture housekeeping personal service laundry service materials handling
Reliability	This test has proven reliability (mentally retarded individuals' range = .72 to .95). Test- retest reliability ranges from .70 to .97 across all groups.
Validity	Concurrent validity was demonstrated when the R-FVII was compared with the Geist Picture Interest Inventory (Geist, 1964), and many significant correlations were found.
Interpretation	Raw scores are transformed into standard scores to enable comparison with "normal" groups. Provides T scores, percentiles, and ratings. The individual profile sheet provides a snapshot view of a client's vocational preferences in relation to each other. Scores above the 75th percentile are described as significant and are said to indicate strong preferences. Scores below the 25th percentile are significant in that they reveal a client's lack of preference. Scores between the 25th and 75th percentile are in the average range, and the manual suggests that many of the interests within this area will gravitate toward one end or the other, given additional time and experience by the client.
Supporting Materials	The manual discusses in detail how other types of validity were examined.

Case of Using the R-FVII in a Classroom with Students Diagnosed With Mild Retardation

In beginning a unit on career development, Mr. Carroll, a classroom teacher for a ninth-grade class of students diagnosed with mild mental retardation, asked the counselor if there was a career test that his students could take to help them identify career options. The counselor talked with Mr. Carroll about the developmental level and other characteristics of the class and decided that a class administration of the R-FVII would be the most appropriate tool.

The counselor and the teacher discussed what activities might help the kids prepare for the R-FVII and what follow-up activities might help them integrate what they learned. They decided that having the children cut pictures out of magazines and newspapers that showed people working would be a good show-and-tell project that would help them become familiar with different types of work.

Following this activity, the counselor would administer the inventories in class and explain the purpose of the R-FVII and how to complete it. The counselor then would train the teacher's aide on how to score the profiles and train the teacher on how to interpret them. After the R-FVII, the counselor, teacher, and aide prepared a one-page summary sheet for each student, including a list and description of his or her highest preferences and sample occupations. Students were told to star the occupations they were most interested in and were then shown various ways to get information about the occupations. Finally, they were assigned the task of making a presentation to the eighth-grade class on their favorite occupation and why.

Suggestions for Career Development

Many of the following suggestions for fostering the career development of students and adults can be modified and used interchangeably to meet the needs of both groups. These suggestions should not be considered all the possibilities for using assessment results to enhance career development; rather, they are examples from which exercises can be developed to meet local needs and needs of other groups.

For Schools:

- Ask students to identify interests as components of personal uniqueness. Share the results with others.
- Ask students to use interest results to match their personal goals and needs. Summarize in a paragraph, verbally or artistically.
- Ask students to identify and compare interest results with selected occupations. Share in groups.
- Ask students to compare interest results with achievement scores. Discuss results.
- Ask students to compare interest results with aptitude scores. Write about findings, or create a chart or graph that demonstrates the comparison.
- Ask students to link interests to a variety of occupations. Share in group discussions.
- Ask students to develop a list of on-site community visits from their interest inventory results. Share their findings.
- Ask students to relate how different interests among individuals must be respected to maintain positive peer relationships.
- Ask students to discuss how interests influence career behavior patterns.
- Ask students to link occupational interests to academic interests.
- Ask students to interview someone they know about his or her interests and how that person meets those interests (through work, leisure, etc.). Share results in class.

For Adults:

- Ask adults to give examples of how interest inventory results can verify and reinforce self-concepts.
- Ask adults to give examples of how interests can influence adjustments, adaptations, and socialization in work environments.
- Ask adults to discuss how interests influence career and life goals.
- Ask adults to discuss how interests are related to learning and leisure.
- Ask adults to discuss how some interests have remained the same over the life span and others have changed.
- Ask adults to discuss how interests influence relationships with peer affiliates in the work place.
- Ask adults to discuss how interests have influenced career decision-making. Use current inventory results as an example.

Other Interest Inventories

The following are examples of other interest inventories currently being used. This list is far from complete, as a considerable number of interest inventories are currently published. Some measure general interests, whereas others measure interests in specific occupational fields.

- *Ashland Interest Assessment*. This assessment includes 144 pairs of work-related activities and was developed for use with people with learning disabilities or developmental delays, brain injuries, limited English ability, limited education, chronic employment and similar conditions. The inventory consists of 12 scales, including: Arts and Crafts, Personal Service, Food Service, Clerical, Sales, General Service, Protective Service, Health Care, Mechanical, Construction, Plant or Animal Care and Transportation. Ellison (2013) provides a detailed review of this inventory.

- *California Occupational Preference Survey.* The target population for this inventory is middle school, high school, and college students and adults. Reported scores are raw scores and percentiles for science, consumer economics, outdoor, business, clerical communications, arts, service, and technology. Scoring can be done on site or by computer.

- *Career Assessment Inventory-Enhanced Version.* This inventory (paper-and-pencil or online administration) can be administered in 45 minutes. It is for individuals 15 years and older. Four types of scales are provided. One is a general occupational theme scale based on Holland's RIASEC model, providing a measure of an individual's orientation to work. Basic interest scales provide measures of interest and their relationship to specific careers. Occupational scales compare a person's interests to those of people who have been happily employed in an occupation for several years. Non-occupational scales are also provided.
  - o There are currently two versions: The enhanced version focuses on careers requiring various amounts of postsecondary education, and the vocational version focuses on careers requiring two years or less of postsecondary of training. This inventory is designed to be used primarily with individuals who are not planning to go to college.

- *Career Directions Inventory-Second Edition.* The CDI is a machine-scorable inventory for high school and college students. 100 triads of job-related activities are presented for which the client selects the most and least preferred. The report provides a "sex-fair" profile of 15 basic interest scales, including: Administration, Art, Assertive, Clerical, Food Service, Industrial Arts, Health Service, Outdoors, Personal Service, Persuasive, Sales, Science & Technology, Systematic, Teaching/Social Service and Writing. Carlstrom and Hughey (2013) provide a detailed review of this inventory.

- *Career Exploration Inventory-3rd Edition (CEI).* This 128 item inventory allows clients to reflect on past, present, and future activities that they might enjoy doing. The CEI is designed to integrate work, learning, and leisure. Test results link to O*NET codes for use with high school and adult populations.

- *Career Targets*. Career Targets is an interest inventory housed within a planning guide for middle school students reading on a 6th grade level that includes an aspirations section, information/exercises on career clusters, knowledge-building games such as matching occupational titles to a 1-line job description skills activities, understanding and responding to want ads, a next steps page, and other relevant activities meant to expand thinking about potential career options.

- *COIN Clue.* Designed for elementary students reading at a third grade level, COIN Clue is a self-administered and self-scored booklet (available in English and Spanish) that helps students connect what they currently do and enjoy doing at school, home and for leisure, to the world of work. In addition to many fill in the blank self-reflection exercises, there are word finds of occupations in a certain career field, matching games (between job titles and descriptions), poster finds, and many other activities.

- *Geist Picture Interest Inventory-Revised Eighth Printing.* This self-administered pictorial inventory seeks to help children-through adults, and especially those with barriers (disabilities, low reading ability, or educationally deprived), to identify primary interests from general interest areas. The general interest areas are persuasive, clerical, mechanical, musical, scientific, outdoors, literary, computational, artistic, social service, and dramatic. A second optional measure examines one of seven key motivations behind each of the individual's answers, such as past experience, family and prestige. Vacha-Haase and Enke (2013) provide a detailed review of this inventory.

- **Interest Determination, Exploration, and Assessment System (IDEAS).** This 128-item (drawn from the Career Assessment Inventory-Enhanced), paper-and-pencil inventory is designed to introduce the concept of career exploration to students and adults. It is appropriate for students 13 years and older and adults who are beginning the career exploration process, but it can also be used with special education students and students who are at risk.

- **Jackson Vocational Interest Survey-Second Edition.** This inventory is designed to assist high school and college students and adults with educational and career planning. Scores are reported by raw score,

111

and percentiles by 34 basic interest scales and 10 general occupational themes. This inventory also compares the individual's score to college and university student groups by 17 major areas such as engineering, education, and liberal arts, 32 occupational group clusters that are ranked, and an academic satisfaction score. The inventory can be hand or machine scored, and a basic mail-in scoring report is available as well as an online extended report. Sanford-Moore (2013) provides a detailed review of this inventory.

- **Korean Strong Interest Inventory (K-SII).** The K-SII is a translated and adapted version of the Strong Interest Inventory. Simply translating an inventory into another language does not ensure automatic generalizabilty to another country or culture. Along with the translation, items on the Strong that were not appropriate for Korean culture, such as "Latin language" or "football" were replaced with more culturally relevant but also similar terms, such as "Chinese letter" and "soccer." Tak (2004) provided a validation study of the K-SII with 4,619 college students from 33 universities and 2 colleges.

- **Occupational Aptitude Survey and Interest Schedule—3 (OASIS-3).** This instrument is designed to measure 12 interest areas: Artistic, Scientific, Nature, Protective, Mechanical, Industrial, Business Detail, Selling, Accommodating, Humanitarian, Leading-Influencing, and Physical Performing. The survey is untimed, but most students finish the inventory in 30 minutes. Norms for junior and senior high school students are available by male and female and combined sex. Scores expressed in percentiles and stanines can be used for vocational exploration and career development.

- **O*NET Interest Profiler**. Based on the O*NET Interest Profiler (http://www.onetcenter.org/IP.html), this self-administered and self-interpreted inventory includes 180 activities that a client rates as either liking, disliking or unsure and results in the RIASEC types as well as a 24 page score report onto which the user transfers their scores. The inside of the inventory includes job titles related to each type and divided by "zones"- ranging from zone 1 (little or no preparation needed) to zone 5 (extensive preparation needed). According to Rounds, Walker, et al. (1999), internal consistencies on the RIASEC codes range from .93 to .96. A short version is also available online (http://www.mynextmove.org/explore/ip). Crockett (2013) provides a detailed review of this inventory.

- **Vocational Preference Inventory (VPI)**. A measure of vocational interests, the VPI summarizes people's interests in terms of Holland codes by assessing their preferences for or against 160 occupations. It takes about 15 to 30 minutes, and only one minute to hand score. The VPI consists of 11 scales: Realistic, Investigative, Art, Social, Enterprising, Conventional, Self-Control, Status, Masculinity/Femininity, Influence, and Acquiescence. The VPI scales have an average internal consistency of .88.

- **WRIOT-II.** A pictorial interest inventory developed for measuring interests and attitudes (motivators) of people aged 9 to 80 who are academically disadvantaged and people with learning disabilities, the WRIOT-II provides information on 17 Occupational Clusters, 16 Interest Clusters and 6 Holland Type Clusters. Bugaj (2013) provides a detailed review of this inventory.

Summary

Interest inventories have a long association with career counseling. Strong and Kuder were pioneers in the interest measurement field. Holland's RIASEC theory of careers has greatly influenced the presentation of many of the current interest inventories.

Questions and Exercises

1. In what instances would you choose the Strong Interest Inventory® or the KCIA? Give reasons for your choice.
2. How would you explain to a high school senior that measurements of interests do not necessarily indicate how successful one will be in an occupation?
3. A college student states that he knows what his interests are but can't decide on a major. How would you justify suggesting that he take an interest inventory?
4. How would you interpret an interest inventory profile that has no scores in the "above average" category? What would you recommend to the individual who took the inventory?
5. Defend or criticize the following statements: Interests are permanent over the life span. An individual will have the same interests in 2025 as in 2015.
6. What are the benefits and drawbacks of online interest inventories, such as the Kuder Career Interests Assessment, or the online version of the Self-Directed Search? How would you determine which clients would benefit from an online version? How could you integrate such a tool into your counseling? How could you minimize the negatives?
7. Carole, who wants to return to the workforce after her children have started school, tells you the occupations she is currently considering include office manager, teacher, and nurse. She'd like to take an

112

interest inventory to help her find out which might be the best fit for her. Do you have an initial reaction to Carole's aspirations? How would you balance what you would actually say to Carole with what your initial reaction was? Which interest inventory would you recommend, and why? How would you help Carole expand her options without directly or indirectly negating the validity of her first choices?

8. John Switch, a 23-year-old male, has taken the Strong Interest Inventory® in hopes of learning more about possible career options. His profile is as follows: R = 68; I = 70; A = 51; S = 54; E = 72; C = 27. His top five interest areas were listed as: Entrepreneurship (E), Management (E), Research (I), Science (I), and Protective Services (R). His *Personal Style* scales included Work Style (54), Learning Environment (20), Leadership Style (88), and Risk Taking, (72). How would you interpret his profile? (Refer back to Table 6-11). What occupations might be suggested based on his scores? What next steps might you suggest? What impact might that have on his options? How would you interpret his personal style scales? From the information given in this report, how do you think John is in interpersonal relationships, on the job, in a job search? What are his strengths and weaknesses?

9. Consider the two profiles of the Self-Directed Search presented below. What are your basic interpretations of these profiles? In each of these scenarios, how might the client present in counseling? What affective and behavioral characteristics might also be present? What other concerns (in addition to career) might need to be addressed? Using the Occupations Finder or other appropriate tools, identify potential occupations or majors that might be appropriate for each client to consider. How would your counseling approach differ with each case?

	R	I	A	S	E	C		R	I	A	S	E	C
Activities	10	9	10	10	10	10	Activities	3	2	1	1	2	3
Competencies	9	10	10	8	10	10	Competencies	1	1	2	1	0	2
Occupations	9	8	7	9	7	10	Occupations	1	3	3	3	2	1
Self-Estimates	7	7	7	6	5	6	Self-Estimates	2	4	3	2	1	2
	7	7	6	5	7	6		2	2	1	3	2	1
Summary Scores	42	41	40	38	39	42	Summary Scores	9	12	11	10	5	9

10. The Kuder Career Interests Assessment compares an individual's results to people in the norm group who had similar response patterns. Is this preferred over comparing the individual to people in similar occupations, or gender/racially similar groups? Why or why not? What are the benefits/drawbacks of this approach?

11. Consider the following interests (I) and skills (S) scores on the Orientation Scales of the CISS: Influencing (I=74; S=73); Organizing (I=42, S=51), Helping (I=76, S=78), Creating (I=72, S=81), Analyzing (I=75, S=77), Producing (I=79, S=32), Adventuring (I=48, S=82). How would you interpret this profile? What type of suggestions would you make to this person with respect to the four-factor model of CISS?

12. Should pictorial interest inventories for nonreaders include activities that depict high-level jobs requiring college degrees? Explain your answer.

13. A client with a severe visual impairment comes to you for career counseling. Her interest inventory results confirm the educational options she has been considering: medicine and engineering. She is particularly interested in becoming a physician. How would you advise this student? What potential barriers does she face? What type of accommodations might she need for success? How probable is success, or is that a question you can answer?

14. A client has completed the short version of the O*NET Interest Profiler Online. Her results are presented below. Based on her results, what are your observations about the types of careers she might be interested in exploring? What assumptions might you make about her personality, based on these results? Using Holland's terminology, how consistent are her scores? Go to http://www.mynextmove.org and input her scores into the database to see what options emerge next.

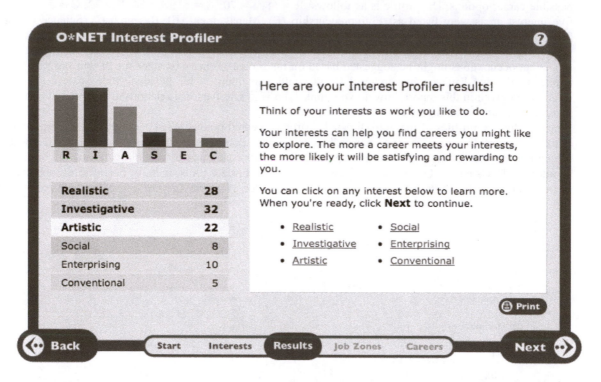

15. A male client has completed the Ashland Interest Assessment. His profile is presented below. How might you approach interpreting these results with the clients? What questions might you ask? What are your working hypotheses about his interests and how they might overlap? Which areas of interests does the profile suggest he should explore in greater detail, as opposed to the areas in which he has the least interest?

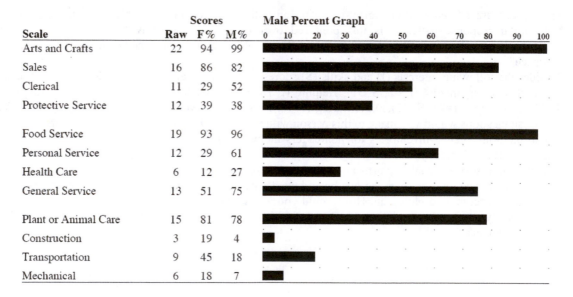

	Scores			Male Percent Graph										
Scale	Raw	F%	M%	0	10	20	30	40	50	60	70	80	90	100
Arts and Crafts	22	94	99											
Sales	16	86	82											
Clerical	11	29	52											
Protective Service	12	39	38											
Food Service	19	93	96											
Personal Service	12	29	61											
Health Care	6	12	27											
General Service	13	51	75											
Plant or Animal Care	15	81	78											
Construction	3	19	4											
Transportation	9	45	18											
Mechanical	6	18	7											

The column marked **Scale** lists the name of each Basic Interest Scale. The next column is your **Raw Score** for each scale. This number can be from 0 to 24. The next 2 columns are **Percent Scores**, one for females, **F%**, and one for males, **M%**. These numbers show how you scored compared to a group of females and a group of males. The numbers range from 0 to 100. The bars on the right show the scores in the Male Percent column.

CHAPTER 7

USING PERSONALITY INVENTORIES

Counselors turn to personality inventories to measure individual differences in social traits, motivational drives and needs, attitudes, and adjustment—vital information in the career exploration process.

Advanced Organizer

In this chapter, we will cover:

- The Role of Personality and Career Theory
- Research on Personality Inventories
- Using Personality Assessments in Career Counseling
- Suggestions for Career Development
- Other Personality Inventories
- Summary
- Questions and Exercises

Prior to diving in, let's hear from a practitioner and her use of one personality inventory in helping a second year college student gain clarity on her career path.

A second year female student (Jessica) visited Career Services expressing significant anxiety about choosing a major. As she stated, "I have no idea what to do, I have lots of ideas but feel like I change my mind every other day." Jessica was able to state fairly clearly some of majors she found particularly interesting, which included English, Psychology and "teaching something, but I don't know what." Having tested out some of these areas through coursework, she particularly found that her literature classes stimulated her intellectual curiosity and allowed her to use one of favorite skills, writing. Jessica had also been working as a tutor for students in the entry-level campus writing course. She spoke a great deal about her desire to "be brave" and pick something because she likes it, even if she was unsure about the availability and desirability of her career options. In listening to Jessica, I felt that she had a sense of what she would like to do, but was having trouble moving forward with that decision.

I suggested that Jessica take the MBTI® primarily because I wanted her to have the opportunity to explore and understand more about her natural way of making decisions as well as give her the opportunity to, in a sense, increase her vocabulary regarding how she describes and sees herself. Jessica's results indicated preferences for INFP, all clearly indicated except for the Extraversion/Introversion dimension that fell in the slight range. After a discussion and series of exercises, Jessica agreed that her best fit type was INFP. Through the course of our conversation, Jessica began see how her decision-making style related to her type preferences. Her desire to keep her options open at all costs and her fear that making a decision would lock her in and prevent her from exploring and pursuing other possible paths was clearly understood in the context of her preferences for Intuition and Perceiving. In addition, when discussing her type and reading the INFP description on her own, she said, "what is most important to me above all else is that I enjoy what I am doing, really love my classes, and just stay true to myself." This values centered statement is highly consistent with the language of introverted feeling, the dominant mental function for INFP.

Because of impending credit limits (students must have a major by 60 credits) and possible financial aid implications, Jessica needed to pick a preliminary major fairly quickly. By owning her own natural tendency to want to keep her options open, she understood more that it was not really the major she was hesitant about but the act of committing to ANY major. By the end of our discussion of the MBTI, Jessica felt that she really wanted to allow herself to move forward with the English major, and that she was prepared to live with the uncertainty of what she would do with that major for a bit longer. We discussed her desire to know all of her career options related to this major and how we could begin researching some of those opportunities while honoring her more open-ended style. Jessica expressed relief that she was "normal" and she seemed to really embrace the person that she saw through the lens of her type preferences

Lauren Johnson
Career Services Counseling Manager
University at Buffalo

The Role of Personality and Career Theory

A number of career theorists have stressed the importance of considering personality factors and characteristics in career guidance. Super (1990) emphasized the importance of self-concept in career counseling, Holland (1997) related modal personal style to work environments, and Dawis (2002) suggested that personality style determines how one interacts within an environment. Prediger (1995), when reviewing trait-and-factor theory, observed that clients should evaluate occupations from a broad perspective—that is, by giving consideration to a broad range of human traits. In addition, identifying and understanding personality or life themes is a major goal of having clients tell their stories as described by the constructivist theory.

Research on Personality Inventories

An earlier review by Lowman (1991) focuses specifically on the use of personality inventories for the clinical practice of career assessment. Although there appears to be an increased interest in the use of personality inventories for career counseling, they have not been extensively used for two main reasons:

a. Because personality inventories were originally developed primarily to measure psychopathology, their use for career assessment has been limited. Although efforts were made to relate personality measures to career-fit projections, the results have not been impressive (Lowman, 1991).

b. More personality measures are needed that are specifically designed to evaluate those personality traits that are relevant to success in certain careers.

A few studies have begun to examine this. For example, one set of researchers (Judge, Higgins, Thoresen & Barrick, 1999) examined the relationship between the "Big Five" personality factors as measured by the NEO Personality Inventory-Revised (PI-R) and career success, defined as intrinsic (job satisfaction) or extrinsic (income and occupational status). They found that intrinsic and extrinsic career success was predicted by higher levels of conscientiousness, general mental ability predicted extrinsic career success, and a negative relationship existed between neuroticism and external career success.

Kitchel (2010) found career and technical education student teachers most frequently had the following Myers Briggs Types: ESTP, ENFP, and ESFJ. Agricultural education student teachers were most often ESTPs, while Family and Consumer Science student teachers were most often ESFJs. Other researchers (Major, Holland, & Oborn, 2012) found commitment to college STEM majors was positively correlated to having a proactive personality. Others (Taber, Hartung, & Borges, 2011) found personality traits of first year medical students predicted whether the individual was person or technique-oriented. Finally, Prather-Jones (2011) conducted a qualitative study of teachers of students with emotional and/or behavioral disorders as to why they remained in the field. She found the teachers consistently indicated the importance of personality in being successful in this particular job.

More research is needed to establish relationships between personality variables and specific occupational fit/career satisfaction and commitment, and also among abilities, interests and personality variables. Table 7-1 outlines research focusing on the relationship between personality and several career-related issues.

Table 7-1: Specific Career Issues and Related Research Studies Focusing on the Relationship Between Personality and Career-Related Issues

Career Issue	Related Research
Aptitudes	Carson, Stalikas, & Bizot, 1997
Career adaptability	Duffy, 2010
Career change	Carless & Arnup, 2011
Career choice	Katz, Joiner, & Seaman, 1999; Krug, 1995; Paige, 2000; Stilwell, Wallick, Thai, & Burleson, 2000
Career decidedness	Lounsbury, Tatum, Chambers, Owens, & Gibson, 1999; Neuman, Gray, & Fuqua, 1999
Career Holland type	Blake & Sackett, 1999; Nauta, 2012
Career maturity	Lundberg, Osborne, & Minor, 1997
Career obstacles	Healy & Woodward, 1998
Career orientation	Pulkkinen, Ohranen, & Tolvanen, 1999
Career planning	Hirschi, 2010
Career self-efficacy	Tuel & Betz, 1998
Career stability	Pulkkinen et al., 1999; Wille, De Fruyt, Few, 2010
Career transitions	Heppner, Fuller, & Multon, 1998
Career type and colleague type preference	Wampold, Mondin, & Ahn, 1999

Education and earnings	Silles, 2010
Elevated interest profiles	Fuller, Holland & Johnston, 1999
Job satisfaction	Krug, 1995

Although the list is impressive, most of the topics have only one or two studies associated with them, which translates into a great need for more research in this area to confirm these findings, and which means that the outcomes of these studies should be viewed as preliminary data.

Using Personality Assessments in Career Counseling

While the research thus far does not support the idea that personality (as measured by personality inventories such as the Myers-Briggs or NEO) predicts occupational satisfaction or success, personality measures can be used as additional information in support of or opposition to a career under consideration. For example, an individual may find support for a sales career from a high score on a personality trait that is related to interpersonal skills. Nevertheless, personality alone should not be viewed as a predictor of success or failure in a sales career. Like interest inventories, personality measures provide topics for stimulating dialogue. Through discussion, the individual confirms or disagrees with the results and comes to understand the relationship of personality characteristics to career decisions. In addition, as Table 7-1 demonstrates, personality impacts career concerns beyond that of making a career choice.

In this chapter, three commonly used personality inventories are used as examples to illustrate how these measures can be used in career development counseling. Keep in mind that these inventories provide opportunities for clients to experience a view of self as they discuss relevant issues about themselves and others in the search for an appropriate work environment, or in processing other career-related issues, such as work adjustment, career transition, dissatisfaction, relationships with co-workers or employers, and so forth. In addition, this chapter includes exercises for career development and a list of several personality inventories. To begin with, we'll start with the California Psychological Inventory 434 (See Table 7-2).

Table 7-2: California Psychological Inventory 434™ (CPI™ 434)

Author/Publisher	Gough/Consulting Psychologists Press
Test Purpose	By describing individuals as others see them, the CPI assessments provide a portrait of personal and work-related characteristics, motivations, and thinking styles – as well as of how people manage themselves and deal with others.
Versions	Revised 3rd Edition. CPI 260 is a short form of the CPI 434
Administrator Requirements	C level
Appropriate Age Range	13 years old and over
Norms	The norm groups include 3000 male and 3000 female high school (50% of the normative group), college, and adult individuals (thus, care should be taken when using with individuals prior to high school level) and several representatives from special populations. The 431 page manual includes new norms for 52 samples of males and 42 samples of females, including graduate students in various fields, college majors, members of different occupations, and so on.
Administration	Individually or group-administered
Time to Complete	About 50 minutes
Test Scales & Subscales	*3 Vector Scales* • Internality-Externality; Norm Questioning-Norm Favoring; and Self-Realization

	20 Folk scales
	• Class 1: Interpersonal style and how the client interacts with others: Dominance, Capacity for Status, Sociability, Social Presence, Self-Acceptance, Independence, Empathy
	• Class 2: Individual endorses and internalizes normative conventions: Responsibility, Socialization, Self-Control, Good Impression, Communality, Well-Being, Tolerance
	• Class 3: Cognitive/intellectual functioning and need for achievement: Achievement via Conformance, Achievement via Independence, Intellectual Efficiency
	• Class 4: Reflects broad styles of thinking or behavior: Psychological-Mindedness, Flexibility, Femininity/Masculinity
	7 Special Purpose scales
	• Occupational issues: Managerial Potential, Work Orientation, Law Enforcement Orientation
	• Personal characteristics: Creative Temperament, Leadership Potential, Amicability, Tough-Mindedness
Test Scales & Subscales, continued	Vectors 1 and 2 combine to form 1 of 4 lifestyle quadrants, Alpha, Beta, Gamma and Delta. Savickas, Briddick and Watkins (2002) examined the relationship between personality type (as measured by the CPI™ 434 Inventory) and career maturity. They found that Alphas had the highest level of career maturity, Betas demonstrated better developed decisional and information competencies than Alphas, and were the highest on informational competence. Deltas showed the lowest degree of career maturity, and Gammas being more divided in their responses. They did note that external Gammas displayed "more mature attitudes toward planning" (p. 39). They also found that the four types were similar in career development competence and level of realization supports, suggesting that individuals in each type can "develop the competencies needed to realize their potential at work and in relationships" (p. 38).
Reliability	Sixteen of the 20 folk scales and 9 of the specialty scales' internal consistency estimates ranged from were at or above .7. Internal consistency estimates for the 3 vector scales ranged from .77-.88. Retest reliabilities were reported for 1, 5 and 25 year retests, with the highest seen for the first year scores, ranging from .6 to .8.
Validity	The construct validity of the CPI™ 434 Inventory has been well explored, and tends to have moderate to strong correlations with instruments measuring similar constructs, ranging from .4 to .8 for the Folk and Vector scales (Atkinson, 2003).
Interpretation	The CPI™ 434 Inventory Profile provides a five page snapshot. In general, higher scores on each of the scales, and a higher scores overall suggest greater levels of interpersonal functioning. Separate charts comparing the individual's scores to same-gender and total male/female scores are included. Raw and standard scores are also included. Part I describes the reliability/validity of the individual's protocol, including the number of items left blank. If the protocol is deemed unreliable, the counselor should not proceed with an interpretation, but should seek to understand the reasons for this. For example, were there too many missed items, inconsistency in responses due to boredom or lack of understanding or motivation,

	or did the client present themselves in an overly favorable light? Part II describes the Classification Type and Level for the individual, and a chart that shows where the individual scores among the four quadrants. Part III includes an analysis of the individual's scores on the 20 folk concept scales. Two different graphs are included that allow the client to see his/her scores as compared to same sex gender and both genders. The information is divided into 4 classes. In Part IV, seven of the special purpose scales are described and presented in conjunction with gender specific and both gender standardized scores. Higher scores are reflective of greater levels of the variable. For example, a standard score of 85 on Work Orientation reflects that the person is well above average on that scale, and is seen by others as reliable and conscientious with respect to work.
Interpretation, continued	It is recommended that the results and descriptions of the CPI™ 434 Inventory be combined with other information about the individual, such as information from interest inventories, work samples and structured interviews. Another recommendation is to tell clients that the CPI™ 434 both describes characteristics specific to the individual as well as comparing those results to larger groups of similar individuals (such as managers and executives).
Supporting Materials	CPI manual, A Practical Guide to CPI Interpretation
Research/Reviews	For in-depth reviews of the CPI™ 434, see Atkinson (2003), Chope (2009; 2013) and Hattrup (2003).

Case of a High School Teacher Contemplating a Career Change

Marc has been teaching high school for several years. While he enjoys his work, and values the interaction he has with his students, the desire to make a better income has become more salient to him. He has been contemplating moving into administration within the school system, but is not sure that he has the personality for management. He has been consulting with the school counselor on the issue, and completed the CPI™ 434 Inventory to assess his personality. As the counselor reviewed the results prior to the interpretation session, a validity check suggested that Marc had tried to answer the results in a socially acceptable way to the extent that the results were impacted and rendered un-interpretable.

COUNSELOR: Hi, Marc. I have the results of the CPI™ 434 Inventory that you completed last time.
MARC: Great! I'm looking forward to seeing what it has to say about me.
COUNSELOR: It is interesting how your answers to questions can result in consistent themes about your personality. As I looked over your results, though, I have some concerns about some of the scores. Do you see this Gi score? It is above 70, which suggests that you may have answered the questions in a way to make yourself be seen in a good light.
MARC: What do you mean?
COUNSELOR: Most of us want to make good impressions on others. Is it possible that you were trying to make a good impression on me?
MARC: I guess I was nervous that the results might not come out right if I didn't exaggerate just a little.
COUNSELOR: That's certainly understandable, but the problem is that we can't place much confidence in the results. Let me ask you, would you be willing to complete the inventory again, but this time give yourself permission to answer the questions as honestly as possible - knowing that you could fake out the test, but that you are choosing to be as transparent as possible so that the results will better reflect your personality?
MARC: Yes, I think that would be a good idea.

Marc retook the CPI 434 Inventory, and this time, though the scores were still very close to the threshold for being called fake good, the report was found to be valid.

COUNSELOR: Marc, can you tell me how you approached the CPI™ 434 Inventory differently this time around?

MARC: Yes. Even though I was tempted to answer in a certain way - when I knew I "should" be more this way than that, I went ahead and answered as honestly as I could.

COUNSELOR: I can see that we can have more confidence in these results. You've had a chance to look over your report. Your scores were very high on leadership and management as indicated in your Leadership and Managerial Potential scales. What are your initial reactions?

MARC: I guess I'm excited. I thought that I had some leadership qualities, but I didn't realize they were very high. It's good to hear that I'm heading in the right direction, I suppose. I wasn't sure what the lower score on Cm meant. Can you help me with that?

COUNSELOR: Sure. I have a brief description of each of those scales to help you better understand the results. Let's walk through each part of the report. In Part 1, you see that the report is reliable. That's important - if it was unreliable, we wouldn't be able to proceed because we couldn't have confidence in the results. In Part 2, you see that your scores classify you as an "Alpha" type. I have a highlighter here - why don't you look through that description and highlight the parts that seem to really reflect your personality?

MARC: OK. I guess I am pretty entrepreneurial and I generally follow the rules. And, I guess my wife would tell you that I can be stubborn at times, too. I'd like to think I have a "talent for leadership" - but I guess only time will tell.

COUNSELOR: Let's think about that - I'm sure you can think of some times when you shown some "talented leadership."

MARC: Well, sometimes it is difficult to lead high school students into a deeper reflection of World History, so I guess it takes a certain degree of talent to lead them there. I also enjoy leading our Boy Scouts troop, too.

COUNSELOR: All right! So, maybe you don't have to wait and see if you have that potential - you have some examples right now. As you can see, you scored at a level 7 on vector 3, which means that you feel comfortable and satisfied with your personality type. In Part 3, you see the detail of personality indicators. There's one graph that shows your scores in comparison to other males, and a second graph that illustrates how your scores compare to both males and females. You can see that you are above average on all of the scales, with the exception of Communality and Femininity/Masculinity as indicated by the Cm and F/M scales.

MARC: Yeah - what does that mean?

COUNSELOR: Generally, the scores closer to the heavy line in the graph are more like those of the general population. For example, if you scored a 90 on the Do or Dominance scale, that would mean that you are probably very aggressive and bossy, while a 10 on that scale would suggest that you get stepped on a lot because you let people dominate you. It's probably better to be closer to the average. Here's a highlighter. Why don't you read through the description of the scales and highlight the characteristics that you think are most like you?

After doing this, the counselor asks:

COUNSELOR: What themes did you note?

MARC: Being responsible and reliable seems to come up a lot. I set goals, follow the rules and am a good guy. Also, that I'm open and positive. I guess you could say I "play well with others."

COUNSELOR: I think you are correct in noticing those. Let's take a look at another score. See, your score on the Gi or Good Impression scale is 75. This is one of the scales that alerted me to the idea that you were over-self representing. Even though you retook the inventory, your results here are still quite high. It suggests that you tried really hard to make yourself look as good as possible, probably exaggerating to achieve that, and that you are quite concerned about the reactions of others. Are there times that you use manipulation to get your way?

MARC: That's what it suggests? Yes, I've always been "seen" as a rock, the one people run to. I can't be seen as weak, I have to put up a good front. As for manipulation, yes,

120

sometimes I resort to that, but only if it seems like the only way to make things happen.

COUNSELOR: Well, we can spend some more time talking about how that approach is working for you, and how it may adversely affect your managerial and leadership qualities that we briefly mentioned earlier. But for right now, let's go on with the report. What did you think about the descriptions I gave you for the Communality (Cm) and Femininity/Masculinity (F/M) scales?

MARC: I don't think I'm that much of a non-conformist, and I guess, yes, I'm not one to sit back and daydream. I'm a doer. I don't like that it said that I'm not creative, though.

COUNSELOR: Ok, Yes, you can see that while the Cm score dipped below the average, it is still close to that line — so you are "within normal limits for the general population" on that one. And your action-oriented, task/goal-oriented approach is suggested by your lower F/M results.

Let's go on to Part 4. In this section, you see a report of some special scales. Not all of them apply to you, but there are a few of interest. 50 is still our midpoint for comparison. As you can see, you have several above 50. On the back of the handout I gave you is a description of the scales in this part of the report. What do you think about your results?

MARC: I guess it's saying that I've got what it takes to be a good leader.

COUNSELOR: Yes, you do have some qualities that are useful for managers and leaders, being decisive and confident. Can you think of some times when those characteristics might not be as positive?

MARC: Sure. I've been told that sometimes I'm bossy and insensitive. I guess at times, I'm overly direct.

COUNSELOR: So, there are two sides to the coin. When you take those strong leadership qualities to the extreme, your efforts at being an effective leader can be thwarted.

MARC: Yeah, I see that. It's something I need to be aware of.

After finishing the review of the CPI™ 434 report, the counselor and Marc began to discuss other ways of exploring whether or not moving into administration was a good decision at this time. In this case, the CPI™ instrument provided Marc with an organization of his personality strengths, highlighted some potential areas of weakness and confirmed his current career aspiration.

The second instrument we will review is the Myers-Briggs Type Indictor®. A review of the properties and relevant research of the MBTI as related to career is presented in Table 7-3.

Table 7-3 Myers-Briggs Type Indicator®

Author/Publisher	Isabel Briggs Myers & Katharine Cook Briggs/Consulting Psychologists Press
Test Purpose	A measure of normal personality traits.
Versions	MBTI Complete Step 1(Form M), Step 2 (Form Q), Combined Reports available: Form M: Profile, Career Report, Interpretive Report, Report for Organizations, Team Report, Work Styles Form Q: Profile, Interpretive Others: Decision-Making Style, Communication Style, Strong/MBTI combined
Administrator Requirements	B; CPP offers MBTI certification
Appropriate Age Range	High school to adult

121

Norms	Stratified sample of 3009 adults similar to US Census percentages for age, gender and ethnic group and across the U.S.
Administration	Self, online, group administration
Time to Complete	About 30 minutes for most forms
Test Scales & Subscales	Four preference dimensions serve to identify: • Extraversion vs. Introversion (E vs. I, how a person energizes) • Sensing vs. Intuition (S vs. N, perceives information) • Thinking vs. Feeling (T vs. F, makes decisions) • Judging vs. Perceiving (J vs. P, demonstrates his or her lifestyle)
Reliability	According to Mastrangelo (2009), one study found that the internal consistency estimates for single scales ranged from .83-.97 for a four week interval. However, the consistency for all four scores occurred in 65% of 424 respondents after four weeks, and 35% having consistency with three types. He suggests that this finding is somewhat troubling given the emphasis on the interactions among the four preferences as opposed to the specific four preferences. He goes on to state that the four preference interaction only predicted 3 of 73 dependent variables, as opposed to the individual preferences predicting 16-36. Carpraro and Carpraro (2002) confirmed strong retest reliability estimates and internal consistency for the MBTI ® Instrument in their meta-analytic analyses across several studies.
Validity	The issue of validity is complex with this inventory. The problem has to do with violations of a key MBTI® Instrument assumption, that the outcome of the MBTI® Instrument is types, not a continuous score. A criticism of many reliability and validity analyses for the MBTI® Instrument centers on the use of the type scores as continuous variables, instead of predicting consistency of types (Fleenor, 2001; Mastrangelo, 2001; Mastrangelo, 2009).
Interpretation	Preferences are classified as very clear, clear, moderate, and light. Responses to items are rated according to a prediction ratio, and the total rated scores provide an index to the respondent's preferences. For example, higher total points for E compared with I would translate into an individual having a preference for Extraversion rather than Introversion. Numbers are also assigned to preferences to indicate the strengths of the preference. A low score can indicate that there is no or little difference between preferences. There are 16 possible combinations of a person's summary code, taking one type from each of the four dimensions. According to Jungian theory of psychological types, each type has gifts and strengths as well as potential for vulnerability. The differences between types provide clues for developmental activities as well as being indicators of preferences for career direction. The manual recommends that counselors become familiar with Jung's theory before using this instrument.
Supporting Materials	Introduction to Type and Leadership, Introduction to Type and Decision Making, Introduction to Type and Innovation, The Leadership Advantage: Leader's Resource Guide, Introduction to Type and Careers
Research/Reviews	Carlson (1989), Fleenor (2001), Healy (1989); La Guardia (2013); Mastrangelo (2001; 2009), Thompson & Ackerman (1994).

Myers-Briggs Type Indicator® (MBTI®) Instrument

The Myers-Briggs Type Indicator (MBTI) is a very popular personality inventory. Many people can state their MBTI type as easily as an astrological sign. Just recently, I saw a license plate with "ENFP" front and center! A variety of reports are available for the MBTI, including one that pairs the MBTI with the Strong Interest Inventory, and a Career Report. A career counselor should be cautious against relying on the MBTI to provide potential occupations, as there have been repeated warnings by reviewers about the lack of empirical support to do so (Healy, 2001; Mastrangelo, 2009). In addition, while some researchers (Buboltz, Johnson, Nichols, Miller, & Thomas 2000) found that MBTI types were correlated with the Personal Style scales of the Strong Interest Inventory, other researchers (Pulver & Kelly, 2008) found that while the Strong Interest Inventory was statistically significant in predicting academic major, the MBTI did not add significantly to that prediction. La Guardia (2013) also stated that the MBTI "should not be used as a tool to predict what type of job or environment would be best suited for the client based on the typological result" (p. 388), and that this tool was not designed to "delineated concrete areas for clients" (p. 388). However, the MBTI can be helpful in processing client preferences about work as well as relationships with others at work.

Case of a Confused Adult Concerning a Future Work Role

Chuck had considered going for counseling for several months before making an appointment. "Why am I having difficulty holding on to a job?" he mused. "I can't seem to be satisfied with anything anymore — my whole life seems to be a waste of time. Maybe, just maybe, a counselor can help me." With much ambivalence, Chuck reported for his first counseling session. After appropriate introductions and small talk, the counselor began:

COUNSELOR: Chuck, I noticed on your request form that you want to discuss your future. Could you be more specific?

CHUCK: Huh—well—yes—I've had problems settling down and finding something I like to do.

COUNSELOR: You've not been able to find a satisfactory job.

CHUCK: Yes—but it's more than that—I don't know how to say it, but I feel different than other people I've worked with. I don't seem to fit in, and I'm not sure what I do that irritates others.

As the conversation continued, Chuck stated that he had had numerous jobs but soon became bored with them and either was fired or quit. He made reference to a lack of interest in work.

CHUCK: It's more than just identifying interests—I don't understand myself and how and why I think the way I do. I seem to be out of sync with other people.

The counselor made note of Chuck's desire for identifying interests and later in the conversation made the following comment:

COUNSELOR: Chuck, earlier you mentioned identifying interests—would you like to take an interest inventory?

CHUCK: Not now, but maybe later. I'm more interested in knowing what kind of person I am—like maybe my personality.

As the conversation continued, it became apparent that Chuck would benefit from an inventory that would provide insights into his perception of the world around him. The counselor suggested an inventory that might help clarify perceptions of self and provide him with a better understanding of his judgments concerning the behavior and actions of peer affiliates in the workplace. For this purpose the counselor chose the MBTI® Instrument.

The results of the MBTI® Instrument indicated that Chuck's preference scores were INTJ. After the counselor explained how to interpret the report form, Chuck read the description of his reported type.

CHUCK: One thing is for sure—I prefer Introversion and I like to think things over a long time— sometimes too much because I never get anywhere.

COUNSELOR: Do you agree with the description of your identified type?

CHUCK: Some of it, I guess, but one point is really true; I'm stubborn and I like to come out on top.

Chuck continued to reflect on the results of the inventory, and the counselor encouraged him to express his thoughts fully concerning his self-evaluations. This instrument helped establish rapport between Chuck and the counselor, and after several more counseling sessions a career decision-making model was introduced to Chuck to provide direction for career exploration.

The results of the MBTI® Instrument reinforced Chuck's strengths and pointed out some areas for improvement. Chuck was now better prepared to further evaluate his interests, experiences, and other factors in pursuit of the career decision. In this case, the MBTI® Instrument was used to provide a basis for discussing perceptions of peer affiliates in the workplace.

The final personality inventory we will review is the NEO. A description of psychometric properties and research relevant to careers is presented in Table 7-4.

Table 7-4: NEO

Author/Publisher	Costa & McCrae/PARinc
Test Purpose	The NEO provides an assessment of normal personality and is applicable for individuals or in a group setting where career counseling, employee training and learning about self is the focus.
Versions	<ul><li>NEO-3PI-3 measure 5 domains (Neuroticism, Extraversion, Openness, Agreeableness, and Conscientiousness) as well as 6 facets for each of those scales. and focuses on positive traits.</li><li>NEO-FFI-3 – 60 item version of the NEO-PI-3</li><li>NEO-4 – for use in business organizations</li><li>Self-administered version is form S; form R is for observer reports.</li></ul>
Administrator Requirements	Level S or B
Appropriate Age Range	12-99
Norms	For the NEO-PI-3, three samples (adolescent, N=500; adult, N= 635; and Middle School, N = 424) were used.
Administration	Self-administered or individually administered
Time to Complete	Varies according to instrument, but around 35-45 minutes.
Test Scales & Subscales	Five domains: Neuroticism, Extraversion, Openness to Experience, Agreeableness and Conscientiousness with six facet scales per domain, interpreted through six personal styles (Interests, Interaction, Activity, Attitudes, Learning and Character)
Reliability	According to the technical manual, internal consistency coefficients for the NEO-PI-3 Form S ranges from .89 to .93 for the five domains, and from .54 to .83 for the 30 facets. Form R had slightly higher numbers. The manual states that there are no test-retest reliability numbers for this version as of yet.
Validity	The manual reports that due to its recent development, there is limited validity evidence for the NEO-PI-3. The validity of the previous version (NEO-PI-R) is well established.
Interpretation	A counselor would begin by transferring raw scores to the appropriate columns on the profile sheet, which includes the 5 domains and 30 facets. When interpreting the NEO, a counselor

	would likely start by reviewing the 5 main domains in order to provide a broad framework. Results are presented in t-scores (below, low, average-45-55, and high-above 56). However, when sharing with a client, the publishers recommend using the profile summary sheet which categorizes the person's scores into different types. This is because terms like "high" or "low" may have negative connotations to them. A Style of Interests profile is also available, which is a graph comprised of concentric circles and then divided into quadrants and t-scores (with the center equaling a "T" of 50) exists for each of the styles, and respondents can plot their results onto each graph.
Interpretation, continued	The concentric circles on personal style graphs are used to help interpret an individual's scores on each of the domains. T scores between 45 and 55 are found in the inner-most circle, between 35 and 65 are found in the middle circle and beyond 35 and 65 are found in the outer area. Among the information provided is the T score (related to the appropriate norm group) for the client's scale scores. The further away the t score is from 50, the more distinct the characteristic is, and the more an accurate interpretation can be made. Visually speaking, this would apply to intersecting scores that are plotted closer to a line drawn in the middle of a quadrant and that also are in the outer circle.
Supporting Materials	NEO Job Profiler, NEO Style Graph Booklet, NEO Summary feedback sheet and NEO Problems in Living Checklist. A bibliography is available on the publisher's website.
Research/Reviews	For earlier reviews of the NEO PI, see Leong and Dollinger (1991) and Ben-Porath and Waller (1992). Leong and Dollinger (1991) summarize their impression of the NEO PI by stating that "the NEO PI must be regarded as one of the best state-of-the-art tests available for the general and systematic assessment of normal personality" (p. 536). For a more extensive review of the NEO 4, see Bahns (2001), Henington (2001), and Stebleton (2009).

Using the NEO in Career Counseling

The NEO was designed as a personality inventory to be used in career counseling. The developers suggest several ways to use the NEO (See Table 7-4 on the next page). For its use in career counseling, they provide some general ideas about how the scales might relate. Table 7-5 shows the subscales for the major scales. Prior to reviewing the results, a counselor could provide this table and have clients indicate or highlight which areas they believe are most like them, and then compare to the actual results.

Table 7-5: NEO Factors and Sub-Scales

Extraversion		Agreeableness	
• Warmth	• Excitement Seeking	• Trust	• Modesty
• Gregariousness	• Positive Emotions	• Straightforwardness	• Tender-mindedness
• Assertiveness	• Total	• Altruism	• Total
• Activity		• Compliance	
Openness to Experience		**Conscientiousness**	
• Fantasy	• Ideas	• Competence	• Self-Discipline
• Aesthetics	• Values	• Order	• Achievement Striving
• Feelings	• Total	• Dutifulness	• Total
• Actions		• Deliberation	

The relationships between main traits and an individual's career-seeking behaviors may be anticipated. For example, "open" people might be open to exploring a wide range of career opportunities to the point of being indecisive, whereas closed individuals might be reluctant to expand their options. Extroverted individuals might be more likely to enjoy "enterprising" careers such as sales, politics, and so on, whereas an introverted person might be more interested in "investigative" careers such as science or research.

Fuller, Holland, and Johnston (1999) found that those with elevated profiles were likely to score higher on openness and extraversion and lower on depressive features. A meta-analytic study (Larson, Rottinghaus, & Borgen, 2002) also showed overlap, with the strongest relationships between the following pairs: Artistic and Openness, Enterprising and Extraversion, Social and Extraversion, Investigative and Openness, and Social and Agreeableness scales. As with most personality inventories, the NEO results should not replace the results of traditional career inventories but should *confirm* or *clarify* career inventory scores.

Research on the NEO-PIR is worth mentioning. Research with the Conscientiousness scale has yielded some interesting results. There is a correlation between the Conscientiousness scale and the Military Leadership scale (Gough & Heilbrun, 1983). Also, scores on the Conscientiousness scale were found to consistently predict job performance ratings (Barrick & Mount, 1991). Although the developers do not link scores on the Neuroticism scale with career interests, they do suggest that someone with a high neuroticism score will probably be unsatisfied in all the careers he or she is considering. Another interesting finding came from a research question investigating the relationship between personality and career transitions (Heppner, Fuller, & Multon, 1998). The researchers found that four of the five factors predicted self-efficacy. The developers discuss several options for interpreting profiles, including noting a few traits, comparing spouse ratings (from Form R), and examining facet scales across domains.

Suggestions for Career Development

Many of the following suggestions for fostering the career development of students and adults can be modified and used interchangeably to meet the needs of both groups. These suggestions do not exhaust all possibilities for using assessment results to enhance career development but, rather, provide examples from which exercises can be developed to meet local needs and needs of other groups.

For Schools:
- Using identified personality traits, ask students to write a composition describing themselves.
- Ask students to develop an ideal work environment that matches their personality characteristics and traits.
- Ask students to develop a list of occupations that match their personal characteristics and traits.
- Ask students to identify and discuss personal uniqueness by comparing personality characteristics and traits with abilities, achievements, and interests.
- Ask students to share, describe, and discuss how differences among people can influence lifestyle and work-related goals.
- Ask students to form groups according to personal characteristics and traits and to share future goals.
- Ask students to write a short paragraph identifying what they consider to be personal characteristics and traits of someone in a chosen occupation. Have them compare and contrast these with their personal traits and characteristics.
- Have students role-play "Who Am I?" based on personal characteristics and traits.
- Using personality results, ask students to project their future lifestyle in five or ten years.

For Adults:
- Ask adults to describe how their personal characteristics and traits influenced their career development.
- Ask adults to describe how their personal characteristics and traits influenced perceptions of their work role.
- Ask adults to share how their personal characteristics and traits influenced lifestyle preferences.
- Ask adults to describe the match or lack of match between their personal characteristics and traits and past work environments and peer affiliates.
- Ask adults to describe how their and their spouses' personality characteristics and traits influenced perceptions of dual career roles.
- Ask adults to share and discuss how their personal characteristics and traits can influence their interactions with supervisors and peer affiliates in the workplace.
- Ask adults to identify personal characteristics and traits that have contributed to their desire for a career change.
- Ask adults to discuss and identify how their personal characteristics and traits could influence choices in the career decision-making process.

Other Personality Inventories

In addition to the personality inventories discussed in this chapter, the reader may find the following inventories useful in career counseling. The evaluation of the normative sample and the description of the scales will help determine their usefulness.

- **16 PF Adolescent Personality Questionnaire.** Designed for ages 11-22, this self-report personality inventory measures personal style or normal personality, problem-solving abilities and preferred work activities. An optional "Life's Difficulties" section addresses problematic issues for this age group, allowing them indicate which specific ones are areas of concern.

- **Adult Personality Inventory.** This is a computer-scored and interpreted self-report questionnaire for ages 16 and above, examining factors such as personality, interpersonal style, and career lifestyle preferences. It includes 21 scales, 4 validity scales, pattern codes and item responses.

- **16PF Children's Personality Questionnaire.** This instrument is designed to measure 14 primary traits of children. Broad trait patterns are determined by combinations of primary scales. Scores are presented by percentile and standard scores. Separate and combined sex tables are available.

- **Clifton StrengthsFinder 2.0.** 34 talent themes are identified to promote development and productivity. It is available in 24 languages. Instead of summary scores, a report presents the highest five talent themes based on ratings.

- **Coopersmith Self-Esteem Inventory.** This inventory is designed to measure attitudes toward self and social, academic, and personal contexts. The scales are reported to be significantly related to academic achievement and personal satisfaction in school and adult life. One form is designed for children ages 8-15, and the adult form is designed for ages 16 and above.

- **Early School Personality Questionnaire.** This instrument is designed to measure personality characteristics of children ages 6 to 8. Questions are read aloud to students by teachers or can be administered by an audiocassette tape. This questionnaire is untimed, and scores are presented in 13 primary personality dimensions similar to the 16PE Separate and combined-sex tables are available.

- **Gordon Personal Profile—Inventory.** The newest version contains both the Gordon Personal Profile, which measures four aspects of personality: ascendancy, responsibility, emotional stability, and sociability, and the Gordon Personal Inventory, which measures cautiousness, original thinking, personal relations, and vigor. This inventory contains a forced-choice format in which respondents react to alternatives by indicating which choice is most like themselves and which is least like themselves. Percentile ranks for high school, college, and certain occupational groups are provided.

- **Guilford-Zimmerman Temperament Survey.** This self-report survey is a measure of the following traits: general activity, restraint, ascendance, sociability, emotional stability, objectivity, friendliness, thoughtfulness, personal relations, and masculinity. Norms were derived from high school, college, and adult samples in several occupations. Single scores and total profiles may be used to determine personality traits to be considered in career decision making.

- **PeopleMapper.** A brief assessment from the UK of how people are most likely to behave in work situations. Eleven work-related dimensions are assessed: Change Oriented, Risk Taking, Competitive, Socially Confident, Work Oriented, Stamina, Perfectionist, Time Managed, Outgoing, Warm, and Worrying. A summary report provides information on five key areas: impact at work, motivation and energy, approach to work, interaction with others and coping with pressure.

- **Vocational Implications of Personality.** A personality inventory with two levels, one for adults and one for students. It is computer-administered inventory, available in English and Spanish. The report includes a personality classification, descriptions of learning style, decision-making style, and operational style. A personality graph shows how a client's type relates to other types. Finally, a list of careers organized by GOE interest clusters relevant to the client's personality type is represented.

Summary

Several career theorists have stressed the consideration of individual characteristics and traits in career exploration. Personality measures provide individuals with the opportunity to examine their views of themselves and to see how their qualities impact their career choices, work with others, and career preferences. While personality inventories have not been directly linked with career satisfaction, results can be used as a springboard for useful discussion.

Questions and Exercises

1. How would you explain the suggestion that personality measures act as mirrors to help individuals examine their views of themselves? What are the implications for career counseling?

2. Give an example of a counseling case in which you would recommend using a personality inventory.

3. A faculty member has recommended using a personality inventory as a predictive instrument for academic success. What would you reply?

4. Explain how you would establish the need for a personality inventory during a counseling interview.

5. What would your strategy be for interpreting personality inventory results that conflict with an individual's career goals?

6. Consider that a client is showing you one of her personal style graphs for Style of Interests from the NEO-PI-3. You notice that the Extraversion T score is 23 and the Openness T score is 78. Knowing this, what assumptions might you make about this individual? Would this person be excited or frustrated in a career counseling group? How might she be in a job interview?

7. The MBTI® Instrument is often given to work teams as a way to improve communications. A team of four members completes the MBTI and has a group type of ESFP. The number of people with each preference are listed in Table 7-6. The individual types are INFP, ENFP, ESTJ and ESFJ. Think about each individual on the team and compare to the other workers. Based on the results, how well do you think each person fits in with the organizational climate at work? Where might each person flourish, and in what types of situations might there be confusion? What might this group look like as they approach and work on a specific project?

Table 7-6: MBTI Team Results

Extraversion	3	Introversion	1
Sensing	2	Intuition	2
Thinking	1	Feeling	3
Judging	2	Perceiving	2

8. Review the results of one or more personality inventories you have taken. If they were taken several years ago, do you think the results may have changed? What are the implications of your scores with respect to your career choice, interactions with others, strengths, and areas for growth?

9. How might you link personality inventory results with the results from interest or aptitude inventories?

10. What are your thoughts about personality testing and children? Given the results of the Children's Personality Questionnaire in Table 7-7, what type of careers might be suggested that would fit this child's emerging personality? What interventions would he respond most positively/negatively to? How would he best learn about careers?

Table 7-7: Children's Personality Questionnaire

Factor	Sten	Percentile
Warm	5	40
Abstract Thinking	7	77
Calm, Stable	9	96
Excitable	6	60
Dominant, Assertive	7	77
Enthusiastic, Cheerful	9	96
Conforming	2	4
Bold, Adventurous	4	23
Sensitive	1	1
Guarded, Withdrawn	2	4
Shrewd, Astute	8	89
Self-Blaming, Insecure	2	4
Self-Disciplined	4	23
Tense, Driven	6	60

11. John is trying to decide what to do after high school. He's not sure if he wants to go straight to a 4-year college, a 2-year college, or take some time to work and figure out what he wants to do. His

profile of the Adolescent Personality Questionnaire shows the following sten scores: Extraversion (4.4), Anxiety (6.5), Tough-Mindedness (3.1), Independence (4.8), and Self-Control (6.8). Other sten scores of interest include Tension (9), Perfectionism (8), Openness to Change (4). His Holland themes were Scientific, Manual, and Artistic. What observations can you make about his personality? What might be contributing to his indecision? Based on his personality, what type of interventions are suggested? Part of his report includes suggestions for the counselor. How useful do you find this information?

12. Consider Jane's MBTI® Type of ENFP. What general observations can you make about her personality? Strengths? Weaknesses? Which career counseling interventions might work best with Jane if she was seeking to make a career choice, or engage in the job search process? What type of work activities might Jane enjoy more than others, based on her personality profile?

CHAPTER 8

CAREER BELIEFS AND DECISION-MAKING INVENTORIES

Career counselors are passionate about helping individuals figure out what they would like to do with their lives. We want to help clients identify their interests, skills, aptitudes, values and strengths, and then help them see the variety of options that are available to them. For the majority of individuals, this process works quite well. However, there are others who seem to get stuck in the process of making a career decision. They may take a career inventory only to result in a flat profile, or to yield occupations that they don't like or don't believe is possible. Or, they may present to the career counselor saying, "I have no idea what I'm good at or interested in doing." It is in these cases that a career decision inventory may help the client and counselor determine how best to proceed.

Advanced Organizer
In this chapter, we will cover the following:
- Theoretical Aspects of Career Decision Making
- Impact of Beliefs on Career Decision Making
- Review of Specific Career Decision Making Inventories
- Other Career Decision Inventories
- Summary
- Questions and Exercises

But before we begin, let's hear from a career counselor who also serves in a supervisory role of other career practitioners, as she shares a story of how she's helped her supervisees use an inventory about negative career thoughts with their clients.

Stacey is a graduate Career Counseling student and has an assistantship as a Career Advisor in the university's career center and provides direct career advising and counseling to students, alumni, and community members on a drop-in and individual basis. As Stacey's semester supervisor, we met weekly to discuss her clients and further develop her career counseling skills. During our first supervision meeting, Stacey shared her desire to enhance her skills in the administration and interpretation of the Career Thoughts Inventory (CTI), which is a commonly utilized assessment in our career center.

Since the CTI is a part of the client intake process, Stacey and I agreed that exploring the use of the CTI with her individual client would be beneficial. The client's CTI Total Score of 102 (college norms are $T = 66$; percentile rank = 95), DMC score ($T = \geq80$; percentile rank = >99), and CA score ($T = \geq80$; percentile rank >99) required a high degree of assistance in thinking more helpful thoughts about career decision making. Given the elevated negative thoughts and the client's history of depression, Stacey disclosed her nervousness about reviewing the CTI scores with her client for fear of bringing more negativity to the situation. To help Stacey feel more comfortable, we role played the initial conversation she might have with her client and discussed Stacey's prior use with interpreting the CTI. It was helpful to allow Stacey some space to process her own feelings and confidence level related to the assessment.

Moving forward, Stacey briefly discussed the results of the CTI with her client but focused more on various career planning activities over the course of about six counseling sessions (e.g. Strong Interest Inventory, card sorts, seeking occupational information). However, in supervision Stacey continued to feel stuck because her client, who wanted to choose a major, continued to state she was *"doing the same things the academic advisors did"* with her! As her supervisor, I wanted Stacey to begin thinking differently. I asked her to conceptualize the client from a Cognitive Information processing (CIP) theoretical approach and drew the Pyramid of Information Processing on a white board.

Next, I asked Stacey to fill each section of the pyramid with the activities her client had done and/or the information she gathered. After filling in the information I posed the following question to Stacey "have you discussed this aspect of career development with your client" and "did it feel different for your client." Stacey looked up at me and said "we've been missing the top of the pyramid…the metacognitions." When Stacey saw the diagram on the white board, she understood why she had felt so "stuck" in session and knew this was the piece that would be "different" for her client.

As homework, I asked Stacey to read each Chapter of the CTI Workbook to fully understand the sections before assigning the same homework to her client. Additionally, I tasked her with reading the following sections of the CTI Professional Manual: *Interpretation and Use of the CTI in Service Delivery* and *Rational and Use of the CTI Workbook*. Stacey introduced the CTI Workbook in session and explained it to her client as *"something you haven't tried yet, and something we are going to address which is different"*. Over several sessions, Stacey assigned sections of the CTI Workbook for her client to engage in which slowly began to challenge and alter her negative career thoughts.

After considerable item analysis, cognitive restructuring, and rehearsal and practice in session, we decided in supervision that it would be helpful to administer a post-test CTI to see if the client had reduced some of the negative thinking. The client's lowered post-test CTI Total Score of 63, DMC score ($T = 54$; percentile = 66) and CA score ($T = 67$; percentile = 96) was evidence to both of us that the Career Thoughts Inventory was a helpful tool to measure career choice readiness. Stacey's client shared her excitement in seeing the lowered CTI scores and admitted that she had finally done something different that actually helped her think more clearly about career planning and decision making.

When thinking back on this supervision experience, Stacey shared that reading the CTI Workbook and CTI Professional Manual paired with visually mapping the client's career problem within a CIP theoretical context helped her further develop her comfort level with the CTI.

Casey Dozier, Ph.D., NCC
Psychology Resident
Psychological Center
Thomasville, GA

Theoretical Aspects of Career Decision Making

Career development theories outline what are necessary elements for making a career decision (see Table 8-1). One possibility for why individuals are struggling to make career decisions is that there are gaps in knowledge in the areas highlighted by these theories. By identifying the gaps that a client has, a career practitioner can work with the client to fill in the missing information and decrease indecision. Test developers have identified inventories to help with identifying deficits and needs a client may need to address to make an effective career decision.

Table 8-1: Theoretical Components of Career Decision Making

Career Constructivism	Life themes
	Vocational Personality
	Career Adaptability
Cognitive Information Processing (CIP)	Knowledge of Self
	Knowledge of Options
	Decision Making Approach
	Addressing Dysfunctional Thinking
	Career Readiness
Holland	Matching personality/interests to environment
Parsons' Trait/Factor Model	Knowledge of Self
	Knowledge of the Conditions of Success
	True Reasoning
Super	Clarified self-concept
Social Cognitive (Lent, Brown & Hackett)	Self-efficacy
	Outcome expectations
	Personal goals

Impact of Beliefs on Career Decision Making

A major cause of career indecision that has received a great deal of attention from theorists and researchers is the impact of beliefs on one's abilities to make decisions. Correlates of career indecision have included anxiety, lack of self-knowledge, lack of structure, personal conflict, perfectionism, fear of commitment, and perceived occupational barriers. Walker and Peterson (2012) found that significant relationships among dysfunctional (or negative) career thoughts, depressive symptoms and career indecision. Career indecision has also been found to be related to emotional stability (Di Fabio, Palazzeschi, Asulin-Peretz, & Gati, 2013), as well as lower work engagement and less involvement in leisure activities (Konstam, & Lehmann, 2011). Studies exploring correlates and predictors of career indecision in diverse groups have enhanced our understanding of issues that may be specific to that group (See Table 8-2 for examples).

Table 8-2: Studies of Career Indecision with Diverse Groups

Diverse Group	Correlates of Indecision	Reference
African Americans	Perceived occupational barriers, career self-efficacy, career-related emotional maturity, information needs, vocational identity development	Constantine, Wallace and Kindaichi, 2005 Hammond, Lockman, & Boling, 2010
Greek high school students	Absence of structure, a need for career guidance, having diffused interests and more personal conflicts	Argyropoulou, Sidiropoulou-Dimakakou, and Besevegis, 2007
Italian youth	Career search self-efficacy	Nota, Ferrari, Solberg, & Soresi, 2007
Puerto Rican college students	Anxiety	Corkin, Arbona, Coleman and Ramirez, 2008
White, Hispanic and African American college women	African American women reported more barriers	Lopez and Ann-Yi, 2006
Korean college students (validation of the Korean Career Indecision Inventory)	Lack of career information, lack of necessity recognition, lack of self-identity, and external barriers	Tak and Lee, 2003

The majority of these studies were based on self-report measures, which could also be a form of self-talk. Individuals complete a survey to reflect what they believe is true about their situations. These are perceptions and may not be reality. Still, regardless of how real the barrier is, people's self-talk can have a dramatic impact on how they view themselves, as well as on their options and how they make career decisions. This is a key component of Cognitive Information Processing Theory (Peterson, Sampson, Reardon, & Lenz, 2002). According to this theory, negative thinking impacts all other domains of making a career decision, including knowledge about self, knowledge about options, and knowledge of how to make decisions. If the self-talk is peppered with "I should," "I ought," or always, never, or other absolutes, it is likely that the person's thinking is acting as a barrier in making an effective career decision. If a person constantly believes that he or she is not good at anything, or if the person is depressed, how will that impact the way that he or she completes an interest or skill inventory? How will those beliefs impact the person's thoughts about occupational information and their ability to make career decisions?

Review of Specific Career Decision Making Inventories

In this chapter, we review several inventories related to career beliefs as well as career decision-making. Table 8-3 below offers a brief comparison of the scales being reviewed in this chapter.

Table 8-3: Comparison of Career Decision Inventories

Title	Publisher/ Distributer	Grade/Age Range	Items	Time	Scoring
Barriers to Employment Success Inventory	List	High school to adult	50 items. Likert scale: no concern to great concern	20-30 minutes	Paper and online
Career Decision-Making Difficulties Questionnaire	Gati/Yissum	17+	34 items; Likert scale 1-9, with 1=Does not describe me to 9= Describes me well	6-8 minutes	Paper and online
Career Decision Scale	Psychological Assessment Resources, Inc.	High school-adult	18 items. Likert scale: 1=not at all like me to 4= exactly like me	About 15 minutes	paper
Career Decision Making Profile	Gati/Yissum	17+	36 items. Likert scale: 1-9, with 1=Strongly Disagree to 9= Strongly Agree	6-9 minutes	Paper and Online
Career Thoughts Inventory	Psychological Assessment Resources, Inc.	High school to adult	48 items. Likert scale: strongly disagree to strongly agree	7-15 minutes	Paper

To address career beliefs, we will review the Barriers to Employment Success Inventory, the Career Decision-Making Difficulties Questionnaire, and the Career Thoughts Inventory. For career decision-making, we will look at the Career Decision Scale and the Career Decision Making Profile. We'll start with a review of the BESI. Psychometric properties and relevant information is presented in Table 8-4.

Table 8-4: Barriers to Employment Success Inventory, 4th Edition

Author/Publisher	John Liptak/Jist.com
Copyright date	2011
Test Purpose	Measures barriers and challenges to obtaining and retaining a job
Versions	Paper/pencil and also available online
Administrator Requirements	None listed
Appropriate Age Range	High school-adult; 8th grade reading level
Norms	Male and female college students, long-term unemployed, offenders and ex-offenders, welfare-to-work clients.
Administration	Self-administered, self-scored, self-interpreted
Time to Complete	20-30 minutes
Test Scales & Subscales	Personal & Financial Barriers Emotional & Physical Barriers Career Decision Making & Planning Barriers Job Seeking Knowledge Barriers Training and Education Barriers
Reliability	According to the manual, coefficient alphas range from .87 (Job Seeking Knowledge) to .95 (Career Decision Making & Planning). Reliability of all 5 scales equal or greater than .87. Test-retest reliability at 6 months: .79 to .90 (N=150 unemployed government-sponsored job training program attendees)
Validity	Content validity described in the manual through the interscale correlations ranging from .45 to .69, which shows that the scales are measuring different constructs.
Interpretation	10-19 = fewer barriers than most adults 20-30=about the same level of barriers in that category as most adults 31-40=more barriers in that category than most adults.
Supporting Materials	Barriers to Employment Success Administration Manual
Research/Reviews	Green (2009; 2013)

Using the BESI with a Job Search Strategies Class

Mrs. Halon is teaching an undergraduate course on job search strategies. She decides to use the BESI in the first class so that she can gain awareness of issues that are specific to each student, as well as those that many might share in the group. After students complete the BESI, she shows them how to score the five scales, and reminds them that high scores are not better or worse than low scores. She then has students divide into small groups according to their scale with the highest number of points. She decided to divide one of the groups, the career decision-making and planning group, in half because of the large number of people in it. Once students were in their groups, she reminded the class that the inventory identified barriers that they saw in their way of getting a job. She then passed out copies of a worksheet with a grid on it (see Table 8-5), and gave the students 15 minutes to complete it.

Table 8-5: Sample Comparison Worksheet

	Concern #1:	Concern #2:	Concern #3:
Strategy #1			
Strategy #2			
Strategy #3			
Strategy #4			
Strategy #5			

When time was up, Mrs. Halon asked them to talk with each other and keep notes on any themes that they saw in their tables, and to be prepared to share with the large group. She gave them 10 minutes to complete the task and then asked the first group to share one theme. She wrote that theme on the board, asked how many other groups had a similar theme and jotted the number of people who raised their hands beside that theme. She then moved to the second group and repeated the pattern. She continued this process until all themes were exhausted. After adding some of her ideas to the list and asking for additional thoughts, Mrs. Halon gave the following homework assignment:

1. Go back through your BESI inventory and highlight barriers you endorsed as a 4, or a 3 if you did not mark any 4s.
2. In your journal, write down the barrier and an accompanying strategy you believe you can use to help tear down that barrier.
3. Write down what you have learned from taking the BESI and the activities we have done.

Mrs. Halon's use of the BESI accomplished many goals. First, students were not only made aware of their perceived barriers, but through the group activity, realized that they were not alone, and that others also shared similar barriers. Second, the students were able to gain a sense of control over the barriers as they worked with each other to identify strategies to address them. Third, they found that there was a great deal of overlap in the strategies, and that many required skills that they already possessed. Fourth, they expanded their ideas of potential strategies from hearing from others. Finally, they were able to take the strategies shared in class and personalize their approach to addressing the barriers noted on their own inventories. Later that week, Mrs. Halon emailed the entire list of brainstormed strategies from each of the groups to the entire class. A week later, she asked the students to complete a two-minute writing assignment where they talked about one strategy they had either tried and the result.

The next inventory we will review is the Career Decision Making Difficulties Questionnaire. Psychometric properties and relevant information is presented in Table 8-6.

Table 8-6: Career Decision-Making Difficulties Questionnaire

Author/Publisher	Gati/Yissum
Test Purpose	The CDDQ's goal is to locate the foci of the client's career decision-making difficulties. The online Internet version of the CDDQ provides feedback that includes some first-step recommendation on ways to overcome identified career decision-making difficulties.
Versions	Paper and pencil (email the author); online; translated into 14 languages
Administrator Requirements	None noted
Appropriate Age Range	16+
Norms	Interpretation is ipsative (within client)
Administration	Individually, group, or online
Time to Complete	6-8 minutes
Test Scales & Subscales	Lack of Readiness • Lack of Motivation • Indecisiveness • Dysfunctional Beliefs Lack of Information • About the decision making process • About the self • About the occupations • About ways of obtaining information Inconsistent Information • Unreliable information • Internal conflicts • External conflicts
Reliability	Total score Cronbach alpha's in 7 studies ranged from .88 to .96. Retest reliabilities for total score was around .8.
Validity	Several studies focusing on the construct, concurrent, and predictive validities of the CDDQ are described in the online supporting materials www.cddq.org/cddqinfo.htm
Interpretation	A mean response of 6.34 or higher is considered a "salient" concern, 3.33 or less is considered "negligible" and any score in between the two is considered moderate.

Supporting Materials	www.CDDQ.org
	Youtube video: http://youtu.be/Jn3MEtJFcEI
Research/Reviews	Undecided students have been shown to have higher scores on the CDDQ, indicating decision-making difficulties, Career Decision Scale scores, and lower career decision-making self-efficacy scores (Osipow & Gati, 1998). Reliability and validity of the CDDQ have been supported (Lancaster, Rudolph, Perkins, & Patten, 1999). Creed &Yin (2006); Gati, Osipow, Krausz & Saka (2000); Osipow & Gati (1998); Tien (2005). For a recent summary see Gati & Levin (2014), and for a full list see www.cddq.org/addinf1.htm

Case of an Undecided Transferring Student

Maria is completing her Associate's degree and in the process of applying to a nearby university. She utilizes an online chat service within her college career center that allows her to talk in *real time* with a career practitioner from the career center utilizing the Internet.

MARIA:	I'm filling out my application for the university, but they are requiring that I choose a major. I haven't decided on that yet.
PRACTITIONER:	What options are you thinking considering?
MARIA:	I don't know. I've sort of been considering nursing, or maybe something with technology.
PRACTITIONER:	What do you know about each of those fields?
MARIA:	I know that nursing allows you to help people, and that there are always lots of jobs available in that field. Technology seems to be everywhere, so I would think I'd be able to find a job in that area, too.
PRACTITIONER:	So, being able to find a job is very important to you.
MARIA:	Absolutely.
PRACTITIONER:	What else do you know about these fields?
MARIA:	Well, that's about it. I guess you need to major in nursing to be a nurse, and maybe computer science to get a job in technology?
PRACTITIONER:	We can find out some more information about those two fields, but first, tell me how you usually go about making important decisions. For example, how did you choose to go to our community college?
MARIA:	Um, I don't really have what you might call a planned approach. I was enjoying high school and before I knew it, it was time to graduate. I hadn't really paid much attention. No one around me was applying to universities, so I guess I didn't give it much thought. I came here because it seemed like the right thing to do, plus I'd be with a lot of my friends, and I figured I would be able to make small steps towards getting my bachelor's degree.
PRACTITIONER:	OK – so looking back on that time, how would you evaluate your decision making process?
MARIA:	I wasn't very purposeful about it. I mean, I wasn't very proactive. I have really enjoyed my time here, but I guess, looking back, that was sort of a gamble.
PRACTITIONER:	So how do you want this decision to be different?
MARIA:	That's why I'm here! I want to be more thoughtful and planful about it. I want to make a decision rather than just fall into it. I just don't know where to start. Should I take a career test? Should I contact the nursing and computer science departments? What should I ask them? Should I volunteer in both areas first? What do you think?
PRACTITIONER:	I can see that you are ready to get started! But, let me recommend that we work together to determine a plan, instead of running around in many directions. I have an idea of what might be a helpful starting place. I will send you the link to an online inventory that will help us focus our discussion what you will need in order to help you with this decision. Then we can decide on the next step.

The practitioner sent Maria the link to the CDDQ. Maria completed the CDDQ (see Figure 8-1) and emailed the practitioner with the results prior to their next appointment.

Figure 8-1: Sample CDDQ Results

Your responses reflect significant difficulties involving:

Type of difficulty	Score 1-9	
Lack of Information about the Decision Making Process - A high score in this area reflects a **lack of knowledge about how to reach a decision wisely**, and specifically about the steps involved in the career decision-making process. For instance, you may not know what factors to take into account, or may encounter difficulties in combining the knowledge you have about yourself (for example, your strengths and weaknesses) with information on the various career options (for example, what abilities are required for a specific occupation).	8	
Lack of Information about the Self - A high score in this area reflects a situation where **you feel that you do not have enough information about yourself**. You may not know what you want - for example, what work conditions you prefer or whether you are talented enough in a certain field, or whether you possess certain personality traits that are critical for a specific occupation.	6	
Lack of Information about Occupations - A high score in this area reflects a **lack of information about existing career options**: what alternatives exist and / or what each alternative is like.	8	
Internal Conflicts - A high score in this area reflects a **state of internal confusion**. Such conflict may stem from difficulties in compromising between the many factors you view as important, (for example, you have been accepted at a particular college, but your partner lives in a different city). Internal conflicts may also arise when an attractive occupation involves a certain unattractive element (such as the long training needed to become a physician).	6.8	

PRACTITIONER: Thank you for sending the results. What did you think about the CDDQ summary?

MARIA: I think it is right on target. I am overwhelmed with making this decision. I know I need more information about the areas I'm thinking about.

PRACTITIONER: That's what I was seeing in the results as well. We talked last time about how you make important decisions, and how you would like this decision to be different. May I share with you a career decision making model that other students have found helpful?

Maria agreed, and the practitioner shared the client version of the CASVE Cycle from Cognitive Information Processing Theory, available at http://www.career.fsu.edu/techcenter/.

PRACTITIONER: You can see that there is also a need for more information about yourself. May I suggest a plan, in that first you take an online assessment to see how your interests match up with occupations? You can use the *MBCD* (http://mbcd.intocareers.org) to do this, which will result in a list of promising occupations that match your preferences and thus worth further, in-depth exploration. Second, you should narrow down the list of occupations that come from that assessment to those you'd like to learn more about, and third, I will send you some links for researching those occupations. I will also send you a table to complete before next time (https://sites.google.com/site/debbieosborn/teaching-tools, entitled "Occupational Comparison Sheet"). You should identify what is important for you to know, such as job duties, length of education, salary – or whatever is most important to you, and then complete the table. How does that sound?

MARIA: That sounds like a plan!

In this example, the practitioner utilized the CDDQ to help highlight specific areas of decision making in which Maria was experiencing difficulty. Because of the issues with information as well as with understanding the decision making process in general, the practitioner was able to target the interventions to those specific areas. Before moving on, let's hear from one practitioner about how they use the CDDQ in practice.

For the past 4 years I have worked as a career counselor at a research university. As part of my work, I interacted with young adults considering enrollment in the university and current students considering changing their major. The number of individuals asking for my services greatly exceeds the scope of my employment, and thus I try to integrate various assessments and Internet resources to provide better service for more clients. In fact, if I consider it appropriate, I encourage them to fill out pertinent career assessments before the first counseling session.

Over the years, the cases I encountered have demonstrated that better career counseling involves helping individuals deal directly with the specific difficulties they encounter while making their career decisions, rather than telling them what to do. Most of the young adults I have met professionally, although they were hoping to get expert advice on what they should be doing in their lives, were more interested in finding ways of increasing their confidence in their career choice. In other words, most clients wanted my help in dealing with career indecision. To this end, as I see it, one of the most important steps in facilitating clients' career decision-making is helping them to overcome the difficulties that prevent them from entering, advancing in, or finishing the process.

The CDDQ is a theory-based measure of career indecision. It allows me to reliably assess in just minutes what are most likely the salient difficulties that the individual is facing. Before I started using the CDDQ, I needed at least one session to assess these difficulties. Once I started using it, I needed only ten minutes (and sometimes even less) to verify the results of the CDDQ.

One of the advantages of the CDDQ, as I see it, is that it provides each individual with language to better understand what his or her career-decision difficulties are. Most individuals report being undecided, and I have wondered why. I have heard from many clients that they find the feedback, which reflects the sources of their career indecision alone, to be extremely valuable.

I personally ask my clients to fill out the online version of the CDDQ. This version provides feedback which can be printed out, and I ask the client to bring it for the first session. The feedback has a numerical section and verbal section. Since I use the CDDQ frequently, I rely on the numerical results and then validate them in a semi-structured intake interview. Based on the validated results of the CDDQ, I plan the counseling sessions, tailoring the interventions to the unique needs of each individual.

Yuliya Lipshits-Braziler M.A.
Career guidance counselor
Student Administration Department
The Hebrew University of Jerusalem

The second inventory we will review that looks at career decision making and areas that might impact one's ability to make career decisions, such as procrastination and a desire to please others, is the Career Decision Making Profile, presented in Table 8-7.

Table 8-7: Career Decision Making Profile (CDMP)

Author/Publisher	Gati/Yissum
Test Purpose	The goal is to enable individuals and their counselors to learn about the way they tend to make career decisions.
Versions	Paper and pencil (email the author); online
Administrator Requirements	None noted
Appropriate Age Range	17+
Norms	Interpretation is ipsative (within client)
Administration	Self-administered
Time to Complete	6-9 minutes
Test Scales & Subscales	Information Gathering Information Processing Locus of Control Effort Invested in the Process Procrastination Speed of Making the Final Decision Consulting With Others Dependence on Others Desire to Please Others Aspiration for an "Ideal Occupation" Willingness to Compromise Using Intuition
Reliability	Cronbach's alphas ranged from .72-.91 with a median of .81 for all the scales (based on 3 items). Median two-week retest reliability was .82. More recently, Gati and Levin (2012) found retest reliability at 2 weeks to be .90, and at 1 year, .81.
Validity	Confirmatory Factor Analyses supported the distinctness of the 12 dimensions. The *CDMP* better predicted clients' decision status than the GDMS (Scott & Bruce, 1995). Gati and Levin (2012) found the 12 dimensions of the CDMP to be compatible with the theoretical framework.
Interpretation	The extreme scores on the dimensions highlights the unique way the individual makes career decisions.
Supporting Materials	Online resources such as an administrative manual, psychometric properties, etc.: http://kivunim.huji.ac.il/cddq/cdmpinfo.htm
Research/Reviews	Gati, Landman, Davidovitch, Asulin-Peretz, & Gadassi (2010).

Case of "I've got to choose by Thursday"

Rebeccah came into the career center during the last week of classes to choose a major. The career advisor asked her what prompted her to come in at this time.

REBECCAH: I'm going home on Thursday and my parents are going to bug me all through the vacation if I don't have a plan.

ADVISOR: Well, what do you think? Do you believe that you need to have a plan?

REBECCAH: They're probably right. I really don't have a clue as to what I want to go into, and I guess I might as well get started now.

The advisor asked Rebeccah to describe how she typically makes decisions, and it seemed that Rebeccah's approach to decision making was random. Sometimes she went with her gut, and at other times, she depended heavily on what others suggested. The advisor suggested that they begin by determining Rebeccah's decision-making style, as that would help to identify next steps that would be more meaningful to her. After the advisor explained the instrument, Rebeccah agreed to take the CDMP. Her report indicated Table 8-8.

Table 8-8: Rebeccah's CDMP Scores

Information gathering:	Comprehensive	Consulting with others:	Frequent
Information processing:	Holistic	Dependence on others:	High
Locus of control:	External	Desire to please others:	High
Effort invested in the process:	Little	Aspiration for an "ideal occupation":	Low
Procrastination:	High	Willingness to compromise:	High
Speed of making the final decision:	Fast	Use of intuition:	Much

Rebeccah's scores indicated that she felt a need to make a choice now, and her dependence on others' input was clear on multiple scales of the CDMP. The advisor decided to ask Rebeccah about her desire and readiness to make a choice at this time.

ADVISOR:	Rebeccah, how do you feel about being undecided?
REBECCAH:	I need to decide, I guess. Then I could start taking classes toward my major. I just need to have something in mind to tell my parents when I go home. I guess I can always change my mind later.
ADVISOR:	Sounds like it might be more important to your parents that you make a decision now, than it is for you.
REBECCAH:	I know that I need to choose something, but I feel like I've still got some time to check things out.
ADVISOR:	Deciding when is the right time to choose is up to you. If you decide to take more time, are there things you could be doing to help you learn more about yourself, programs of study, and the variety of occupations that are out there?

Rebeccah and the advisor established a timeline and made a goal for choosing a major by the end of the next semester. In addition, because the CDMP highlighted Rebeccah's tendency towards pleasing others, the career advisor and Rebeccah spent time discussing the pros and cons of relying on others when making her decisions. To get at this, the advisor asked Rebeccah to describe a time when she had relied on someone else's opinion in making a decision. Rebeccah shared about how she chose her first major, after several people had told her that the best major to go into was business. The advisor asked what happened, and Rebeccah stated that she quickly found out that not only was business boring to her, but that she really struggled to understand the formulas. "I wasted an entire semester's worth of time and am still rebuilding my GPA because of the low grades I got that semester."

The advisor and Rebeccah then discussed how she wanted this decision to be different, to which Rebeccah stated that this time around, she wanted to find something that would better fit her personality, and not make a choice based completely on what other people thought was a "good" major. They decided to meet after the break to begin the process of finding some alternatives that were a better fit. They also discussed the balance between finding something that would satisfy Rebecca and hopefully also her parents. Rebeccah decided to show her plan to her parents, believing that they would be satisfied in seeing that she was "working on it."

The fourth inventory we will review that focuses on concerns relevant to career decision-making is the Career Decision Scale (CDS). Psychometric properties and relevant information on the CDS is presented in Table 8-9.

Table 8-9: Career Decision Scale

Author/Publisher	Osipow /Psychological Assessment Resources, Inc.
Test Purpose	The CDS was designed to measure career indecision, identify career decision-making difficulties, and act as a follow-up procedure to evaluate the effectiveness of a career intervention.
Administrator Requirements	Self-administered; Level B
Appropriate Age Range	14- 23 years old
Norms	High school, college students, adults seeking to continue their education, and women who were returning to college.
Administration	Individually
Time to Complete	About 15 minutes

140

Test Scales & Subscales	19 items, Likert scale, item 19 is open-ended for any additional information the person would like to add. Two scales: • Certainty (add the first two items for a score of 2-8) • Indecision (add items 3-18 for a score of 16-64)		
Reliability	Test-retest reliabilities for total CDS scores (Osipow, Carney, & Barak, 1976) ranged from .82 to .90 for college students in psychology courses, and were approximately .70 for another group of college students at the end of six weeks (Slaney, Palko-Nonemaker, & Alexander, 1981). Item correlations for the Certainty and Indecision scales range from .34 to .82, with the majority of correlations falling between .60 and .80.		
Validity	According to Harmon (1994), the evidence for the validity of the CDS is "impressive."		
Interpretation	Scale scores for the Certainty scale that are at or below the 15th percentile are considered significant, as are Indecision scores that are at or above the 85th percentile. For scores in between, the counselor should talk with the clients more about their purposes for seeking career counseling and their specific career needs.		
		Low Indecisiveness Score	**High Indecisiveness Score**
	Low Certainty Score	Undecided, but comfortable with that indecision (Savickas, 2000)	targeted interventions with more counselor support may be warranted
	High Certainty	May not need in-depth assistance at this point with making a decision	May make strong commitments to several options over a short period of time (Savickas, 2000)
Research/Reviews	More extensive reviews of the CDS, which also summarize the subscale arguments, have been provided by Savickas (2000), Harmon (1994), Allis (1984), Herman (1985), Slaney (1985), and Osipow and Winer (1996).		

The CDS (Osipow, Carney, Winer, Yanico, & Koeschier, 1987) was designed to measure career indecision, identify career decision-making difficulties, and act as a follow-up procedure to evaluate the effectiveness of a career intervention. Osipow believed that "a finite number of relatively discrete problems" keep people from being able to make or commit to a career decision (1980, 1987, p. 4). When he designed the CDS, he hoped that the CDS would point clients to issues that they should explore when trying to understand their career indecision (Osipow & Winer, 1996).

Case of a Confused Community College Student

Sari, a second-year student at a community college, met with a counselor for the purpose of deciding on a career. Sari told the counselor that she planned to apply to several universities.

SARI: I discovered that the universities I planned to attend require that you identify a major, and I haven't done that yet. I'm just not sure.

COUNSELOR: You have come to the right place! We should be able to help you make a decision. To start the process, perhaps you can identify options you have considered.

Sari was able to identify business, education, and English as possible majors. As they continued their discussion about Sari's future plans, the counselor introduced the possibility of taking an inventory to help in the career decision process. She then informed Sari of the purpose of the CDS, and Sari agreed that the results should help her decide, or at least provide some directions for her future plans.

The counselor was not surprised with the CDS results of a low certainty score and a high indecision score. To help Sari identify reasons for a high indecision score, the counselor suggested they discuss items on the indecision scale that was marked "exactly like me." After a thorough discussion of each identified item, the counselor asked Sari to summarize her needs that had emerged from their discussion. Sari identified two needs, "more information about specific careers and to learn more about my abilities." The counselor agreed and added two more—self-confidence and approval of her choice from others.

In this case, the CDS served as a springboard for identifying which interventions might be helpful (occupational information and self-assessment), as well as an indicator for what issues might be interfering with Sari's ability to make a successful decision. Although a lack of information about her personality and career options can be easily remedied, the issues of self-confidence and a need for external approval will need to be discussed further in counseling and revisited throughout Sari's decision-making process to ascertain their separate and combined impact.

The authors of the CDS caution clinicians to remember that indecision is not always a negative indicator and may even be appropriate, depending on the client's developmental level. Savickas (2000) suggested examining the discrepancy between ratings on major choice certainty versus career choice certainty. If the major choice certainty score is higher by 2 or 3 points, Savickas recommends examining whether the client has a plan ("I'm going to major in communications"), but not a clear goal ("but I have no idea what I'll do after I graduate"). The opposite would be true for someone with higher career certainty than major choice certainty; that person has a goal ("I want to be a manager"), but no plan ("Which major would best prepare me for that?"). In either case, Savickas suggested talking with the client about how he or she made that first decision and trying to identify the factors that affect the decision. For example, was the choice of major to please someone else, or was the career choice a completely informed one?

The Career Thoughts Inventory (CTI) was designed to measure the existence of dysfunctional career thinking, which is a key component in Cognitive Information Processing Theory (Peterson, Sampson, Reardon, & Lenz, 2002). Psychometric properties and relevant information is presented in Table 8.10.

Table 8-10: Career Thoughts Inventory (CTI)

Author/ Publisher	Sampson, Jr., Peterson, Lenz, PhD, Reardon, & Saunders/Psychological Assessment Resources, Inc.
Copyright date	1996
Test Purpose	Assist in career problem solving and decision making in adults, college students, and high school students
Administrator Requirements	B
Appropriate Age Range	High school through adults; The reading level is sixth grade, and it takes about 7 to 15 minutes to complete.
Norms	Include 571 adults, 595 college students, and 396 high school students. Information on client norms (N = 376) is also provided.
Administration	Self-administered.
Time to Complete	7 to 15 minutes
Test Scales & Subscales	The CTI consists of 48 items and 3 scales: *Decision-Making Confusion*: difficulty beginning or continuing with career decision making due to negative feelings or confusion about decision making *Commitment Anxiety*: difficult to commit to a specific career choice, along with strong worries about decision making *External Conflict*: difficult to balance the importance of one's ideas with the importance of the ideas of family members and/or friends, making a choice more difficult
Reliability	Test-retest reliabilities for the CTI total after a four-week period were reported as .86 (college students) and .69 (high school). Test-retest reliabilities for the other scales ranged from .74 to .82 for college students, and from .52 to .72 for high school students. Internal consistency coefficients for the CTI total score ranged from .93 to .97, with the following ranges for the other scales: Decision-Making Confusion, .90 to .94; Commitment Anxiety, .79 to .91; and External Conflict, .74 to .81.
Validity	The manual provides sufficient information on content, construct, convergent, and criterion-related validity, indicating that the CTI is a valid instrument for measuring dysfunctional thinking.
Interpretation	Higher scores indicate higher levels of dysfunctional career thinking. Once scored, the total and scaled scores are transferred to the profile sheet. Separate profiles (including T scores and percentiles) are shown for high school, college, and adult clients. The manual identifies four

	levels of intervention, based on the client's total score. Level 1 requires the least intensive intervention, and Level 4 requires the most intensive intervention. Suggested interventions for each level are provided in the manual.
Supporting Materials	Career Thoughts Inventory Workbook; CTI Manual
Research/ Reviews	The CTI total scores have demonstrated a negative correlation with vocational identity, career certainty, and knowledge about occupations and training, which means that the higher the CTI score, the lower the scores on these other factors. In addition, the CTI total score was positively correlated with indecision, neuroticism, and vulnerability; a person with high CTI scores is more likely to have high scores on those particular factors. The manual provides more information on career and personality factors that are related to the CTI total and scale scores. The design and psychometric properties of the CTI are described in an article by the creators of the inventory (Sampson, Peterson, Lenz, Reardon & Saunders, 1998). A regularly updated bibliography on the CTI is available from authors at http://www.career.fsu.edu/ and searching for the bibliography. Peila-Shuster and Feller (2013) provided a thorough review of the CTI.

Case of the Diving Board Syndrome

Keith, a college junior, came to the career center to discuss his career plans with a counselor. When the counselor asked Keith what career options he was considering, Keith stated, "Film directing." After a pause, he also stated that he was interested in real estate, advertising, possibly management and that teaching was always an option. Then he commented that he had read that management information systems were a hot field for the future, and he wanted to learn more about that subject. When asked about his first choice, he stated that being a film director was a dream, but so few people are successful at it, and he wasn't sure it was the best choice for him anyway.

Based on his comments, which clearly indicated a lack of focus career decision-making difficulty, the counselor suggested that he complete an inventory that would help clarify his needs. Keith agreed. The counselor decided upon the Career Thoughts Inventory because of the negative comments Keith was making, which indicated negative thinking. Keith took the CTI during the session. The counselor scored the inventory with Keith, first tearing the perforated edges on the top, bottom and right side, opening the booklet, scoring the total and subscales, and then transferring the scores to the graph on the back.

Keith's CTI scores are shown in Table 8-11.

Table 8-11: Keith's CTI Scores

	T score	Percentile
CTI Total	60	84
DMC	61	86
CA	73	99
EC	50	50

Before offering an explanation, the counselor was able to quickly determine that the overall level of dysfunctional thinking was on the high end of average, but that one scale indicated significant concerns.

The counselor first reminded Keith about the purpose of the inventory: to identify thoughts that get in the way of making effective career decisions. Then counselor provided a brief description of the meaning of each scale. The counselor stated that Keith's high score on the Commitment Anxiety scale suggests that he seemed to be having difficulty committing to a career option and that he might have some anxiety about what would happen when he made the decision. The counselor asked how much research Keith had done on his first option, film director. Keith pulled out a notebook that had articles, names of contacts, job task descriptions, and job outlook information on the field of film.

> COUNSELOR: You have an impressive amount of information on the field of film. Based on what you know about yourself and what you know about this option, do you think this is a good choice for you?
>
> KEITH: It would be awesome! It sounds like it involves a lot of things I enjoy doing and that I'm good at, but still, I just don't know...

COUNSELOR:	It's almost like getting to the edge of a diving board. You look at the water in the pool, but something inside, perhaps fear, is keeping you from diving in.
KEITH:	What if I go for it, major in film, do all the right things, and I still fail?
COUNSELOR:	What do you mean by failing?
KEITH:	Well, that I can't get a job. I'd hate to go through all this education to end up living with Mom and Dad again.
COUNSELOR:	Are there some things you could do to increase the odds that you'll be successful?
KEITH:	Are you talking about an internship?
COUNSELOR:	Sure, that's one way. You'll get some work experience, and start to build your network. What else can you do?

In this example, the counselor was able to address the negative thoughts by gently confronting that there are ways to decrease the chances of failure, and to engage Keith in active career planning. The CTI was used as a screening tool to identify the client's needs for support and assistance in the process of decision-making. Second, the CTI identified problems that needed attention and specific intervention.

The counselor should also review the individual items in each scale and address any that were circled as agree or strongly agree. The reason for this is that even one dysfunctional thought can represent an insurmountable boundary to a person. Consider if a person strongly agreed with "I never make good decisions" or "Someone significant to me is always getting in the way of my choices." A counselor could conceivably spend the rest of the session unpacking the thoughts and feelings associated with that one thought – and that one thought might be impacting a person's view of self and options to the point that it must be addressed first before further assessment can continue.

If negative thoughts are found, a counselor might engage in this follow up process:
1. Choose two or three items that were endorsed as "strongly agree" or "agree."
2. Ask the client to talk about his or her feelings and thoughts about each item.
3. Using the CTI Workbook, discuss the process of reframing negative thoughts.
4. Taking the items identified in Step 1, have the client practice reframing the statements. Consider assigning homework that focuses on reframing other highly rated statements, or possibly the Career Thoughts Workbook.

Other Career Decision Inventories
The following inventories reflect the variety of career development issues discussed in this chapter, including decision-making, self-efficacy, and indecision.

- **Adult Career Concerns Inventory (ACCI).** This instrument assesses an individual's career state and vocational maturity. This inventory, a research edition in developmental stage, is a measure of Super's (1990) hierarchy of life stages: exploration (crystallization, specification and implementation), establishment (stabilizing, consolidating, advancing) maintenance (holding, updating, innovating), and disengagement (decelerating, retirement planning, retirement living). One research study identified three potential patterns of career exploration: those who were maintaining a current position, those who were recycling through a current position, and those who were moving into a new position (Niles, Anderson, Hartung, & Staton, 1999). For a review of the development of the ACCI, see Cairo, Kritis, and Myers (1996), and for a recent review, see Baker (2013). The inventory is available at www.vocopher.com.

- **Career Attitudes and Strategies Inventory (CASI).** This inventory is designed to measure a variety of attitudes, experiences, and obstacles that affect adults' careers. There are nine scales of work adaptation rated from 1-4 in terms of degree of concern: Job Satisfaction, Work Involvement, Skill Development, Dominant Style, Career Worries, Interpersonal Abuse, Family Commitment, Risk-Taking Style, and Geographical Barriers. Counselors use this instrument to help predict whether a client is more likely to continue in a certain work environment or seek to change jobs. In addition, the client's profile can be used to identify obstacles that are hindering career development. For a review of the CASI, see Gottfredson (1996).

- **Career Beliefs Inventory** - The CBI was designed as a counseling tool to help clients identify faulty beliefs that interfere with career decision making and subsequent career development. The CBI is untimed, consists of 96 items and is answered by using a five-point rating scale from strongly agree to strongly disagree. The results are reported by 25 scales organized under five headings: "My Current Career Situation," "What Seems Necessary for My Happiness," "Factors That Influence My Decisions," "Changes I Am Willing to Make," and "Effort I Am Willing to Initiate." Appropriate for grades 8-adult.

- **Career Development Inventory – College and High School Editions.** According to the manual, the purpose of the CDI is to help individuals evaluate how well they are "constructing" their career path. It consists of the following scales: Career Planning (CP) - knowledge of personal career plans; Career Exploration (CE) – using good and poor sources of information; Decision Making (DM) – ability to apply knowledge to decision making; World of Work Information (WW) – a test of career awareness and occupational knowledge; Career Development – Attitudes (CDA) – combines the CP and CE scales; Career Development – Knowledge and Skills (CDK) –combines the DM and WW scales; Career Orientation Total (COT) – combines CP, CD, DM, and WW and serves as a measure of 4 aspects of career maturity. Scores between the 40th and 60th percentiles suggest that the client's scores are similar to others in his or her grade level. Lower scores indicate deficits; higher scores indicate awareness and appropriateness of choices.

- **Career Decision Profile (CDP) -** an inventory composed of 16 questions with three scales, including a Decidedness scale (how clearly clients view their vocational plan), and a Comfort scale (how certain a client is of career choice). Both of these scales consist of two questions each, and have a response range from 1 (strongly disagree) to 8 (strongly agree), which means each scale score (Decidedness and Comfort) can range from 2 to 16. These first two scales can then yield four possible subtypes: decided-comfortable, decided-uncomfortable, undecided-comfortable and undecided-uncomfortable.

- **Career Decision Self-Efficacy Scale (CDSE).** The CDSE was created by Taylor and Betz (1983) to evaluate the degree of confidence a person voices in making career decisions. The 50-item CDSE Scale was developed from the Social Constructivist Career Theory. The CDSE Scale also includes questions that reflect the degree of confidence a person has in performing specific tasks that are associated with making career decisions. A short form (25 questions) has been developed and has strong psychometric properties. Individuals rate themselves on a scale of 1 (no confidence) to 5 (complete confidence). Watson (2013) provides a review of the CDSE.

- **Career Factors Inventory (CFI).** The CFI was developed by Chartrand, Robbins, and Morrill (1989) to provide a measure of self-identified difficulties that people experience when making career decisions. It is appropriate for high school students and beyond, and may help those considering a career change or a first career or unemployed persons seeking a job. The self-scorable CFI consists of 21 questions that are supposed to measure emotional and informational needs associated with making a career decision. It consists of two major scales, "Lack of Information or Self-Knowledge," which breaks into two subscales (Need for Career Information and Need for Self-Knowledge) and "Difficulty in Making Decisions," which also divides into two subscales (Career Choice Anxiety and Generalized Indecisiveness). A review of the CFI is provided by D'Costa (2013).

- **My Vocational Situation (MVS).** MVS (Holland, Daiger, & Power, 1980) is intended to measure the degree to which three factors— lack of vocational identity, lack of information or training, and barriers—might be affecting a person's ability to make an effective career decision. The Vocational Identity scale consists of 18 true/false items, such as "I don't know what my major strengths and weaknesses are." The "falses" are scored to produce a maximum score of 18. The higher the score is, the higher the level or the clearer the sense of a person's identity will be (Holland, Johnston, & Asama, 1993).

Summary

The concept of career development has evolved from developmental approaches to career guidance and career education programs. Several emerging career development inventories reflect a more inclusive approach to career development counseling. Inventories now include such factors as dysfunctional thinking, anxiety, and cognitive clarity. The current emphasis on assessing a person's level of career development includes examining potential and real obstacles or barriers that might hinder the career decision-making process and exploring the person's level of career maturity. Inventories provide a rich source of information from which counselors may build group and individual counseling programs.

Questions and Exercises

1. What are career decision inventories designed to measure?
2. Defend or criticize the following statement: Issues affecting career decidedness are limited and can be measured. Defend your position with illustrations.
3. At what stage in the career counseling process can career decision inventory results be used in career counseling programs? Illustrate with three examples.
4. How might you justify the use of a career development inventory to evaluate career education programs? Career counseling interventions?
5. What are the advantages of using questions taken directly from a career development inventory to stimulate group discussion? Are there any concerns about the reliability/validity of this issue that a counselor should consider?

6. How do career beliefs, career self-efficacy, or career thinking affect a person's decision-making ability?
7. Think of three creative ways to help clients reframe their negative career thoughts.
8. How might someone's culture or gender affect how that person scores on a career beliefs or decision making inventory?
9. Interview a counselor who uses one of the career development inventories reviewed in this chapter. What instrument does this counselor use? Why? How does he or she determine when it's appropriate, introduce it, score it, and go about interpreting it?
10. Annie has completed the Career Decision Profile. Her scores include:
    - Self-Clarity: 7
    - Knowledge About Occupations and Training: 6
    - Decisiveness: 15
    - Career Choice Importance: 15

    Based on these scores (refer back to the description of the CDP earlier in the chapter), how decided and comfortable would you say Sarah is with her career choice at this time? What do her subscale scores suggest? Which of the four groups (as described in the CDP section) is Sarah likely to fall into? What are the implications of that? What type of interventions or next steps might you recommend?
11. A client's CDS scores include Certainty = 2 and Indecision = 76. How would you interpret this person's scores? What does it say about his or her level of indecision and certainty? What next steps might you recommend?
12. A 16-year-old female has taken the CDSE-short form. The individual rates each item on a scale of one to five, with 1 being no confidence, and 5 being complete confidence. Each total subscale ranges from 5 to 25 points, and the total score can range from 25-125, with higher scores showing greater levels of career decision-making self-efficacy. This client's scores (along with the local means and standard deviations) are presented in Table 8-12.

Table 8-12: Sample CDSE Scores

	Client Score	Mean	Standard Deviation
Self-Appraisal	23	23.5	1.4
Gathering Occupational Information	19	24.1	.78
Goal Selection	15	23.9	1.4
Making Plans for the Future	12	18.2	5.2
Problem Solving	4	20.4	4.9
TOTAL	14.6	22.7	2.7

How would you interpret these results? What direct and indirect interventions might you employ?
13. A client has taken the CTI as part of a screening inventory. His raw score/percentile results include Total=78 (93rd percentile), DMC=22 (93rd percentile), CA=16 (73rd percentile), and EC=5 (79th percentile). How would you interpret these results if the client were a high school student? A college student? An adult? How would your interventions vary for each? If the scores were DMC at the 12th percentile, CA at the 50th percentile, and EC at the 80th percentile, how would you interpret the results? What cultural issues might be impacting the scores? What interventions might you make?
14. An individual facing a career transition takes the CASI. In reviewing the client's scores, the counselor notices that family commitment and career worries have the most "fours" circles. In addition, the individual has checked off appearance, lack of self-confidence, criminal record and emotional problem as career obstacles. How would you proceed with this client? Looking over the career obstacles listed, what type of interventions would you provide? Are there any career obstacles that you would want to refer to another counselor with specialties different from yours? How would you go about that?
15. Take some time and research the tenets of Super's theory of career maturity. After exploring the different tenets, consider the ACCI profile in Figure 8-2.

Figure 8-2: Sample ACCI Results

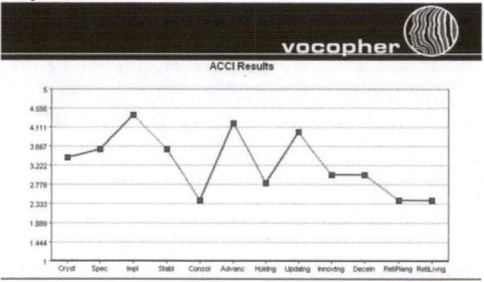

Adult Career Concerns Inventory. ACCI copyright by Vocopher 2005, reproduced by permission of Vocopher.com.

What might be the concerns of this 50-year old female? What would the next steps be?

16. Given the CDI profile in Figure 8-3, how would you summarize this high school student's career decision plans thus far? What interventions might you use? What recommendations might you make?

Figure 8-3: The Career Development Inventory

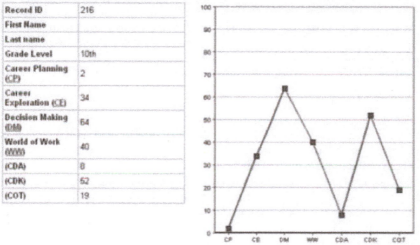

Career Development Inventory: High School, CDI copyright by Vocopher 2005, reproduced by permission of Vocopher.com.

147

CHAPTER 9

COMPUTER-ASSISTED CAREER GUIDANCE AND ONLINE ASSESSMENTS

In the last three decades, the use of computer-assisted career guidance systems (CACG) and online assessments has steadily increased. One of the primary reasons for the growth of computer-based assessment is that results are immediately available to clients. Also, with the explosion of Internet access, many so-called "tests" as well as career information and job searches are readily available with just a click of a mouse. Career counselors need to have an awareness of the technological and online career assessments – not only to help distance counseling clients but also for the face-to-face clients who may access these resources (Gati & Asulin-Peretz, 2011).

Advanced Organizer
In this chapter, we will discuss:
- Online Inventories versus Online Career Systems
- Ethical Issues with Computerized Assessments
- Using Computerized or Online Assessments in Career Counseling
- Other Types of Technological Assessments-Social Media, Apps and Games
- Review of Specific CACGS and Online Assessments
- Other CACGS and Online Assessments
- Summary
- Questions and Exercises

Online Inventories versus Online Career Systems

Career practitioners should understand the difference between an online version of an inventory and an online career system. An online inventory is somewhat static in nature. An individual completes the inventory by clicking a radial button or rating an item. A script in the program calculates scores for the total and for subscales, and a report is generated based on these results. The report may have hyperlinks in it that allow for further exploration of specific occupations. Some examples of online inventories that we have previously discussed are the Self-Directed Search, the Campbell Interest and Skill Survey, and the Career Decision-Making Profile. Also, many inventories, including paper/pencil, computerized and online, offer the client a website with extended information. A good example of this is the Kuder Career Planning System (Chapter 6). Once a client has completed one of the Kuder inventories, they have access to the Kuder site (www.kuder.com), and can use their results to identify various options, read daily articles, identify training opportunities, and learn about people who are in careers of interest.

An online career system tends to be more comprehensive and interactive. Gati and Asulin-Peretz (2011) state that online systems should go beyond ust having assessment results, and should provide an interpretation of these scores, as well as suggested interventions to help clients with difficulties. These systems usually include assessments of interests, values and skills, as well as an interactive component in which an individual can change their profile based on a combination of preferences. For example, a person may be able to create a profile and resulting list based off of his or her primary interest, top two values, and educational goals. In this way, that person is able to see how his or her ratings and choices impact the list of resulting occupations. CACGs are similar to online career systems and may be available online as well as in stand-alone mode within a career center computer lab. Examples of these online assessment systems and CACGs include Sigi3, Choices, Kuder Career Planning System, and MyPlan.

Because we have covered the computerized versions of specific inventories in previous chapters, this chapter will focus on CACGs and on online career assessment systems. But before we dive in, let's hear from one practitioner and how he uses one of these systems to help students with their career decision.

Typically college undergraduates and even some graduates students who I work with have difficulty identifying and developing career goals, or perhaps they have declared their academic major but have limited knowledge of what they can or would like to do through their major or still others I see have declared one major but realize that it was a mistake and are confounded by the prospect of choosing another. Many in this group are challenged by the task of identifying a particular area and occupation to pursue related to majors whether they are declared in management, sociology or philosophy. In addition to these students, I also make use of MyPlan when working with students who may have had little or no experience outside of a classroom, students who did not participate in extracurricular activities in high school or never held a summer job at the mall and are bewildered with the overwhelming prospect of choosing careers that will take them through the rest of of their lives.

I present MyPlan to my students as an option to consider and am very clear in telling students that in the end this tool may not provide a perfect solution to all their career planning problems but that it may expose them to a process of assessment, exploration and choice that could lead to their career satisfaction if they are willing to put time and effort into the process. If students agree to complete the online My Plan assessment I offer them a demonstration of what the results may look in the form of a sample version that I completed in advance. Within the sample is a personality profile summary that lists a detailed report on the four sections associated with the MBTI model that this test emulates. I also display the career match section which lists occupations that would be a good fit according to personality type which are arranged top to bottom by percentages of levels of satisfaction. One of the benefits associated with this instrument and the career match section is that it provides students with objective information on a variety of occupations, and the required qualifications, skills, knowledge, and salaries that are associated in a very concrete manner. Along with this list of occupations there is also an education section that allows students to select undergraduate as well as graduate level degrees which produces different sets of occupations to consider. I also review the results contained within the Interest section of My Plan which is drawn from the theoretical model established by John Holland who devised the RIASEC combination of career interests which range from Realistic to Investigative, Artistic, Social, Enterprising, and Conventional. This section provides a detailed numerical scoring on the interest types for each individual and is accompanied by a career match section that lists occupations that would satisfy interests from highest to lowest percentage levels. Following the Interest section, I display the Composite section which combines both Personality and Interests sections while yielding an additional list of occupations in the career match section that for some clients is the only section that they want to consider.

Once the students have been oriented on the instrument along with the nature of the results to be generated, I instruct them to complete the actual online version which consists of 70 questions per section and caution them to answer in genuine fashion or as I usually phrase it "go with your gut" when responding to the questions in order to illicit the most genuine and accurate results. Students complete the online assessment then return for a follow up session in order to go through the results of the assessment. While explaining the results within the Personality section I will and point out the strengths and weakness of their Personality type and how the strengths and weaknesses of an Introvert are related to careers and occupational exploration. While interpreting this information I also ask the students to raise questions or bring up any areas of disagreement with the results. Upon completion of the interpretation students are instructed to go through the information on their own and to eventually create a least occupations that appeal to them so that we might compare and contrast these occupations and eventually pare down their lists to an occupation or a series of occupations in a field such as marketing so that they might develop a more focused approach to selection of an academic major or to choose marketing research rather than brand management. There are also students who go through this assessment interpretation process and confirm the original ideas and plans that they brought with them in the first place. In the numerous interpretation sessions that I have administered using My Plan, I've come to see it as a multifaceted tool that introduces students to the concepts of self-awareness, insight reflection, and choice as well as the overarching concepts that are contained in the career development process. It has been used to help students choose careers and academic majors and has also been used to assist more experienced alumni clients in career transition as well.

Terry Dowling
Career Counselor, M.A.
Career Services
University of South Florida

Ethical Issues with Computerized Assessments

Chapter 4 includes a thorough discussion of ethical issues as related to computerized and online assessments. As a reminder, we will highlight a few specific guidelines to remember when using these types of assessments. First, career practitioners must be aware that validity of CACG assessment systems should meet the same set of standards used for other psychometric measures. For instance, the validity of scoring standardized instruments includes the weighting of items into scales and assurance of error-free scoring. However, errors in these two processes are difficult to identify in computer-based assessment. Thus, career service providers might not be aware of potential errors and subsequent misleading results.

Secondly, interpretive statements generated by computer-based testing systems should be carefully evaluated for their validity. One should request evidence that interpretative statements have been carefully evaluated and are indeed valid results that clients can fully understand and apply to their search processes. Other areas of concern include client privacy/confidentiality and client readiness to use online or computerized inventories.

Also, given that the Internet knows no geographical boundaries, online tests are available internationally. However, the same validation and reliability issues should apply for tests originating in one country that are used in another. For example, high internal consistency is a psychometric property which counselors should be considering when using any inventory, regardless of its origin. In addition, counselors should remember that educational systems, occupational structures and options that are available in America may not be available to clients in other countries. Use of these inventories in a culturally inappropriate way may raise false hopes and expectations, or increase career confusion.

Career counselors must also be ready to discuss printouts that a client may present from an online "test" that the client found. Ethically speaking, a career counselor should not try to interpret results of any inventory on which they have not been trained. Also, the career counselor should first investigate the test and the site for reliability and validity information. Some website may generate a code such as a RIASEC or MBTI code, but the tool wasn't one that was developed by the publisher. Career decisions have an impact on an individual's time, happiness, family and financial outcomes. Encouraging a client to make that decision based off of a questionable inventory is completely unethical.

Career service providers must insist that system developers and independent researchers meet the testing standards that have been clearly defined by the American Psychological Association, American Counseling Association, National Career Development Association, and the Alliance of Career Resource Professionals. Evidence of valid testing standards should be clearly delineated in promotional materials of CACGs and online assessments as well as in professional manuals. In general, counselors should examine evidence of reliability and validity of the system, how current and accurate the information is, any evidence of bias, the amount of support that is needed, and what confidential or personal information is requested and how profiles are scored (security). In addition, counselors should consider how ready an individual client is to use a CACG or online system before encouraging them to use one, as well as the fit between what the online system does and what the client needs. As with other instruments, if the counselor has not been trained on a CACG or online too, the counselor should not ask a client to complete it. Many other standards exist regarding the use of assessments, CACGS and online assessments, and counselors should take time to make sure that they understand and examine any tool they are using for evidence that these standards are upheld. Most standards are available online for free on the associations' websites.

Using Computerized or Online Assessments in Career Counseling

When a client expresses a desire to use a CACG, they have certain expectations about the outcomes, including increased career options, enhanced self-knowledge and strengthened occupational knowledge (Osborn, Peterson, Sampson & Reardon, 2003). If a career counselor approaches the use of a CACG or online assessment system within the decision making model presented in Chapter 1, specific components or modules of the system can be matched with the specific needs of the client.

When using a computerized assessment, there are three likely points of intervention: prior to system use, during system use, and following system use. Prior to system use, the counselor should provide an orientation to the computerized or online assessment. This orientation should include an overview of the system components, and the counselor should highlight which aspects of the system will address the client's stated needs. Other topics during orientation might include common keys/commands, how and what to print, and where to find help. Consider the interaction between a career advisor and Kwabena, who is planning to use a CACG outside of his session time with the advisor to see what occupations match his interests in the goal of finding a major that relates. The advisor pulls up the website and also hands Kwabena a paper that has several screenshots on it.

ADVISOR: So, Kwabena, let me show you some of the basics of the website so you'll know what to expect when you get home. As you can see, there are buttons here that are links to the different aspects of the program that might interest you. Here's the self-assessment link, and when we click on it, you can see that it allows you to answer questions on your interests, values and skills. You can choose to complete any or all of these, but it seemed like in our conversations that what was most important to you was finding a career that was related to your skills.

KWABENA: Yes, I want to be in a career that uses my skills. I figure, if I'm good at something, I'll probably be interested in it as well.

ADVISOR: Has that been your experience?

KWABENA: For the most part. There are some things I do well, like singing, but that's not a skill I want to use in my career. Then there's typing. I can type really fast, but I don't want to be sitting all day behind a computer.

ADVISOR: But is it possible that there are careers out there that might use that skill in a way that would interest you?

KWABENA: I guess so – and I guess that there may be jobs out there that use the skills that I have in ways that wouldn't be interesting to me.

ADVISOR: I agree. The point is that you don't want to eliminate any choices prematurely. Perhaps you want to start with the abilities section and see what occupations are suggested. If you don't like the list, or if the list is still too long, consider doing one of the other sections. It would be interesting to see where the overlaps occur.

KWABENA: That sounds reasonable to me. So I start with the assessment section?

ADVISOR: You could. That seems like a logical place to begin. However, you did say that you were interested in learning more about mechanical engineering. See the link on careers? You could start with that section and get some information about that career. (Advisor clicks on the link to demonstrate). See when you scroll down, it has other occupations that are similar? You could start exploring by choosing occupations and seeing what's related to them. There's really no wrong way to go about this.

KWABENA: So what do you want me to bring back to you when we meet?

ADVISOR: It'd be helpful for me to see the results of your assessment or assessments, or your summary profile and the list of occupations those results generate. Aside from those, you can bring back whatever printout you would like to discuss. If you can focus this week on the assessment piece and start narrowing down the list of options, next week when we meet we can pick up where you leave off, and discuss the next step. Pay attention as you go through the careers to the types of majors that are required for those careers you like. You may find some overlap.

A counselor might also intervene during system use. Of course, this is only possible if the person is completing the CACG in a location where the counselor is present, or if the person is completing the activity remotely but sending the counselor updates after each section. It is a good idea to check with clients at least once during their interaction with the CACG to address any frustrations, misperceptions, or to allow them to talk about their experience thus far. Social types, for example, may be very excited to share what they have learned about themselves, or the occupations generated. Consider this example, where Krystle has been working on a CACG in the computer lab within a career center for about 30 minutes. The career advisor comes in to check on her.

ADVISOR: Hi. I wanted to see how it's going.

KRYSTLE: I think it's going well. I have finished taking the values sort.

ADVISOR: How was that for you?

KRYSTLE: It was harder than I thought it would be. I guess I was a little too picky in the beginning. I rated everything as being "Essential," but the computer wouldn't let me do that. I had to go back and really think about what I wanted in work. I mean, I really want it all.

ADVISOR: Do you think it's possible to have it all in a job?

KRYSTLE: Evidently not! (laughing) I see why I need to figure out what I must absolutely have. If I'm interviewing for a job, and it doesn't have everything I want, I should know before going in what isn't negotiable, what I must have in order to be happy.

ADVISOR: That makes sense. You need to know what really is essential for your happiness in a job. So where are you now?

KRYSTLE: I was just starting to look at the occupations. I see some here that I want to learn more about.

ADVISOR: OK. Well, I was just checking to see how things are going. I'm right outside if you need me.

151

KRYSLE: Sounds good.

Following system use, a career practitioner might proceed in the following way:

1. Ask the client about their interaction with the system. What was their experience, their reactions to the way the system work, and their satisfaction with what they found?
2. Have the client read through the results and highlight descriptors and/or occupations that are of particular interest.
3. Ask the client to talk about how the descriptors relate to what she or he already knew about her or himself, what new knowledge was found, and how that relates to the career decision being made.
4. Move on to the list of highlighted occupations, and have the client describe what is appealing about each of those occupations. The counselor may choose to take notes or write on the report beside each of the highlighted options.
5. Compare the reasons given for liking specific occupations to determine themes and further clarify self-knowledge, e.g., "It's really important to you that your career choice offers you opportunities for advancement and independence."
6. Determine next steps. Review the model for using assessments, and the purpose for using this particular assessment. Was the stated need met completely, partially or not at all? Were additional needs discovered (e.g., a need for information about training opportunities or scholarships) during the process? Is a different assessment or a follow-up activity on the system warranted? What will help the client move towards making the career decision?

Consider the example below.

ADVISOR: So, Ricky, tell me about what that was like for you.
RICKY: It was interesting. I didn't do everything on there, but I spent some time doing the self-assessment. Here's my list.
ADVISOR: (Glancing at the list) What did you think of these?
RICKY: Well, I was surprised that it suggested for me to be a curator. I don't like going to museums. I'd much rather be outside. Why would it say that?
ADVISOR: Well, remember that the purpose of these types of tools is to expand your options, not to narrow it down to the perfect career for you. It's just making suggestions of possible occupations based on the information that you gave it.
RICKY: So it's saying that I'm secretly interested in being a curator?
ADVISOR: No, just that your interests and skills match up with some of the activities that curators do. There are many things involved in deciding whether or not a career is the right one for you. I think what you brought up is a good example for evaluating the careers on this list. Have you ever shown any interest in your leisure time in activities related to these careers? If not, it could be that this isn't the best choice for you. At the same time, it could be that this is something you haven't considered, but that might be worth at least taking a look at. Why eliminate an option? For example, you seem to want to delete curator from the list. How come?
RICKY: Because their job is boring. They lead tours of elementary kids and do the same job day after day. Plus, I want to be outside, and they are always stuck inside a museum.
ADVISOR: Let's think about what you said here and critically analyze it. Where did you get the information you just shared?
RICKY: OK, I guess I got it from watching movies. But you have to agree, most curators are inside.
ADVISOR: I would assume that's probably true – but I don't know that the other pieces are true. Don't volunteers lead the tours? I don't know that curators do the same thing day after day. Some may even travel to determine whether or not to purchase an item for their museum. The truth is, I haven't researched what curators do, and I haven't interviewed one to find out about what a typical day is like for them.
RICKY: So you're saying my perception is biased?
ADVISOR: A bit. Some of it is probably true, some of it isn't. The main point to me is that I would hate to see you shut the door on an option that could be really exciting and satisfying to you just because you have a bias towards it. You're making an important career decision here, and about to invest several years in training for that career. Personally, I think you owe it to yourself to at least investigate it a little more, and only close the door once you have enough information to be pretty sure that the option isn't for you.
RICKY: I suppose that makes sense.

152

ADVISOR:	So, you've completed this step. There are many ways to approach making a career decision. You could do another assessment, or spend some time researching some of these careers. What would you like to do?
RICKY:	I think I'd like to take these printouts home and think about them some. Maybe I can start narrowing down my list. Two pages of occupations are just too much to think about!
ADVISOR:	I hear you. Let me give you a couple of websites that have information on occupations. Start with O*NET (writing the url on Ricky's printout) and use that to narrow down your list.

In this example, the advisor was able to offer a gentle confrontation about elimination options prematurely. It's also very important that the advisor did not immediately dismiss the results generated by the system. In this case, the advisor demonstrated a balanced response between supporting the client's experience and/or emotional reaction and describing how the system works. In the last part of the conversation, the advisor sent a message to Ricky that showed a belief in Ricky's ability to make a good decision, and also showed a willingness to support the plan that Ricky came up with by giving him a tool (i.e., O*NET) to help him accomplish that plan.

Other Types of Technological Assessments-Social Media, Apps and Games

With the improvement of technology has also come an explosion of new possibilities for career assessments. Social media sites such as Facebook regularly have online "tests" that tell users careers they should follow. Many career assessment publishers have LinkedIn groups, and professional groups on LinkedIn or Twitter may host discussions about how to use a certain inventory. Test publishers are now providing trainings via blogs, webcasts and YouTube channels. In addition, social media sites such as Pinterest, Vine, Instagram and even blogs can provide snapshots or even whole albums about a person's interests, skills, values and personality.

We've introduced the idea of shared folders such as through Google Drive or Dropbox. While this would not be for taking an assessment, this could allow the results of the assessment to be shared between the counselor and the client, as well as additional resources, Web links, and other related information (such as the client's resume). A counselor would need to be careful to make sure that the confidentiality of the client's records are secure. For example, if you share an office with someone or use your laptop (with client files saved on it) at home and at work, you'd want to make sure no one could access those files.

Another area of explosion are apps. At this point, it's unlikely to see validated career inventories that link to occupations as an app. There are a few out there, but the ratings are low. Most people want to download an app with the hope of being able to use it multiple times. How many times would you want to re-take a career inventory? That being said, having an app for a CACG or interactive website where you can toggle between your assessment results and occupational information, portfolio, educational opportunities, and so forth, might be an app that people would be interested in seeing. More likely are apps to help address issues like cognitive restructuring for negative thinking, or general apps like Oprah's "Unstuck" app that help with decision-making.

Do you want to play a career game? That doesn't sound very fun, does it? And yet, people are playing games that simulate living all the time. Three career games that are online currently include realgame.com, driveofyourlife.com, and Sims 3 Ambitions. Webkinz is a popular online children's game in which the characters have to take on different jobs to earn money to buy clothes and food for their pets. There hasn't been any research to examine the impact of playing these or other games on career decision-making, but the research may be just around the corner.

Review of Specific CACGS and Online Systems

The format for the tables in this chapter will vary for each system being reviewed because of the unique features of these systems. For example, the Career Key is an instrument that has been researched for its psychometric properties. In discussions with some of the CACG developers, the emphasis of these systems was not on the psychometric properties of the instrument, but on the entire system. They do not claim to have reliability or validity, but the purpose is to provide a starting place for exploration. They are set up more as a learning tool instead of prescriptive assessment. For example, an individual might indicate a primary interest in careers that involve helping. Once that selection is made, the person sees that the original list of 500 occupations has been reduced to 267. The person makes another selection, perhaps this time from a values portion of the CACG, and the list is narrowed down to three. So, the person re-adjusts that ranking from *Essential* to *Preferred* and sees that the occupational list increases back to 20 occupations. This type of flexibility in the system makes calculating reliability and validity virtually impossible. Still, if an inventory is used as part of the CACG or online system, the developers should seek and provide such information.

Career Key is the first CACG system we'll review. Basic information on Career Key is included below in Table 9-1.

Table 9-1: The Career Key

Copyright Date	2011
Website Mission	**www.careerkey.org** We strive to be the nation's source for professional help in making career and educational choices -- affordable to all.
Website Sections	• Matching personality with careers, career clusters/pathways, college major or training program, and green jobs • Career advice on various topics including military transition • College major match • Major & training match
Appropriate Age Range	Middle school to adult
Reliability/Validity	Internal Consistencies (KR20's) ranging from .69 to .92 for the six scales, with a mean of. 74. Test-retest correlations (3 weeks) averaged .82. Another study (Levinson, Zeman, & Ohler, 2002) showed retest reliability ranging from .75 to .94. Comparison with other Holland type inventories has shown a "reasonable match" between types. One study showed similar outcomes among the Career Key and 2 other measures (Jones, Sheffield, & Joyner, 2000). Levinson, Zeman, & Ohler, 2002 cited a validity coefficient above .65.
Interpretation	After the person completes the Career Key inventory, the computer scores the responses and creates a brief profile, indicating the scores (a three-letter code is not calculated). The person can then choose to see occupations that match his or her highest scored type.
Research/Reviews	Levinson, Zeman, and Ohler (2002)

Case of a Determined Middle-Schooler

A middle-schooler walked into his counselor's office one day, asking for a career test. He wanted to see what occupations might fit his personality and to learn about those occupations. Unfortunately, the computers at the middle school did not have the memory needed to run career programs. The counselor suggested the student visit the local library, access the Career Key on the Internet, and then make an appointment with her to discuss the results. After the student returned from the library with his printouts, he made an appointment with the counselor.

COUNSELOR: Tell me about your experience at the library.

MATIAS: Well, the librarian showed me how to get on the Web, and from there, it was pretty easy. I took the Career Key and it showed me that my main group is Realistic.

COUNSELOR: What does that mean to you?

MATIAS: Well, it means that I like to do things with my hands, and I like to see things happen. It's neat, because that's what my dad and grandpa are into as well.

COUNSELOR: And what about the occupations it suggested?

MATIAS: They seemed OK. After I got my list, I picked some careers that really looked good to me, and when I clicked on them, it took me to another area that told all about them. It was neat.

COUNSELOR: Well, where do you think you want to go from here?

MATIAS: Right now, I think I want to keep going with this hands-on stuff. I really like it, and I think I'm good at it, too. So, I guess for my elective, I'm going to look at mechanics, shop, or maybe computers. I'm gonna talk with my Dad as well about maybe helping out in the shop, too.

In this case, the use of the Career Key helped Matias to learn about his personality, as well as occupations of interest, and to make some educational plans to further clarify that knowledge. Through talking with his counselor, Matias also realized some common interests he shared with other family members, and created an opportunity for him to learn hands-on through his network. Counselors who suggest an Internet tool should be familiar with it and be willing to help the client interpret and use the results. Finally, career practitioners who are interested in learning more about using the Internet in career counseling and advising are referred to *The Internet: A Tool For Career Planning*, available from the National Career Development Association.

The next system we will review is CHOICES. Basic information on CHOICES is presented in Table 9-2.

Table 9-2: CHOICES

Website Mission	**https://access.bridges.com** CHOICES helps clients explore their options for work and education.
Website Sections	Work Learn Assessments: Interest Profiler, Basic Skills Survey (based on the 10 O*NET basic skills), Workplace Skills Checklist, Work Values Sorter (based on the Minnesota Importance Questionnaire), Transferable Skills Checklist, Ability Profiler (optional add-on), Do What You Are (optional add-on), and Learning Style Inventory (optional add-on). FAQ Spanish version Search Tools: Career Finder, School Finder, Scholarship Finder, Cluster Finder, Guide ways, Course Plan Builder, Portfolios
Appropriate Age Range	Middle school through adult
Reliability/Validity	Online documents describe the process of developing the assessments. Internal consistency for the Interest Profiler was reported at .93-.96, and test-retest reliability ranged from .91 to .92.

Case of a Client with Time Constraints

Myra, a 37-year-old architect, has begun to consider a career change. "I like the creativity and seeing my ideas being transformed into reality, but I'm starting to grow tired of all the legal aspects that I have to work around, and the demands of customers. I'd like to find a job that would incorporate my creativity and something hands-on, but with less contact with people."

After talking with Myra, her counselor decided that she might benefit from taking a values inventory and an interest inventory.

COUNSELOR: After we see where your main values and interests lie, we can then see what occupations use your preferred values and interests. It would also be helpful for you to read about some of the occupations that emerge, as well as reorganizing your résumé and brushing up on interview skills.

MYRA: I think all of that's important, but it seems like it will take a lot of time—and that's one thing I don't have a lot of right now. I can barely find the time for my session with you, much less to be thumbing around on a computer or making appointments to talk with other people, unless they're willing to meet later at night or on the weekends.

COUNSELOR: I may have a solution that will help. We have an online program called CHOICES that has several assessments and links to occupations that are easily researchable. Do you think you would have time to take the Interest Profiler prior to our next session?

MYRA: I think so. I may be able to do more than one.

COUNSELOR: Well, why don't we start there? You can go further if you have time, but if not, we'll just pick up where you left off.

In this case, CHOICES was an excellent option for this client as it allowed her to complete the assessment at home in her own leisure. The counselor made sure to give Myra a handout outlining the basic functions of CHOICES, and highlighting which sections would most likely be of most use to her.

Next, we will examine the Kuder Career Planning System (KCPS). Information on the KPCS is presented in Table 9-3.

Table 9-3: Kuder Career Planning System

Website Mission	**www.kuder.com** Kuder Career Planning System offers innovative and comprehensive educational and career planning for all levels of involvement – elementary, middle school, high school, postsecondary, adults, and parents.
Website Sections	Navigator (middle through high school) • Learn About Myself (Kuder Career

	Search with Person Match,
	• Kuder Skills Assessment, Super's Work Values Inventory)
	• Explore Options
	• Plan for Education
	• My Portfolio
	• Plan for Work (9th-12th grade)
	• Find a Job (9th-12th grade)
	Journey (college and adult)
	• Assessments
	• Occupations
	• Majors
	• Education & Financial Aid
	• Job Search Tools
	• Jobs
	• My Portfolio
Appropriate Age Range	Middle school to adult; Kuder Galaxy system is available for elementary (focusing on exploration, not assessments)
Reviews/Research	Schenk (2009); Zytowski (2001); Zytowski and Luzzo (2002)

Case of a Person Needing to Reinvent Herself

Marty is a 52-year-old woman who, during tough economic times, was let go of her job in pharmaceutical sales. She had been very successful financially in her career, making a six-figure salary. She had secured several interviews for similar positions, but no job offers. She believed that her number of years of experience plus her previous salary were costing her job offers as employers sought younger sales reps whom they could pay a great deal less. She has come to career counseling to explore what other options might be available to her using her existing skills. She is realistic about her salary, realizing that she will likely need to take a significant cut in pay, at least temporarily.

MARTY:	It's not that I don't want to go back to school – I'm open to that, but I'd first like to see what options are out there that may not require retraining. I've thought of a few positions, but I'd like to have more options on my plate. Maybe I'm overlooking some careers that might be just as fun as pharmaceutical sales that use my skills, but that I don't know about.
COUNSELOR:	So, you are open to going back to school, but first you'd like to see what other careers match with the skills and experiences you currently have?
MARTY:	Yes. Do you have a test or something that I could take to see what might match up with my skills?
COUNSELOR:	We have several different inventories available, but I'm thinking you might particularly enjoy the Kuder Career Planning System and Career Journey. It's an online system that you can complete at home, and utilizes interest, skills and values inventories that are well-researched. Plus, the system saves your assessments results into a personal portfolio. That way you can keep track of your results and explore occupations easier.
MARTY:	That's good to know. I searched for career tests online and came up with hundreds. Some of them were obviously very low quality, but others – I couldn't tell whether I should be making a decision based on the results or not.
COUNSELOR:	That's true. I'm glad you were able to see that when you searched. There are definitely some factors to keep in mind when looking at career-related websites, whether for career testing or career information or job searching. First and foremost, you want to know that the information is valid and reliable. The information should come from a trustworthy source. I have a handout on how to evaluate online career sites. Would you be interested in having a copy of that?
MARTY:	Oh, yes. I'm sure that will come in handy, especially as I get more into this.
COUNSELOR:	(Handing her the information) There are other tools in the Kuder Journey as well that you might find interesting. I'll give you some basic information on it, and feel free to explore any area that you think would be helpful, but if you could focus on the assessment section

156

and start looking at the person-career matches, that will give us a good starting point for our next session.

In this case, the Kuder Career Planning System was perfectly matched with the client's needs. She wanted to see how her skills might be used in different ways, and by seeing the profiles of people who matched her characteristics, she could learn about what some of the pros and cons might be of those jobs and decide whether or not to continue to consider that occupation.

The next system we will examine is MyPlan. Basic information on MyPlan is presented in Table 9-4.

Table 9-4: MyPlan

Website Mission	www.myplan.com helps students and professionals plan more fulfilling lives by making well-informed decisions about their education and careers.
Website Sections	**Careers**-career database with over 900 careers, video library of about 500 careers, salary calculator, top ten lists, career community, industry, and online resources. **Assessment**-career personality test, career interest inventory, career skills profiler, career values assessment, career match (see careers that match assessment results) **Colleges**-college database, college resources (college rankings, famous alumni directory, financial aid guide, college media library, college community, college resource center) **Majors** – college majors database, what can I do with a major in?, top ten lists, majors community, majors & degree resource center
Appropriate Age Range	College
Reviews/Research	None found

Case of a Dabbling Designer

Shanté remembers being interested in design since she was a young child. She loved dressing up dolls, and finding scraps from her mothers' quilts to create new designs. As she grew, she found herself watching TV shows about all kinds of design – architecture, landscape, cakes, and interior – but her favorite was always the shows about costumes and fashion. She loved watching the fashion award shows as well as shows about what you shouldn't wear. She was the person her family and friends went to when they weren't sure about an outfit, and Shanté was well known for having the PERFECT accessory for any outfit. So, when she got to college, everyone was surprised that she didn't immediately declare fashion design as her major.

COUNSELOR:	So, it seems like, from what you've told me, that everyone is surprised – even you're surprised – that you weren't the first one to sign up for fashion design.
SHANTÉ:	Yes, I am, too. I mean, I love it, but everything I've seen on TV about the lives of fashion designers seems like it's not me.
COUNSELOR:	What do you mean?
SHANTÉ:	Well, they're running all over the place with high stress all the time, and I'm not like that. I like to be still and think through my designs. Also, a lot of them are always blaming others for when their designs don't do well, and to me, I'm going to take responsibility for my designs, for better, or for worse. That's really important to me, but I guess it's not a big deal to them.
COUNSELOR:	I see. What do you think the chances are that most fashion designers are similar to the ones you see on TV?
SHANTÉ:	Probably pretty slim.
COUNSELOR:	There's probably some truth in it, but remember that the goal of these shows is to have viewers, so they'll probably ramp things up a bit to keep the viewers interested. It sounds like you're interested in seeing if what's important to you is similar to what's important to fashion designers.
SHANTÉ:	Is there a way I can find that out?
COUNSELOR:	Well, you can always ask different fashion designers about their values, but it's probably useful to first know what your own values are, and then you can see how well they match up with those of fashion designers. We actually have a system here called MyPlan that will let you compare your values to those of fashion designers.
SHANTÉ:	Sounds great!

The counselor reviewed the overall system with Shanté, but encouraged her to focus on the values career assessment and the match. She decided to compare her values to those of fashion designers. Those results are presented in Figure 9-1. She and the counselor reviewed the results at their next meeting.

Figure 9-1: Sample My Plan Values Comparison

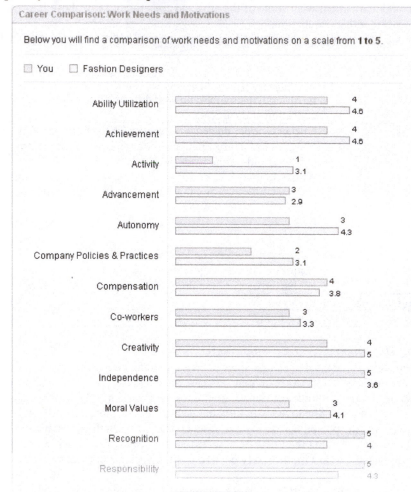

COUNSELOR: So what did you think of the comparison?

SHANTÉ: It was interesting. I guess I'm closer to fashion designers than I originally thought. There weren't a lot of perfect matches, though.

COUNSELOR: There aren't usually, but like you said, there isn't a lot of spread between your scores and theirs – mostly a point or less a part. So what do you think would be a reasonable next step?

Together, they brainstormed how Shanté could use social media to connect with fashion designers that were near to her geographically as well as doing the type of work she wanted to do. She decided she would ask them questions related to her strongest values to see how much discrepancy was between hers and theirs. As a first year student, she still had plenty of time to declare a major, so she decided to hold off on declaring, and to spend her time developing her network of fashion designers, researching the field other occupations that were generated in the MyPlan match that seemed to be better fits with her profile.

The final system we will be reviewing is SIGI3. Information about SIGI3 is presented in Table 9-5.

Table 9-5: System of Integrated Guidance and Information (SIGI3)

Website Mission	**sigi4.org** Valparint: To help students and other job seekers create a plan that's right for them.
Website Sections	• My Stuff (results from SIGI3): Portfolio, bookmarks, usage summary • Assessments: Values, Interests, Personality, Skills, FastStart (see all factors at once)

158

	• Job comparison
	• Occupational Information
	• Analysis (Skills Check, Preparing, Deciding)
	• Getting There (Coping, Next Steps, Résumé Basics, School Search, Military Careers)
	• Additional Resources (Find Employers, SAT/ACT/GRE Prep)
Appropriate Age Range	High school to adult
Reviews/Research	Lokan and Fleming (2003)

Case of an Occupation Explorer

Eugene wanted to see what occupations might be "good" for him. After talking with a counselor, Eugene agreed that SIGI3 might be a good place to start to help him organize information about himself and to generate some new options. Through Self-Assessment, Eugene learned that the values of security and independence were essential to him in his job. During Search, he identified occupations related to his major (English) and occupations that matched his two highest values, which were Variety (Essential) and Independence (Very Important). Once he had his list of occupations, he met with the counselor to discuss the options on his list. He went through his printout and crossed through the options that "just weren't him." The counselor asked him to go back through the ones he'd crossed out and discuss the reasons he crossed them off the list. The counselor wrote down the reasons and kept track of those that Eugene repeated.

The counselor then asked Eugene what he thought he needed to help him narrow down his options. Eugene stated that he needed to learn more about the occupations that were left on his list. He returned to SIGI3 and used the Information, Preparing, and Next Steps sections. At that point, he and the counselor created a plan of activities to help him decide among his options.

Eugene used information in the career center and narrowed his list to five options. At that point, he decided to meet with people who were involved in those five occupational fields to get a personal flavor of what each was like. The counselor encouraged Eugene to ask questions that were reflective of his values, such as, "It's important to me to have a great deal of variety on the job. How much variety do you have in your position?"

After the interviews, Eugene had narrowed his options to two and decided to revisit SIGI3 again. He used the Deciding section, which allowed him to weigh the pros and cons of each of his options. SIGI3 provided a framework for helping Eugene learn about himself, expand his career options, and focus on the occupations that most reflected his values.

Other CACGS and Online Assessments

In addition to the CACGS and Online Assessments reviewed in the chapter, several other systems are described briefly in this section. The reader should note that sites and links change frequently.

- **Career Cruising** (www.careercruising.com). For use in the United States and Canada, includes interest assessments, occupation profiles, multimedia informational interviews, portfolio tools and information on education.
- **CareerStorm Navigator** (http://www.careerstorm.com). From Finland, utilizes four assessments (interests, skills, style, values) to help clients map out a career path after exploring options.
- **Making Better Career Decisions (MBCD).** An Internet-based career planning system, available at mbcd.intocareers.org, created by Gati at the Hebrew University. The 90-minute assessment (called a "dialogue") results in a listing of potential occupations and majors for further exploration. Gati, Kleiman, Saka and Zakai (2003) reported that the MBCD increased decidedness for about half of 712 participants.
- **MySkills MyFuture** (www.myskillsmyfuture.org). This is a career one-stop site developed by the U.S. Department of Labor Employment and Training Administration to help job seekers find new options based on experiences and skills. An individual enters a job title into the search box (recommended to use the job in which the person has the most experience) to see a list of careers and job listings that use similar skills and knowledge similar to the job entered.
- **O*NET Inventories.** This website (http://www.onetcenter.org/tools.html) includes links to the following career exploration tools: O*NET Ability Profiler, Interest Profiler, Computerized Interest Profiler, Work Importance Locator and Work Importance Profiler.
- **Vocopher.** A professional website for researchers and counselors, available at www.vocopher.com. The site currently houses several versions of the Career Development Inventory, the Adult Career Concerns Inventory and the Career Maturity Inventory.

Summary

In this chapter, we explored the use of CACGS and online assessments as viable tools in counseling. CACGS allow individuals to quickly expand their career options by seeing what occupations "match" their values, interests, and skills. As with any psychometric instrument, a practitioner should be familiar with the different components a CACG or Internet assessment offers and should take all associated assessments before asking a client to do the same. CACGS and websites can hold immense amounts of data about occupations. The counselor must help clients make sense of the data and use the data in a way that helps the client progress toward his or her career goals. Finally, the counselor should be knowledgeable of the ethical issues involved with CACG and Internet career testing as well as using online information.

Questions and Exercises

1. A woman trying to choose a career path comes to you with her printout of occupations. How do you proceed?
2. What are the pros and cons associated with having a client use a CACG or online assessment versus a traditional paper/pencil interest inventory? Versus a non-standardized approach?
3. What would you say to a person who came to your counseling office and said, "I heard there was a computer that will tell me what I should be?"
4. What types of client characteristics might suggest that a CACG or online career testing are not appropriate tools?
5. Suppose your organization is thinking about purchasing a new CACG. Create a plan for selecting, implementing and evaluating the new system.
6. Consider that a client is undecided about her career path. Choose one of the computerized programs reviewed in this chapter and go to its website to see a sitemap of the system. Create at least two different possible ways she might use the site to help her with the decision. How would these plans compare to the other systems?
7. A client has completed the Making Better Career Decisions online inventory. Her results are presented in Figure 9-2.

Figure 9-2: Sample MBCD Results

= Your preferred level
= Your acceptable levels

Wages	$5,000	$4,000	$3,000	$2,000	Minimum
Your Choice					

Problem solving	A great deal		Somewhat		Hardly ever
Your Choice					

Education and training	5+ Years	4 Years	2-3 Years	4-12 Months	0-3 Months
Your Choice					

Teach	A great deal		Somewhat		Hardly ever
Your Choice					

Advise	A great deal		Somewhat		Hardly ever
Your Choice					

Artistic	A great deal		Somewhat		Hardly ever
Your Choice					

Flexible hours	A great deal		Somewhat		Hardly ever
Your Choice					

Variety	A great deal		Somewhat		Hardly ever
Your Choice					

Communicate	A great deal		Somewhat		Hardly eve Unaccep
Your Choice					

Supervise	A great deal		Somewhat		Hardly ever
Your Choice					

Indoors or outdoors	Outdoors		Both		Indoors
Your Choice					

How would you go about interpreting her results? What's most important to her? What do her results suggest about her work preferences? As she entered in preferences, the MBCD narrowed her list down to those presented in Figure 9-3. What questions would you ask to help her process her results?

Figure 9-3: Sample MBCD Occupational List

View Occupations On Your List

The occupations matching your preferences are listed below. Click on ▦ to see how your preferences match the occupation's requirements. Click on the occupation title to view a complete description.

Compare Occupations ▦
Stage Three Options ◉

Number of occupations on your list: 10

Occupations On Your List

Animators and Multimedia Artists ▦
Archeologists ▦
Geographers ▦
Landscape Architects ▦
Mental Health Counselors ▦
Naturopathic Physicians ▦
Political Scientists ▦
Sociologists ▦
Urban and Regional Planners ▦
Web Developers ▦

8. A student has come to you for help in making a career choice. He is a member of the 4-H club, volunteers for a charity that builds homes for disadvantaged people, and enjoys drawing, especially during his business class. While working on Career Targets within COINJR, the counselor comes by and sees that the student has highlighted two career clusters, Business/Finance and Education & Training. Based on the career clusters, how would you characterize this student's interests? What occupations might link with his interests? What advice might you give this student in narrowing down his options? What type of counseling interventions would you make with this student that would help him progress? What type of interventions would coincide with his interests? How would your counseling style change? What other information would you like to have about this student?

9. Jason has completed the Values game of SIGI3. His *essential* values were High Income, Security and Flexible Hours. He rated Staying Put and Contribution to Society as *not important.* How would you proceed in advising/counseling Jason? What would your next steps be as his counselor? What types of rewards are likely to motivate for him on the job? What types of jobs might be a good match for someone with these values? Are any of the values likely to conflict?

10. A middle-school student completes the Career Key. His highest scores are Investigative (16), Artistic (9) and Realistic (7). What does this suggest about his interests and possible careers of interest? What next steps might you recommend?

11. Figure 9-4 shows a sample report for a person who has completed the SIGI3 Values assessment. How would you proceed with this individual? With what types of positions would this individual most likely be satisfied? What advice would you have for this individual if she or he were in high school or college and had a couple of years left before graduating?

Figure 9-4: Sample SIGI3 Values Report

Values FAQs Job Search	Results
Contribution to Society	1
High Income	2
Independence	E
Leadership	2
Leisure	2
Prestige	2
Security	2
Variety	1
Ratings: 1 - Not Important 2 - Desirable	3 - Very Important E - Essential

12. If you have an existing social media website, look over the pictures and videos you've posted within the last month. What do these suggest about your personality, interests, and so forth? If you haven't used one of these tools, consider creating one. You could focus it on the present, or also have separate boards or albums for your past, your present and future/dreams.

CHAPTER 10

CARD SORTS AND OTHER NON-STANDARDIZED APPROACHES IN CAREER COUNSELING

Having clients identify occupational likes and dislikes does not always require paper and pencil. The hands-on approach of sorting cards into various piles or constructing a collage offers a nice alternative to traditional testing approaches. Given that clients might not prefer to engage in "testing" (Galassi, Crace, Martin, James & Wallace, 1992), the card sort might be a more innocuous way to help clients organize their thoughts about interests, skills, values, occupations, or other issues. Interventions such as card sorts, ideal days and the like are typically not seen or interpreted as standardized instruments but are more often pictures that are symbolic of a client's thought process and, more specifically, about perceptions of careers and work. In this chapter, we will explore the use of card sorts and other non-standardized approaches that are designed to help clients learn more about themselves, their options, and the way they make career decisions.

Advanced Organizer

In this chapter, we will cover:

- Description of Card Sorts
- Using Non-Standardized Self-Assessment Inventories
- Other Non-Standardized Approaches
- Summary
- Questions and Exercises

Description of Card Sorts

What are card sorts? At their simplest, they are exactly how they sound – they are cards made out of a thick material (like card stock) that a client then sorts into different piles. The cards can be any shape, size or color, although most are similar to playing cards in shape. Figure 10-1 gives an example of some simple looking cards in an occupational card sort.

Figure 10-1: Sample of Simple Occupational Cards

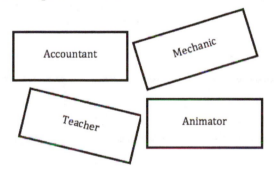

Usually, a word representing an occupation, interest, hobby/leisure activity, value, skills, etc., is typed on one side of the card. The back of the card may have a description of the occupation or word. Other information might include Holland type, salary, or training required. For other samples of card sorts created by students, see http://careerresource.coedu.usf.edu/linkteachingtools/ExamplesofLessonPlans.htm.

Advantages and Disadvantages of Card Sorts

Card sorts have many advantages for the career counseling process, but also have disadvantages that should be considered (see Table 10-1).

Table 10-1 Advantages and Disadvantages of Card Sorts

Advantages
• Immediacy of results—no waiting for a printout or return profile (Crouteau & Slaney, 1994)
• Client sees a connection between their results and the decisions they made during the sort, validating the exploration process (Osborn & Bethell, 2010)
• The client is in obvious control of how she or he organizes his or her perception of the

world of work (Hartung, 1999)

- Client is actively engaged in producing, monitoring, and evaluating the results (Slaney & MacKinnon-Slaney, 1990)
- Assessment and counseling become more seamless with increased collaboration, and the counselor can help the client explore why he or she placed in the occupations in a certain pile (Goldman, 1995)
- Clients have often been stimulated to openly express and evaluate their preferences when sorting and during the discussion of results
- When used with other standardized assessments, can enhance the career counseling process by providing subjective information that complements and serves as a framework for the objective results
- Flexibility of the card sort approach (Able to sort in different ways with diverse clients)
- Inexpensive
- Instructions easy to follow
- Card sorts can be created by the counselor and made specific to the client's interests such as medical careers or scientific careers (Osborn & Bethell, 2010)

Disadvantages

- Lack of research proving reliability or validity
- Because card sorts are not high tech, they may be seen by clients as unsophisticated or a waste of time
- While there are basic approaches to interpreting card sort results, results are never predictable, and thus the counselor may feel stuck on how to proceed when the sort is completed.
- In most cases, there is no report generated, so the counselor or client must record the results for future reference.

Basic Instructions

The basic instructions for an occupational card sort are as follows:

1. Clients are first instructed to sort the cards into three piles under the headings "Would Not Choose," "Would Choose," and "No Opinion." Other headers might range from "Not like me at all" to "Exactly like me," or from "Extremely Important to me" to "Not at all important."
2. Clients are instructed to sort the remaining cards under each of the categories. See Figure 10-2.

Figure 10-2: Traditional Card Sort Process

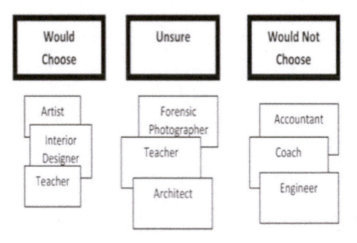

3. Clients might be asked to go back through the three main piles to form subgroups within those piles, based on the client's reasoning. For example, clients would take the occupations in the "Would Not Choose" category and identify why they rejected each occupation that was placed in that category. During the process, common themes for rejecting may begin to emerge.
4. Together with the counselor, the client discusses the subgroups and looks for other themes, such as education, Holland type, prestige, gender typing, and so forth.
5. Next steps are determined, which might include additional self-assessment or researching occupations.

164

Sorting Behaviors

Counselors can instruct clients to sort the cards in a variety of manners. Goldman (1983) described the process of sorting the cards as a type of projective activity, in which one projects a subjective sense when evaluating an occupation in terms of personal values, goals, interests, abilities, and so on. Thus, although the cards to be sorted remain the same for each client, the meaning each client attributes to the cards can be vastly different. Slaney and MacKinnon-Slaney (1990) offer several suggestions for sorting, including:

1. Sort the cards by different time periods, to show how they would have sorted them five or ten years ago compared with how they would sort them now.
2. Sort the cards with relation to feelings, to contrast the results of the sort when clients are feeling optimistic versus pessimistic.
3. If the client reports some pressure from important others regarding his or her decision, the client can be instructed to sort and label the cards from his or her own perspective first, and then to repeat the task but imagine doing it from the important other's perspective.
4. People with disabilities might sort the cards as if they had no disability, and women might sort the cards from a man's perspective to reveal potential thoughts that are limiting current options.

Sorting Alone or with the Counselor Present

Card sorts can be administered with or without the counselor being present. Both approaches have advantages and disadvantages as described in Table 10-2.

Table 10-2 Advantages and Disadvantages of Sorting Alone Versus with a Counselor Present

	Advantages	Disadvantages
Sorting Alone	• Foster a sense independence and reinforce the idea that the client has "the capacity to find the answer to [his or her] own career problems" (Slaney & MacKinnon-Slaney, 1990, p. 349). • That a counselor may have more time to attend to other tasks, including seeing other clients, while a client is working on the card sort.	• It may be difficult to ascertain the degree to which a client energetically investigates his or her reasons behind the choices of card placement. • The client may feel lost or abandoned.
Sorting with the Counselor Present	• The counselor and the client can become co-facilitators during the process, with both sharing the problem-solving responsibilities (Slaney & MacKinnon-Slaney, 1990). • The counselor can alert the client to "here and now issues of decision-making style, as well as historical and future concerns" (Slaney & MacKinnon-Slaney, 1990, p. 366). • The counselor can help clients clarify reasons behind their choices, including why they chose to accept some occupations and reject others, and to provide support for clients during the process (Pinkney, 1985). Counselors can listen for clues to assist clients to explore, and then confront any negative self-talk that clients might be imposing on themselves.	• The client may feel pressure to do the activity "correctly," or quickly. • The client may belabor the activity by checking in with the counselor every few minutes.

165

Task Approach Behaviors

How people approach the task of sorting cards also provides important clinical information (Goldman, 1983). Some behaviors to watch for include:

- Are they impulsive, quickly sorting the cards into piles, or are they slow and more deliberate about the process?
- How organized are the piles (do you see hints of perfectionism or obsessiveness?)
- Do they seem hesitant or seem to need confirmation that they are "doing it right," and what kinds of questions do their behaviors raise for the counselor?
- Do they ask a lot of questions or make responses that indicate that they need more information about the world of work?

All these "task approach" factors may be important to consider when working with a client.

Interpreting Card Sort Results

Goldman (1983) suggested that the accuracy of a client's interpretation of what is presented on a card is not the most important measure; rather, the client's interests, values, and skills that are exposed by the stimuli are significant for the counseling process. During interpretation, the counselor asks the client about the themes and the client's reasoning.

- If you haven't done so as part of the sort, ask the client to re-sort the cards into subgroups according to commonalities that the client sees within the main headings.
- Ask the client to describe what each subgroup represents, and examine for themes for choosing and avoidance themes (discussed below). Record that information for later use (because once the sorting activity is completed, the cards are removed and without a written record, it's unlikely that the client and counselor will remember the card sort results).
- Have the client discuss the options in the "unsure" pile. What information is needed to help move the cards in that pile to one of the other piles? Jones (1980) suggested that asking why these options have been identified as possibilities for a future occupational choice becomes an exercise in values clarification.
- The "would not choose" cards are then re-sorted into smaller piles according to the person's reasons for rejecting them.
- Continue to ask questions to further clarify the client's view of himself or herself in the world of work. These questions could be about other family members employed in the cards chosen, the information the client knows about each of the options, and so forth.
- Ask the client to prioritize his or her top choices in the would choose pile, and then ask what information is needed to narrow down the choices to a first choice and backup – most likely, the need will be information.

Avoidance Themes

Pinkney (1985) labeled the type of themes identified for the "Would Not Choose" pile as "avoidance themes," stating that clients are often more comfortable describing avoidance themes and "often seem well-prepared to defend such themes" (p. 337). Slaney, Moran, and Wade (1994) state that in the process of labeling "negative" subgroups, clients' confidence in their abilities to make logical, successful choices is reaffirmed. According to Pinkney (1985), the focus of the discussion of avoidance themes is "to explore the issue of over-generalization" (p. 337). He states that having a desire to avoid certain activities is appropriate, but that clients with flat profiles "seem to carry on avoidance to an extreme with little exploration" (p. 337). A counselor's role in this situation is to help the client see how avoiding affects the career development process, including limiting options.

The Peterson and Lenz Approach

Peterson and Lenz (1992) encourage clients to approach the card-sorting task in a different manner. According to Peterson (1998), the main purpose of the card sort task is not to expand occupational alternatives but, rather, to "assess cognitive process and structure" (p. 4). In other words, the focus is on how the client proceeds through the task and imposes structure on the ambiguous situation at hand.

1. After giving the client 36 occupational cards (from the Occ-U-Sort; Jones, 1980), the client is asked to sort the cards into "groups of related occupations" (p. 1). While the client is sorting, the counselor focuses on the following:
   a. How does the client make sense of the somewhat ambiguous directions?
   b. Was the client's approach methodical, or did it appear to be unorganized?
   c. Does the client use a linear or circular approach to sorting?

166

     i. Peterson stated that in his experience, the manner in which a person approaches the task provides an initial picture of how this person goes about the decision-making process, particular personality traits this person is likely to have, and what type of interventions might be most successful.

    ii. Linear problem solvers tend to be logical and methodical in their approaches and might prefer detailed, individual plans of action in which recommended steps are written and prioritized. A circular problem solver, most evident from the way the person places all the cards on the table first and then begins to see and create emerging patterns, might reject the predictability and seemingly inflexible (uncreative) boundaries a written plan may impose. Instead, this person might opt for more creative, spontaneous interventions.

  d. How is the way in which the client sorts the cards similar to the way the client makes decisions?

  e. Also, what emotions are expressed during the task?

2. Once the cards are sorted, the client is asked "to arrange the piles in some relation to each other, and then to label each pile" (p. 1).

3. The counselor then draws a "map," or a visual representation of how the cards are arranged, and writes down the occupational titles in each pile and the label the client gave each pile. The counselor should be aware of the total number of piles of cards. According to Peterson and Lenz (1992), the median is between five and seven piles, which they state is a picture of occupational maturity. A person with less than five piles might need more specific information on the world of work, whereas a person with more than seven might need help integrating the pieces of knowledge he or she has.

4. Ask the client about which pile they identify with the most and least and how those two piles are different to gain an understanding of how clients view themselves and the world of work. Peterson and Lenz (1992) recommend that the way to get the most out of this step is to listen carefully to the words the person is using when contrasting the two piles. Listening to "sort talk" is one of the counselor's most important roles.

5. Ask the client to point out where different family members would fit in each pile. A counselor should listen for information about important people in the client's life, as well as any family rules about career decisions. In addition, the counselor can help the client identify gender patterns—for example, that all the women in the client's life are found in a certain pile—and discuss how these patterns relate to the client's current options and decision-making process.

6. Peterson (1998) modified the task by asking the client to describe each occupation in the pile that was identified as most similar.

  Similar to other card sorts, but emphasized more heavily in this approach, the client's verbalizations during the sorting are seen as critical pieces of information because they provide a "semantic network of their world of work" (Peterson, 1998, p. 3). By paying attention to client verbalizations before, during and after the card sort, the counselor can identify areas that need to be discussed more thoroughly, such as negative self-concept, parental conflict, or lack of self-confidence as a good problem solver.

  Figure 10-3 presents a sample cognitive map. The clouds represent what the client had to say about each pile. In this example, the counselor can see that the "helping jobs" are more Social in nature, and the "creative jobs" are more Artistic. This client seemed to lump the other Holland types together, and did not indicate that this area was of primary interest. The client does identify with "Crazy Uncle Tim," though. There may be some issues related to that identification to explore during the session. The client is choosing a group of careers clearly different from those in the immediate family, and there may or may not be repercussions (real or imagined) for this choice.

Figure 10-3: Sample Cognitive Map via Card Sort

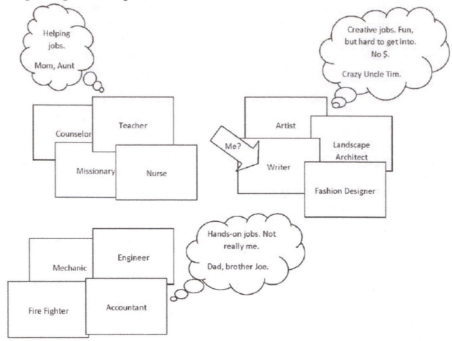

It is also clear that there are some gender patterns in the family, with the females in the helping careers and the males in the hands-on jobs. If the client was a female and choosing a job in the male-dominated group or if the client was male and choosing a job in the female-dominated group, this would also merit discussion. The discussion would not be to dissuade the individual from pursuing the career of interest, but should be framed in the way of an observation. For example, "I see that the women in your family tend to go into the helping careers. You've placed yourself in a career similar to those that the men in your family have chosen. What are your thoughts about that?" It may be that the client does not perceive any issue with this, but the counselor should at least point out the obvious.

Clients Who Might Benefit from Card Sorts

Pinkney (1985) suggested that the use of a card sort is especially helpful when a client has obtained a flat profile on an interest inventory. By exploring the client's reasons for grouping cards in a certain way, a counselor can gain information about the client's thoughts and beliefs that might have led to a flat profile. We have found that a person with an elevated flat profile is likely to have several cards, and thus several themes, in the "Would Choose" file.

Slaney (Slaney & MacKinnon-Slaney, 1990), in describing his Vocational Card Sort, identified the following clients for whom the card sort experience would be an "appropriate career intervention":

1. Undecided clients, especially those who have not developed a strong sense of their vocational identity and who have not experienced nor explored the occupational possibilities within the world of work.
2. Older clients, who can draw upon their previous work and life experiences.
3. Female clients, who might have stereotypical thoughts about occupations and therefore limit their opportunities.
4. Clients with "psychopathology" or limits in mental abilities (however, Slaney cautions that the counselor must make a clinical judgment regarding the level of impairment or comprehension).
5. Younger clients who are trying to assess their interests, values, skills, and so on.
6. "Intellectually oriented clients who like to control their own decision-making" (p. 341).
7. Those clients whose "inventoried interests" differ from their "expressed interests" (p. 341).

Sample Card Sorts

In addition to occupational card sorts, a variety of other card sorts are available that have been developed to explore values, skills, and majors. Because the availability of research on the use and effectiveness of card sorts is limited, most of the card sorts reviewed have not been researched adequately. The categories of card sorts reviewed include occupational, values, skills, and majors.

The Career Values Card Sort Planning Kit

The Career Values Card Sort Planning Kit (Knowdell, 2010a) allows users to clarify their values by sorting 41 cards into one of five categories. Each card identifies a value and briefly describes the value. The five categories are labeled: "Always Valued," "Often Valued," "Sometimes Valued," "Seldom Valued," and "Never Valued." Clients are instructed to place the five categories in a row, making five columns, and then to sort the value cards into the appropriate column. Clients are further instructed to have no more than eight values in the "Always Valued" column. After the cards are sorted, clients are told to prioritize the cards within each column, and then copy the results onto a summary sheet. A sample summary sheet is seen in Figure 10-4.

Figure 10-4: Sample Summary Sheet of Prioritized Values

SUMMARY SHEET OF PRIORITIZED VALUES

Always Valued	Often Valued	Sometimes Valued	Seldom Valued	Never Valued
Work on frontiers of knowledge	Location	Profit/gain	Adventure	Stability
Creativity	Security	Affiliation	Competition	Working under pressure
Independence	Advancement	Aesthetics		
Time freedom	Help society	Change/variety		
Exercise competence	Moral fulfillment			
Influence others	Friendships			
Help others recognition	Working with others			

After clients complete the summary sheet, they complete the following steps:

1. Clients are given a Career Values Worksheet, which asks them to write the type of career decision they are trying to make.
2. Clients are asked to write down their eight most important values and describe how they apply to that decision.
3. Third, a client would list potential conflicts and a place to brainstorm how those conflicts might be resolved.
4. Fourth, clients are asked to express what they have learned and to identify the next step.

Using the Career Values Card Sort in a Career Advising Session

Claire, a 30-year-old woman, came to the career center "seeking a career change." In the intake interview, Claire indicated that she had spent several years in a sales job that had provided good financial returns but caused her to be away from her family a considerable amount of time. As Claire put it, "I want to focus more on balancing family and career." Furthermore, she informed the counselor that she was ready to start having children and to devote her work outside the home to "something new and different." As Claire reasoned, the time had arrived for a change.

As the intake interview continued, Claire made statements that indicated that she was not completely sure about her value orientation. For instance, she stated, "I think I have my priorities in order, but I am not sure—I think I am right to change positions now, but there are times when I regret losing the contacts I made in sales work." After the intake interview was completed, the career advisor suggested that a measure and discussion of career values could be productive for answering some of her basic questions about the future.

Claire strongly agreed and liked the idea of a card sort. The Career Values Card Sort was suggested because of its focus on career values orientation. After the purpose of the instrument was explained, Claire chose to begin as soon as possible. The counselor gave Claire the Career Values Card Sort and explained that an important first step is to identify what factors are important to her when considering career options. Claire sorted and prioritized the cards. After completing the remaining instructions, the counselor helped her process the results.

ADVISOR: Claire, tell me what you learned about your values.

CLAIRE: Well, there are a lot of things that are important to me—things I didn't even realize. There are also things that don't appeal to me at all. I guess my highest values right now are time, freedom, security, and working with others.

ADVISOR: How are those values different from the ones you had, say, five or ten years ago?

CLAIRE: I guess these values were always here but were not the priority at the time. Let's see … five or ten years ago, my main values would have been status, fast pace, and advancement. I guess those are still important to me (pointing to the "Often Valued" pile), but they are not priorities right now.

ADVISOR: So, what you need in a job has changed. How will this affect the careers you are currently considering?

CLAIRE: I'll need to find out whether or not those careers will meet my values—what's important to me and my family right now.

As the dialogue continued, the advisor decided to discuss the degree to which Claire's husband's values matched her own and how their likes and dislikes might affect her decision. The advisor also focused on conflicting values such as high salary versus working predictable hours. Finally, the advisor let Claire decide if she wanted further self-exploration or to go on with the identification of specific occupations or career fields. Claire opted for further self-exploration, for, as she put it, "Now that I have started this process, I may as well get to the underlying reasons for change." In this case, a card sort encouraged self-exploration by introducing values that are very meaningful for inclusion in career exploration and lifestyle. Claire decided that she needed more time to sort out a variety of considerations in making career and family changes that could affect her life for many years in the future.

Motivated Skills Card Sort Planning Kit

With the Motivated Skills Card Sort (Knowdell, 2010b), the client deals the cards twice. The first time, the cards are placed in the following categories (placed in a column, forming five rows): "totally delight in using," "enjoy using very much," "like using," "prefer not to use," and "strongly dislike using." By sorting into these categories, a person identifies his or her level of motivation for each skill, that is, how much the person enjoys or does not enjoy using a particular skill. The client then places three other categories of cards into three columns. These categories include the following headings: Highly Proficient, Competent, and Little or No Skill. The cards in the "totally delight in using category" are then resorted relative to the three "proficiency" categories. The same procedure is followed with the remaining four rows.

The client is then instructed to re-sort the cards within each "cell," observing related skills and creating subgroups to reflect the similarities. A matrix sheet allows the client to record the results, and the manual includes several worksheets to aid the client in interpreting the results. The manual also includes eight supplementary activities to help the career planner in the process. One example is a skill wheel, such as the one shown in Figure 10-5.

Figure 10-5: Sample Skill Wheel

The purpose of the skill wheel is to broaden a person's ideas about how a particular skill can be used and be marketable in the working world. Although a skill in organizing closets and cabinets in a home might not seem very marketable, the person who came up with the organizing system for shoes, hangers, and so on made a handsome profit from that skill. Field (2013) reviewed Knowdell's card sorts (Values Card Sort, Occupational

170

Interests Card Sort, and Motivated Skills Cards Sort). He noted that the cards are packaged to look like household card games, which may have the affect of creating a playful and relaxed atmosphere during the process of sorting. He also suggested that some of the activities in the manuals may require knowledge outside of the client's realm of experience. For example, with the Motivated Skills Cards Sort, knowledge of a variety of occupations that may use the skills would be useful to move from the card sorting activity to exploring careers related to those skills.

SkillScan- Advance Pack

This card sort includes a set of 60 skills cards describing one of six types of skills. The goal of SkillScan is to help users gain an understanding of their specific skills and "general areas of strength" and to increase their awareness and understanding of how their transferable skills could be applied to a variety of work tasks. In other words, the goal for this card sort is to help clients identify transferable skills. The categories include communication, relationship, management/leadership, analytical, creative, and physical/technical. The cards are color coded according to a category. SkillScan results integrate with Holland, Personality and Values themes to provide a holistic picture of client preferences. Skillscan comes with a facilitator handbook and instructions on how ideas of how to move forward with the results. But instead of going into those details, why don't we hear from someone who has a great deal of experience in using SkillScan with her clients?

When working with individuals launching, changing or advancing in their careers, they need a clear understanding of their transferable skills and unique strengths and interests to identify best-fit career options. In this case study, I used SkillScan's Advance Pack transferable skills card sort and the Holland RIESEC descriptors to clarify potential roles and industries. I have that found by integrating themes from different assessments, it helps to reinforce clients' core preferences for targeting best-fit career options. The following case study illustrates this process in greater detail.

Kate is a 27 year old, college graduate with a Bachelor's degree in Psychology. During college and 5 years following graduation, Kate worked for a high production, fast food chain restaurant. She had started as a cashier, progressed to cook and was considering the next step of management trainee. While serving as a cook she injured her wrist and could no longer perform the job. The injury forced her to evaluate whether she wanted to stay in the restaurant business or look for another job in a new industry. Although Kate liked the collaboration and team work of the restaurant business, she disliked the fast pace, repetition and unpredictable hours.

Kate decided to make a change. Within three months, she found a job as a bank teller and was hopeful that this entry level position would be a platform for launching a career in commercial banking. She liked learning the computer system, working with fewer customers and colleagues, having greater responsibility and performing the variety of tasks. Unfortunately, after one year, she was let go during a reorganization.

She came to see me at a low point. She was angry about being let go and felt that she had been singled out by the new manager. She asserted that it was time to figure out a career where she could be happy, advance in the organization, work with people and help others.

In our initial session, I first let Kate vent her anger and frustration about the loss of her banking job. I then assessed Kate's abilities to clearly articulate her skills, interests and other career preferences. Kate responded in generalities, describing herself as "a people person with good customer service skills who liked to help others". She was adamant that she didn't want a clerical or customer service job – as these were "dead end jobs" and "not careers".

In our next session, Kate agreed to conduct some self-assessment exercises. We started with a Holland interests exercise to narrow down her areas of interest and then used SkillScan's Advance Pack transferable skills card sort to clarify her strengths and preferences for spotting potential roles. Kate's results from the Holland (RIESEC) exercise, were: Social, Conventional and Enterprising. With SkillScan, we assessed her level of proficiency and enjoyment on 60 skills that spanned 6 skill competency areas; Relationship, Communication, Management, Analytical, Creative and Physical/Technical skills. Kate's results indicated a clear preference in Relationship, Communication and Management competencies which nicely aligned nicely with her Holland themes. Then for each of her top preferred skills, I asked her to provide me with specific examples of how she enjoyed using these skills. I organized a profile of her interests and skills to help Kate see the core themes.

(Continued on next page)

Kate's Holland Interest Themes	Kate's Preferred Skills from SkillScan's Advance Pack
Social – Work with people, inform, help, train and develop	**Relationship Competency** **Collaborate**: Collaborated with team member to produce the order for the "board person" – with accuracy and under pressure. As a teller, communicated with team members to brainstorm ways to achieve "wait time" goals.
Conventional – Clerical skills, carrying things out in detail, following through on instructions	**Counsel**: As a cook, provided counseling and guidance to younger associates on personal and/or work issues. As a bank teller, enjoyed counseling new employees on how to navigate the company culture.
Enterprising – Work with people, managing for organizational goals	**Communication and Management Competencies** **Coach/Train**: Coached and trained new employees on order taking, serving, cleaning, etc., and coached tellers on preparing for weekly procedural quizzes. **Organize/Plan**: Organized and implemented new policy and rules to meet production and safety goals. Set up a plan for associates to keep their stations organized and clean to increase accuracy and balance at end of the day.

Kate's overarching themes pointed to a preference for working directly and collaboratively with customers and colleagues to provide a practical service; coach, train or help them. She was very organized and enjoyed managing details and accomplishing specific tasks. In terms of interests, we discussed healthcare, human resources and education as possibilities. Using her interests and top skills, we brainstormed a list of options which included medical and dental assisting, optician and other allied health services jobs. Although Kate was unwilling to pursue a graduate degree, she was open to attending a vocational training program to support her transition.

Over the course of a few weeks, Kate had two informational interviews in Optometrist offices. She utilized her annual eye exam in her optometrist's office to speak to the opticians about their jobs. Fortunately a little serendipity conspired and the opticians mentioned there would be two openings in the next couple of months and encouraged her to apply. In the meantime, Kate signed up for an Optometric Assistant Vocational training program.

Within three months of starting career counseling, Kate landed a job in her Optometrist's office. She discovered that she enjoyed learning about the technical aspects of assisting with eye exams which helped to overcome her initial nervousness. More importantly, she loved using her coaching and training skills to provide a practical service to her patients.

Lesah Beckhusen, M.S.
Career Counselor in Private Practice and Associate Director
Haas School of Business, Career Management Group

Other Card Sorts

Although one advantage of card sorts is that counselors can create them with relative ease, several published versions are available, complete with supporting materials and activities.

- **Intelligent Career Card Sort.** This online (intelligentcareer.net) card sort exercise that aims to have clients take control of their career decision-making process. They do this by helping clients examine and enhance three ways of knowing – knowing why, how and whom. Completion time is about 45 minutes for 115 cards that represent a current career behavior or belief. This is an online system that requires active participation by counselors and clients.

- **Occupational Interests Card Sort Planning Kit (OICS).** This card sort consists of 113 Occupational Interest Cards, each listing an occupational title. According to the manual, there are five objectives for using the card sort: "to define and cluster occupations holding high appeal for you; to identify characteristics shared in common by these occupations; to identify fields holding high appeal for you; to clarify degree of readiness, skills, and knowledge needed, and competency-building steps for entry into highly appealing occupations; and to apply learning from the OICS to your career decisions" (p. 5).

- **O*NET Career Values Inventory.** Based on the Work Importance Locator (http://www.onetcenter.org/WIL.html), this inventory includes 20 values cards that a client places in one of five columns, ranging from *Most Important* to *Least Important.* Scoring boxes yield scores for the RIASEC types. The inside of the inventory includes job titles related to each type and divided by "zones" - ranging from zone 1 (little or no preparation needed) to zone 5 (extensive preparation needed).

- **Values Driven Work.** The goal of the Values Driven Work card sort is to help clients identify and then align their values with their careers. Congruence between a person's values and his or her work leads to more satisfaction, whereas lack of congruence leads to less satisfaction and, often, more frustration. This card sort allows clients to examine values in four different areas: intrinsic values, work environment, work content, and work relationships. This card sort is available at http://novaworks.org/EmployerServices/EmployeeTraining/ValuesDrivenWork.aspx.

- **VISTA Life/Career Cards.** This card sort system consists of four packs of RIASEC-color coded cards, including Values, Interests, Skills and Traits. Clients sort one pack at a time into three piles. For example, if sorting the Skills cards, a client would sort the cards under one of these header cards: "Most Proficient," "Somewhat Proficient" and "Not Proficient." After sorting all the cards in one pack, the client would take the cards in the "Most" category, choose 10 that best describe him/her, and then organize them in the form of a pyramid with the most important card on top and the least important four cards on the bottom. The client then transfers the name of the cards and the primary Holland RIASEC type from the cards to a worksheet. The client would repeat these steps for each pack, and then summarize his or her total Holland scores. Available at http://www.vista-cards.com/.

Using Non-Standardized Tools in Career Counseling

For years, career counseling programs have incorporated tools created on-site to identify individual characteristics and traits. Examples include a variety of self-scored questionnaires, checklists, and rating/ranking formats that evaluate specific characteristics for use in career counseling. Personal career/life autobiographies have been used in many undergraduate career classes. The purpose of these tools are not to undermine the use and value of standardized assessment devices. Rather, using non-standardized approaches can enhance our understanding of results from standardized inventories, and may be of greater use to certain clients. They provide another way of understanding the client, and can be used to stimulate discussion of career options and supplement or raise questions about information obtained in other ways. Furthermore, non-standardized instruments can be used effectively with standardized inventories. Career decision-making is a process in which all aspects of an individual should receive consideration. When career counseling programs incorporate all relevant information, including non-standardized self-estimates, the chances of the career decision being dominated by any one source decreases.

In this section, examples of non-standardized approaches to self-assessment are presented. Some are illustrated with a brief case study, whereas others are simply described.

Career Construction Interview

The Career Construction Interview (CCI) is a self-portrait that an individual creates in response to questions that were created as part of the theory of Career Construction (Savickas, 2005). This portrait was originally a verbal construction (Rehfuss, 2009), but has also been adapted to include visual images (Osborn, 2009). It is available in a self-guided booklet format at vocopher.com, and was reviewed by Rehfus (2013), who recommends also using the My Career Story workbook that walks individuals through the process in greater detail. Rehfuss states "Overall, the assessment in its newer forms has become more rigorous and helpful as a qualitative career assessment" (p. 468).

The client is asked to answer questions about hobbies, favorite story, favorite motto, heroes/heroines, most/least favorite subjects in school, favorite magazines and television shows, early memories, and the like. The focus of the discussion is not simply on getting answers to the questions, such as TV titles or a book title, but to have the client describe each in detail. The CCI is a projective tool. As the client describes her or his favorite story, s/he is asked to identify main characters in the story, give the story line along with the moral of the story, and tell with which character s/he identifies most and how. Clients also estimate a Holland code and construct a success formula using terms associated with the Holland types. For example, "I feel happy and successful when I use technology in creative ways to teach others." A counselor interested in using this approach is strongly encouraged to read more about the theory and the Career Style Interview for the background on the CCI as well as a detailed example on using the CCI.

Work History via Resumé Analysis

Resumés can be used as a career exploration tool. They provide a snapshot of a client's work experiences. In addition to noting general themes about job titles and places of employment, a counselor can help the client generate personal themes about values, interests and skills. One technique is to have the client outline in detail the job activities or duties for each paid and unpaid activity on the résumé. The client can then place a checkmark or an asterisk by those activities he or she enjoyed doing, and an x by those activities he or she disliked immensely. Duties without a mark are considered neither really liked nor disliked. After each job duty has been marked, a summary list of likes and dislikes could be created, and then prioritized.

COUNSELOR:	Raphael, I see you brought your résumé with you. That's great–I think it will help us gain a clearer picture of what you've done and help us figure out where you're headed.
RAPHAEL:	Well, it forced me to put my résumé in order and to update it some.
COUNSELOR:	That's true. You know, many times you'll see résumés that begin with a summary of professional skills. Looking over the different tasks you've done, how would you describe your skills?
RAPHAEL:	Well, I'm a good communicator, and a creative problem solver. I am resourceful, persistent and thorough.
COUNSELOR:	Which of those do you think you thrive at?
RAPHAEL:	Creative problem-solving. I always seem to come up with out-of-the box ideas that people really gravitate towards.
COUNSELOR:	What I'd like you to do now is to look over your résumé, and use this yellow highlighter to mark job tasks that you really enjoyed doing. When you're done, we'll use a blue highlighter to mark the job tasks you just detested – you may not have listed those on your résumé, but you can write them back in.
RAPHAEL:	Wow–I think I'm starting to see some themes here.
COUNSELOR:	OK, tell me about it.
RAPHAEL:	I really enjoyed being assigned to short-term projects, where I was pretty independent to do my own thing. I didn't prefer the team approach where everyone's ideas had equal weight, because I enjoy bringing my own ideas to life.
COUNSELOR:	I'd like you to go through each of your job listings one more time, and write down one to two word descriptors that immediately come to mind on how you feel about that job.
RAPHAEL:	That's very telling. Those jobs, the ones where I lacked independence or creativity—the words that came to mind were "jail" and "stifled." The other jobs had descriptors of "fun," and "energetic."
COUNSELOR:	You've just demonstrated why it's important to be doing work that you enjoy.
RAPHAEL:	Yeah, I guess I have.
COUNSELOR:	So, as we move on and begin to look at occupational alternatives, and as you interview and consider job offers, you should keep in mind what made you thrive at work, and what specific factors stifled your creativity at work.

In this example, the resumé served as a career exploration tool in which Rafael began to see some patterns in his interests and skills, and solidified what he was looking to have—as well as looking to avoid—in a career.

Five Lives

The "Five Lives" activity is perhaps most useful at the onset of career counseling, even before asking the typical questions of "What are you interested in?" or "What are you good at?" With this activity, the career practitioner asks the client, "If you were able to live five completely different lives, what would they be?" A simple question, but the answers are often rich with meaning.

A main goal of this technique is to introduce the process of career counseling in a less formal and traditional manner, giving the client permission to dream about his or her potential, versus "getting down to business" and staying focused in reality. This is important because many clients will dismiss aspirations that are actually quite within the realm of possibilities. This happens because of real or perceived barriers, such as "I won't be able to provide for my family if I just quit my job and open my own business."

The career practitioner's role is to then help the client entertain how the client can work around that barrier. By giving permission to be anything, with no reality pressures, the counselor allows for creative thinking and problem solving by the client to overcome the obstacles and actualize his or her dreams. Other goals include assessment of self and occupational knowledge, identification of barriers, identifying potential sex role stereotyping, assessment of client's confidence level, increasing motivation in the process, and determining the client's career counseling need(s) and appropriate next steps.

The question in itself is very important. One might say, "Well, I ask my clients what options they are considering at the time, and that's the same thing." Sort of. Although both questions ask the person to elaborate past one option, only the first question allows the person to temporarily dismiss real or perceived barriers and to entertain their realistic and idealistic aspirations. It is crucial to identify the "idealistic" or unrealistic aspirations. These dreams offer a window into what the person values. The Happenstance Approach holds that people's curiosity becomes blocked by asking too many "What" questions, such as "What are you good at?" or "What do you want to do?" These questions tend to lead to pat answers and uncreative solutions. Usually, the Five Lives question leads to more than one word responses, probably because they are envisioning what their life might be like as they think about each one. Once the person has identified five occupations (either writing them down or stating them), the counselor has many options from which to proceed. We usually find it helpful to be more open-ended, asking the client to tell me about each of the options, including what's attractive about each, as well as what they believe their life would be like in that occupation.

Ideas for interpreting include:

- Looking for positive themes or patterns (i.e., the client's interests, values, skills, and goals);
- Asking how much the client knows about each occupation (to determine world of work knowledge);
- Examining the degree of congruence between his or her self-knowledge and occupational aspirations;
- Identifying real or perceived barriers ("What's keeping you from following each of these aspirations?");
- Helping the client learn how to implement certain aspects of the aspirations into their life via leisure; and
- Linking the aspirations and the client's current occupation to Holland codes and examining them for congruence.

By using this activity, the next steps seem to emerge naturally. What does the client need most at this point—assessment of interests, information about occupations, decision-making strategies, or more discussion on barriers?

We have used this technique in individual counseling and classroom settings. The actual process of listing can take anywhere from 5 to 15 minutes, with the average time being around 8 minutes. In individual counseling, the follow-up continues with various questions as just described. In addition, we ask the client to find out the "Five Lives" of his or her parents, siblings, partner, and so forth. Often, some overlap exists, which contributes to the client's sense of connectedness to important others. In the classroom, we ask the class how they might follow up with this question. After brainstorming ideas, we have them pair up and ask the questions. This often takes 20 to 30 minutes to complete. Then we ask volunteers to share their observations with the class.

Example of Five Lives Activity

Heather came to a career counselor very frustrated with her inability to narrow down an occupational choice. "There are just so many options. I'm afraid I'll miss the best one for me. I mean, there are careers I think I'd enjoy, but how do I know if I'd enjoy that one the most?"

COUNSELOR: Let's go with that. If you could have five different lives to live, what would they be?

HEATHER: I only get to choose five? Well, I'll just go with what comes to mind. First, I'd be a rich, single woman. Second, I'd be the President of the United States. Third,

	I'd be an advertising executive. Fourth, I'd be a consultant. I guess my fifth life would be a private investigator.
COUNSELOR:	Very interesting lives! Tell me more about the first one.
HEATHER:	Well, if I could be rich and single, I'd be free to do what I wanted, and I wouldn't have anything keeping me from doing it. Shoot, I could make all of my career interests into hobbies, and if I didn't like it, no big deal, I'd move on to the next one.
COUNSELOR:	So, having freedom in making choices and permission to make mistakes without receiving a lot of punishment is something you dream about.
HEATHER:	Well, I don't know if I dream about it or not, but it sure would make things easier if I didn't have to worry about failing.
COUNSELOR:	Which brings us to life number two. Seems like being the President would add a lot of pressure about failing.
HEATHER:	Yeah, you'd end up failing somebody all the time. That's not why I chose that one. I liked the power, the definitiveness that goes with being President. When he signs a bill, it's law, and it takes a literal act of Congress to change it.
COUNSELOR:	So, it'd be nice to be certain about what you're doing.
HEATHER:	Yeah. But I guess, now that I think about it, that being the President wouldn't really make my top five lives. Knowing that my decisions affected others so much would be a terrible burden.
COUNSELOR:	Which goes back to life number one.
HEATHER:	Yep. Rich and single. No dependents, no strings attached.

The counselor and Heather continued discussing her five lives. Through the conversation, Heather began to realize the amount of pressure she was putting on herself to find a perfect job and how she tended to obsess about the impact of her potential failures on others. An issue of wanting to be in control emerged in her lives as well. Heather acknowledged that she was feeling completely out of control with this decision, and that she liked the confidence associated with people in those careers. In this example, the use of the Five Lives activity opened a discussion and allowed for insight into what was keeping Heather stuck.

Ideal Day

A common technique that career counselors use as a non-standardized way of assessing a client's interests, values, and life roles is through their descriptions of an ideal day. The instructions, although simple, can vary according to counselor and client. The simplest instruction is to ask a client to either write or record his or her thoughts about an ideal workday, starting when she or he wakes up in the morning and ending when she or he goes to sleep that night. Another approach is to use guided imagery to "walk" the client through the ideal day. Some suggested guides might be "You're waking up. How do you wake up? Is there an alarm, or do you wake up naturally? Before you get out of bed, look around your room. What does it look like? Is anyone with you?" One problem with guiding them through the ideal day is that the counselor could spend too much time on one topic (of his or her interest), and might go too quickly past another topic (of particular interest to the client).

Sample Case of an Ideal Day

Jacques was more of an Artistic type—that was plain to see by the way he dressed, wore his hair, and communicated. He was very resistant to being categorized, and so wanted no part of traditional inventories. Still, he did want a clearer picture of his future. For an early activity, the counselor asked Jacques to create a collage that would be a picture of who he was. Jacques was very excited about this activity and created a 3-D design out of various objects. In the next session, he shared with his counselor meanings he attached to the sculpture. Based on his creative approach, the counselor decided to use the non-standardized approach of an ideal day.

COUNSELOR:	Jacques, I think it might be useful to talk about your ideal day. I'm going to turn the lights down a little bit and have you relax. You're going to close your eyes and using your imagination, walk through that perfect workday somewhere in your future.
JACQUES:	OK. Just don't let me fall asleep.

The counselor played some soft music in the background, dimmed the lights slightly and began with some general relaxation techniques, having him begin by tensing and then releasing muscles in his body, beginning in his feet and ending with his face. As Jacques relaxed, the counselor began, speaking softly and leaving pauses in between the directions and questions.

176

COUNSELOR: OK, Jacques. I want you to imagine that it's about seven months after you graduated. It's a regular workday for you. You've had a good night's sleep, and it's time to wake up. How do you wake up? Is there an alarm, or a partner? What time are you waking up? Before you get up, look around you. What does your room look like? What smells, sounds and colors are you aware of? Do you look different than you do now?

All right. You move through your place, getting dressed and eating breakfast. What clothes are you wearing as you prepare for work? What do the other rooms look like?

You're ready to go to work. Do you leave your place, or do you work at home? What happens next? Do you drive or walk to work? If you drive, what are you driving? How far is it to work? As you walk outside, take notice of your neighborhood, what it looks like.

You're at work now. Are you alone or with people? Do you have an office? What does it look like? It's time to start working. You're excited, because you are going to be doing your favorite thing. What type of work are you doing? Are you working by yourself or with a team? What are you feeling?

It's time to go home now. Take a look at your watch. What time is it? What are your plans after work?

You're headed home now, and the evening is yours. What will you be doing?

At last, it's time for bed. As you fall asleep, you reflect on what a good day it has been, and what made it such a good day.

The counselor pauses and waits for Jacques to open his eyes, which he does after several seconds.

JACQUES: That was something—I could really see some things very clearly, and others were kind of hazy. I really enjoyed looking at my surroundings along the way.

COUNELOR: Tell me about what you saw.

Jacques described his ideal day to the counselor. As they talked, they were able to reveal some values Jacques had that previously the counselor had not known, such as his need for independence. They went on to discuss what occupations might lead him to the dream living environment he hoped for.

Life/Career Collage

About a year ago, I (Debbie) had the luxury of engaging in a one hour training on using career collages to help individuals in their career decision-making. The facilitator had brought in tons of magazines, scissors, construction paper, and glue sticks. We were told to grab a couple of magazines, a glue stick, scissors, and construction paper. The instructions from that point were few. We could focus on a career decision we were considering at that point, try to create a picture of our present or future selves, our values, and so forth. I decided to think about my life in retrospect, and to find symbols that represented a life well lived. I thought about pictures and symbols I hoped to have – family, spirituality, and lots of pretty, girly, beautiful things. To my disappointment, when I went back to the table to grab magazines, there were only fishing and hunting magazines left. I grabbed two of them and began flipping through the pages, cutting out a few words, a picture in an ad, a little here and a little there. To my surprise, my piece of paper began filling up! Not having the "right" magazine forced me to become even more creative in my symbols. Fortunately, a few minutes into the activity, people started trading and passing along magazines. At the end of the activity, the facilitator had us pair up and share our collages, and we also had a couple of people share with the large group. I was amazed at the different ways people approached the task. One person made a book, with one picture per page. I, on the other hand, used one piece of paper and crammed every inch of it full. The facilitator shared that she does one at the end of each year to represent what happened in the previous year. I found the activity to be incredibly rewarding, and enabled me to think about who I am and who I am hoping to become. That's my perspective, but let's hear from that facilitator!

As a career counselor with a constructivist bent, my goal in the counseling process is helping people to understand how they use personal constructs or theories they have created about life to organize and account for their experiences and associate meaning through decisions and actions. Understanding a client's career constructs is reflective of their social, psychological, historical, and cultural relationships and experiences. Unlike norm-referenced models, constructivism celebrates all of these aspects of clients in a holistic, empowering model. By letting clients use their own language and other forms of expression, they take a greater ownership of the process and become active agents in building the next part of their narrative.

Using collage in career counseling has been especially powerful with my clients. By supplementing discussion with action and creative energy, you can help to get clients out of their heads and into the core constructs that make them who they are. While it can be assigned as homework, I prefer having people at least start their projects in group or individual session with me so that I can watch how they go about the process of choosing what they will include in their project. When finished, I can ask all kinds of probing questions about the content as well as the process. Clients are excited to share their creation and having an external, visual representation of their career construct can really give you some deep concepts to process. The most vivid example I can remember involved a client who was able to quickly fill most of the page with words and images, leaving a profound white space right in the middle. He was clearly frustrated by the omission. I asked him to describe the other parts of the page and we had a great discussion before I asked, "What's happening there in the middle." With great frustration, he replied, "I just don't know what should go there in the middle." He then sat back, smiled, looked me straight in the eye, and said in a quiet voice repeated, "I don't know what should go in the middle." Our work together then became the process of discovering and creating what should go in the middle, which was a profound and meaningful process for us both.

Lisa Severy, PhD
Assistant Vice Chancellor of Student Affairs
Director of Career Services
University of Colorado Boulder
President, National Career Development Association (NCDA)

Career Genogram

Another non-standardized assessment that is a useful tool is the career genogram. Genograms are used extensively in family counseling, with the purpose of obtaining a graphic picture of a person's heritage. With career counseling, the purpose is to gain a graphic picture of the client's career heritage (see Figure 10-8). What have family members done in the past? What themes are evident among gender, or other, factors? The counselor would work with the client to create a genogram, in the same way a genogram is normally created (start with either self or relative, indicating marriages, children, divorces, etc.). What gives a genogram a career emphasis is going back through the genogram and identifying each person's career. Many other options exist. For example, it might be interesting to note highest level of education achieved, career paths each took, any dominant values, stress-related illnesses, and so forth. Using this tool can help the client see a connection between where he or she is relative to where his or her predecessors have been.

Figure 10-6: Sample Career Genogram

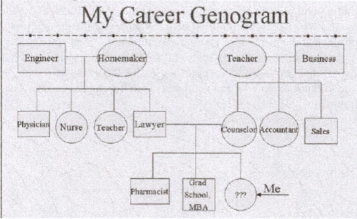

178

When introducing the career genogram, you should start with the client's primary relationship (partner/spouse), followed by children. Then the counselor would have the client start diagramming his family background, going back a generation at a time. Once the genogram has been completed, the client should go back and write in the careers/jobs, skills, talents and other relevant information for each person on the genogram. If the extended family is small, the client could also include close friends.

Some questions/activities might include:

- Writing down perceived work/education values for each person and then noting themes.
- Analyzing occupations for Holland type and then comparing to personal type.
- Have the client identify people on the genogram who are most like the client, and then ask how satisfied they are in their career, how they make career decisions, and what advice they would give to the client.
- Are there any pressures toward or away from certain careers?
- How do family members balance work and play?

Other Non-Standardized Approaches

Holland Party Game. A great career group or classroom guidance activity involves a non-standardized intervention with the six Holland types. Participants are given a basic, one-sentence description of each of the Holland types. Before the session, the counselor has placed cards with the first letter of each type around the room. After reading through the types and selecting their top three choices, participants are asked to find their letter and stand there. What happens next is up to the counselor and client. It could be relatively non-structured, letting participants talk with others in their group before moving on to their second choices, or it could be more structured. One particularly interesting activity is to assign each group the task of organizing for a party. I have found, on a fairly consistent basis, that the "S" types typically don't get much planned, as they are having fun talking about the party, while the "A" types tend to focus on the party theme, and "E" types discuss who they can bring in to speak, and how they can get funding for the party. Regardless of the approach, the counselor can make notes of how many are in each group, and then use the class numbers as examples describing consistency and differentiation. The party game could be used with individuals as well as groups.

Checklists. These are often counselor-created tools developed out of necessity when funds are limited and a need exists. For example, a counselor might not be able to afford a values inventory, so he or she creates a list of values and has students prioritize their top and bottom five. This then serves as ground for discussion. Other checklists might include interests, skills, hobbies, career beliefs, career worries, coping strategies, or majors. The list could be exhaustive. The purpose for these checklists is not to achieve high reliability, but to provide the client and counselor with a springboard for discussion. Counselors can also use information to create self-assessment checklists. For example, if a counselor knows that a client is interested in a particular occupation, she can go to a reliable source, such as the Occupational Outlook Handbook and the O*NET Center, and create a card sort or a checklist of each of the job descriptions or skill items for the occupation.

Life Role Analysis. Gysbers (2006) designed this assessment to help clients explore their expectations towards the different life roles they have played, are playing currently, and expect to play in the future. This approach has its foundation from constructivist, Adlerian, lifespan (Super), and feminist theories (Lorelle, 2013). Clients are instructed to draw three separate circles, to identify roles 5 years back, currently, and projecting 5 years into the future. Within each of those circles, clients draw smaller circles to represent the roles they are playing during those time periods, arranging the smaller circles to show relationships among the roles and importance as compared to the other roles. Lorelle (2013) praises this tool as a holistic approach that encourages discussion of cultural and social factors that might be impacting the client.

My Career Chapter. McIlveen (2008) developed this writing tool as a narrative approach to use with clients, with an emphasis on self-reflection. Consisting of seven steps, clients are asked to respond to different prompts. Steps may include completing a matrix of personal influences versus environmental/societal influences, writing a manuscript in response to sentence completion stems, "channeling" a self that is five years younger to act as an editor of the manuscript, and reviewing themes. Bayne (2013) notes that this assessment has been minimally tested, and may also be cumbersome for clients to move through on their own. She suggests that this tool might be excellent for those clients who are interested in longer and more thorough career counseling.

My System of Career Influences. This tool is a brief workbook that is grounded in the systems theory framework of career development. Clients are guided to think about their past, present and future with headings such as "My Present Career Situation," "Thinking About Who I Am," and "Thinking About the People Around Me. After exploring the influences that are in their lives, clients then create a visual representation of how their system of these influences relate personally. Henfield (2013) reviewed the MSCI and noted that while it is difficult to determine its effectiveness due to a lack of research, it does have the potential to be effective with diverse populations.

20 Things. Goodman (1993) presents an intriguing method of assessing interests adapted from Simon, Howe, and Kirschenbaum (1972). She suggests that activities she has devised stimulate students to want to know more about their interests. Clients are instructed to write down 20 things they like to do. They can list activities done at work; leisure activities, such as movies, parties, reading; or taking classes. She assigns the following codes to each interest listed.

1. Put a T next to each item on your list that you would enjoy more with more training.
2. Put an R next to each item on your list that involves risk—physical, emotional, or intellectual.
3. Put a PL beside those items that require planning (for planning).
4. Indicate with an A or a P or A/P whether you prefer to do the activity alone, with people, or both.
5. Next to each activity, put the date when you last engaged in it.
6. Star your five favorite activities. Discussion can ensue from any or all of these codings or from the list itself. The implications for career decision making are, hopefully, obvious, but perhaps a mini case study will make the point clearer.

Summary

Non-standardized tools and card sorts have been a part of the career counselor's bag of interventions for decades. A key benefit of non-standardized assessments and home-made card sorts is that they are relatively easy and inexpensive to create and offer a number of possibilities for administration and interpretation. A counselor should be aware of the limitations of using a non-standardized assessment, specifically those that generate a list of "suggested occupations" based on the results of a non-standardized assessment, is dangerous and unethical. A person might be making a career choice based on the results of these assessments and, without reliability and validity backing up the non-standardized tools, a counselor should not use these tools as the sole basis for a career decision. That being said, the non-standardized approaches and card sorts can open up the conversation about issues impacting the career decision that might not be easy to access with a standardized instrument. Plus, they can be personalized to the client's interests or concerns.

Questions and Exercises

1. Think about the setting in which you would like to work. Create a card sort (and accompanying instructions or worksheet) that might help clients in your setting. For more ideas of sample card sorts, see http://careerresource.coedu.usf.edu/linkteachingtools/ExamplesofLessonPlans.htm. Practice giving the card sort to a colleague. How would you interpret the process and outcome? What changes would you make, based on the practice session?
2. What are the major advantages of using self-assessment measures in career counseling? What are the disadvantages?
3. List at least three reasons why a client might be willing to try a card sort or non-standardized approach rather than a computer-assisted career guidance (CACG) system.
4. Build a self-assessment instrument for measuring the values of high school seniors. Explain how you would incorporate this instrument into a career counseling program.
5. Work through the non-standardized self-assessments discussed in this chapter. What have you learned about yourself that you might not have learned with standardized assessments?
6. How would you use a person's results on a values card sort with a printout of occupational titles he or she obtained after interacting with a CACG or other interest inventory?
7. Experiment with the ideal day experience. Which approach is more effective, writing the ideal day down or describing it to a partner?
8. As technology advances, card sorts might become computerized, such as with the Virtual Card Sort. Describe the positives and negatives of this possibility.
9. After reading about the Career Construction Interview, answer the following questions:
    a. If you were to see a career counselor today, what career concern would you want to discuss?
    b. Identify 3 people you consider role models and whom you admire, and tell what it is you admire about each. How are you similar/different from each of these people?
    c. What is your favorite story? Tell me about it. Describe the main characters. Which character is most like you and why? What's the moral of the story?
    d. What are your favorite magazines? What is each of them about? What do you like about each?
    e. What are your favorite TV shows? What are they about? What do you like about each of them? Who are the main characters? Tell me about their personalities. Which character is most like you?
    f. Describe your favorite hobbies, or what you like to do in your free time. What do you like about each of them?
    g. What is your favorite saying? What is it that you like about that statement?

h. What were your favorite subjects in school (any grade level is fine) – and what was it about each that you liked?

i. What are three early memories that you have? Create a headline or title for each.

j. If you know your Holland type, use descriptions from your three types to create a success formula: "I feel happy and successful when I use ___ and ___ to ___."
Review your answers to the above questions, and then summarize the key themes you notice, along with repeated words. Try to provide a tentative answer to questions about who you are, what your quest is, and how you can grow and flourish. Finally, create a collage to represent your answers to the questions. You could also copy and paste your answers into wordle.net to make a word cloud to identify themes. Then, try this procedure on a volunteer client.

10. What types of clients might benefit from using a card sort? Discuss your opinions with a colleague. What types of clients might not find a card sort a useful intervention?

11. Review the client's values card sort results in Figure 10-4. How would you proceed with this client? (Assume she has just finished filling out this values card sort sheet, and says to you, "Well, here it is.") Role play with a colleague.

12. Is it possible to be in a job that violates important work values? Explain your answer. How might you counsel a person in that situation?

13. Review the list of skills at http://online.onetcenter.org/skills/, and choose one or two that you think you possess and enjoy using. Create a skill wheel as described in this chapter, brainstorming ways you might use that skill in work. When you've exhausted your list of activities that utilize that skill, ask a colleague to add to it.

14. Savannah has decided it is time to make a career change. She is sure of her interests and skills. She enjoys writing, creating, and leading - and describes herself as organized but also a dreamer. She is currently an accountant in a state department. She reports feeling like she is just a number, and that she doesn't feel excited about what she does. There's been a lot of internal stress lately at the office, and she says her work is very repetitive with no real opportunities to "shine." She is considering several career options, including opening her own business, working with the elderly, and consulting. She's open to other ideas. How would you proceed?

15. A client's five lives are given in the following list. What kind of interpretations can you make from her descriptions?

a. If I could be anything at all, I'd be a homemaker. I'd have lots of children, and a husband that had a good paying job. I'd write books on the side, but mostly I'd be at home, enjoying myself in my children and other hobbies. I'd learn to be a great chef, and actually try some of the recipes that I carefully copy down all the time and then shove into that little box.

b. I guess my second life stems from the first. I'd love to be a chef– a pastry chef. I'd like to own a comfy little shop where people come in and relax from the pressures of the outside world. They'd enjoy coffee and one of my pastries. We'd have good conversations and there would be a great deal of comfort in the routine.

c. I guess I've always thought about being a missionary, getting out there and working with those who don't have as much as I do. I guess that's about as adventurous as I get. It'd be cool to think that you were doing something that had God's stamp of approval on it.

d. I think I'd like to be a writer. Not a reporter, but a writer of what I want to say. Maybe children's books, maybe a novel.

e. Last one! I would love to be a singer. Well, I am a singer now, but just haven't been recognized by anyone with connections. I guess I really wouldn't like all the touring and demands on my personal life. Maybe if I could just go record some songs and then hang out at home while my CDs sold millions. Yes, that'd be the life.

16. Find a career of interest either on the O*NET or the Occupational Outlook Handbook. Use the descriptors to create a checklist. Then take the checklist. What surprises or gaps were there if any? Use this information to develop a personal career plan for yourself.

17. Using social media sites such as Pinterest or Instagram, create a board or an album that represents your interests, values, skills, and personality. Write down or discuss with a colleague to discover relevant themes.

CHAPTER 11

COMBINING ASSESSMENT RESULTS

In each preceding chapter, the discussion of assessment was necessarily limited to one type of inventory or test. We do not want to give the impression, however, that segregating individually measured characteristics and traits is good practice. On the contrary, career counselors should consider the totality of an individual when helping them relate to their options. Each measured characteristic provides a rich source of information for stimulating discussion about goals and for enhancing self-understanding.

Along those lines, it is becoming more common for inventories to measure more than one factor. For example, clients can choose to take the Strong Interest Inventory along with the Myers-Briggs Type Indicator, which yields a report of interests and personality. The Differential Aptitude Test is paired with the Career Interest Inventory, and many of the computer-assisted career guidance programs include measures of values, interests and skills that culminate in an overall profile. Even within a single-focused inventory, like the Self-Directed Search, there may be subscales and combinations (such as profile elevation) that offer information on more than the explicit construct being measured. In addition, classic and current career theories emphasize that the self is complex and unique. No inventory, no matter how thorough, will capture the complete uniqueness of an individual. A career counselor can use multiple inventories, both standardized and non-standardized approaches, as well as solid questioning and basic counseling skills of paraphrasing and reflecting feelings, to better understand the client and her or his view of self and options. In this way, the career counselor's aim is to encourage combining all of the available information in the career planning process.

In this chapter, a counseling case illustrates the use of a conceptual model for using assessment results in a university counseling center. In addition, the use of a combination of assessment results is illustrated by cases that use the results of several tests and inventories discussed in preceding chapters. Finally, the use of a computerized assessment program is illustrated.

Advanced Organizer
- Using a Model for Combining Assessment Results
- Combining Separate Tests and Inventories
- Summary
- Questions and Exercises

Using a Model for Combining Assessment Results

In the following illustration of a conceptual model for using assessment results, both major and minor components of the model are identified to demonstrate a sequential order of events. Although this is a contrived situation, it closely resembles an actual counseling case at a university counseling center.

Marvin, a 20-year-old college sophomore, was referred to the counseling center by one of his instructors. He informed the receptionist that he needed help choosing a major. The receptionist assigned Masoud, a career counselor, to Marvin's case.

Step 1. Analyzing Needs
A. Establish the Counseling Relationship

COUNSELOR:	Hi, Marvin. I'm Masoud. Come into my office and let's talk. I see that you were referred by Mr. Goss.
MARVIN:	Yes, sir. He's my math instructor.
COUNSELOR:	I know Mr. Goss well. He's a great professor, isn't he?
MARVIN:	I really like him! I guess because he's so fair to everyone and he's real easy to talk to.
COUNSELOR:	Right. Most students have told me that. Do you live in the city, Marvin?
MARVIN:	No. I live out on Hunter Road.
COUNSELOR:	That's a nice area. Now, let's see how we can help you. You mentioned to the receptionist you need help in choosing a major.
MARVIN:	Yeah. I just can't decide. But, let me tell you the whole story. Do you have the time?
COUNSELOR:	You bet. We'll take as much time as we need. Tell me, how do you go about making decisions?

Marvin informed the counselor that he was interested in forestry but wasn't able to attend a college that offered forestry as a major, because he was financially unable to live away from home and felt he should not leave his aged parents. He was somewhat disappointed but seemed to accept the reality of the situation.

MARVIN: Well, I really look up to my big brother. If I'm leaning one way, and it's a real important decision, I always call him.

B. Accept and Adopt the Counselee's View

COUNSELOR: I understand your concern. That's not the ideal situation for you perhaps, but let's follow up on your interest in forestry. Tell me something about that.

MARVIN: Well, I like to be outdoors—growing up in the woods and all—our house is right on a river, and I've fished and hunted all my life. I just like it outside. I probably couldn't make it being penned up in an office all day long.

COUNSELOR: Okay, you like the outdoors, and that's a good point we need to keep in mind when you are considering college majors or careers. What else can you tell me about forestry?

The counselor's question was an attempt to determine whether Marvin had investigated the nature or work involved in forestry. Also, the counselor wanted to measure the depth of Marvin's commitment to this kind of work.

MARVIN: Okay, see, I read up some on forestry in a career book and it sounded just like the kind of work I'd like. You know, watch the growth of trees and how they survive. And I also looked at some college catalogs to find out which ones offered it as a major. That's about when I realized I couldn't go with forestry because I just can't leave my parents now.

Following further discussion of forestry, the counselor was satisfied that Marvin was indeed committed. The counselor concluded that occupations related to forestry would be a good point for discussion in the future.

C. Establish Dimensions of Lifestyle

COUNSELOR: Earlier, you mentioned that you like to hunt and fish. What other leisure activities do you enjoy?

MARVIN: Oh, I collect rocks and I go horseback riding; plus I like to watch basketball, and I play a little tennis.

COUNSELOR: Do you belong to any clubs on campus?

MARVIN: Yes, I'm a member of the science club, and I've thought about joining a fraternity.

During these discussions, the counselor made occasional notes reflecting pertinent information about Marvin. Included in the notes are the following statements:
- Expressed an interest in forestry
- Likes the outdoors
- Grew up in a country home
- Has given considerable thought to a career
- Commitment to outdoor work seems firm
- Interested in science
- Likes to be around animals
- Collects rocks
- Likes team sports
- Some interests are fairly well crystallized
- Is disappointed about inability to pursue forestry degree, but has accepted the situation fairly well
- Family considerations are important

D. Specify Needs

COUNSELOR: Let's get back to your reason for coming here. You mentioned that you wanted help in choosing a major that is available at this university. One of the first

	things we can do is to further explore your interests. For example, you stated a strong need to work outdoors and a definite interest in forestry. Would you like to explore other interests and link them to possible major and career options?
MARVIN:	Right. That's what I came here for. I'd like to take one of those interest tests.
COUNSELOR:	I believe that would be a good first step, and we can arrange for you to take an interest inventory during your next appointment. But before we decide on a specific interest inventory, tell me how you are doing academically in college.

Marvin informed the counselor that he had maintained a high B average in all of his course work. He explained that he did best in math and science courses.

MARVIN:	I've always liked math and science, and I make my best grades in these courses. So far, I have an A in biology, chemistry, and math.

The counselor decided that an aptitude or achievement test was not necessary at this time, since Marvin had established a good academic record. The counselor would review Marvin's transcript before the next appointment.

Step 2. Establishing the Purpose

COUNSELOR:	Now, let's get back to the interest inventory. How do you think an interest inventory will help you in choosing a major?
MARVIN:	Well, I hope it will give me some ideas about possible majors.
COUNSELOR:	Right, it will. We usually expect that results will verify some previously expressed interests and will also introduce new possibilities to explore. How does this sound to you?
MARVIN:	Let's go for it!
COUNSELOR:	Great! Later we can decide if another assessment is necessary. Now, let's see about scheduling a time for taking the assessment.

Step 3. Determining the Instrument

When selecting an interest inventory for Marvin, the counselor reviewed the notations he had made earlier and, in fact, reconstructed the entire conversation with Marvin. He concluded that Marvin could benefit most from an interest inventory that provided person-career match as presented by the Self-Directed Search. His rationale was that Marvin had crystallized his interests fairly well at this point in his life and was more in need of specific information, such as college major scale scores, and less in need of information pertaining to broad areas of interest such as general occupational themes. The counselor decided that the SDS would also be a good instrument to provide Marvin with specific college majors to consider in the career decision-making process.

Step 4. Using the Results

During the pre-interpretation phase, the counselor reviewed the profile scores from the SDS. He noticed that Marvin's highest codes were I and R. Suggested occupations included forestry worker, civil engineer, county agricultural agent, mathematician, and veterinarian, with suggested fields of study as forestry, mathematics, biological science, civil engineering, animal husbandry, and physical science. These results seemed to verify Marvin's expressed interest in the outdoors, mathematics, and sciences.

In reviewing Marvin's transcript of earned college credits, the counselor found that Marvin's grade point average was a high B. Marvin had done extremely well in mathematics and science courses, earning grades of A's. His outstanding performance in mathematics and science courses linked well with his interest in mathematics, civil engineering, and biological and physical sciences.

Marvin reported promptly for the next counseling session. After asking Marvin what had transpired since their last meeting, the counselor presented the profile of interest scores.

COUNSELOR:	As you recall, in our discussion of interest inventories, we agreed that we could get some suggestions for college majors from the results. I believe you will be pleased to find that there are a number of majors indicated for your consideration. But, remember, this information is only one factor we should consider in the career decision-making process.
MARVIN:	Right.

The counselor then explained the SDS results as follows.

184

COUNSELOR:	Your code suggests that you enjoy hands-on activities as well as problem solving. Math and Engineering are two areas of potentially satisfying fields for you. According to these results, a major in one of these areas may be one of the majors for you to consider.
MARVIN:	(Pause.) Yeah, I do like math, but I'm not really all that interested in being a mathematician. What do they do besides teach?
COUNSELOR:	Good question. I think you will find our career library helpful in answering questions like this one. In fact, I think it would be a good idea for us to make a list of all the college majors and related careers you might want to explore further, as well as important questions that you have about them, like what exactly they do. We can also go online with your report and you can see that these occupations link right to O*NET, which is a national career information database.

Marvin agreed that he would be interested in researching several majors suggested from the results of the interest inventory. The counselor also discussed how interests in certain college subjects could be related to the occupational scales on the interest inventory.

COUNSELOR:	Another of your highest interests is on the Investigative scale – if you look at some of the occupations listed, you'll see there's several types of engineers matching your code. Can you link high interests in college major scales to this occupation?
MARVIN:	Oh, I see. Yeah, civil engineers have to be sharp in mathematics.
COUNSELOR:	That's right. The point is, if you don't want to be a mathematician, you can link this interest and your proficiency in math to a number of occupations.

Using this procedure to discuss the results of the interest inventory, the counselor assisted Marvin in developing a list of majors and occupations he would research in the career library. It was agreed that Marvin was to do his research within a 30-day period. After three weeks, Marvin came in for an appointment.

COUNSELOR:	Hi, Marvin. I've been wondering how you made out. I noticed you busy at work in the career library several times.
MARVIN:	Yes, I went through quite a bit of material.
COUNSELOR:	Before you tell me what you found, let's review the list of majors and occupations you were to research.
MARVIN:	Okay, but I eliminated several right away.

As they looked over the previously prepared list of majors and occupations, Marvin also reviewed the notes he had made from his research.

MARVIN:	I still would like to be a forester, but I found that civil engineering might be a good substitute.
COUNSELOR:	Tell me more about how you came to that conclusion.
MARVIN:	Well, as you know, I like the outdoors and I'm pretty good in math. I read that civil engineers do spend a lot of time surveying in the open country. Also, our college offers a degree in civil engineering. This appeals to me. I think I might like a job like this, but I'm not completely sure.
COUNSELOR:	Your conclusions sound logical. The civil engineer occupation does fit the pattern of your expressed interests that we reviewed from the interest inventory, and you have a good background in math and sciences. But, you still seem to have doubts.
MARVIN:	Yeah, I'd like to know more about it.
COUNSELOR:	Would you like to talk to someone who is a civil engineer?
MARVIN:	Hey, that'd be great!

The counselor arranged for Marvin to visit a civil engineer assigned to the state highway department. Then the counselor and Marvin identified some private surveying companies in the phone book and after a few calls, found an engineer who was willing to meet. He also suggested that Marvin visit the chairman of the civil engineering department. Marvin opted to visit the practicing engineers first. In addition to discussing civil engineering, Marvin and the counselor explored several other career options. However, Marvin, preoccupied with visiting the civil engineers, gave little attention to other possible alternatives.

Two weeks later, Marvin was back for another counseling session after having visited the work sites of two civil engineers. Surprisingly, Marvin lacked his usual enthusiasm when he greeted the counselor.

COUNSELOR: It's good to see you again, Marvin. I hope you found the visits to the engineers to be informative.

MARVIN: It was okay, I guess.

COUNSELOR: You don't seem to be too excited about what you found.

MARVIN: No, I'm not. I don't really think now that I'd like being a civil engineer.

COUNSELOR: Would you mind sharing your observations with me?

MARVIN: Well, it turns out they have to be inside and do more office work than I had thought, looking up materials, reading land titles, and plotting grades. That part of it sure doesn't appeal to me. I just have this thing about working outdoors. Also, they don't make much money, either!

As Marvin and the counselor continued to discuss civil engineering and other occupations, it became clear to the counselor that Marvin was in need of further clarification of interests, values, and preferred lifestyles. The counselor shifted the discussion to analyzing needs.

COUNSELOR: Marvin, during this conversation there have been some key factors discussed that are most important for you to consider in planning for the future. For example, you found several work requirements in civil engineering that were not to your liking. You also brought up the fact that the pay scale of civil engineers does not meet your financial requirements. The point is that, on this visit, you learned a great deal about a particular occupation and some very important factors about yourself. Would you agree?

MARVIN: You're right. I had the wrong impression about civil engineering, and I guess it took a trip out there to make that clear. Besides, when I started researching in the career library, I realized that I hadn't thought about a lot of things concerning work.

COUNSELOR: We all learn through experience.

MARVIN: Yeah, I guess that's right, but now what?

COUNSELOR: You mentioned that you learned more about yourself when you made the on-site visitation. Could you explain more fully?

MARVIN: Oh, I guess I started thinking about a lot of things, like I know now that I want to make a lot of money, you know. I need to be able to afford to buy some land, and have a nice car and even a stable full of horses. I just didn't realize that this was all a part of what I was supposed to be deciding. I suddenly realized that the decisions I make right now will have a lot to do with all this stuff in the future like for the rest of my life, even. Whew, heavy stuff.

COUNSELOR: Perhaps I can help you clarify more of these important factors like the ones you mentioned.

MARVIN: Yep, that's what I need, all right. I'm just not ready to make that big a decision yet.

The counselor had returned to the first step in the model for using assessment results: Analyzing Needs. He was now ready to further specify needs, part of Step 1.

COUNSELOR: What we have been discussing are values. You have verified your interests and now we have shifted to considering a most important dimension—values clarification. For example, how strongly do you value a variety of tasks on a job, or prestige, independence, creativity, and a feeling of accomplishment?

MARVIN: (Pause.) I never even thought of those things before.

The counselor was now in the position to again establish the purpose of using assessment results.

COUNSELOR: Would you like to learn more about your values?

MARVIN: That sounds interesting.

186

COUNSELOR:	We have found that values clarification is an important part of career decision-making. Many individuals find that the discussion of values is an enlightening experience that helps clarify expectations of life and work. I believe that an inventory that measures satisfaction one seeks from work would be helpful to you.

Marvin agreed that value clarification would help him at this point in the decision process, and an appointment was made for administering a values inventory. In determining the instrument, the counselor decided using the values component in the self-assessment section of SIGI3 (VALPAR International, 2010) would be most helpful for Marvin, primarily because the focus of attention at this point was on values associated with work.

The values section measures several work values by having a person rank traits from *"Essential"* to *"Not Desired"* for personal job satisfaction. The counselor's strategy was to link specific work values with college majors and occupational interest patterns as measured by the previously administered interest inventory. The counselor's rationale was that Marvin needed a values measure that could provide direct association with work to stimulate discussion about satisfactions derived from work.

When Marvin completed that section of SIGI3, he gave a copy of the printout to the counselor, who then began preparation for using the results. The counselor made notes of the three highest values—leisure, security, and working in main field of interest—and the three lowest values—high income, prestige, and independence. Using these results, the counselor felt that he could stimulate discussion concerning work values and their relation to career choice.

When Marvin came to the next appointment, the counselor explained the purpose of the values exercise and began reviewing the printout.

COUNSELOR:	Marvin, I'd like you to look at this and tell me your definition of each of these values.

Marvin spent considerable time looking over his printout and describing each value. When he finished, he had the following discussion with the counselor.

MARVIN:	This is interesting. I'm surprised about some of the results, but yet when I think of what I really like and value, I guess I'm not all that surprised.
COUNSELOR:	Could you be more specific?
MARVIN:	Remember when I came back from the visit with the civil engineer, I said they didn't make enough money for me? Well, that's not really a big thing with me. I guess that I was just frustrated because civil engineers turned out to not be a good substitute for what I really want. Anyway, my low ranking of high income as a value is right, I think.
COUNSELOR:	What about the other values?
MARVIN:	Time for leisure and working in my field of interest are right on target.
COUNSELOR:	Can you relate these values to college majors and occupations as measured by the interest inventory?
MARVIN:	I guess you probably have opportunities for leisure in almost any occupation, so that's no big deal. As for working in my field of interest, forestry, that's real important to me—essential. Isn't there some way I could still go into forestry?

The depth of Marvin's commitment to forestry was again made very clear in this discussion and others that followed. Assessment of interest and work values stimulated Marvin to consider alternative college majors and occupations, but he also came to the conclusion that his dream of becoming a forester was an overwhelming desire for which there was no substitute.

Step 5. Making a Decision

Marvin decided to continue college on a part-time basis in order to find a job from which he could save the necessary funds to attend a university that offered forestry. Even though he was reluctant to leave his parents to attend college, they encouraged him to pursue his interest.

Case Summary

This case illustrates how assessment results can be used at various stages in the career decision-making process and, in particular, how they can encourage further exploration and clarification. In Marvin's case, assessment results were used when the need was established. An interest inventory focused attention on career alternatives that Marvin had not considered and reinforced his expressed interest in outdoor work. When Marvin and the counselor agreed that value clarification was an important dimension to consider in the career decision-making process, a values exercise was used. In each instance, the purpose of assessment results was clearly established. As Marvin experienced a greater sense of awareness, he was greatly assisted in the career decision-making process by the use of carefully selected assessment inventories.

Combining Separate Tests and Inventories

Inventories and computer-assisted career guidance systems are becoming more complex and including multiple measures of interests, skills, and so on, but another way to obtain results on the various components of career choice is to combine several tests and inventories. Let's look at four cases in which the results of more than one test or inventory are combined. The results of an interest inventory and a career development inventory were used to assist Janeesha in career planning. The results of the DAT, the Strong Interest Inventory and a values card sort were combined to provide information designed to stimulate Ari's career exploration. For Kwok, achievement and aptitude test results were combined with the results of an interest inventory to enhance the self-awareness so vital to career decision making and educational planning. Computerized inventories measuring abilities, interests, and values were used to help Flo decide on a career direction.

Case of a High School Senior Lacking Career Orientation

Janeesha was both confused and infuriated by her poor scores on the Career Development Inventory (CDI)—specifically with her low scores on the decision-making scale. She thought she was as ready as anyone was to make a career decision. "What's all this nonsense about self-evaluation?" she asked herself as she waited outside the counselor's office. "After all, I have been in school almost 12 years, my grades are good, and I'm ready to go to college. Or am I ready to go to college? Maybe I should go to work? Oh well, I'm just like the rest of my classmates: I'll know what to do when I graduate."

The counselor sensed that Janeesha was upset. He realized that Janeesha had rarely received what she considered low scores on a test. She had been a model student throughout her school career. With emotional overtones, Janeesha immediately brought up the issue of low scores. The counselor acknowledged her concerns and suggested that they evaluate her scores by studying the content of the inventories.

The counselor explained that the CDI was different from tests on which one received grades; the CDI was used primarily as a counseling tool to help students develop skills for career planning and decision-making. This information seemed to have little effect on Janeesha's emotional state. The counselor allowed considerable time for Janeesha to express her feeling of frustration. She eventually returned to the content of the inventories. As they discussed the profile, the counselor asked Janeesha if she would like to look at some of the item responses. They started with the results of the career-planning and decision-making scales.

JANEESHA: I missed quite a few of the questions dealing with understanding how to make career decisions. I don't know what that means.

COUNSELOR: Okay, let's look at some of the items.

Their review revealed that Janeesha had difficulty recognizing various aspects of work and working conditions. Although she was threatened by her answers on the items, she recognized the differences between her responses and those considered appropriate. As Janeesha became increasingly defensive, however, the counselor decided to set up another meeting to give himself time to plot strategy and create a more productive atmosphere.

Janeesha seemed relaxed at the beginning of the second conference. The counselor hoped that she would be able to accept suggestions for programs that could help her. He began by informing Janeesha that career decision-making was a learned skill and that knowledge of working conditions came with experience.

While discussing the results of an interest inventory, Janeesha commented that she had low scores there, too. The counselor agreed that Janeesha had a flat profile, but again he emphasized that this was not a test used to give grades for high scores. In fact, the counselor commented that the results of the CDI and the interest inventory were somewhat similar because she had admitted to having little knowledge about the world of work and had narrow, well-defined interests. This, he stated, could be the main reason for the "low scores," or flat profile. Finally, he explained that she had difficulty responding to questions and choices on the interest inventory because of her lack of involvement in work activities; she simply had little knowledge of occupations and work environments.

The combined results of the interest inventory and the CDI pointed out problems Janeesha would have in career planning. As she recognized her lack of knowledge of occupations and lack of career decision-making skills, she became convinced that action was necessary. The counselor was now in a position to suggest methods to overcome her inexperience, including visits to workplaces. In this case, the results of two inventories provided both Janeesha and the counselor with specific information to be used in planning intervention strategies to overcome recognized deficits.

Case of a High School Senior with Unclear Post-Graduation Plans

During the fall semester of his senior year in high school, Ari made an appointment to see the career counselor for help in planning his future. He informed the counselor that he thought about going to college "like everyone else," but he also thought about going to work after graduation. His parents were indifferent about his plans and left these decisions to him. After a rather lengthy conversation concerning Ari's likes, dislikes, and options, Ari agreed with the counselor that a battery of tests and inventories would help with decision making. Specifically, Ari was to take the Differential Aptitude Test (DAT) to help him understand his abilities and then relate these abilities to his interests as measured by the Strong Interest Inventory (SII) and his values as measured by a values card sort.

As the counselor reviewed the results of the DAT, she questioned whether Ari currently possessed the aptitude necessary for college work. She was particularly concerned about the low scores in verbal reasoning and numerical ability, as these two scores provide a fairly reliable index for predicting academic success. She was aware that colleges vary in their requirements and did not want to eliminate this option, but at the same time, Ari's low scores had to be considered in their discussion. She also noticed that his highest score was in mechanical reasoning.

The results of the SII indicated a primary code of IRS. Ari highlighted the following jobs on his printout: engineer, mechanical engineer, industrial, and auto mechanic. Ari also highlighted the following majors/fields of study: engineering, mechanical engineering, civil engineering, and physical education. The counselor wondered whether Ari's apparent interest in occupations that require a college degree reflected a current interest Ari had in attending college, rather than his true interests, especially given his low aptitude for college work.

On the values card sort, Ari preferred supervision-human relations (values a supportive supervisor), social status (values recognition in the community), and working conditions (values pleasant work environments). His lowest values were in creativity (values ability to try out own ideas), responsibility (values being able to make own decisions), and independence (values working on his own). These results were of particular interest to the counselor because Ari placed a high value on the working environment but a low value on intellectual stimulation.

Ari seemed somewhat embarrassed by the DAT scores, but he stated that he did not consider himself a good student. The counselor then asked about his interest in attending college. Ari replied: "Well, all of my friends are going to college, and I figure that I ought to go, too. I got through high school somehow, and I ought to be able to make it in college." These remarks indicated that Ari did not know what college would be like. His reason for going to college reflected little knowledge of college requirements and a lackadaisical attitude toward exploring other options available to him.

When the counselor mentioned Ari's high score on mechanical reasoning, Ari expressed an interest in mechanics and other jobs such as television repair and electric engine repair. The counselor followed this expression of interest with a description of occupations in technical fields—auto mechanics and related trades. Her purpose was to introduce several career options Ari had not considered. A discussion of values as related to work environments held Ari's attention.

ARI: Yeah, I like to work around people who are friendly and visit a lot. The way I see my life is a job 8-to-5, five days a week, and a chance to go fishing and hunting.

COUNSELOR: Okay, now that you have come to that conclusion, we should examine other parts of the inventory. Your lowest value was in intellectual stimulation, which means that you do not place a high value on work that permits independent thinking.

ARI: I guess that's right. That doesn't interest me. I just want a job that's not too complicated. I don't care about being independent, and I'm not interested in artistic things.

The counselor then linked the results of the assessment instruments to occupational requirements. She suggested that Ari attempt to develop a list of occupations that would be related to his high mechanical reasoning score. Next, he was to relate these occupations to his interests and work values. The counselor helped Ari begin this assignment by suggesting several occupations to consider, including jobs that would require apprentice training and for which technical training courses were offered.

Ari reported for the next counseling session early. He seemed eager to get started.

ARI: Do you think everybody should go to college? I've been thinking that maybe college isn't for me. This assignment you gave me helped me see that I'm

189

actually more interested in jobs that require some education and training, but not necessarily a four-year program.

When the counselor asked Ari to explain how he arrived at this conclusion, Ari replied: "When we started talking about my values, I realized that I was thinking about college because most everyone else was. That isn't really me; besides, my grades and test scores are not very high."

The counselor and Ari continued their discussion and reached some tentative conclusions. Ari would not give up the idea of college completely, but he would explore other options also. He therefore looked into occupations that require college training as well as technical occupations and trades.

In this case, the combined test results provided the stimulus for considering career options from several perspectives. Measuring aptitudes, interests, and work values provided Ari with information he had never considered for career exploration. The discussions of the results helped Ari relate his characteristics and traits to occupational and educational information. He was stimulated to explore several different options and gained an understanding of the complexities of the world of work.

Case of a High School Senior with a Poor Attitude Towards School

Being the last one to enter the classroom and the first one to leave typified Kwok's attitude toward school. Most teachers wondered why he bothered to stick around for his senior year. Perhaps it was the good time he was apparently having, or maybe it prevented him from having to go to work. The counselor had made numerous attempts for two years to get Kwok interested in coming in for counseling, but Kwok managed to evade the counselor's office. Thus, the counselor was quite surprised when Kwok's name appeared on the appointment list.

Kwok further amazed the counselor when he asked for help in planning what to do after high school. He informed the counselor that he began thinking about his future because of the results of a test he had taken. He explained that the entire class had been required to take several tests and that his teacher informed him that he had scored high on the aptitude test. The counselor and Kwok set up another meeting in a few days so that the counselor could gather the test data. In the meantime, the counselor suggested that Kwok take an interest inventory. The counselor was interested in maintaining Kwok's enthusiasm as well as in obtaining a measure of his interests.

The counselor discovered that Kwok did indeed do well on the DAT, which had been administered to all seniors. The counselor was surprised to find that his scores were above the 90th percentile for verbal reasoning and numerical ability. Abstract reasoning and mechanical reasoning also were significantly high (above the 75th percentile). The counselor wondered why Kwok let all this talent go to waste during his school career.

Achievement test scores reflected Kwok's poor academic performance. Most scores were below the 50th percentile (national group) with the exception of mathematics reasoning, which was at the 75th percentile. The counselor concluded that even Kwok's high aptitude could not make up for the academic work he had not done.

The Self-Directed Search (SDS) provided insights into Kwok's modal personal style; Enterprising was his dominant personality type. An Enterprising person, according to the SDS description, is adventurous, extroverted, and aggressive—a good description of Kwok. Although Kwok didn't use these characteristics in academic endeavors, he was considered a leader by his peer groups. His summary code, ECS (Enterprising, Conventional, Social), suggested that he would prefer sales jobs such as insurance underwriter or real estate salesperson.

In the next session, Kwok told the counselor that he was planning to attend college and devote much more of his energy to college courses than he had to high school courses. The counselor took this opportunity to point out the discrepancies between Kwok's aptitude test scores and his grades and achievement test scores. He emphasized that Kwok had the potential for making much better grades than he had in the past. Kwok was quick to agree that he had goofed off and would have to pay the price now. The counselor suggested that Kwok enroll in a summer course sponsored by the community college learning resource center to upgrade his basic skills and improve his study habits.

Kwok was undecided about a career because he had given little thought to his future. The SDS results provided him with several specific occupations to consider.

KWOK: I think I would like sales work of some kind or to have my own business. Do you think I should study business?

COUNSELOR: That may be a good possibility. However, I think you should take the time to research what is offered in a typical school of business at a university. But first, let's consider what's involved in career decision-making.

The counselor continued by emphasizing the importance of self-understanding in career planning. He discussed the significance of modal personal style, as identified by the SDS. Kwok recognized that the results of the aptitude and achievement measures also contributed to his self-understanding; they provided stimulus for further discussion. As a result, Kwok was challenged by the counselor to devote time to researching the world of work in relation to his personal characteristics. Kwok thanked the counselor for helping him establish some direction and set up several appointments to discuss and evaluate the careers he was exploring, as well as to make an educational plan.

Case of a Divorced Woman Searching for a Career Direction

Flo had been encouraged by her sister and friends to attend a job club at the nearby women's center. She experienced immediate support from the job club group and found that other divorced women with children were in the process of deciding future alternatives. Eventually, Flo was given an appointment with a volunteer counselor. She related information about her background to the counselor, who summarized it as follows:

- *Marital status:* divorced for eight months after a 10-year marriage.
- *Children:* four children, ages 9, 7, 4, and 2.
- *Financial situation:* child support payments and state welfare assistance.
- *Work experience:* has never worked outside the home.
- *Educational level:* high school graduate—grades were above average in the A and B categories, and she was on the honor role several times.
- *Strongest and most interesting subjects:* science courses, such as chemistry and biology.
- *Living accommodations:* renting an apartment owned by her sister who lives next to her. Good schools are nearby.
- *Occupations considered:* none seriously because she was devoted to raising her children. In high school, she had considered being a nurse, medical doctor, or dentist. She expressed an interest in helping others and *working* with people, but at this point in her life, she did not have a career preference or direction.

The women's center was fortunate enough to have the computerized career guidance system for adults, CHOICES. This computer-assisted career guidance program is designed to assist individuals through a systematic career exploration and decision-making process. It contains large databases that provide up-to-date information about occupations and educational opportunities and contains inventories that measure interests, abilities, and work-related values.

Under the counselor's direction, Flo entered the CHOICES system with the approach that she was completely undecided, and decided to complete three of the assessments: the Interest Profiler, Skills Survey, and the Values Sorter. The counselor explained, "Each of these inventories will provide us with different snapshots of factors that are important to you, that you might want to consider. We'll also be able to see how all three of these fit into the whole picture. For example, you might have interests in the medical field, but not the skills. By taking these inventories, we can see how your interests, values and skills overlap and how they differ."

At their next session, the counselor began by asking Flo what she thought about the results.

FLO:	Well, I guess that there weren't any fields that captured my interests, values and skills.
COUNSELOR:	True—in the best-case scenario, you'd find several occupations that match all three of these areas. Remember, though, that not every occupation is listed here. Tell me what observations you can make about the other combinations or themes that you see.
FLO:	I guess where I have interests and values, that's two out of three. I'd just have to focus on building my skills in that area. As for themes, I think it's interesting that it didn't come out that I was interested in medical treatment or medical technologies and yet I do have interests in health care.
COUNSELOR:	What do you make of that?
FLO:	That maybe there's a lot of different jobs within the medical field? I guess I need to learn more about that.
COUNSELOR:	I think you're right. Occupational fields are complex. There may be certain jobs within the medical field that match your interests, values and skills, and others that do not match at all. Doing some research on occupations in health care and the medical field would make sense as a next step.

In the sessions that followed, Flo and the counselor discussed several occupational options from the list presented by the computer-assisted career guidance system. Other occupations were added for exploration purposes. Flo found more information from the computerized database concerning work tasks, employment outlook, income potential, and paths of training. She had verified and learned some new things about herself from the results of the inventories that she had completed. She kept these results in mind as she explored

191

occupations, and she felt that the major benefit from talking with the counselor and using the computerized career guidance system was the fact that she was able to develop a frame of reference to use in career decision-making. As she read job descriptions that were linked in her profile on CHOICES, she was able to evaluate each one from the vantage point of how she could accomplish the job training requirements and still care for her four children.

FLO: This has been a completely new experience for me. During my marriage I never considered working because my husband had a marvelous income and I was happy with raising a family. I'm excited about a future career role, but I still want and have the responsibility of raising my children.

COUNSELOR: It sounds like the next step would be for you to talk with some people in the field to find out how feasible it is to balance work and family in those occupations.

Flo eventually decided to choose dental assistant primarily because of the availability of training at a nearby community college. For the time being, she would aspire to this occupation, but she recognized that the future might provide opportunities in the field of dentistry. She had for the first time in her life developed a potential career direction.

Case of Harold, Unemployed for Over a Year

Harold came to his first appointment at the workforce office with a sad demeanor. The career counselor greeted him and gently suggested, "Tell me what's going on." It was obvious that Harold was embarrassed at sharing his situation. He barely looked at his counselor in the eyes, and sat slouched in his chair. At times, she had trouble understanding him because he spoke with his head on his chest in low tones. What the counselor did make out was that Harold had been unemployed for over a year, and been burning through his savings. At 50, he was very concerned about having to start at the bottom again. He shared that applied for every opening that he could find, but was told many times that he was over-qualified for the job. His goal for coming to the workforce office was to see if there were other jobs out there that he might be qualified for, and to learn how to strengthen his changes of getting hired.

Because the counselor heard several negative statements throughout his story, she decided to administer the Career Thoughts Inventory. His T scores were Total Score: 80, Decision-Making Confusion: 83, Commitment Anxiety: 45, External Conflict: 40. Knowing that there was a correlation between the CTI and depression, as well as the research on chronic unemployment and the impact on mental health, the counselor asked if he was receiving mental health services; he indicated that he was not. She also decided, based on his non-verbals, to inquire about depression and suicidality. He stated that his doctor had diagnosed him with depression, and that he was currently on medication to address the depression. The counselor shared with him research that showed that the best combination for managing depression was medication and therapy, and offered to help him find a counselor in the area, to which he agreed.

Harold brought in his resume at the request of the counselor, and together they reviewed each of his previous jobs, including what he liked and disliked about each. His work history revealed that he had worked his way up through the ground floor at a local retail store to the management levels. He reported that the company started making cutbacks 2 years earlier, and that he was one of the last to be let go. The discussion revealed that he enjoyed finding ways to inspire his sales team to exceed company goals, as well as the mentoring aspect of his work. "I'm a good salesperson. I can sell anything – but I really prefer managing people, and I think I'm pretty good at it."

Over the course of career counseling, the counselor used both standardized and non-standardized inventories. She started with addressing the negative career thoughts she heard, such as "No one will want to hire an old man like me when they can get somebody fresh and at half the price right out of college." They worked on cognitively reframing his negative thoughts and she checked in monthly (with his permission) with his counselor to make sure that they were working cooperatively with the interventions.

About a month into career counseling, the negative thoughts seemed to be occurring much less frequently, and Harold's mood and body language seemed slightly improved. At this point, he completed and started reviewing various career assessments. His interest inventory results revealed that he had strong Enterprising and Social interests/skills. He worked with his wife to create a life/career collage. He was very excited to share the collage with his counselor, and said that the collage activity with his wife was very meaningful, in that she had also created one for herself, and then the two of them decided to do a joint collage. In doing the collage, they were able to think about where they wanted to be in the next few years, and also cement what values were important to them.

The counselor reviewed Harold's interest inventory results and asked the degree to which he had been involved with people in the last year. It was no surprise to find out he had started pulling out of meetings and gatherings with friends. He said he got tired of telling them he had no job, and knew they didn't want to be

© 2016 Cengage Learning. All Rights Reserved. May not be scanned, copied or duplicated, or posted to a publicly accessible website, in whole or in part.

around a loner such as himself. The counselor explained that by withdrawing from others, he also had closed off his support group, as well as his network for finding potential work. He had stopped managing a kids' basketball team, which had given him great pleasure, too. With the counselor's encouragement, Harold started re-engaging in the activities and friendships he had enjoyed. Two months later, he had his first interview, which he found through the parent of one of the kids on the team.

In this case, the counselor was able to use standardized and non-standardized instruments to help Harold clarify his values and goals, and to create strategies for addressing his depression. Not always do cases work out this well, but more often than not, a positive intervention in one area (such as career) will effect a positive change in another (such as mental health).

Summary

In this chapter, we discussed using combinations of assessment results to help individuals consider their characteristics and traits during career counseling. We emphasized that assessment results should not be used in isolation; counselors and clients should consider the totality of individual needs. Assessment results taken from different types of tests and inventories provide useful information in the career decision-making process. Consider the model for comparing suggested occupations from various assessments. Table 11-1 shows a sample way to combine the results from different assessments into one table.

Table 11-1 Sample Occupational Table that Combines Results

Potential Occupations to Pursue

SDS	MIV	ASVAB	CACG	CARD SORT	*OTHER*
1.	1.	1.	1.	1.	*1.*
2.	2.	2.	2.	2.	*2.*
3.	3.	3.	3.	3.	*3.*
4.	4.	4.	4.	4.	*4.*
5.	5.	5.	5.	5.	*5.*

Occupations to Avoid

SDS	MIV	ASVAB	CACG	CARD SORT	*OTHER*
1.	1.	1.	1.	1.	*1.*
2.	2.	2.	2.	2.	*2.*
3.	3.	3.	3.	3.	*3.*
4.	4.	4.	4.	4.	*4.*
5.	5.	5.	5.	5.	*5.*

Once the client has filled out the table, she or he can look for common occupations to consider in more depth. In addition, counselor and client can discuss the potential reasons certain occupations kept turning up on the "avoid" list, thus turning the process full circle again as self-knowledge is clarified.

Questions and Exercises

1. Following the steps of the conceptual model for using assessment results, develop a counseling case that illustrates each step.
2. How would you determine which instruments to use if you were requested to recommend tests and inventories for a group of tenth-graders interested in career exploration?
3. Defend the following statement: Multidimensional assessment results are more effective in career counseling than are the results of only one instrument.
4. How would you explain to an individual the differences in norms when using a combination of assessment results, some of which are based on local norms and others on national norms?
5. Illustrate how assessment results from two different instruments can support each other and how they can point out conflicts.
6. Micanel, a senior in high school, has come in for career counseling and has taken the middle-school version of the Self-Directed Search. In addition, he completed the CISS, Choices, O*NET Skills Search, and an online card sort. He completed a summary table shown in Table 11-2 on the next page. How would you interpret his results? What next steps might you recommend? Do you have any concerns about the tests he took? Are there others you would have suggested, and if so, why?
7. Pull together all of the assessment inventories you have taken. Pretend that you are a counselor, and that this information has been presented to you. How would you go about organizing the

information in a way that would make sense? Create a form or chart that would allow you to concisely show the results.

Table 21-2 Micanel's Summary Table

	Main Interests, Personality Descriptors or other (include actual scores for main scales) or results	Occupations to Consider or Pursue	Occupations to Avoid (if applicable)
SDS	Holland code: SAR S – 39, A – 36, R – 26 Interests & Personality: Likes to help, teach and counsel people, works cooperatively with others, sympathetic, and warm. Likes to come up with original ideas, make art, and self-expression. Likes to work with hands, hardworking, modest, and shy.	Art Teacher, English Teacher, Family and Marriage Counseling, Music Therapy, Artist, Painter	
CISS	Writing, fashion, art, helping people	Child care worker, Guidance counselor, Teacher K-12, Social worker, psychologist, artist, fashion designer, professor, musician, writer, restaurant manager, chef, carpenter	Influencing, organizing, analyzing, adventuring
Choices	Top work values: Achievement, Support	Fire Fighter, Conservation Worker	
ONET Skills Search	Skills Search for: Reading comprehension, active listening, writing, speaking, critical thinking, active learning, learning strategies, social perceptiveness, coordination, negotiation, instructing, service orientation, complex problem-solving	Mental Health Counselor, Mental Health and Substance Abuse Social Worker, Child, Family, and School Social Worker, Anthropologist, Fire Fighter	
Virtual Card Sort	Interests: Social, Artistic	Would choose: Teacher, Psychologist, Photographer, Fashion Designer, Career Counselor, Artist	Web Editor, Underwriter, Ultrasound Technologist, Special Agent, Public Relations, Physician, Pharmacist, Nurse Pilot

REFERENCES

Association for Assessment and Research in Counseling. (2012). *Standards for multicultural assessment.* Retrieved from http://www.theaceonline.com/multicultural.pdf

Abu-Hilal, M. M. (2000). A structural model of attitudes towards school subjects, academic aspiration and achievement. *Educational psychology: An international journal of experimental educational psychology,* 20, 75–84.

Argyropoulou, E., Sidiropoulou-Dimakakou, D., & Besevegis, E. (2007). Generalized self-efficacy, coping, career indecision and vocational choices of senior high school students in Greece: Implications for career guidance practitioners. *Journal of Career Development, 33,* 316-337.

Allis, M. (1984). Review of the Career Decision Scale. *Measurement and Evaluation in Counseling and Development, 17,* 98–100.

American Counseling Association. (2014) *Code of ethics and standards of practice.* Alexandria, VA: Author.

American Psychological Association. (1985). *Standards for educational and psychological tests.* Washington, DC: Author. Retrieved 1/6/15 from http://www.apa.org/science/programs/testing/standards.aspx

American Psychological Association. (1986). *Guidelines for computer-based tests and interpretations.* Washington, DC: Author.

American Psychological Association. (2002). *Ethical guidelines of the American Psychological Association.* Washington, DC: Author. Retrieved 1/6/15 from http://www.apa.org/ethics/code/

Anastasi, A. (1988). *Psychological testing (6th* ed.). New York: Macmillan.

Anseel, F., & Lievens, L. (2007). A within-person perspective on feedback seeking about task performance. *Psychologica Belgica, 46,* 269-286.

Association for Assessment in Counseling (2012). *Standards for Multicultural Assessment.*
Alexandria, VA: Author.

Atkinson, M. J. (2003). Review of the California Psychological Inventory Third Edition. In B.S.
Plake, J.C. Impara, and R.A. Spies (Eds.), *The fifteenth mental measurements yearbook.*
Lincoln, NE: Büros Institute of Mental Measurements. Retrieved December 15th, 2004,
from Mental Measurements Yearbook database. Accession number: 15122723

Baker, C. A. (2013). [Self-Directed Search, Fourth Edition, and Career Explorer]. In C. Wood &
D. G. Hays, (Eds.), A *counselor's guide to career assessment instruments, 6th Ed.* (pp. 275-
278). Broken Arrow, OK: National Career Development Association.

Baker S. R. (2013). [Adult Career Concerns Inventory]. In C. Wood & D. G. Hays, (Eds.), A
counselor's guide to career assessment instruments, 6th Ed. (pp. 302-305). Broken Arrow,
OK: National Career Development Association.

Bahns, T. M. (2001). Review of the NE04. In B.S. Plake and J.C. Impara (Eds.), *The fourteenth*
mental measurements yearbook. Lincoln, NE: Büros Institute of Mental Measurements.
Retrieved December 15th, 2004, from Mental Measurements Yearbook database. Accession
14122273.

Barak, A. (2003). Ethical and professional issues in career assessment on the Internet. *Journal of*
Career Assessment, 11, 3–21.

Barrick, M. R., & Mount, M. K. (1991). The big five personality dimensions and job
performance: A meta-analysis. *Personnel Psychology, 44, 1–26.*

Bayne, H. B. [My Career Chapter]. In C. Wood & D. G. Hays (Eds.), *A counselor's guide to*
career assessment instruments. Sixth Edition (pp. 493-497). Broken Arrow, OK : National
Career Development Association.

Bennet, G. K., Seashore, H. G., & Wesman, A. G. (2002). Review of the Differential Aptitude
Tests (DAT) & Career Interest Inventory (CII). In J.T Kapes, & E. A. Whitfield (Eds.), A

counselor's guide to career assessment instruments (pp. 123–131). Alexandria, VA: National Career Development Association.

Ben-Porath, Y S., & Waller, N. G. (1992). "Normal" personality inventories in clinical assessment: General requirements and potential for using the NEO-PI. *Psychological Assessment, 4,* 4–19.

Betz, N. E. (1992a). Career assessment: A review of critical issues. In S. D. Brown & R. W Lent (Eds.), *Handbook of counseling psychology* (pp. 453–484). New York: Wiley.

Betz, N. E. (1992b). Counseling use of career self-efficacy theory. *Career Development Quarterly, 41, 22-27.*

Betz, N. E. (1994). Basic issues and concepts in career counseling for women. In W. B. Walsh & S. H. Osipow (Eds.), *Career counseling for women: Contemporary topics in vocational psychology* (pp. 1–41). Hillsdale, NJ: Erlbaum.

Betz, N. E. (1997). What stops women and minorities from choosing and completing majors in science and engineering? In D. Johnson (Ed.), *Minorities and girls in school: Effects on achievement and performance* (pp. 105–140). Thousand Oaks, CA: Sage.

Betz, N. E. (2000a). Contemporary issues in testing use. In C.E. Watkins, Jr., &V L. Campbell (Eds.), *Testing and assessment in counseling practice,* (481–516). Mahwah, NJ: Erlbaum.

Betz, N. E., & Gwilliam, L. R. (2002). The utility of measures of self-efficacy for the Holland themes in African American and European American college students. *Journal of Career Assessment, 10,* 283–300.

Betz, N. E., & Hackett, G. (1997). Applications of self-efficacy theory to the career assessment of women. *Journal of Career Assessment,* 5, 383–402.

Betz, N. E., Schifano, R, & Kaplan, A. (1999). Relationships among measures of perceived self-efficacy with respect to basic domains of vocational activity. *Journal of Career Assessment, 7,* 213–226.

Blackwell, T. L., & Lutyhe, T. D. (2003). Test review: Review of Occupational Aptitude Survey and Interest Schedule - third edition. *Rehabilitation Counseling Bulletin, 46,* 247–50.

Blake, R. J., & Sackett, S. A. (1999). Holland's typology and the five factor model: A rational-empirical analysis. *Journal of Career Assessment, 7,* 249-279.

Boggs, K. R. (2002). Review of the Campbell Interest and Skill Survey. In J.T. Kapes, & E. A. Whitfield (Eds.), *A counselor's guide to career assessment instruments. Fourth Edition* (pp. 195–201). Alexandria, VA: National Career Development Association.

Bouffard, T., Markovitz, H., Vezeau, C., Boisvert, M., & Dumas, C. (1998). The relation between accuracy and self-perception and cognitive development. *British Journal of Educational Psychology, 68,* 321–330.

Brew, S. (1987). *Career development guide for use with the Strong Interest Inventory.* Palo Alto, CA: Consulting Psychologists Press.

Bridges (2014). Choices. [Computer Program]. Ontario, Canada: Author.

Brown, D. (Ed.). (2002). The role of work values and cultural values in occupational choice, satisfaction and success. In D. Brown's (Ed.), *Career choice and development* (4th ed.) (pp. 465–590). San Francisco: Jossey-Bass.

Brown, F. G. (1993). Stanford Achievement Test. In J. J. Kramer & J. S. Conoley (Eds.), *The eleventh mental measurement yearbook* (pp. 861–863). Lincoln: Büros Institute of Mental Measurement, University of Nebraska.

Brown, S.D., & Ryan Krane, N.E. (2000). Four (or five) sessions and a cloud of dust: Old assumptions and new observations about career counseling. In S.D. Brown & R.W. Lent (Eds.), *Handbook of Counseling Psychology* (3rd ed., pp. 740-766). New York: Wiley.

Buboltz, W. C, Jr., Johnson, P., Nichols, C, Miller, M. A., & Thomas, A. (2000). MBTI personality types and SII Personal Style Scales. *Journal of Career Assessment, 8*, 131–145.

Bugaj, A. M. (2013). In C. Wood & D. G. Hays (Eds.), *A counselor's guide to career assessment instruments. Sixth Edition* (pp. 296-299). Broken Arrow, OK : National Career Development Association.

Bullock, E., E., & Reardon, R. C. (2008). Interest profile elevation, big five personality traits, and secondary constructs on the Self-Directed Search: A replication and extension. *Journal of Career Assessment, 16,* 326-338.

Burck, A. M. (2013). [TESTS of Adult Basic Education].]. In C. Wood & D. G. Hays (Eds.), *A counselor's guide to career assessment instruments. Sixth Edition* (pp. 147-151). Broken Arrow, OK : National Career Development Association.

Cairo, P. C, Kritis, K. J., & Myers, R. M. (1996). Career assessment and the Adult Career Concerns Inventory. *Journal of Career Assessment, 4,* 189–204.

Campbell, D. P. (1992). *Campbell Interest and Skill Survey (CISS).* Minneapolis: National Computer Systems.

Campbell, D. P. (2002). The history and development of the Campbell Interest and Skill Survey. *Journal of Career Assessment, 10,* 150–168.

Campbell, V. C., & Perry, Q. A. (2013). [Harrington-O'Shea Career Decision Making System-Revised]. In C. Wood & D. G. Hays (Eds.), *A counselor's guide to career assessment instruments. Sixth Edition* (pp. 251-254). Broken Arrow, OK : National Career Development Association.

Campbell, V. C., & Raiff, G. W. (2002). Review of Harrington O'Shea Career Decision-Making System Revised (CDM). In J.T. Kapes, & E. A. Whitfield (Eds.), *A counselor's guide to career assessment instruments. Fourth Edition* (pp. 230–234). Alexandria, VA: National Career Development Association.

Cantwell, Z. M. (1994). Review of the Reading-Free Vocational Interest Inventory-Revised. In J. T. Kapes, M. M. Mastie, & E. A. Whitfield (Eds.), A *counselor's guide to career assessment instruments* (pp. 326–330). Alexandria, VA: National Career Development Association.

Carless, S. A., & Arnup, J. L. (2011). A longitudinal study of the determinants and outcomes of career change. *Journal of Vocational Behavior, 78,* 8-91.

Carlson, J. G. (1989). Affirmative: In support of researching the Myers-Briggs Type Indicator./owrna/ *of Counseling and Development, 67,* 484–486.

Carlstrom, A. H., & Hughey, K. F. (2013). [Career Directions Inventory, Second Edition]. In C. Wood & D. G. Hays (Eds.), *A counselor's guide to career assessment instruments. Sixth Edition* (pp. 233-237). Broken Arrow, OK : National Career Development Association.

Carpraro, R. M., & Carpraro, M. M. (2002). Myers-Briggs Type Indicator score reliability across studies: A meta-analytic reliability. *Educational and Psychological Measurement, 62,* 590–602.

Carson, A.D, Stalikas, A., & Bizot, E. B. (1997). Correlations between the Myers-Briggs Type Indicator and measures of aptitudes. *Journal of Career Assessment,* 5(1), 81–104.

Chang, D. H. E (2002). The past, present, and future of career counseling in Taiwan. *Career Development Quarterly, 50,* 218–225.

Chartrand, J. M., Robbins, S. B., & Morrill, W. H. (1989). *The Career Factors Inventory. Concord,* Ontario: 2000 Career/LifeSkills Resources.

Chope, R. C. (2009). [California Psychological Inventory, Third Edition]. In J.T. Kapes, E. A. Whitfield, & R. Feller (Eds.), *A counselors guide to career assessment instruments. Fifth Edition* (pp. 382-387). Alexandria, VA: National Career Development Association.

Chope, R. C. (2013). [California Psychological Inventory, Third Edition]. In C. Wood & D. G.

    Hays (Eds.), *A counselor's guide to career assessment instruments. Sixth Edition* (pp. 368-

    371). Broken Arrow, OK : National Career Development Association.

Chung, Y. B. (2003). Ethical and professional issues in career assessment with lesbian, gay and

    bisexual persons. *Journal of Career Assessment, 11,* 96–112.

Ciechalski, J. C. (2002). Self-Directed Search. In J.T. Kapes, & E. A. Whitfield (Eds.), *A*

    counselor's guide to career assessment instruments. Fourth Edition (pp. 282–287).

    Alexandria, VA: National Career Development Association.

Ciechalski, J. C. (2009). Self-Directed Search. In E. A. Whitfield, R. W. Feller, & C. Wood (Eds.),

    A counselor's guide to career assessment instruments (5th ed., pp. 296-308). Broken Arrow,

    OK: National Career Development Association.

Clinedinst, M., & Hawkins, D. (2013). *State of College Admission 2013.* Arlington, VA: National

    Association for College Admission Counseling.

Cole, J. S., Bergin, D. A., & Whittaker, T. A. (2008). Predicting achievement for low stakes

    test with effort and task value. *Contemporary Educational Psychology, 33,* 609-624.

Constantine, M. G., Wallace, B. C., & Kindaichi, M. M., (2005). Examining contextual

    factors in the career decision status of African American adolescents. *Journal of Career*

    Assessment, 13, 307-319.

Cooper, H., Lindsay, J. J., Nye, B., & Greathouse, S. (1998). Relationships among attitudes about

    homework, amount of homework assigned and completed, and student achievement.

    Journal of Educational Psychology, 90(1), 70–83.

Corkin, D., Arbona, Coleman, N., Ramirez, R. (2008). Dimensions of career indecision

    among Puerto Rican college students. *Journal of College Student Development, 49,* 1-15.

Creed, P. A., & Yin, W. O. (2006). Reliability and Validity of a Chinese Version of the Career Decision-Making Difficulties Questionnaire. *International Journal for Educational and Vocational Guidance, 6*, 47-63.

Crockett, S. A. (2013). [O*NET Interest Profiler and Computerized O*NET Interest Profiler]. In C. Wood & D. G. Hays (Eds.), *A counselor's guide to career assessment instruments. Sixth Edition* (pp. 261-267). Broken Arrow, OK : National Career Development Association.

Cronbach, L. J. (1984). *Essentials of psychological testing* (4th ed.) New York: Harper & Row.

Crouteau, J. M., & Slaney, R. B. (1994). Two methods of exploring interests: A comparison of outcomes. *Career Development Quarterly, 42,* 252–261.

Darcy, M., & Tracey, T. J. G. (2003). Integrating abilities and interests in career choice: Maximal versus typical assessment. *Journal of Career Assessment, 11,* 219–237.

Dawis, R. V (2002). Person-environment-correspondence theory. In D. Brown's (Ed.), *Career choice and development* (4th ed.) (pp. 427–464). San Francisco: Jossey-Bass.

D'Costa, A. (2013). [Career Factors Inventory]. In C. Wood & D. G. Hays, (Eds.), A *counselor's guide to career assessment instruments, 6th Ed.* (pp. 325-328). Broken Arrow, OK: National Career Development Association.

Dell, C. A., Harrold, B., & Dell, T. (2008). Wide Range Achievement Test--Fourth Edition. *Rehabilitation Counseling Bulletin, 52,* 57-60.

Diamond, E. E. (1982). Review of the AAMDBecker Reading-Free Vocational Interest Inventory. In J. T. Kapes & M. M. Mastie (Eds.), A *counselor's guide to vocational guidance instruments* (pp. 162–165). Falls Church, VA: National Vocational Guidance Association.

Di Fabio, A., Palazzeschi, L., Asulin-Peretz, L., & Gati, I. (2013). Career indecision versus indecisiveness: Associations with personality traits and emotional intelligence. *Journal of Career Assessment, 21,* 42-56.

Domino, G. (1988). Review of the Reading-Free Vocational Interest Inventory, Revised. In J. T.

Kapes & M. M. Mastie (Eds.), *A counselor's guide to career assessment instruments* (2nd

ed.). Alexandria, VA: National Career Development Association.

Donnay, D. A. C. (1997). E. K. Strong's legacy and beyond: 70 years of the Strong Interest

Inventory. *Career Development Quarterly, 46,* 2-22.

Dozier, V. C., Sampson, J. P., & Reardon, R. C. (2013). Using two different Self-Directed

Search (SDS) interpretive materials: Implications for career assessment. *The*

Professional Counselor Journal. 3, 67-72.

Drummond, R., J., & Jones, K. D. (2009). Assessment procedures for counselors and helping

professionals. 7th Ed. Prentice Hall.

Duffy, R. D. (2010). Sense of control and career adaptability among undergraduate students.

Journal of Career Assessment, 18, 420-430.

Dumenci, L. (1995). Construct validity of the Self- Directed Search using hierarchically nested

structural models. *Journal of Vocational Behavior, 47,* 21–34.

Ehrhart, K. H., & Makransky, G. (2007). Testing vocational interests and personality as

predictors of person-vocation and person-job fit. *Journal of Career Assessment, 15,* 206-

226.

Ellison, L. (2013). [Ashland Interest Assessment]. In C. Wood & D. G. Hays (Eds.), *A counselor's*

guide to career assessment instruments. Sixth Edition (pp. 416-419). Broken Arrow, OK :

National Career Development Association.

Field, J. R. (2013). [Knowdell card sorts: Career Values Card Sort, Motivated Skills Card Sort,

and Occupational Interests Card Sort]. In C. Wood & D. G. Hays, (Eds.), A *counselor's guide*

to career assessment instruments, 6th Ed. (pp. 481-486). Broken Arrow, OK: National Career

Development Association.

Fish, L.A., & Wilson, F. (2009). Predicting performance of MBA students: Comparing the part-time MBA program and the one-year program. *College Student Journal, 43*, 145-160.

Fleenor, J. W. (2001). Review of the Myers Briggs Type Inventory Form M. In B.S. Plake and J.C. Impara (Eds.), *The fourteenth mental measurements yearbook.* Lincoln, NE: Büros Institute of Mental Measurements. Retrieved August 15th, 2004, from Mental Measurements Yearbook database. Accession number: 14122331

Flores, L. Y., Spanierman, L. B., Armstrong, P. I., & Velez, A. D. (2006). Validity of the Strong Interest Inventory and Skills Confidence Inventory with Mexican American high school students. *Journal of Career Assessment, 14,* 183-202.

Flores, L. Y., Spanierman, L. B., & Obasi, E. M. (2003). Ethical and professional issues in career assessment with diverse racial and ethnic groups. *Journal of Career Assessment, 11,* 76–95.

Fouad, N. A. (1993). Cross-cultural vocational assessment. *Career Development Quarterly, 42,* 4-13.

Fouad, N. A. (1999). Validity evidence for interest inventories. In M. L. Savickas & A. R. Spokane (Eds.), *Vocational interests: Meaning, measurement, and counseling use* (pp. 193–209). Palo Alto, CA: Davies-Black.

Fouad, N. A., & Mohler, C. J. (2004). Cultural validity of Holland's theory and the Strong Interest Inventory for five racial/ethnic groups. *Journal of Career Assessment, 12,* 423–439.

Fuller, B. E., Holland, J. L., & Johnston, J. A. (1999). The relation of profile elevation in the Self-Directed Search to personality variables. *Journal of Career Assessment, 7,* 111–123.

Fuqua, D. R., & Newman, J. L. (1994). Review of the Campbell Interest and Skill Survey. In J. T. Kapes, M. M. Mastie, & E. A. Whitfield (Eds.), *A counselor s guide to career assessment instruments* (pp. 139–143). Alexandria, VA: National Career Development Association.

Fuller, B. E., Holland, J. L., & Johnston, J. A. (1999). The relation of profile elevation in the Self-Directed Search to personality variables. *Journal of Career Assessment, 7,* 111–123.

Galassi, J. P., Crace, R. K., Martin, G. A., James, R. M., & Wallace, R. L. (1992). Client preferences and anticipations in career counseling: A preliminary investigation. *Journal of Counseling Psychology,* 39, 46–55.

Gati, I., & Asulin-Peretz, L. (2011). Internet-based self-help career assessments and interventions: Challenges and implications for evidence-based career counseling. *Journal of Career Assessment, 19,* 259-273.

Gati, I., Kleiman, T., Saka, N., & Zakai, A. (2003). Perceived benefits of using an Internet-based interactive career planning system. *Journal of Vocational Behavior, 62, 272–86.*

Gati, I., Landman, S., Davidovitch, S., Asulin-Peretz, L., & Gadassi, R. (2010). From career decision-making styles to career decision-making profiles: A multidimensional approach. *Journal of Vocational Behavior, 76,* 277-291. *http://dx.doi.org/10.1016/j.jvb.2009.11.001*

Gati, I., & Levin, N. (2012). The stability and structure of Career Decision-Making Profiles: A 1-year follow-up. *Journal of Career Assessment, 20,* 390-403.

Gati, I., Osipow, S. H., Krausz, M., & Saka, N. (2000). Validity of the career decision-making difficulties questionnaire: Counselees' versus career counselors' perceptions. *Journal of Vocational Behavior, 56,* 99-113.

Geist, H. (1964). *The Geist Picture Inventory.* Beverly Hills, CA: Western Psychological Publishers. (ERIC Document Reproduction Service No. ED 5005 9234) Gianakos, I. (1999). Patterns of career choice and career decision-making self-efficacy. *Journal of Vocational Behavior, 54,* 244–258.

Gibbons, M. M. (2013). [Kuder Skills Confidence Assessment]. In C. Wood & D. G. Hays (Eds.), *A counselor's guide to career assessment instruments. Sixth Edition* (pp. 203-210). Broken Arrow, OK : National Career Development Association.

Glavin, K. W., & Savickas, M. L. (2011). Interpreting Self-Directed Search profiles: Validity of the "rule of eight." *Journal of Vocational Behavior, 79,* 414-418.

Goldman, L. (1972). *Using tests in counseling* (2nd ed.). New York: Appleton-Century-Crofts.

Goldman, L. (1983). The vocational card sort technique: A different view. *Measurement and Evaluation in Guidance, 16,* 107–109.

Goldman, L. (1995). Comment on Crouteau and Slaney (1994J. *Career Development Quarterly, 43,* 385–386.

Good, C., Aronson, J., & Harder, J. A. (2008). Problems in the pipeline: Stereotype threat and women's achievement in high-level math courses. *Journal of Applied Developmental Psychology, 29*, 17-28.

Goodman, J. (1993, April 29). Using non-standardized appraisal tools and techniques. Presentation to Michigan Career Development Association Annual Conference. Kalamazoo, MI.

Gottfredson, G. D. (1996). The assessment of career status with the Career Attitudes and Strategies Inventory. *Journal of Career Assessment, 4,*363–381.

Gottfredson, G. D., & Jones, E. M. (1993). Psychological meaning of profile elevation in the Vocational Preference Inventory. *Journal of Career Assessment, 1,* 35-49.

Gratz, Z. S. (2013). [Reading-Free Vocational Interest Inventory, Second Edition]. In C. Wood & D. G. Hays (Eds.), *A counselor's guide to career assessment instruments. Sixth Edition* (pp. 447-450). Broken Arrow, OK : National Career Development Association.

Green, K. E. (2009). [Barriers to Employment Success Inventory, Second Edition In J.T. Kapes, E. A. Whitfield, & R. Feller (Eds.), *A counselor's guide to career assessment instruments. Fifth Edition* (pp. 328-33). Broken Arrow, OK : National Career

Development Association.

Green, K. E. (2013). [Barriers to Employment Success Inventory, Fourth Edition]. In C.

Wood & D. G. Hays (Eds.), *A counselor's guide to career assessment instruments. Sixth*

Edition (pp. 307-310). Broken Arrow, OK : National Career Development Association.

Groth-Marnat, G. (2009). *Handbook of psychological assessment.* New Jersey: John Wiley &

Sons.

Gysbers, N. C. (2006). Using qualitative career assessments in career counseling with adults.

International Journal for Educational and Vocational Guidance, 6, 95-108.

Hackett, G., & Lonborg, S. D. (1994). Career assessment and counseling for women. In W. B.

Walsh & S. H. Osipow (Eds.), *Career counseling for women* (pp. 43–85). Hillsdale, NJ:

Erlbaum.

Haile, G.A., & Nguyen, A. N. (2008). Determinants of academic attainment in the United

States: A quantile regression analysis of test scores. Educational Economics, 16, 29–

57.

Hambleton, R. K. (1985). Review of Differential Aptitude Tests: Forms V & W. In J. V. Mitchell,

Jr. (Ed.), *The ninth mental measurement yearbook.* Lincoln: Büros Institute of Mental

Measurement, University of Nebraska.

Hammond, M. S., Lockman, J. D., & Boiling, T. (2010). A test of the tripartite model of career

indecision of Brown and Krane for African Americans incorporating emotional intelligence

and positive affect. *Journal of Career Assessment, 18,* 161-176.

Hansen, J. C. (1985). *User's guide for the SVIB/SII.* Palo Alto, CA: Consulting Psychologists

Press.

Hansen, J. C. (1990). Interpretation of the Strong Interest Inventory. In W. B. Walsh & S. H.

Osipow (Eds.), *Career counseling for women.* Hillsdale, NJ: Erlbaum.

Hansen, J. C. (2000). Interpretation of the Strong Interest Inventory. In C. E. Watkins, Jr., & V. L. Campbell (Eds.), *Testing and assessment in counseling practice.* 2nd ed. (pp. 227–262). Mahwah, NJ: Erlbaum.

Hansen, J-I. C., & Lee, W. V. (2007). Evidence of concurrent validity of SII scores for Asian American college students. *Journal of Career Assessment, 15*, 44-54. doi: 10.1177/1069072706294514

Hansen, J-I. C, & Neuman, J. L. (1999). Evidence of concurrent prediction of the Campbell Interest and Skill Survey (CISS) for college major selection. *Journal of Career Assessment, 7*, 239–247.

Harmon, L. W (1994). Review of the Career Decision Scale. In J. T. Kapes, M. M. Mastie, & E. A. Whitfield (Eds.), *A counselor's guide to career assessment instruments* (pp. 259–262). Alexandria, VA: National Career Development Association.

Harmon, L. W, Hansen, J-I. C, Borgen, F. H., & Hammer, A. L. (1994). *Strong Interest Inventory: Applications and technical guide.* Palo Alto, CA: Consulting Psychologists Press.

Harrington, T. F. (2006). A 20-year follow-up of the Harrington-O'Shea Career Decision Making System. *Measurement and Evaluation in Counseling and Development, 38,* 198-202.

Harrington, T., & Long, J. L. (2012). The history of interest inventories and career assessments in career counseling. *Career Development Quarterly, 61,* 83-92.

Harrington, T. E, & O'Shea, A. J. (2000). *The CDM2000 manual.* Circle Pines, MN: American Guidance Service.

Härtung, P. J. (1999). Interest assessment using card sorts. In M. L. Savickas & A. R. Spokane (Eds.), *Vocational interests: Meaning, measurement, and counseling use.* Davies-Black Publishing/Consulting Psychologists Press, Inc, Palo Alto, CA: 235–252.

Hattrup, K. (2003). Review of the California Psychological Inventory Third Edition. In B.S. Plake, J.C. Impara, and R.A. Spies (Eds.), *The fifteenth mental measurements yearbook.*

Lincoln, NE: Büros Institute of Mental Measurements. Retrieved December 15, 2004, from
Mental Measurements Yearbook database. Accession number: 15122723

Hattrup, D. (1995). Review of Differential Aptitude Tests: Fifth Edition. In J. C. Conoley & J. C.
Impara (Eds.), *The twelfth mental measurements yearbook* (pp. 302-304). Lincoln, NE: Buros
Institute of Mental Measurements.

Hay, I., Ashman, A. F, & Van Kraayenoord, C. E. (1998). Educational characteristics of students
with high or low self concepts. *Psychology in the Schools, 35,* 391–400.

Healy, C. C. (1989). Negative: The MBTI: Not ready for routine use in counseling. *Journal of
Counseling and Development, 67,* 487–489.

Healy, C.C. (2001). *Myers-Briggs Type Indicator*. In J. T. Kapes & E. A. Whitfield (Eds.), *A
counselor's guide to career assessment instruments* (4th ed.; pp. 363-368). Columbus,
OH: National Career Development Association.

Healy, C. C., & Chope , R. C. (2006). Implications of the articles for interpreting interest
inventories: Consequential validity and meaning making. *Measurement and Evaluation in
Counseling and Development, 38,* 247-252.

Healy, C. C., & Woodward, G. A. (1998). The Myers-Briggs Type Indicator and career obstacles.
Measurement and Evaluation in Counseling and Development, 31, 74–85.

Henfield, M. S. (2013). [My System of Career Influences]. In C. Wood & D. G. Hays (Eds.), *A
counselor's guide to career assessment instruments. Sixth Edition* (pp. 499-502). Broken
Arrow, OK : National Career Development Association.

Henington, C. (2001). Review of the NEO4. In B.S. Plake and J.C. Impara (Eds.), *The
fourteenth mental measurements yearbook.* Lincoln, NE: Büros Institute of Mental
Measurements. Retrieved December 15th, 2004, from Mental Measurements Yearbook
database. Accession # 14122273.

Heppner, M. J., Fuller, B. E., & Multon, K. D. (1998). Adults in involuntary career transition: An analysis of the relationship between psychological and career domains. *Journal of Career Assessment, 6,* 329–346.

Herman, O. D. (1985). Review of the Career Decision Scale. In J. V Mitchell, Jr. (Ed.), *The ninth mental measurement yearbook,* (Vol. II) (p. 270). Lincoln: Büros Institute of Mental Measurement, University of Nebraska.

Hirschi, A. (2010). The role of chance events in the school-to-work transition: The influence of demographic, personality and career development variables. *Journal of Vocational Behavior, 77,* 39-49.

Holden, R. H. (1984). Review of the Reading-Free Vocational Interest Inventory, Revised. In D. J.Keyser &R. C. Sweetland (Eds.), *Test critiques II* (pp. 627–630). Kansas City, MO: Test Corporation of America.

Holland, J. L. (1994b). *The Self-Directed Search: Professional user's guide.* Odessa, FL: Psychological Assessment Resources.

Holland, J. L. (1997). *Making vocational choices: A theory of vocational personalities and work environments.* Odessa, FL: Psychological Assessment Resources.

Holland, J. L., Daiger, D. C, & Power, P. G. (1980). *My Vocational Situation.* Palo Alto, CA: Consulting Psychologists Press.

Holland, J. L., Johnston, J. A., & Asama, N. F. (1993). The Vocational Identity Scale: A diagnostic and treatment tool. *Journal of Career Assessment, 1,* 1-12.

Holland, J. L., & Messer, M. A. (2013). *The Self-Directed Search: Professional manual.* Odessa, FL: Psychological Assessment Resources.

Holland, J. L., Powell, A., & Fritzsche, B. (1994). *The Self-Directed Search (SDS): Professional user's guide.* Odessa, FL: Psychological Assessment Resources.

Holmgren, R. L., & Dalldorf, M. R. (1993, October). *A validation of the ASVAB against supervisors' ratings in the General Aptitude Test Battery (GATB)*. Washington, DC: United States Employment Service. Ihle-Helledy, K., Zytowski, D. G., & Fouad, N. A. (2004). .Kuder Career Search: Test-retest reliability and consequential validity. *Journal of Career Assessment, 12,* 285–297.

Jenkins (2008) – [Strong Interest Inventory and Skills Confidence Inventory]. In J.T. Kapes, E. A. Whitfield, & R. Feller (Eds.), *A counselors guide to career assessment instruments. Fifth Edition* (pp. 309-319). Alexandria, VA: National Career Development Association.

Jenkins, J. A. (2013). [Strong Interest Inventory and Skills Confidence Inventory]. In C. Wood & D. G. Hays (Eds.), *A counselor's guide to career assessment instruments. Sixth Edition* (pp. 279-284). Broken Arrow, OK : National Career Development Association.

Jones, L. K. (1980). Issues in developing an occupational card sort. *Measurement and Evaluation in Guidance,* 22, 200–213.

Jones, L. K., Sheffield, D., & Joyner, B. (2000). Comparing the effects of the Career Key with Self-Directed Search and Job-OE among eighth grade students. *Professional School Counseling, 3,* 238–247.

Judge, T. A., Higgins, C. A., Thoresen, C. J., & Barrick, M. R. (1999). The big five personality traits, general mental ability, and career success across the life span. *Personnel Psychology,* 52, 621–652.

Kaplan, R., & Saccuzzo, D. (1993). *Psychological testing.* Pacific Grove, CA: Brooks/Cole.

Kantamneni, N. (2014). Vocational interest structures for Asian Americans, Middle-Eastern Americans and Native Americans on the 2005 Strong Interest Inventory. *Journal of Vocational Behavior, 84,* 133-141.

Katz, L., Joiner, J. W., & Seaman, N. (1999). Effects of joint interpretation of the Strong Interest Inventory and the Myers-Briggs Type Indicator in career choice. *Journal of Career Assessment, 7,* 281–297.

Kelly, K. R. (2005). Review of the Harrington-O'Shea Career Decision Making System-Revised. In R. A. Spies & B. S. Plake (Eds.). *The sixteenth mental measurements yearbook* (pp. 434-438). Lincoln, NE: Buros Institute of Mental Measurements.

Kelly, K. R. (2009). [Differential Aptitude Tests and Career Interest Inventory]. In J.T. Kapes, E. A. Whitfield, & R. Feller (Eds.), *A counselors guide to career assessment instruments. Fifth Edition* (pp. 129-136). Alexandria, VA: National Career Development Association.

Kelly, K. N. (2013). [Differential Aptitude Tests and Career Interest Inventory]. In C. Wood & D. G. Hays, (Eds.), A *counselor's guide to career assessment instruments, 6th Ed.* (pp. 183–190). Broken Arrow, OK: National Career Development Association.

Kitchel, T. (2010). Psychosocial differences by CTE discipline and personality type in student teachers. *Journal of Career and Technical Education, 25,* 35-46.

Knowdell, R. L. (2010a). *Career Values Card Sort Planning Kit.* San Jose, CA: Career Research and Testing.

Knowdell, R. L. (2010b). *Motivated Skills Card Sort Planning Kit.* San Jose, CA: Career Research and Testing.

Konstam, V., & Lehmann, I. S. (2011). Emerging adults at work and play: Leisure, work engagement, and career indecision. *Journal of Career Assessment, 19,* 151-164.

Konstantopoulus, S., & Chung, V. (2009). What are the long-term effects of small classes on the achievement gap? Evidence from the Lasting Benefits Study. *American Journal of Education, 116,* 125-154.

Krug, S. E. (1995). Career assessment and the Adult Personality Inventory. *Journal of Career Assessment, 3,* 176-187. DOI: 10.1177/106907279500300205

La Guardia, A. C. (2013). [Myers-Briggs Type Indicator]. In C. Wood & D. G. Hays (Eds.), *A counselor's guide to career assessment instruments. Sixth Edition* (pp. 385-389). Broken Arrow, OK : National Career Development Association.

Lancaster, B. P., Rudolph, C. E., Perkins, T. S., & Patten, T. G. (1999). The reliability and validity of the Career Decision Difficulties Questionnaire. *Journal of Career Assessment, 7*, 393–413.

Larson, L. M., Rottinghaus, P. J., & Borgen, F. H. (2002). Meta-analyses of big six interests and big five personality factors. *Journal of Vocational Behavior, 61,* 217–39.

Lent, R. W., & Brown, S. D. (2008). Social cognitive career theory and subjective well-being in the context of work. *Journal of Career Assessment, 16,* 6-21. DOI: 10.1177/1069072707305769

Leong, E T. L., & Dollinger, S. J. (1991). Review of the NEO-PI. In D. J. Keyser & R. C. Sweetland (Eds.), *Test critiques VIII* (pp. 527–539). Austin, TX: PRO-ED

Leong, F. T. L., & Hartung, P. J. (2000). Adapting to the changing multicultural context of career. In A. Collin & R. A. Young (Eds.), *The Future of Career* (pp. 212-227). Cambridge, UK: Cambridge University Press.

Leung, S. A. (2002). Career counseling in Hong Kong: Meeting the social challenges. *Career Development Quarterly, 50,* 218–225.

Levin, A. (1991). *Introduction to the Strong for career counselors.* Palo Alto, CA: Consulting Psychologists Press.

Levinson, E. M. (1994). Current vocational assessment models for students with disabilities. *Journal of Counseling and Development, 73,* 94–101.

Levinson, E. M., Zeman, H. L., & Ohler, D. L. (2002). A critical evaluation of the web-based version of the Career Key. *Career Development Quarterly, 51, 26–35.*

Lindley, L. D., & Borgen, F. H. (2002). Generalized self-efficacy, Holland theme self-efficacy and academic performance. *Journal of Career Assessment, 20*, 301–314.

Linn, R. L. (1982). Differential Aptitude Tests/DAT career planning program. In J. T. Kapes & M. M. Mastie (Eds.), A *counselor's guide to vocational guidance instruments* (pp. 37–42). Falls Church, VA: National Vocational Guidance Association.

Logue, C. T., Lounsbury, J. W., Gupta, A., & Leong, F. T. L. (2007). Vocational interest themes and personality traits in relation to college major satisfaction of business students. *Journal of Career Development, 33,* 269-295. DOI: 10.1177/0894845306297348

Lokan, J., & Fleming, M. (2003). Issue in adapting a computer-assisted career guidance system for use in another country. *Language Testing, 20*, 167-177.

Lopez, F. G., Sujin, A-Y. (2006). Predictors of career indecision in three racial/ethnic groups of college women. *Journal of Career Development, 33,* 29-46.

Lorelle, S. (2013). [Life Role Analysis]. In C. Wood & D. G. Hays, (Eds.), A *counselor's guide to career assessment instruments, 6th Ed.* (pp. 487-491). Broken Arrow, OK: National Career Development Association.

Lounsbury, J. W., Tatum, H. E., Chambers, W., Owens, K., & Gibson, L. W. (1999). An investigation of career decidedness in relation to "Big Five" personality constructs and life satisfaction. *College Student Journal, 33,* 646-652.

Lowman, R. L. (1991). *The clinical practice of career assessment: Interests, abilities, and personality.* Washington, DC: American Psychological Association.

Lundberg, D. J., Osborne, W. L., & Minor, C. U. (1997). Career maturity and personality preferences of Mexican-American and Anglo- American adolescents. *Journal of Career Development, 23*, 203–213.

Major, D. A., Holland, J. M., & Oborn, K. L. (2012). The influence of proactive personality and coping on commitment to STEM majors. *Career Development Quarterly, 60,* 16-24.

Manuelle-Adkins, C. (1989). Review of the Self- Directed Search: 1985 revision. In J. C. Conoley & J. J. Kramer (Eds.), *The tenth mental measurement yearbook.* Lincoln: Büros Institute of Mental Measurement, University of Nebraska.

Marsella, A.J., & Leong, F.T.L. (1995). Cross-cultural Issues in Personality and Career Assessment. *Journal of Career Assessment, 3,* 202-218.

Marsh, H. W., & Yeung, A. S. (1998). Longitudinal structural equation models of academic self-concept and achievement: Gender differences in the development of math and English constructs. *American Educational Research Journal, 35(4),* 705–738.

Mastrangelo , P. M. (2001). Review of the Myers Briggs Type Inventory Form M. In B.S. Plake and J.C. Impara (Eds.), *The fourteenth mental measurements yearbook.* Lincoln, NE: Büros Institute of Mental Measurements. Retrieved August 15th, 2004, from Mental Measurements Yearbook database. Accession number: 14122331

Mastrangelo , P. M. (2009). [Myers-Briggs Type Indicator]. In E. Whitfield, R. Feller, & C. Wood (Eds.), *A counselor's guide to career assessment instruments. Fifth Edition, pp. 400-406).* Broken Arrow, OK : National Career Development Association.

Mattson, C. E. (2007). Beyond admission: Understanding pre-college variables and the success of at-risk students. *Journal of College Admission,* 8-13.

McKee, L. M., & Levinson, E. M. (1990). A review of the computerized version of the Self-Directed Search. *Career Development Quarterly, 38,* 325–333.

McIlveen, P. (2008). *My Career Chapter: A dialogical autobiography* (Doctoral dissertation). University of Southern Queensland, Toowoomba, Australia.

Miller, R. J. (1992). Review of the Reading-Free Vocational Interest Inventory, Revised. In J. J. Kramer & J. C. Conoley (Eds.), *The eleventh mental measurement yearbook.* Lincoln: Büros Institute of Mental Measurement, University of Nebraska.

Moller, J., Pohlmann, B., Koller, O., & Marsh, H. W. (2009). A meta-analytic path analysis of the internal/external frame of reference model of academic achievement and academic self-concept. *Review of Educational Research, 79,* 1129-1167.

Nauta, M. M. (2012). Are RIASEC interests traits? Evidence based on self-other agreement. *Journal of Career Assessment, 20,* 426-439.

Neuman, J. L., Gray, E. A., & Fuqua, D. R. (1999). The relation of career indecision to personality dimensions of the California Psychological Inventory. *Journal of Vocational Behavior,* 54(1), 174–187.

Niles, S. G., Anderson, W P., Jr., Härtung, P. J. & Staton, A. R. (1999). Identifying client types from adult career concerns inventory scores. *Journal of Career Development, 25*, 173–185.

Niles, S. G., & Goodnough, G. E. (1996). Life-role salience and values: A review of recent research. *Career Development Quarterly,* 45(1), 65–86.

Noel, N. M., Michaels, C, & Levas, M. G. (2003). The relationship of personality traits and self-monitoring behavior to choice of business major. *Journal of Education for Business,* 78,153–57.

Nota, L. Ferrari, L., Solberg, V., S. H., & Soresi, S. (2007). Career search self-efficacy, family support, and career indecision with Italian youth. *Journal of Career Assessment, 15,* 181-193.

Ohler, D. L., Levinson, E. M., & Barker, W. F. (1996). Career maturity in college students with learning disabilities. *Career Development Quarterly,* 44(3), 278–288.

Okiishi, R. W (1987). The genogram as a tool in career counseling. *Journal of Counseling and Development,* 66,139–143.

Oliver, L. W., & Zack, J. S. (1999). Career assessment on the Internet: An exploratory *study. Journal of Career Assessment,* 7(4), 323–356.

Olson, G. T., & Matlock, S. G. (1994). Review of the 16PF. In J. T. Kapes, M. M. Mastie, & E. A. Whitfield. *A counselor's guide to career assessment instruments* (3rd ed.) (pp. 302–305). Alexandria, VA: National Career Development Association.

Organist, J. E. (1985). Review of the Wide Range Interest-Opinion Test. In D. J. Keyser & R. C. Sweetland (Eds.), *Test critiques IV (pp.* 673–676). Kansas City, MO: Test Corporation of America.

Obsorn, D. S., & Bethell, D. B. (2009). Using card sorts in career assessment. *Career Planning and Adult Development Journal, 25,* 101-114.

Osborn, D. S., Peterson, G. W, Sampson, J. P., Jr., & Reardon, R. C. (2003). Client anticipations about computer-assisted career guidance outcomes. *Career Development Quarterly, 51, 356–67.*

Osipow, S. H. (1980). *Manual for the Career Decision Scale.* Columbus, OH: Marathon Consulting and Press.

Osipow, S. H. (1987). *Manual for the Career Decision Scale.* Odessa, FL: Psychological Assessment Resources.

Osipow, S. H., Carney, C. G., & Barak, A. (1976). A scale of educational-vocational undecidedness: A typological approach. *Journal of Vocational Behavior, 27,*233–244.

Osipow, S. H., Carney, C.G., Winer, J.L., Yanico, B. J., & Koeschier, M. (1987). *Career Decision Scale* (3rd rev.). Odessa, FL: Psychological Assessment Resources.

Osipow, S. H., & Gati, I. (1998). Construct and concurrent validity of the career decision making difficulties questionnaire. *Journal of Career Assessment, 6,* 347–364.

Osipow, S. H., & Temple, R. D. (1996). Development and use of the Task-Specific Occupational Self-Efficacy Scale. *Journal of Career Assessment,* 4(4), 445–456.

Osipow, S. H., Temple, R. D., & Rooney, R. A. (1993). The short form of the Task-Specific Occupational Self-Efficacy Scale. *Journal of Career Assessment, 2*(1), 13–20.

Osipow, S. H., & Winer, J. L. (1996). The use of the Career Decision Scale in career assessment./owrna/ *of Career Assessment, 4,* 117–130.

Osipow, S. H., Winer, J. L., & Koschier, M. (1976). *Career Decision Scale.* Odessa, FL: Psychological Assessment Resources.

Overton, T. (1992). Social and Prevocational Information Battery (SPIB). In J. J. Kramer & J.S. Conoley (Eds.), *The eleventh mental measurement yearbook* (pp. 834–836). Lincoln: Büros Institute of Mental Measurement, University of Nebraska.

Paige, B. E. (2000). Psychological types of dental hygiene students. *Journal of Psychological Type, 52,* 32–35.

Parish, L. H., & Lynch, P.S. (1988). Review of the Pictorial Inventory of Careers. In J. T Kapes &M.M. Mastie (Eds.), A *counselor s guide to career assessment instruments* (2nd ed.). Alexandria, VA: National Career Development Association.

Parish, P. A., Rosenberg, H., & Wilkinson, L. (1979). *Career information resources, applications, and research, 1950–1979.* Boulder: University of Colorado.

Park, H., Khan, S., & Petrina, S. (2009). ICT in science education: A quasi-experimental study of achievement, attitudes toward science, and career aspirations of Korean middle school students. *International Journal of Science Education, 31,* 993-1012.

Parsons, F. (1909). *Choosing a vocation.* Boston: Houghton Mifflin.

Parsons, E., & Betz, N. E. (1998). Test-retest reliability and validity studies of the Skills Confidence Inventory. *Journal of Career Assessment, 31(3),* 150–163.

Patrick, J., Blosel, C. W., & Gross, C. L. (2009). [Armed Services Vocational Aptitude Battery Career Exploration Program]. In E. Whitfield, R. Feller, & C. Wood (Eds.), *A counselor's guide to career assessment instruments. Fifth Edition, pp. 94-104).* Broken Arrow,

OK : National Career Development Association.

Patrick, J., Samide, J., Muth, D. L., Comito, N. S., & Gross, C. L. (2013). [Armed Services

Vocational Aptitude Battery Career Exploration Program]. In C. Wood & D. G. Hays

(Eds.), *A counselor's guide to career assessment instruments. Sixth Edition* (pp. 127-133).

Broken Arrow, OK : National Career Development Association.

Peila-Shuster, J. J., & Feller, R. (2013). [Career Thoughts Inventory]. In C. Wood & D. G. Hays

(Eds.), *A counselor's guide to career assessment instruments. Sixth Edition* (pp. 333-337).

Broken Arrow, OK : National Career Development Association.

Pennock-Roman, M. (1988). Differential Aptitude Test. In J. T. Kapes & M. M. Mastie (Eds.), *A*

counselor's guide to career assessment instruments (2nd ed.). Alexandra, VA: National

Career Development Association.

Peterson, G. W, & Lenz, J. G. (1992). *Using card sorts: A cognitive mapping task.* Unpublished

manuscript. Tallahassee, FL.

Peterson, G. W, Ryan-Jones, R. E., Sampson, J. P., Jr., Reardon, R. C, & Shahnasarian, M.

(1987). *A comparison of the effectiveness of three computer-assisted career guidance systems*

on college students' career decision making processes (Tech. Rep. No. 6). Tallahassee: Florida

State University, Center for the Study of Technology in Counseling and Career

Development.

Peterson, G. W, Ryan-Jones, R. E., Sampson, J. P., Jr., Reardon, R. C, & Shahnasarian, M.

(1994). A comparison of the effectiveness of three computer-assisted career guidance

systems: DISCOVER, SIGI, and SIGI PLUS. *Computers in Human Behavior, 10,* 189–

198.

Peterson, G. W, Sampson, J. P., Jr., & Reardon, R. C. (1991). *Career development and services: A*

cognitive approach. Pacific Grove, CA: Brooks/Cole.

Peterson, G. W., Sampson, J. P., Jr., Reardon, R. C, & Lenz, J. G. (2002). A cognitive information processing approach to career problem solving and decision making. In D. Brown (Ed.), *Career choice and development* (4th ed.) (pp. 312–372). San Francisco: Jossey- Bass.

Peterson, S. L., & delMas, R. C. (1998). The component structure of Career Decision-Making Self-Efficacy for underprepared college students. *Journal of Career Development, 24(3),* 209–225.

Petrill, S. A., & Wilkerson, B. (2000). Intelligence and achievement: A behavioral genetic perspective. *Educational Psychology Review, 12, 185–199.*

Pinkney, J. W. (1985). A card sort strategy for flat profiles on the Strong-Campbell Interest Inventory. *Vocational Guidance Quarterly, 33,* 331–339.

Pinkney, J. W., & Bozik, C. M. (1994). Review of the Career Development Inventory. In J. T. Kapes, M. M. Mastie, & E. A. Whitfield (Eds.), *A counselor's guide to career assessment instruments. Third Edition* (pp. 265–267). Alexandria, VA: National Career Development Association.

Pitz, G. E, & Harren, V. A. (1980). An analysis of career decision making from the point of view of information processing and decision theory. *Journal of Vocational Behavior, 16,* 320–346.

Pope, M. (2002). Review of the Kuder General Interest Survey, FormE. In J.T. Kapes, &E. A. Whitfield (Eds.), *A counselor's guide to career assessment instruments. Fourth Edition* (pp. 258–264). Alexandria, VA: National Career Development Association.

Popham, W. (2006). Branded by a test. *Educational Leadership 63,* 86-7.

Powell, D. E, & Luzzo, D. A. (1998). Evaluating factors associated with the career maturity of high school students. *Career Development Quarterly, 47,* 145–158.

Prather-Jones, B. (2011). "Some people aren't cut out for it": The role of personality factors in the careers of teachers of students with EBD. *Remedial and Special Education, 32,* 179-191.

Prediger, D. J. (1980). The marriage between tests and career counseling: An intimate report. *Vocational Quarterly,* 28,297–305.

Prediger, D. J. (1994). Tests and counseling: The marriage that prevailed. *Measurement and Evaluation in Counseling, 26(A),* 227–234.

Prediger, D. J. (1995). *Assessment in career counseling.* Greensboro, NC: ERIC Counseling and Student Services Clearinghouse, University of North Carolina.

Prediger, D. J., & Swaney, K. B. (1992). Career counseling validity of Discover's job cluster scales for the revised ASVAB score report (Report No. 92–2). Iowa City, IA: American College Testing Program.

Prediger, D. J., & Swaney, K. B. (1995). Using the UNIACT in a comprehensive approach to assessment for career planning. *Journal of Career Assessment, 3,* 429–452.

Prins, E. (2009). [Tests of Adult Basic Education]. In E. A. Whitfield, R. W. Feller, & C. Wood (Eds.), *A counselor's guide to career assessment instruments. Fifth Edition* (pp. 202-208). Broken Arrow, OK : National Career Development Association.

Pulkkinen, L., Ohranen, M., & Tolvanen, A. (1999). Personality antecedents of career orientation and stability among women compared to men. *Journal of Vocational Behavior, 54,* 37-58.

Pulver, C. A., & Kelly, K. R. (2008). Incremental validity of the Myers-Briggs Type Indicator in predicting academic major selection of undecided university students. *Journal of Career Assessment, 16,* 441-455. doi: 10.1177/10690727083189

Ragothaman, S., Carpenter, J., & Davies, T. (2009). An empirical investigation of MPA student performance and admissions criteria. *College Student Journal, 43*(3), 879-875.

Railey, M.G., & Peterson, G. W. (2000). The assessment of dysfunctional career thoughts and interest structure among female inmates and probationers. *Journal of Career Assessment, 8*(2), 119–129.

Raju, P. M., Asfaw, A. (2009). Recalled test anxiety in relation to achievement, in the context of general academic self-concept, study habits, parental involvement and socio-economic status among Grade 6 Ethiopian students. *Education 3-13, 37,* 269-285.

Ralston, C. A., Borgen, F. H., Rottinghaus, P. J., & Donnay, D. A. C. (2004). Specificity in interest measurement: Basic Interest Scales and major field of study. *Journal of Vocational Behavior, 65, 203–216.*

Rangappa, K. T. (1994). Effect of self-concept on achievement in mathematics. *Psycho-Lingua, 24(1),* 43–48.

Rayman, J., & Atanasoff, L. (1999). Holland's theory and career intervention: The power of the hexagon. *Journal of Vocational Behavior,* 55(1), 114–126.

Reardon, R. C., & Lenz, J. G. (1998). *The Self- Directed Search and related Holland materials: A practitioner's guide.* Odessa, FL: Psychological Assessment Resources.

Reardon, R. C., & Lenz, J. G. (2013). Use and interpretive guide. *Self-Directed Search Professional Manual,* p. 15-29.

Reardon, R. C, Shahnasarian, M., Maddox, E. N., & Sampson, J. P., Jr. (1984). Computers and student services. *Journal of Counseling and Development, 63,* 180–183.

Ree, M. J., &Carretta, T. R. (1995). Group differences in aptitude factor structure on the ASVAB. *Educational and Psychological Measurement, 55,* 268–277.

Rehfuss, M. (2013). [Career Style Interview]. In C. Wood & D. G. Hays, (Eds.), A *counselor's guide to career assessment instruments, 6th Ed.* (pp. 465-469). Broken Arrow, OK: National Career Development Association.

Ricks, J. H. (1978). Review of the Career Development Inventory. In O. K. Buros (Ed.),The *eighth mental measurement yearbook* (Vol. 2). Highland Park, NJ: Gryphon.

Robbins, S. B. (1985). Validity estimates for the Career Decision-Making Self-Efficacy Scale. *Measurement & Evaluation in Counseling & Development, 18,* 64–71.

Rogers, J. E. (2002). Review of the Armed Services Vocational Aptitude Battery Career Exploration Program (ASVAB). In J.T. Kapes, & E. A. Whitfield (Eds.), A *counselor's guide to career assessment instruments* (pp. 93–101). Alexandria, VA: National Career Development Association.

Rojewski, J. W. (1996). Occupational aspirations and early career-choice patterns of adolescents with and without learning disabilities *Learning Disability Quarterly, 19(2),* 99–116.

Rokeach, M. (1973). *The nature of human values.* New York: Free Press.

Rosen, D., Holmberg, M. S.., & Holland, J. L. (1994). *Dictionary of educational opportunities.* Odessa, FL: Psychological Assessment Resources.

Rottinghaus, P. J., Coon, K. L., Gaffey, A. R., & Zytowski, D. G. (2007). Thirty-year stability and predictive validity of vocational interests. *Journal of Career Assessment, 15,* 5-22.

Rounds, J. B., Jr., Henly, G. A., Dawis, R. V, & Lofquist, L. H. (1981). *Manual for the Minnesota Importance Questionnaire: A measure of needs and values.* Minneapolis: Vocational Psychology Research, University of Minnesota.

Rounds, J., Mazzeo, S. E., Smith, T. J., & Hubert, L. (1999). *O*NET Computerized Interest Profiler: Reliability, validity, and comparability.* Raleigh, NC: National Center for O*NET Development.

Rounds, J., & Tracey, T. J. (1996). Cross-cultural structural equivalence of RIASEC models and measures. *Journal of Counseling Psychology, 43,* 310-329. DOI: http://dx.doi.org/10.1037/0022-0167.43.3.310

Ruff, E. A., Reardon, R. C., & Bertoch, S. C. (2008, June). Holland's RIASEC theory and applications: Exploring a comprehensive bibliography. *Career Convergence.* Retrieved April 30, 2014 from http://ncda.org/aws/NCDA/pt/sd/news_article/5483/_self/layout_ccmsearch/false

Sampson, J. P., Jr. (1984). Maximizing the effectiveness of computer applications in counseling and human development: The role of research and implementation strategies. *Journal of Counseling and Development, 63,* 187–191.

Sampson, J. P., Jr. (1994). *Effective computer assisted career guidance* (Occasional paper No. 1). Tallahassee: Florida State University, Center for the Study of Technology in Counseling and Career Development.

Sampson, J. P., Jr., & Johnson, C. S. (1993). *Helping you help people find their way: Training resource guide (SIGI PLUS).* Princeton, NJ: Educational Testing Service.

Sampson, J. P., Jr., & Norris, D. S. (1995). *An evaluation of the effectiveness of Florida CHOICES implementation in high schools* (Tech. Rep. No. 20). Tallahassee: Florida State University, Center for the Study of Technology in Counseling and Career Development.

Sampson, J. P., Jr., & Peterson, G. W. (1984). *Evaluation standard: Computer-assisted career guidance systems.* Unpublished manuscript, Florida State University, Project LEARN—Phase II.

Sampson, J. P., Jr., Peterson, G. W., Lenz, J. G., & Reardon, R. C. (1992). A cognitive approach to career services: Translating concepts into practice. *The Career Development Quarterly, 41,* 67–7A.

Sampson, J. P., Jr., Peterson, G. W., Lenz, J. G., Reardon, R. C, & Saunders, D. E. (1996). *The Career Thoughts Inventory.* Odessa, FL: Psychological Assessment Resources.

Sampson, J. P., Jr., Peterson, G. W., Lenz, J. G., Reardon, R. C, & Saunders, D. E. (1998). The design and use of a measure of dysfunctional career thoughts among adults, college students, and high school students: The Career Thoughts Inventory. *Journal of Career Assessment, 6,* 115–134.

Sampson, J. P., Jr., Peterson, G. W., & Reardon, R.C. (1989). Counselor intervention strategies for computer-assisted career guidance: An information-processing approach. *Journal of Career Development, 16,* 139–154.

Sampson, J. P., Jr., Peterson, G. W., Reardon, R. C, Lenz, J. G., Shahnasarian, M., & Ryan-Jones, R. E. (1992). The social influence of two computer-assisted career guidance systems: DISCOVER and SIGI. *The Career Development Quarterly, 41,* 75–83.

Sampson, J. P., Jr. Purgar, M. P., & Shy, J. D. (2003). Computer-based test interpretation in career assessment: Ethical and professional issues. *Journal of Career Assessment, 11,* 22–39.

Sampson, J. P., Jr., & Pyle, K. R. (1983). Ethical issues involved with the use of computer-assisted counseling, testing and guidance systems. *Personnel and Guidance Journal, 61,* 283–287.

Sampson, J. P., Jr., Reardon, R. C., Lenz, J. G., Peterson, G. W., Shahnasarian, M., & Ryan-Jones, R. (1987). *The impact of two computer assisted career guidance systems on college students' perceptions of the counseling dimensions of computer interaction.* Tallahassee, FL: Florida State University, Center for the Study of Technology in Counseling and Career Development.

Sampson, J. P., Jr., Reardon, R. C, Lenz, J. G., Ryan-Jones, R. E., Peterson, G. W., & Levy, EC. (1993). *The impact of DISCOVER for adult learners and SIGI PLUS on the career decision making of adults* (Tech. Rep. No. 9). Tallahassee: Florida State University, Center for the

Study of Technology in Counseling and Career Development. (ERIC Document Reproduction Service No. ED 363 824)

Sampson, J. P., Jr., Reardon, R. C, Norris, D. S., Greeno, B. P., Kolodinsky, R. W., Herbert, S., Sankofa-Amammere, K. T, Epstein, S., Odell, J., Wright, L., Radice, M., Peterson, G. W, & Lenz, J. G. (1996). *A differential feature-cost analysis of twenty-one computer-assisted career guidance systems* (Tech. Rep. No. 10,7th ed.). Tallahassee: Florida State University, Center for the Study of Technology in Counseling and Career Development.

Sampson, J. P., Jr., Reardon, R. C, Shahnasarian, M., Peterson, G. W., Ryan-Jones, R., & Lenz, J. G. (1987). *The impact of DISCOVER and SIGI on the career decision making of college students* (Tech. Rep. No. 5). Tallahassee: Florida State University, Center for the Study of Technology in Counseling and Career Development.

Sampson, J. P., Jr., Shahnasarian, M., & Reardon, R. C. (1987). Computer-assisted career guidance: A national perspective on the use of DISCOVER and SIGI. *Journal of Counseling and Career Development, 65,* 416–419.

Sander, D. (1985). Review of Differential Aptitude Tests: Form V & W In J. V. Mitchell, Jr. (Ed.), *The ninth mental measurement yearbook.* Lincoln: Buros Institute of Mental Measurement, University of Nebraska.

Sanford-Moore, E. E. (2013). [Jackson Vocational Interest Survey, Second Edition]. In C. Wood & D. G. Hays (Eds.), *A counselor's guide to career assessment instruments. Sixth Edition* (pp. 255-259). Broken Arrow, OK : National Career Development Association.

Saunders, D. E., Peterson, G. W, Sampson, J. P., & Reardon, R. C. (2000). Relation of depression and dysfunctional career thinking to career indecision. *Journal of Vocational Behavior, 56(2),* 288–298.

Savickas, M. L. (1989). Career style assessment and counseling. In T. Sweeney (Ed.). *Adlerian counseling: A practical approach for a new decade* (3rd ed., pp. 289-320). Muncie, IN: Accelerated Development.

Savickas, M. L. (2012). Constructing careers: Actors, agents, and authors. *The Counseling Psychologist, 41,* 1-15.

Savickas, M. L. (2005). The theory and practice of career construction. In R. W. Lent & S. D. Brown (Eds.), *Career development and counseling: Putting theory and research to work* (pp. 42-70). Hoboken, NJ: John Wiley.

Savickas, M. L. (2000). Assessing career decision making. In C. E. Watkins, Jr., & V. L. Campbell (Eds.), *Testing and assessment in counseling practice* (pp. 429–477). Mahwah, NJ: Lawrence Erlbaum Associates.

Savickas, M. L., Briddick, W. C, & Watkins, C. E., Jr. (2002). The relations of career maturity to personality type and social adjustment. *Journal of Career Assessment, 10,* 24–41.

Savickas, M. L., & Härtung, P. (1996). The Career Development Inventory in review: Psychometric and research findings. *Journal of Career Assessment, 4 (2),* 171–188.

Savickas, M. L., & Taber, B. J. (2006). Individual differences in RIASEC profile similarity across five interest inventories. *Measurement and Evaluation in Counseling and Development, 38,* 203-210.

Saxon, J. P., & Spitznagel, R. J. (1995). Transferable skills and abilities profile: An economical assessment approach in the vocational placement process. *Vocational Evaluation and Work Adjustment Bulletin,* 61–67.

Schenck, P. M. (2009). [Kuder Career Planning System.] In E. A. Whitfield, R. W. Feller, & C. Wood (Eds.), *A counselor's guide to career assessment instruments. Fifth Edition* (pp. 163-173). Broken Arrow, OK : National Career Development Association.

Schuerger, J. M. (2000). The Sixteen Personality Factor Questionnaire (16PF). In C. E. Watkins, Jr., & V. L. Campbell (Eds.), *Testing and assessment in counseling practice(2nd* ed.) (pp. 73–110). Mahwah, NJ: Erlbaum.

Seal, B. C. (2004). Psychological testing of sign language interpreters. *Journal of Deaf Studies & Deaf Education, 9,* 39–52.

Severy, L. E. (2009). [Campbell Interest and Skill Survey.] In E. A. Whitfield, R. W. Feller, & C. Wood (Eds.), *A counselor's guide to career assessment instruments. Fifth Edition* (pp. 235-242). Broken Arrow, OK : National Career Development Association.

Severy, L. E. (2013). [Campbell Interest and Skill Survey.] In C. Wood & D. G. Hays (Eds.), *A counselor's guide to career assessment instruments. Sixth Edition* (pp. 226-231). Broken Arrow, OK : National Career Development Association.

Shaffer, M. B. (1995). Review of The Harrington-O'Shea Career Decision-Making System Revised. In J. C. Conoley & J. C. Impara (Eds.), *Twelfth mental measurements yearbook* (p. 457). Lincoln, NE: Buros Institute of Mental measurements.

Sharf, R. S. (1992). *Applying career development theory to counseling.* Pacific Grove, CA: Brooks/Cole.

Schenk, P. M. (2009). Kuder Career System. In J.T. Kapes, E. A. Whitfield, & R. Feller (Eds.), *A counselors guide to career assessment instruments. Fifth Edition* (pp. 168-173). Alexandria, VA: National Career Development Association.

Silles, M. A. (2010). Personality, education and earnings. *Education Economics, 18,* 131-151.

Simon, S. B., Howe, L. W, & Kirschenbaum, H. (1972). *Value clarification.* New York: Hart.

Slaney, R. B. (1980). Expressed vocational choice and vocational indecision. *Journal of Counseling Psychology, 27,* 122–129.

Slaney, R. B. (1985). Relation of career indecision to career exploration with reentry women: A treatment and follow-up study. *Journal of Counseling Psychology, 32,* 355–362.

Slaney, R. B., & MacKinnon- Slaney, E (1990). The use of vocational card sorts in career counseling. In C. E. Watkins, Jr. & V. L. Campbell (Eds.), *Testing in counseling practice* (pp. 317–371). Hillsdale, NJ: Erlbaum.

Slaney, R. B., Moran, W. T., & Wade, J. C. (1994). Vocational card sorts. In J. T. Kapes, M. M. Mastie, & E. A. Whitfield (Eds.), *A counselor's guide to career assessment instruments* (pp. 347–360). Alexandria, VA: National Career Development Association.

Slaney, R. B., Palko-Nonemaker, D., & Alexander, R. (1981). An investigation of two measures of career indecision. *Journal of Vocational Behavior, 18,* 92–103.

Slate, J. R., Jones, C. H., Sloas, S., & Blake, R C. (1998). Scores on the Stanford Achievement Test - 8 as a function of sex: Where have the sex differences gone? *High School Journal, 81 (2),* 82–86.

Sowers, J., Cotton, R, & Malloy, J. (1994). Expanding the job and career options for people with significant disabilities. *Developmental Disabilities Bulletin,* 22(2), 53–62.

Spokane, A. R., & Catalano, M. (2000). The Self- Directed Search: A theory driven array of self-guiding career interventions. In C. E. Watkins, Jr., & V L. Campbell (Eds.), *Contemporary topics in vocational psychology* (2nd ed.) (pp. 339–370). Mahwah, NJ: Erlbaum.

Spokane, A. R., & Holland, J. L. (1995). The Self- Directed Search: A family of self-guided career interventions. *Journal of Career Assessment, 3,* 373–390.

Stebleton, M. J. (2009). [NEO-PI-Revised]. In J.T. Kapes, E. A. Whitfield, & R. Feller (Eds.), *A counselors guide to career assessment instruments. Fifth Edition* (pp. 407-412). Alexandria, VA: National Career Development Association.

Stilwell, N. A., Wallick, M. M., Thai, S. E., & Burleson, J. J. (2000). Myers-Briggs type and medical specialty choice: A new look at an old question. *Teaching & Learning in Medicine, 12,* 14–20.

Stoker, H. (1993). Stanford Achievement Test. In J. J. Kramer & J. C. Conoley (Eds.), *The eleventh mental measurement yearbook* (pp. 863–865). Lincoln: Buros Institute of Mental Measurement, University of Nebraska.

Stone, E. (1993). *The Career Interest Inventory: A review and critique.* (ERIC Document Reproduction Service No. ED 356 255) Strong, E. K., Jr. (1943). *Vocational interests of men and women.* Stanford, CA: Stanford University Press.

Strong, E. K., Jr. (1943). *Vocational interests of men and women.* Palo Alto, CA: Stanford University Press.

Suen, H. K. (2012). *Kuder Career Interests Assessment technical brief.* Idel, IA: Author.

Sullivan, B. A., & Hanse, J-I. C. Evidence of construct validity of the interest scales on the Campbell Interest and Skill Survey. *Journal of Vocational Behavior, 65,*179–202.

Super, D. E. (1983). Assessment in career guidance: Toward truly developmental counseling. *Personnel and Guidance Journal, 61,* 555–567.

Super, D. E. (1990). A life-span, life-space approach to career development. In D. Brown & L. Brooks (Eds.), *Career choice and development: Applying contemporary theories to practice* (pp. 197–261). San Francisco: Jossey-Bass.

Super, D.E., & Nevill, D. D. (1985). *The Salience Inventory.* Palo Alto, CA: Consulting Psychologists Press.

Super, D. E., Osborne, W, Walsh, D., Brown, S., & Niles, S. (1992). Developmental career assessment and counseling: The C-DAC model. *Journal of Counseling and Development, 71,* 74–79.

Super, D. E., Thompson, A. S., Lindeman, R. H., Jordaan, J. P., & Myers, R. M. (1981). *Career Development Inventory, College and University Form.* Palo Alto, CA: Consulting Psychologists Press.

Swanson, J. L. (1999). Stability and change in vocational interests. In M. L. Savickas & A. R.

Spokane (Eds.), *Vocational interests: Meaning, measurement, and counseling use,* 135–158. Palo Alto, CA: Davies-Black.

Swanson, J. L. (1999). Stability and Change in Vocational Interests. In M.L. Savickas & A. R. Spokane (Eds.), *Vocational Interests: Meaning, Measurement, and Counseling Use* (pp. 135-158). Palo Alto: Davies-Black.

Swanson, J. L., & Hansen, J. C. (1986). A clarification of Holland's construct of differentiation: The importance of score elevation. *Journal of Vocational Behavior, 28,* 163-173.

Symes, B. A., & Stewart, J. B. (1999). The relationship between meta-cognition and vocational indecision. *Canadian Journal of Counselling,* 33(3), 195–211.

Taber, B. J., Hartung, P. J., & Borges, N. J. (2011.) Personality and values as predictors of medical specialty choice. *Journal of Vocational Behavior, 78,* 202-209.

Tak, J. (2004). Structure of vocational interests for Korean college students. *Journal of Career Assessment, 22,* 298–311.

Tak, J., & Lee, K-H. (2003). Development of the Korean Career Indecision Inventory. *Journal of Career Assessment, 11,* 328-245. doi: 10.1177/1069072703254503

Takigasaki, T. & Fujimura, K. (2004). Correlations between personal preferences and age for a sample of Japanese Open University students. *Psychological Reports, 94,* 771–774.

Taylor, K. M. & Betz, N. E. (1983). Applications of Self-Efficacy Theory to the understanding and treatment of career indecision. *Journal of Vocational Behavior, 21,* 63–81.

Taylor, K. M., & Popma, J. (1990). An examination of the relationships among career decision-making self-efficacy, career salience, locus of control, and vocational indecision. *Journal of Vocational Behavior,* 37(1), 17–31.

Te Nijenhus, J., Evers, A., & Mur, J. P. (2000). Validity of the Differential Aptitude Test for the assessment of immigrant children. *Educational Psychology: An International Journal of Experimental Educational Psychology, 20,* 99–115.

Tenopyr, M. L. (1989). Kuder Occupational Interest Survey. In J. S. Conoley & J. J. Kramer (Eds.), *The tenth mental measurement yearbook* (pp. 427–429). Lincoln: Büros Institute of Mental Measurement, University of Nebraska.

Thompson, B., & Ackerman, C. M. (1994). Review of the Myers-Briggs Type Indicator. In J. T. Kapes, M. M. Mastie, & E. A. Whitfield (Eds), *A counselor's guide to career assessment instruments* (3rd ed., pp. 283-287). Alexandria, VA: National Career Development Association.

Thompson, A. R., & Dickey, K. D. (1994). Self-perceived job search skills of college students with disabilities. *Rehabilitation Counseling Bulletin, 37,* 358–370.

Thomas, S.W. (1994). Review of the WRIOT. In J. T. Kapes, M. M. Mastie, & E. A. Whitfield (Eds.), *A counselor's guide to career assessment inventories* (pp. 342–345). Alexandria, VA: National Career Development Association.

Thompson, B., & Ackerman, C. M. (1994). Review of the MBTI. In J. T. Kapes, M. M. Mastie, & E. A. Whitfield (Eds.), A *counselor's guide to career assessment instruments.* Alexandria, VA: National Career Development Association.

Tien, H. S. (2005). The validation of the Career Decision-making Difficulties Scale in a Chinese culture. *Journal of Career Assessment, 13,* 114-127.

Tittle, C. K., & Hecht, D. (1994). Review of the Social and Prevocational Information Battery-Revised. In J. T. Kapes, M. M. Mastie, & E. A. Whitfield (Eds.), A *counselor's guide to career assessment inventories* (pp. 332–335). Alexandria, VA: National Career Development Association.

Toossi, M. (2004). Labor force projections to 2012: The graying of the U.S. workforce. *Monthly Labor Review, 127,* 37–57.

Tracey, T. J. G., & Sodano, S. M. (2008). Issues of stability and change in interest development. *The Career Development Quarterly, 57,* 51-62.

Tuel, B. D., & Betz, N. E. (1998). Relationships of career self-efficacy expectations to the Myers-Briggs Type Indicator and the Personal Styles Scales. *Measurement and Evaluation in Counseling and Development, 31,* 150–163.

Tyler, L. E. (1961). Research explorations in the realm of choice. *Journal of Counseling Psychology, 8,* 195–201.

U.S. Bureau of the Census (1990). Projections of the population of states, by age, sex and race: 1989–2010. *Current population representations: Series P-25, no. 1053.* Washington, DC: U.S. Government Printing Office.

U.S. Department of Defense. (1994). *Technical manual for the ASVAB 18/19 career exploration program.* Washington, DC: U.S. Government Printing Office.

U.S. Department of Defense. (1995). *The interest finder.* Washington, DC: U.S. Government Printing Office.

U.S. Department of Defense. (2005). *Exploring careers: The ASVAB career exploration guide.* Washington, DC: U.S. Government Printing Office.

U.S. Department of Labor. (2004–2005). *Occupational outlook handbook.* Washington, DC: U.S. Government Printing Office.

Vacc, N. A., & Newsome, D. W (2002). In J.T. Kapes, & E. A. Whitfield (Eds.), A *counselor's guide to career assessment instruments* (pp. 123–131). Alexandria, VA: National Career Development Association.

Vacha-Haase, T., & Enke, S. (2013). [Geist Picture Interest Inventory, Revised Eighth Printing]. In C. Wood & D. G. Hays (Eds.), *A counselor's guide to career assessment instruments. Sixth Edition* (pp. 433-436). Broken Arrow, OK : National Career Development Association.

VALPAR, International. Sigi Plus. [Computer program]. Tucson, AZ: Author.

Vansickle, T. R. (1994). Review of the Harrington- O'Shea Career Decision-Making System-Revised. In J. T. Kapes, M. M. Mastie, & E. A. Whitfield (Eds.), *A counselors guide to career assessment instruments* (pp. 174–177). Alexandria, VA: National Career Development Association.

Walker, J. V., & Peterson, G. W. (2012). Career thoughts, indecision, and depression: Implications for mental health assessment in career counseling. *Journal of Career Assessment, 20,* 497-506. doi: 10.1177/1069072712450010

Wall, J. E. (1994). Review of the CBI. In J. T. Kapes, M. M. Mastie, & E. A. Whitfield (Eds.), A *counselor's guide to career assessment inventories.* Alexandria, VA: National Career Development Association.

Wall, J. E., & Baker, H. E. (1997). The Interest- Finder: Evidence of validity. *Journal of Career Assessment, 5 (3),* 255–73.

Waller, J. V. III, & Peterson, G. W. (2012). Career thoughts, indecision, and depression: Implications for mental health assessment in career counseling. *Journal of Career Assessment, 20,* 497-506.

Walls, R. T., & Fullmer, S. L. (1997). Competitive employment: Occupations after vocational rehabilitation. *Rehabilitation Counseling Bulletin, 41(1),* 15–25.

Walsh, B. D., Thompson, B, & Kapes, J. T. (1997). The construct validity of scores on the Career Beliefs Inventory. *Journal of Career Assessment,* 5(1), 31–46.

Walsh, J. A. (1978). Review of the Sixteen Personality Factor Questionnaire. In O. K. Buros (Ed.), *The eighth mental measurement yearbook* (Vol. 1). Highland Park, NJ: Gryphon.

Walsh, W. B. (1972). Review of the Kuder Occupational Interest Survey. In O. K. Buros (Ed.), *The seventh mental measurement yearbook.* (Vol. 2). Highland Park, NJ: Gryphon.

Walsh, W. B., & Betz, N. E. (1995). *Tests and assessment,* 3rd ed. Englewood Cliffs, NJ: Prentice-Hall.

Walter, V (1984). *Personal Career Development Profile.* Champaign, IL: Institute for Personality and Ability Testing.

Wampold, B. E., Mondin, G. W., & Ahn, H. (1999). Preference for people and tasks. *Journal of Counseling Psychology, 46,* 35-41.

Wang, L. (1993). *The Differential Aptitude Test: A review and critique.* (ERIC Document Reproduction Service No. ED 56 257).

Wang, L., Ye, M., & Tao, J. (2002). Mental health status, coping style, and personality characteristics of college students. *Chinese Journal of Clinical Psychology, 10,*208–209.

Ward, C. M., & Bingham, R. P. (1993). Career assessment of ethnic minority women. *Journal of Career Assessment,* 2, 246–257.

Watson, J. C. (2013). [Career Decision Self-Efficacy Scale and Career Decision Self-Efficacy Scale – Short Form]. In C. Wood & D. G. Hays, (Eds.), A *counselor's guide to career assessment instruments, 6th Ed.* (pp. 315-318). Broken Arrow, OK: National Career Development Association.

Weiss, D. J. (1978). Review of the Armed Services Vocational Aptitude Battery. In O. K. Buros (Ed.), *The eighth mental measurement yearbook* (Vol. 1). Highland Park, NJ: Gryphon.

Westbrook, B. W (1983). Career maturity: The concept, the instrument, and the research. In W B. Walsh & S. H. Osipow (Eds.), *Handbook of vocational psychology* (Vol. 1) (pp. 263– 304). Hillsdale, NJ: Erlbaum.

Whiston, S. C. (2000). *Principles and applications of assessment in counseling.* Pacific Grove, CA: Brooks/Cole.

Whiston, S. C, & Bouwkamp, J. C. (2003). Ethical implications of career assessment with women. *Journal of Career Assessment, 11,* 59–75.

Whiston, S. C, Brecheisen, B. K., & Stephens, J. (2003). Does treatment modality affect career counseling effectiveness? *Journal of Vocational Behavior,* 62, 390–410.

Whiston, S. C., & Rose, C. S. (2013). Test administration, interpretation, and communication. In C. Wood & D. G. Hays, (Eds.), A *counselor's guide to career assessment instruments, 6th Ed.* (pp. 101-111). Broken Arrow, OK: National Career Development Association.

Wille, B., De Fruyt, F., & Feys, M. (2010). Vocational interests and big five traits as predictors of job instability. *Journal of Vocational Behavior, 76,* 547-558.

Williams, R. T. (1992). Adult Basic Learning Examination (ABLE). In J.J. Kramer &J. S. Conoley (Eds.), *The eleventh mental measurement yearbook* (pp. 21–23). Lincoln: Buros Institute of Mental Measurement, University of Nebraska.

Williams, R. T. (1994). Review of Adult Basic Learning Examination (ABLE) (2nd ed.). In J. T. Kapes, M. M. Mastie, & E. A. Whitfield (Eds.), A *counselor's guide to career assessment inventories* (pp. 59–62). Alexandria, VA: National Career Development Association.

Williamson, E. G. (1939). *How to counsel students: A manual of techniques for clinical counselors.* New York: McGraw-Hill.

Williamson, E. G. (1949). *Counseling adolescents.* New York: McGraw-Hill.

Williams-Phillips, L. J. (1983). *Five career decidedness scales: Reliability, validity, and factors.* Unpublished master's thesis, North Carolina State University at Raleigh.

Willis, C. G. (1982). The Harrington-O'Shea Career Decision-Making System. In J. T. Kapes & M. M. Mastie (Eds.), A *counselor's guide to vocational guidance instruments* (pp. 57–61). Falls Church, VA: National Vocational Guidance Association.

Willson, V L., & Stone, E. (1994). Review of the Differential Aptitude Test and the Career Interest Inventory. In J. T. Kapes, M. M. Mastie, & E. A. Whitfield (Eds.), A *counselor's guide to career assessment instruments* (pp. 93–98). Alexandria, VA: National Career Development Association.

Wircenski, J. L. (1994). Review of the Pictorial Inventory of Careers. In J. T. Kapes, M. M.

Mastie, & E. A.Whitfield (Eds.), A *counselor's guide to career assessment instruments* (pp.

316–319). Alexandria, VA: National Career Development Association.

Wise, Welsh, Grafton, Foley, Earles, Sawin, & Divgi, (1992). *Sensitivity and fairness of the*

Armed Services Vocational Aptitude Battery (ASVAB) technical composites. Seaside, CA:

Defense Manpower Data Center.

Wright, L. K., Reardon, R. C, Peterson, G. W, & Osborn, D. S. (2000). The relationship among

constructs in the Career Thoughts Inventory and the Self-Directed Search. *Journal of Career*

Assessment, 8(2), 105–117.

Wulff, M. B., & Steitz, J. A. (1999). A path model of the relationship between career indecision,

androgyny, self-efficacy and self-esteem. *Perceptual & Motor Skills,* 88(3, Pt 1), 935–940.

Zmud, R. W, Sampson, J. P., Reardon, R. C, Lenz, J. G., & Byrd, T. A. (1994). Confounding

effects of construct overlap. An example from IS user satisfaction theory. *Information*

Technology and People, 7, 29–45.

Zunker, V G. (2014, 2015). *Career counseling: Applied concepts of life planning* (9th ed.). Pacific

Grove, CA: Cengage.

Zwick, R. (2007). College admission testing. *Report for the National Association for College*

Admission Counseling, 1-44.

Zytowski, D. G. (1978). Review of Wide Range Interest-Opinion Test. In O. K. Büros (Ed.),77ie

eighth mental measurement yearbook (Vol. 2). Highland Park, NJ: Gryphon.

Zytowski, D. G. (1999). How to talk to people about their interest inventory results. In M. L.

Savickas & A. R. Spokane (eds.), *Vocational interest: Meaning, measurement, and*

counseling use, pp. 277–293. Palo Alto, CA: Davies- Black/Consulting Psychologists Press.

Zytowski, D. G. (2001). Kuder Career Search with person match: Career assessment for the

21st century. *Journal of Career Assessment, 9,* 229-241.

Zytowski, D. G., & England, R. J. L. (1995). Indices of interest maturity in the Kuder

   Occupational Interest Survey. *Measurement and Evaluation in Counseling and Development,*

   28, 148–151.

Zytowski, D. Gl, & Luzzzo, D. A. (2002). Developing the Kuder Skills Assessment. *Journal of*

   Career Assessment, 10, 190-199.

NAME INDEX

Abu-Hilal, M. M., 69
Ackerman, C. M., 122
Ahn, H., 116
Alexander, R., 141
Allis, M., 141
Anastasi, A., 4, 56, 102
Anderson, W P., Jr., 144
Anseel, F., 90
Arbona, C., 132
Argyropoulou, E. P., 132
Armstrong, P. I., 88
Arnup, J. L., 116
Aronson, J., 69
Asama, N. F., 92, 145
Asfaw, A. 69
Ashman, A. E., 69
Asulin-Peretz, L., 132, 139, 148
Atkinson, M. J., 118, 119
Bahns, T. M., 125
Barak, A., 49, 141
Barrick, M. R., 116, 126
Ben-Porath, Y S., 125
Bennet, G. K., 57
Bergin, D. A., 69
Besevegis, E. G., 132
Bethell, D. B., 163, 164
Betz, N. E., 47, 69, 77, 88,
    105, 116, 145
Bingham, R. P., 21
Blackwell, T. L., 67
Blake, R. J., 71, 116
Blosel, C. W., 60
Boggs, K. R., 94
Boisvert, M., 69
Borgen, F. H., 102, 104, 126
Bouffard, T., 69
Bouwkamp, J. C., 47
Brecheisen, B. K., 12
Brew, S., 102
Briddick, W. C., 118
Brown, D., 2, 4, 31, 54
Brown, F. G., 71
Brown, R. P., 69
Buboltz, W. C, Jr., 123
Bullock, E. E., 92
Burleson, J. J., 116
Cairo, P. C., 144
Campbell, D. P., 92, 94, 95, 96

Campbell, V., 96
Cantwell, Z. M., 110
Carless, S. A., 116
Carlson, J. G., 122
Carney, C. G., 140, 141
Carpenter, J., 69
Carpraro, M. M., 122
Carpraro, R. M., 122
Carson, A. D., 116
Chambers, W., 116
Chang, D. H. E., 25
Chope, R. C., 89, 92, 119
Chung, V., 68
Chung, Y. B., 47
Ciechalski, J. C., 102
Cole, J. S., 69
Coleman, N., 132
Constantine, M. G., 132
Coon, K. L., 88
Corkin, D., 132
Crace, R. K., 26, 163
Cronbach, L. J., 4, 7, 8, 26, 30, 32
Crouteau, J. M., 163
Curran, L. T., 60
Daiger, D. C., 145
Dalldorf, M.R., 60
Darcy, M., 54
Davidovitch, S., 139
Davies, T., 69
Dawis, R. V., 53, 116
Dell, C. A., 74
Dell, T., 74
Diamond, E. E., 110
Dollinger, S. J., 125
Domino, G., 110
Donnay, D. A. C., 104, 105
Drummond, R. J., 8, 36, 53, 55, 71
Duffy, R. D., 116
Dumas, C., 69
Dumenci, L., 102
Earles, J., 60
Ehrhart, K. H., 85
Evers, A., 57
Feller, R. W., 95, 143
Fish, L. A., 69
Fleenor, J. W., 122
Fleming, M., 159
Flores, L. Y., 21, 46, 88

Foley, P., 60
Fouad, N. A., 46, 88, 98
Fritzsche, B., 24
Fuller, B. E., 92, 116, 117, 126
Fuqua, D. R., 94, 116
Gadassi, R., 139
Gaffey, A. R., 88
Galassi, J. P., 26, 45, 163
Gati, I., 132, 133, 135, 136, 139, 148, 159
Geist, H., 109
Gibson, L. W., 116
Goldman, L., 30, 164, 165, 166
Good, C., 69
Goodman, J., 179
Gottfredson, G. D., 144
Gottfredson, L., 92
Gough, H. G., 126
Grafton, F., 60
Gray, E. A., 116
Gross, C. L., 60
Groth-Marnat, G., 8
Gwilliam, L. R., 88
Hackett, G., 47
Hambleton, R. K., 57
Hansen, J-I. C., 88, 90, 92, 93, 102, 104, 105
Harder, J. A., 69
Harmon, L. W., 105, 141
Harrington, T. F., 85, 88, 92, 94, 96
Harrold, B., 74
Härtung, P. J., 21, 46, 116, 144, 163
Hattrup, D., 56, 119
Hattrup, K., 56, 119
Hay, I., 69
Healy, C.C., 89, 92, 116, 122, 123
Heilbrun, A. B., Jr., 126
Henington, C., 125
Heppner, M. J., 116, 126
Herman, O. D., 141
Higgins, C. A., 116
Hirschi, A., 116
Holden, R. H., 110
Holland, J. L., 24, 29, 54, 91, 92, 95, 99, 100, 101, 116, 117, 126, 145
Holmgren, R.L., 60
Howe, L. W., 180
James, R. M., 26, 163
Jenkins, J. A., 104, 105
Johnson, P., 123

Johnston, J. A., 92, 117, 126, 145
Joiner, J. W., 116
Jones, C. H., 71
Jones, E. M., 92
Jones, K. D., 36, 53, 55, 71
Josephs, R. A., 69
Judge, T. A., 116
Kaplan, A., 105
Kaplan, R., 8
Katz, L., 116
Kelly, K. R., 95, 123
Khan, S., 69
Kindaichi, M. M., 132
Kirschenbaum, H., 180
Konstantopoulos, S., 68
Knowdell, R. L., 169, 170
Koeschier, M., 141
Krausz, M., 136
Kritis, K. J., 144
Krug, S. E., 116, 117
Kucinkas, S. K., 60
Kuder, F., 97
Landman, S., 139
Larson, L. M., 126
Lee, P. A., 132
Lee, W. V., 88
Lenz, J. G., 3, 5, 17, 54, 91, 92, 100, 102, 133, 142, 143, 166, 167
Leong, F. T. L, 21, 46, 87, 125
Leung, S. A., 25
Levinson, E. M., 61, 102, 154
Lievens, F., 90
Lindley, L. D., 102
Linn, R. L., 56
Liptak, J., 134
Logue, C. T., 87
Lokan, J., 159
Lonborg, S. D., 47
Lopez, F. G., 132
Lounsbury, J. W., 87, 116
Lowman, R. L., 116
Lundberg, D. J., 116
Lutyhe, T. D., 67
Luzzo, D. A., 159
MacKinnon- Slaney, E., 164, 165, 168
Makransky, G., 85
Manuelle-Adkins, C., 102
Markovitz, H., 69
Marsella, A. J., 46
Marsh, H. W., 69

SUBJECT INDEX

S-2

S-3

CPSIA information can be obtained
at www.ICGtesting.com
Printed in the USA
FFHW011117140619
52977668-58585FF